OBSCENE THINGS

# OBSCENE THINGS

Sexual Politics in Jin Ping Mei

NAIFEI DING

Duke University Press   Durham and London   2002

© 2002 Duke University Press
All rights reserved

Designed by Amy Ruth Buchanan
Typeset in Joanna by Tseng
Information Systems, Inc.
Library of Congress Cataloging-in-
Publication Data appear on the last
printed page of this book.

To my parents, Shih Mei-Chang and Ding Mou-Shih, and to Chen Kuan-hsing, who have been with this book for too long

CONTENTS

Acknowledgments, ix
Preface, xi

PART ONE: PRACTICES

1. Jin-ology, 3

2. The Manic Preface: Jin Shengtan's (1608–1661) Shuihu zhuan, 47

3. A Cure for Melancholy: Yuan Hongdao (1568–1610) and Qifa (Seven Stimuli), 81

4. Tears of Ressentiment: Zhang Zhupo's (1670–1698) Jin Ping Mei, 117

PART TWO: INTERVENTION

5. Seduction: Tiger and Yinfu, 143

6. Red Shoes, Foot Bindings, and the Swing, 165

7. A Cat, a Dog, and the Killing of Livestock, 195

8. Very Close to Yinfu and Ënu; or, How Prefaces Matter for Jin Ping Mei (1695) and Ënu Shu (Taipei, 1995), 225

Notes, 245
Glossary, 297
Works Cited, 305
Index, 325

ACKNOWLEDGMENTS

This book originated in a dissertation on Jin Ping Mei. The greater part of the book as it now stands was written during a year's research leave in 1994–1995, under the auspices of the Center for Chinese Studies at the University of California at Berkeley, and funded by the National Science Foundation of Taiwan. Profound thanks to my dissertation committee; Professors Cyril Birch, Samuel Cheung, D. A. Miller, and Masao Miyoshi gave me space, time, encouragement, and continuing inspiration in often unexpected ways. I also owe a debt of gratitude to my colleagues at the English department of the National Central University in Taiwan for that precious year away; the National Science Foundation for sponsoring the research leave; and the Center for Chinese Studies at Berkeley for providing facilities and helpful discussion opportunities. Deep and abiding appreciation to Patricia Sieber, Kim Besio, Colleen Lye, David Pickell, Maram Epstein, Liu Jen-peng, Amie Parry, Wang Ping, Ni Jiazhen, Chen Yurong, Lucifer Hong, Yu Yu-Shan, Josephine Ho, Karl Ning, Cindy Patton, Jiang Jia-wen, Lin Wen-Ling, and Richard Ding for amoebae aggregation and conversations that have leavened the entire project, and not just. Without the infinite patience of Reynolds Smith and the meticulous reading of Justin Faerber and anonymous readers at Duke University Press, this book would have remained unfinished. Finally, thanks go out to Joy Tu and Chu Yuli for help with finalizing the manuscript. All remaining infelicities, unknowings, and unthinkings are, needless to say, my own.

PREFACE

Jin Ping Mei (JPM) circulates as an extended tale of the rise and fall of a parvenu merchant-militaryman and his family clan set in the last decades of the Sung dynasty. The protagonist is Ximen Qing, an urban opportunist with neither family nor education who nevertheless succeeds at amassing women, a fortune, and an official post through seductive wiles, mercantile savvy, and political bribery. His operative mode is at once sensual and material. But it is the sensual that will ultimately lead to his death, the dispersion of his family, and by implication, the downfall of the Sung empire. His female counterpart and the arch-villainess of the story is the bondmaid-concubine Pan Jinlian. Their encounter had been narrated in another Ming-era narrative, Shuihu Zhuan (or SHZ, refers to the One Hundred Twenty Chapter Shui Hu Zhuan reprinted by Shang Wu Yin Shu Guan [Hong Kong, 1969]), where both die for committing adultery. This episode is then rewritten at length in JPM, postponing their deaths by several years. In JPM, Pan Jinlian becomes Ximen Qing's fifth concubine (sixth "wife"), and the central figure of sexual opportunism and domestic intrigue. In this narrative, she is held accountable for the successive deaths of a former master at whose house she had served as a bondmaid; the cake-seller husband to whom she is given away in punishment; the bondservant's wife with whom Ximen Qing has sex; Li

Ping'er, who is Ximen Qing's favorite as well as the mother of his son; his baby son Guange; and of course Ximen Qing himself. Sex and death are inextricably intertwined, according to this tale, and death is bloody and protracted where sex is nonreproductive, illegitimate, and pleasurably, albeit instrumentally, excessive. Death is not simply that of the individual but of the family and body politic as well. The destructive powers/potency of base yinfu (lascivious women) exemplified in the narrative's various bondmaid-concubine figures, and one's fatal desire for these particular women, are related to the fullest extent in graphic detail.

In its material life, JPM is a book that first appeared on literary record in manuscript form amid a highly select circle of readers at the midpoint Wanli (1573–1620) in the Ming dynasty. Within three decades of its circulation in manuscript, the book was printed in the Jiangnan region and went up for sale on the market. By the Ming Chongzhen period (1628–1645), a significantly altered—carefully edited, and more formally and ideologically consistent—text was printed. One of the candidates for editorship of this version is Li Yu, a writer of fiction, drama, and a manual on connoisseurship of various modes of aesthetic consumption in the not very wealthy yet quite cultured gentleman's life of leisure, but also someone who owned his own troupe of actors and actresses, as well as a bookshop and printing house. Li Yu had been mentioned approvingly by Yuan Hongdao, a leading literatus of an earlier generation.[1] Incidentally, Li Yu was also a family friend of Zhang Zhupo's father, whose talented, poor, and intellectually brilliant though frustrated son set to writing in 1695 (Qing Kangxi 34) a commentaried version of JPM, claiming for this by now "pornographic" book the highest morality—reading it as the product of an embittered filiality. Its "dirt" was, for Zhang Zhupo, that of an ethical abjection. Zhang Zhupo's version of JPM (hereafter ZZJPM) soon became something of a bestseller, repeatedly reprinted despite Kangxi's imperial edict banning its publication along with many other books considered pornographic or treasonous. Zhang Zhupo's commentary edition superseded all previous ones up to the twentieth century (see chapter 4).

If JPM refers to a book (which turns out, on closer examination, to consist of several "books" in many senses), it also signifies an entire range of meanings, from a scholarly "first realist narrative of its kind in China, if not the world," to a "pornographic" narrative that cannot be cleansed, however many passages are cut and censored, and must therefore be restricted to a "mature and/or academic readership" only. In the twentieth-century, in popular media and consciousness in Chinese-speaking places, JPM came to signify a moral and psychophysiological obsession with, and concomitant fear and even hatred of, particular women and female sexuality (*nüse*, or woman-sex)—a view encapsulated and refuted in a 1988 essay in the Taiwan journal *Taibei Pinglun*[2] that analyzes Pan Jinlian, the licentious woman or *yinfu*, as a nymphomaniac. Needless to say, the reputation of the book as being about "women and [female] sexuality" was sufficient in itself to explain its infamy in a space where women are still only legitimate and symbolically valued as reproductive rather than sexual subjects. The function of sexuality and sensualities in general as well as their supplemental relation to the reproductive is foregrounded precisely in the base bodies of licentious bondmaid-concubines who remain barren, unable to bear the man-child that is their sole raison d'être in an extended polygamous family (both in the late Ming era and not so long ago in Taiwan). Sexuality is in such situations by definition foremost among the excessive and potentially harmful sensual expenditures of a semen-centered reproductive economy constituting the master's personal and sociofamilial body politic. Insofar as reproduction entails and encompasses sexual/sensual contact, and to the extent that such contact might be linked to residual Taoist regimes of erotic management and hygienic self-care (as perhaps was so in the case of Yuan Hongdao's reading), moral dictates could be seen as aligned to and ameliorated by practical considerations of hygiene, health, and pleasure. But such acculturated consumption could not have been available for the everyday common man, who must lack the elite cultural wherewithal and sociosymbolic status for the appropriately measured and correctly fertile or even aesthetically appreciative use of sumptuous female objects in the figures of bondmaid-concubines. Thus Li Yu on the acquisition, grooming, and training of bondmaid-concubines, in an age when these had become relatively common and affordable for even your everyday local literatus-gentry as well as merchant-parvenu.[3]

It is perhaps at this particular sociohistorical conjuncture of the Ming-Qing, when bondmaid-concubines appeared in numbers and proximity exceeding those of even elite households and habitual usage, when the familial and social place of women as primarily and/or exclusively reproductive bodies (mothers, wives, daughters) in a strictly bounded internal household economy seems threatened. The movement of female bodies into and out of familial thresholds as bondmaids and/or concubines, their intra-familial incessant competitive dynamics and sexual opportunism, their insidiously long-lasting influence and potency if/when they do give birth, and the violent struggle for uterine power that concubine births might unleash—all of these might be termed a thematics of intimate politics, or what I will call "porous intimacies," whose representation is inaugurated in a definitive vernacular mold in JPM. It is in this text and how this text is remembered that these particular kinds of women—their base "origin" and specific trajectories conveniently forgotten and subsumed or enlarged into general womanhood—are construed to enduring symbolic and discursive effect as potent, powerful, and dangerous sexual agents or yinfu. As if man-killing sexual agency could serve as a deterrent, warning, and counterpart to proper femininity and women (readers), while at the same time servicing a voyeur/masochist masculine sexuality/reading position, and assuaging the latter's fears *and* desires. Had there been no such convenient historic gendered scapegoat of a specific social-class trajectory available for not just familial-social exploitation but as textual and cultural strategies, what would have happened? For example, what would have happened to the increasing class-status performance anxieties of a substratum of the hegemonic elite?

In the seventeenth century, during the Ming-Qing transition period, the frustrations and resentment, the mania and melancholy of distance and alienation from imperial bureaucratic service (signaling a new class-status uncertainty and the blurring of distinctions), and the formation of a new urban culture—all of these were forces most visibly present in transmuted forms in fictional and anecdotal writings.

Writing in 1695, Zhang Zhupo specifically noted that women must not read this book, as much because they could never learn how to read this (or any) book properly, but also because their tendency to a mimetic model of reading would make the familial and social effects of their reading JPM disastrous. Clearly, JPM was read since Wanli (see chapters 2 and 3) as a book primarily for literate, if not literati, men. But just as evidently, certain women had access to such books and could read them; hence Zhang Zhupo's indignation. The recorded readings of elite or not-so-elite men notwithstanding, or perhaps precisely because of such readings, JPM was and continues to be openly or secretly read by mostly (scholarly) men—or so it seems until the twentieth century. It is not a coincidence, then, that this work of all works should continue to circulate and signify in contemporary popular culture as a sign of female (but *not* specifically bondmaid-concubine) desires and sexuality for an acculturated male readership, while signifying at the same time a borderline literary work not suitable for female readers or women scholars. The "class/status-based misogynist continuum" subtending both popular and academic spaces, and their otherwise differently situated male readers, effectively produce the range of meanings that JPM still elicits today.

Yet what do I mean by class/status-based misogyny? Both Wang Yijia writing in contemporary Taiwan and Zhang Zhupo commenting on an edition in 1695 (which would become the best-known version of JPM for the next three hundred years) contribute to the dissemination and circulation of JPM as a popular sign of personally, socially, and politically dangerous desire for morally bad rather than *base* (status-wise) women.[4] The social baseness (*jian*) of particular women is euphemistically rendered into a more generalized and universal moral badness or impropriety (*bu liang*), and thus simultaneously naturalized as an ethical and personal rather than socioeconomic or familial-political problem.[5] This innate moral depravity conflates and substitutes the subject's desire with its improper and dangerous objects, thereby conveniently eclipsing the desiring and reading subject who at least must want (to read of) sexually opportunist things.

There are then at least two kinds of JPMs in terms of their spaces of circulation and spheres of influence. One affects the contemporary popular imaginary and produces shop signs (for betel nut stands and sex paraphernalia stores), as well as revisions in "traditional" forms such as the highly successful Szechuan dramatic version in China but also in modern cinematic and novelistic forms such as Hong Kong–Australia director Clara Law's *The Incarnations of the Golden Lotus*, based on the popular *Pan Jinlian's Previous and Present Life* (*Pan Jinlian zhi Qianshi Jinsheng*) by novelist Li Bihua. The other JPM is the cachet of book collectors, cognoscenti, and academics who may read it openly or on the sly yet seldom talk about it—in public (or print) that is, excepting those who profess to "study" it (myself included). But as JPM's mythic popular aura and influence among a younger generation arguably recedes, it seems to have become the focus of increasing scholarly attention in both Chinese and English (and perhaps other languages as well). Finally, its past cultural migration and incarnations in non-Chinese-speaking Asian sites—in Japan, Vietnam, and Korea, to name just a few—would be a fascinating subject for a follow-up project.

My book owes a great deal to the continued social and political effects of JPM in the contemporary Chinese-speaking popular imaginary—especially its mythic message of the dangers of woman-sex (nüse). Without the gender taboo surrounding JPM, I would not have embarked on the study of what has made and continues to go into the making of that text as constellation of sexual meanings and gender truths in the fulcrum of familial-social hierarchical power negotiations. I should also add that there is no clear dividing line between the fields wherein JPM operates its porous powers or the readers situated in these differentiated spheres. They could be the same though nonidentical subjects—linked by a homologous fear and desire.

Instead of examining contemporary cultural myths spawned in the shadow of JPM, I will be focusing instead on the readings that have cumulatively mediated the text(s) for its twentieth-century readers. I attempt to return to a range of reading positions and investments variously embedded within and around the text(s) in the context of changing cultural and socioeconomic conditions. These include its two most well-known and influential late Ming and early Qing readers, Yuan Hongdao and Zhang Zhupo (see chapters 3 and 4), as well as earlier twentieth-century scholarly efforts to dispel JPM's residual pornographic-erotic aura (see chapter 1). Finally, I offer a counterethical feminist reading position and strategy as one possible (early-twenty-first-century) resistant reading of the narrative's intimate politics—its disciplinary gender and sexual configurations. Such a feminist reading (in part 2) would counter, but also partially continue a "modern" sexual and gender politics in its egalitarian individualist concern. This is not the end of the story as it can be read, however. The last chapter reflects on the possibility of alternative and as-yet-impossible reading positions and illegible sexual practices that are always already in place (or always out of place, exceeding their appointed place) in the last decade of the twentieth century in Taiwan and the first decade of the twenty-first century.

*Obscene Matters*

The distinction between a refined and a greedy consumption is one that was central to a generation of Ming Wanli literati, who began to articulate crucial and self-interested social and moral distinctions through a discourse of connoisseurship that ranged from the pictorial arts and domestic objects to women and vernacular fictional forms. It is no coincidence that the earliest edition of JPM to be published retains the hybrid form of a compendium of songs, drama, and narrative. It is as if the work itself were the product of a "gluttonous" consumption, a regurgitation of some editor-author's favorite pieces, fused by the will, as C. T. Hsia puts it, to ingeniously concoct something never before seen in print.[6] This cutting and pasting of diverse materials and forms itself attests to the influence of a vernacular print culture. Only with the advent of published and therefore more easily available forms of diverse vernacular materials, coupled with a possible market for ever more innovative "pastiche," could JPM appear and, more important, be read by its earliest known elite readers as the "marvelous" work that it was. These readers were themselves Ming Wanli connoisseurs of not only books and literature but also tea and rocks, travel and wine, women and food (see chapter 3). Such readers would "recognize," indeed would adequately appraise, a new and different "objet d'art" if anyone could. Not coincidentally, these readers were socially and culturally positioned to affix to any "new" object on this urban scene the marker of elite approval, whereupon the new object would immediately become "hot stuff."

The histories of readings that may be seen as encrusting the text—forming and adding to it in such a way that a textual archaeology is necessary to separate one from another's lining, to distinguish each reading's relation to its "host" text—constitute part 1 of this book. The moments and structures of reading read in part 1 are parasitic, yet in feeding on their host (JPM), each reading transforms the text to satisfy its specific needs. The parasite changes but so does the host. Reading JPM in the early twenty-first century, it is no longer possible nor is it necessary to separate host from parasite since the former has become the sum of the latter's reformulations.

In part 1, I focus on only two historical moments or sedimentations in what might be called the complex that is JPM as received text. Chapters 2 and 3 both explore the moment of inception, the initial appearance of a marvelous manuscript in the Jiangnan region during the Ming Wanli period. Chapter 2 establishes the practical (prefatorial) and subjective effects of Wanli shifts in the culture and commodification of fiction in print. Chapter 3 closely examines the first circle of readers of JPM, especially one of its earliest readers on record (Yuan Hongdao). This constitutes the text's first layer of literary encrustation, and the fictional text that is embedded within these records of readings is both situated and advertised as a "new" narrative object—somewhat obscene but quite charming, and fit for the most refined literary taste. One such elite reader apparently read and consumed "obscene objects" without preconceptions of "obscenity." Only with subsequent considerations of wider dissemination in print did the readers of the early decades of the seventeenth century begin to concern themselves with questions of the "licentiousness" of the text. In this process, the text is transformed into an offensive against the encroachment of potentially improper parvenu reading subjects in the fictional literary fields then in the making. It is to this moment that one may trace the beginning of JPM's infamy as an "obscene book," a potentially pornographic work. JPM's so-called obscenity, however, had not yet amassed the weight of a coherent and consistently articulated morality that would achieve the simultaneous inflation and deflation of its *aesthetic-ethical* value. This occurs about eighty years later, in the early Qing period after JPM had already been officially banned as a "licentious work" (*yinshu*), when Zhang Zhupo instantiated a systemic aesthetic-ethical defense of this by now thoroughly moral obscene book (see chapter 4). In his process of rewriting the book as filial and therefore ethical, an aesthetics of resentment became the means for a textual innoculation against immoral readings and readers. The text itself was thus saved, and proper readers were both sated and protected.

Part 1 of this book constitutes discrete readings of two historical moments in the changing configurations of reading practices surrounding JPM, with the narrative text as a site for shifting negotiations of gender and social power. Chapters 2, 3, and 4 together suggest how readings of JPM have changed from the Ming Wanli to Qing Kangxi eras, and how such changes must be understood in relation to a vernacular fictional print culture that provided for the social and cultural articulation of differently situated literati subjects in crisis. These crises are brought on and intensified with the continuously redefined relations between a consumer-reader who has had to readjust his previously privileged relation to consumable texts. What happens when a position of virtual monopoly is eroded, and interpretative authority and control (albeit of minor and marginal not-yet-literary forms) fall into the hands of the nonofficially qualified (no degree) and relatively unknown (no fame)? This was the case with some of the editors and commentators of vernacular forms, anthologies, and other miscellaneous writings in cheap editions.[7] This is how I would recast the perennial question of who wrote JPM.

The answers to the question of who or what group of persons wrote JPM by generations of scholars in the twentieth century has, however, provided us with rather significant findings. On the one side are those who continue to come up with singular individual candidates, ranging from the top of the line—the "great" literati figures of Ming Jiajing and Wanli (Wang Shizhen, Tang Xianzu, and Li Kaixian)—to relatively lesser-known figures marginal to the literati establishment, but nevertheless possible candidates in that they have all been involved with vernacular fiction in one way or another, including the publishing of fiction (Jia Sanjin and Tu Long).[8] On the other side are those scholars who argue for a model of collective authorship that originates in oral/folk literature, and the evolving of oral material into textual vernacular forms. What both sides assume seems to be a rupture, a clear-cut divide between the individual literati author and an anonymous collective authorship of lesser social and cultural status and resources. To restate what has already become a cliché of Ming Wanli, this was precisely the moment of the overlap between such entities as individual elites and practices that had belonged to a distinctly lower social status. Urban commercialization, a booming print culture, and imperial political turmoil at least partially account for individual elites such as Wang Shizhen and Yuan Hongdao, or the not-so-elite such as Tu Long, engaging in cultural activities that included publishing and thus publicly championing obscenely marvelous new fictional works. This might have been inconceivable three generations earlier.

What I am more interested in is how this (to the twenty-first-century "modern" novel reader) uncannily "recognizable" product of a late Ming urban book culture was received and read, and by what kinds of readers. For sure, the illustriousness of its first readers has assured it a place among the great works, even with renewed scholarly hedging and qualifications. But successive readers who have wanted to "write" their readings into the text, to inhabit the authoritative position of exegete to a new cultural form, while remaking it for their particular cultural and ideological usage, need to be carefully examined as well. The historical transformations of a text in its different embodiments are the focus of the first part of this book. In exploring the first ascertainable circle of Ming Wanli readers, notably Yuan Hongdao and then Zhang Zhupo of the Qing Kangxi period, such a project is only just begun.

*Porous Intimacies*

JPM is a borderline text between the high literary and pornographic insofar as it is said to thematize obscenities: the sexual practices between a master and his many wives-concubines-bondmaids in an extended narrative form that conforms to cyclical retributive logic. Ultimately, almost all culprits die of their sexual/sensual excesses. It can be read, then, as much for as against the excesses it minutely details. The records of readings extant would actually show it to have been accessible to multiple and conflicting reading positions and investments. These are at least partially determined by the place of each reading position in the sociopolitical and economic state and symbolic order at the particular moment of reading. At the same time, the cumulative weight of differentiated sedimentation of readings has nonetheless produced an apparent devaluation of the text and its objects of textual and readerly desire as obscene and excessive. Only by carefully sifting through and peeling apart the different layers of readings can a previously difficult to read figure of representation—that of the bondmaid-concubine licentious woman—be discerned in shadowy yet vibrant and gyrating movement and speech. She is overshadowed and paradoxically made substantial by repeated readings that assimilate her familial and social baseness (jian) in symbolic and monetary value to an innate gender moral depravity, a feminized ethical impropriety. As such, she is made over, transubstantiated from penumbra (non)subject to the category of the classical "woman" alongside that of "little [petty] men" of whom superior men must always beware.[9] Assimilated to the general category of woman, she becomes nearly illegible in the specificity of her relations to gender, sexuality, and class-status in the urban mercantile (informal) economies in which her kind of persons survived and/or thrived momentarily as well as discontinuously from at least the late Ming to the early twentieth century in "peripheral" Chinese families and societies in the flux of vertiginous socioeconomic and political changes.[10]

A feminist reading would counter not just the cumulative gender-blind recuperative readings of JPM but also the ahistorical egalitarian assumption that would efface a barely perceptible differential shade between the positionalities of good-family women (liang fu) as sexual appendage and domestic reproductive instrument and debased bondmaid-concubine in her sexual opportunism and familial micropolitical machinations—this is what emerges as an urgent necessity rather than a program in these essays. In a sense, feminist readings inattentive to the historical class-status and gender-moral difference between good/chaste and base/unchaste womanhood risk resuscitating the moral high ground of a male literati readership. The sexual opportunism of base marginal gender persons remains illegible or, worse, is encompassed by the same victimization that might have proved her a "chaste victim" of rape in Ming-Qing times.[11] Nowadays, residual "chastity" discourse and sentiment is reformulated to produce the correct feminist "victim" of patriarchal abuse. This, too, is what emerges in attending to readings of JPM in ways that go against the grain of habitual modes of reading and thinking.

In this case, the temporal-spatial differences that merit closer attention are analogous to the spatiotemporal ones that have resulted in the recent proliferation of "feminisms," and I am thinking of the critiques of dominant feminism from the perspectives of postmodern, postcolonial, ethnic-nationalist, and third worldist feminists. The axiomatic of imperialism that, as Gayatri Spivak reminds us, is never far away from an unreflexive high feminist literary critical practice in the "West," might then be considered to parallel and indeed intersect the axiomatic of status-class-caste hierarchy (in Louis Dumont's use of the term) structurally embedded in dynastic Chinese and Confucian-Buddhist ideologies.[12] As Dumont has noted, this hierarchical sense of persons and things does not merely go away in modern democracies. If they are actively repressed in the "Western" democracies, in Asian- and Chinese-speaking regions, class-status and moral hierarchical sense and sentiment have latched onto amazingly contradictory forms and figures. For one thing, the denial of hierarchy in the embracing of egalitarian ideology in progressive readings whether of the May Fourth generation or recent feminists, as much as the positing of universal and therefore equal and liberatory categories (such as woman in contradistinction to man), together obscure the particular formation and representation of residual hierarchical personhoods such as the bondmaid-concubine yinfu.

It is then what Dumont has aptly termed an ideology of individual egalitarianism that subtends and explains an otherwise baffling continuity between disjunctive and even oppositional readings of progressive male intellectuals in the earlier half of the twentieth century and feminist readers in the latter half. Since undertaking this project ten years ago, I have repeatedly been asked: How and when exactly can Pan Jinlian as she is represented in JPM be read as agent in a way that would be meaningful for women (read: urban professional) in spaces like Taiwan in the latter half of the twentieth century? The film director Clara Law has partly answered that query by recasting Pan Jinlian (via Li Bihua's novelistic rewriting) as a reincarnated romantic heroine in twentieth-century Hong Kong. The question has stayed with me because it stumbles against a too easy identification with Pan Jinlian, and hence, an assimilation of such representations into the repertoire available for productive retrieval by twenty-first-century feminist individualists.

The representation of such women as Pan Jinlian in narratives like JPM, however, resists such assimilative readings. These representations resist in their detailing of the situational complexities of the bondmaid-concubine trajectory at a specific moment and place, in the tale of several kinds of bondmaid-concubine and their mythic or mythified "fate." These are the bad ones who come to a bad end, as it were—so bad that it is difficult not to resign their lives, sentiments, and positionalities to the dustbin of "history" and "tradition" or treat them as a kind of myth, an inverted fairy tale, no longer speaking relevantly to any kind of reality. But then, is there not a similar although perhaps reverse assimilatory logic at work in the celebratory study of the positive pole of male literati and elite or literate women's representations of self? Must not these also be treated as carefully, attentively, and suspiciously as those representations occupying the negative pole? There is nonetheless a tendency to have positive representations become the representations of "our" culture to "ourselves" as well as others. This tendency is all the more compelling (for this writer as well) through the invisible screen of not just individualist egalitarianism (thus the focus on individual authors and women writers and selves) but a concomitant identity politics (whereupon writing and representation is seen to emanate from and affirming of identity categories such as "women" and "men" over and above, say, bondmaid and mistress) in the attempt to have the past evidentially conform to and confirm our relatively new world order.

To do so, though, is to epistemologically refuse to know/notice and to politically efface the too obvious differences between, for example, the representation of an idealized mistress-bondmaid relation in the *Peony Pavilion* and the temporally conjunctive, differently compelling inflammatory representation of bondmaid-concubines en masse in JPM. It is also to forget the psychosocial investments of reading in returns variously translated into "disinterested" academic writing that may unwittingly reproduce ideologies (of individual egalitarianism or identity politics) constituting the very questions we now begin with.

To too quickly assimilate the particular formation, trajectory, and representation that is that of the bondmaid-concubine at a certain moment and place to a general category of woman is to first assume that the latter is an a priori with specific givens against which particular exempla are measured. Second, it is to ignore the avowedly shifting distance and placement of bondmaid-concubine in the discursive spectrum or field that makes up and constitutes "general" womanhood, which discursive spectrum or field more often than not is vectored toward the position of socially "valorized" womanhood. And finally, it is to erase the historical transformation and assimilation of the bondmaid-concubine status into moral (commoner) womanhood—in short, the "modernization" of hierarchical gender and sexual Chinese womanhood. The specific contours and fields wherein this transformation occurred needs further study.

As Maria Jaschok has shown in her cultural history of bondmaid-concubines, when the residual practices of bond servitude and bondmaids themselves were ultimately brought to court in the mid–twentieth century in Hong Kong as legal cases usually initiated by their masters/mistresses, the characterization of these surely very diverse women was quite consistent.[13] "[The] list of the girls' characteristics reads like an inversion of what were considered the attributes of respectable females excelling in the virtues of filial piety and obedience, reticence, loyalty, literal adherence to prescribed conventions."[14] The parameters of respectable femininity do not seem to have changed all that much from the late Ming to the mid–twentieth century in some familial-social spaces. Perhaps this can only be said of Hong Kong bond servitude in the early twentieth century as it might well retain strong(er) residual imperial markers ("feudal relations") as a "peripheral" colonial Chinese society. Nonetheless, my point is that given the tendency to represent bondmaid-concubines (in JPM in late Ming Jiangnan or court cases in the twentieth century) as "typically" inversions of proper or respectable femininity, must not this representation itself bear on and negatively mark how these figures as representations, these persons as embodied entities, can be read/understood? Here the reading is not just from the position of male intellectuals, however progressive and well meaning. It is also from the reading position of feminists, many of whom are female *intellectuals*, and as such, women and intellectuals in much greater proximity to, if not entirely within the field of valorized respectable femininity. In the hierarchical Chinese-speaking world (which has not entirely disappeared, at least not in places like Taiwan, for one), it is predominantly literacy and its concomitant ethical acculturation that ensure the training and grooming deemed already in the late Ming both proper and erotic-desirable in new ways (namely, in Li Yu's tract on the acquisition, grooming, and minimal *education* of one's own private concubines).[15]

The question is then one of distance and proximity, as well as how, when, and wherefrom to measure these. To the extent that the bondmaid-concubine trajectory and figure is represented as distant from the order and knowledge that form the core of civility and humaneness, she is tropologically close to domestic animals such as cats and dogs. These can be trained and groomed, and can give pride in ownership; at the other extreme, they can be punished and killed, or given away or sold. Insofar as they are not quite humane, they must never be trusted as such. Intimacy with such an order of persons is dangerous on two grounds. On the one hand, they may forget who they "are" and aspire to what they cannot become; their ambition may make them even more agreeable and instrumental. This gives rise to the other, greater danger for the master, for he may forget who they "are" to the point of becoming gradually assimilated in the reverse, base direction. In this particular hierarchical thinking, baseness is contaminating by an associative logic. It is both powerful (it contaminates) and weak (it cedes to superior force and place). It is a porous intimacy between the subject and its dependent-subjects—the latter being, in the words of a social economist of the Ming, "half-human half-objects." This is an imperial structuration of power at the level of the imperial and its attendant or affinally linked wealthy or powerful families (clans). Bond servant families might, when risen to illicit power via masters, mimic such formations—thus eunuch "families" in the wake of imperial favor (Li Ping'er's wealth and relative prestige). Merchant parvenu families might also tend to mimicry, like Ximen Qing's (thus the appositeness of Ximen's pairing with Li Ping'er). Mimicry in lifestyle and consumption patterns functions toward the transvaluation of forms of prestige and privilege. It does *not always* grant sociopolitical power or only vulnerable "travesties" of the latter; hence the social as well as ideological ephemeral/illusory nature of such "family" fortunes. Yet this vulnerability might itself be a myth maintained in representations such as JPM that seek to distinguish between "real" and "fake," and therefore, the legitimate symbolic hierarchy and its travesties and transgressions, amid the fascinating and frightening blurring of these very distinctions. The proliferation of such myths (of the chaotic blurring and merging, with always already a return embedded within the extended narrative logic) at particular historical moments and places might index an increasing difficulty in maintaining hierarchical distinctions in a sociopolitical matrix such as that of the late Ming.[16]

The porousness of intimate relations sometimes in the transgressive reverse direction extended at this historical conjuncture not just to patriarchal familial relations (the master becoming livestock in his reduced humaneness in the everyday company of catlike concubines; see chapter 7). It could also be metaphorically extended to the relations between reading, writing, authoritative authoring, and publishing in new fields of literary or *wenren* (cultural) work. Certain commentaried editions (by names of cultural renown) could create "masterworks" out of base vernacular genres and pastiches in a new market for popular books, thereby accelerating the "institutionalizing" of commentaries for a more *popular* "private" consumption (consumption not geared toward "public" government service). Yet such editions also affected the way in which fiction commentaries came to be viewed as yet another genre of "writing" or cultural work in the hallowed sense.[17] There is a sense in which urban market relations and literati writing, perhaps especially in the form of intimate records of reading on the margins of heretofore base popular texts, came to be mutually constructed and enhancing. In this context, one could then look for the traces of these porous relations, between new modalities of writing and reading, and commercial or market logic and concerns (see chapters 2 and 3).

*A Counterethics of Reading*

My focus on readings is in alignment with two recent strands of thinking. One is the rethinking of reading and writing beyond or this side of the solitary, individual, and individualist figure emblematic of reading/writing since the sixteenth century in Anglo-European art and civilization. This figure of the solitary reader tends to foreclose what Elizabeth Long has termed the "social infrastructures of reading." That is, how reading must be taught—as socialization occurs within specific social relationships—as well as the ways in which reading is socially framed through collective and institutional processes that legitimate certain texts, and how to read them.[18] The other is the close attention enjoined by Gayatri Spivak among others to the ethico-politics of particular subject positions formed in and enabled by different (positionalities of) readings available in a text, without forgetting the institutional and geographic boundaries that condition and limit such a responsibility in pedagogy and reading.[19]

This book's textual readings of letter notations, prefaces, and commentaried editions of JPM in the late Ming and early Qing periods largely remain within the parameters of a literary discipline that has taken for granted —and perhaps even in its close readings reified—some solitary reader embodied in a text. At the same time, the particularities of each reading's different conditions of possibility at least suggest the institutional and socioeconomic vectors of reading as social practice. This is how JPM is shown to become not one coherent text/myth but an agglomeration of different readings at different times and places, for various social, economic, and psychic uses. Who can accede to such readings, even if only to undo their power and reality effects, and what kind of position of reading in the present can reinscribe an avowedly feminist rewriting? These are the questions addressed in the latter part of the book. Communities (or aggregates not recognizable as such and without the latter's resources) as well as lone practices of readings remain that are difficult to sight/site, and cannot easily obtain academic sanction and social recognition.

Who reads JPM in this particular study is on another level circumscribed by my consideration of the text(s) as narrative. I have primarily used the three major recensions of JPM: the Wanli *Cihua* edition, the Chungzhen lightly commentaried edition, and the Zhang Zhupo fully commentaried version, in both the photocopied and newly typeset modern editions.[20] I have chosen to focus on these texts as narrative without recourse to the "novel" to loosen and dislodge as much as possible unnecessary comparative assumptions that arise in the wake of the analyses of the various readings. JPM appears at a moment and place where a form of hybrid storytelling (prose interlaced with verse) whether in manuscript or print had not quite congealed sufficiently into an easily recognizable literary genre with clearly targeted readers (on the market). It had to be made literary, and its place determined through successive readings, editorial polishing, published notational comments, and commentaried editions.

Yuan Hongdao's reading of JPM as comparable to the *Qifa*—a *fu* or prose poem whose transformational affective powers are at once subject and form of the narrative—suggests the possibility of reading JPM in a way difficult to imagine after Zhang Zhupo. What is interesting is not so much that Yuan was among the first to "value" JPM aesthetically (that is, as "literature"). In fact, I would argue the reverse: that it is Yuan's recommendations, however off-the-cuff, that to some extent set the course for JPM's subsequent literary trajectory. But this is not to disregard Yuan's recommendation. Rather, it opens up the possibility for reconsidering Yuan's comparison, not in the service of retrospectively establishing a fictional aesthetics but in order to approach as much as possible a mode of reading that is no longer readable. Such a heterogeneous reading points beyond the *yin shu* or pornography debate, as well as the ethico-aesthetic principles realized by and instituted in Zhang Zhupo's commentaried edition. Thus, embedded within JPM is a (Yuan's) prose poetic model of reading articulated to psychophysiological transformative powers, which can only perhaps today be approximated to necessarily different exorcistic effect through a psychoanalytic reading.

As a form of storytelling—or more precisely, as the story of a particular kind of domestic hierarchy between one man-master and several categories or symbolic values of women, and among these different women—and also as the story of legitimate sexual services and illicit sexual opportunism as well as the latter's punishment-retribution, JPM has exerted tremendous and lasting influence. Its influence has been a textually verifiable force (in its various editions, its continuing to be circulated and read through the Qing censorship, its rewritings in sequels and personal commentaried editions, the shadow of its influence in the *Dream of the Red Chamber*, its rewritings in contemporary drama and film, and so on). It has also been an infinitely reproducible figuration and plot, an ideologeme. It is this aspect of JPM that has both necessitated its reading as narrative and made that reading itself a narrative, another form of storytelling (see part 2, chapters 5–7).

In going back to the readings that have cumulatively formed JPM as both obscene object and ideological aesthetic-ethical countering of the obscene in the first four chapters of this book, I have been propelled by an alternative feminist rereading (see part 2). At the same time, this feminist reading needed to confront what had implicitly called it into place. What happened in the encounter was an unanticipated transformation of both. The readings of Yuan Hongdao and Zhang Zhupo reading JPM opened up onto a continual questioning and recognition of this project's epistemological assumptions and ignorance. One of these assumptions has turned into a primary preoccupation of this book—that is, an aesthetics-ethics of reading that can be traced to the ethical-political exegesis of "Chinese" canonical texts in general and literature in particular. This particular model of literary theory and critical practice must be understood in the context of a position of the literati always and already as potentially and ideally in service, bureaucratically and ideologically, to the (imperial) state.[21] This usually male intellectual subject position of the reader/writer of a text is often taken for granted if it is not reproduced and reified as a transhistorical structure (see chapter 1). A feminist reading of JPM must necessarily take on both the legacy of readings that have made it the formidably pornographic/antipornographic text that it is, and the problem of countering those readings by instancing a "feminist" reading and reading position of the text.

It is precisely at such a juncture, following the staging of an encounter between a feminist reader of JPM in late-twentieth-century Taiwan and commentators of JPM such as Zhang Zhupo, that further complications arise. These complications stem from the extent to which feminist revisionist work such as this one derive their authority and legitimacy *from* as much as *against* the literati subject position of reading under critique. It is this difficult recognition of the continuity of authoritative (intellectual-academic) positions occupied that is of ethical and political significance, without underestimating the ideological and political discontinuities achieved. Feminism introduces an angle of reading that in its textual and historical impossibility constitute a critique of both JPM's textual ideology and historicity. But it also interjects in its revisionary reading the shadow of its own historical moment and concomitant egalitarian-individualist common sense, just as it might well come to occupy a reformulated yet nonetheless authoritative position of reading. This is how I would now understand the eroto-phobic residues or shadows of a certain feminist revision of JPM. According to such a revision, the force and forms of a misogynist representation would exactly reproduce systemic gender oppression. Such a reading leaves little space for transformative knowledge or practice besides or alongside the position occupied previously by the would-be elite and state-servicing literati, and now inhabited by a feminist reader. Without a critical recognition of the possibility of such continuity, entailing the embodied habits (habitus, too) of authority, statism, and leadership, and the implicit identification with a professional (middle) class, such a feminist position of counterreading could become yet another literati reading position for a new time and place.

In fact, this has already unwittingly as well as strategically happened. The reading of Yang Zhao's preface in chapter 8 is one example of a contemporary (male) literary critic who reads from a position informed by a gender-politics-sensitive position. Yet, as I have argued, Yang obstructs the very possibility of reading a "lesbian" erotic writing to the extent that his reading wishes to recuperate such "lesbianism" as something always already known and knowable (in this case, a particular "Taiwanness" coded in narrative realism). One might say that in Yang's case, a sense of the politics of sexuality welded to nationalist sentiment produces the latter dictating the (again) aesthetic-ethical evaluation of the former. This continuation of the position of the erstwhile literati as always and already in potential service to the state has also occurred in the feminist debates around the licensed prostitutes issues in Taiwan from the fall of 1997 through 1998.[22]

In chapters 6 and 7, the focus is on JPM as a representation of bondmaid-concubine women and agential sexual opportunism with enduring "truth effect" that would erase the "bondmaid-concubine" and "agential" traces of writing-reading thenceforth sublimated into the "mythic truth" of (potentially all) women as embodying a sex that kills (potentially all) men. Such an insistent encircling of specific figures and sequences in JPM works toward undoing the certainty or reification of object and subject with which this study began. The identity of woman as reader and woman's agency as instantiated through rereading can only be sustained through attention to the impossibility of such a project insofar as rereading draws forth difference and particularity. I would like to think that the project is a step toward not the fixing of identities but the forging of connective tissue and political solidarity between a never fully readable Pan Jinlian as bondmaid turned concubine arch-yinfu for all (Chinese) time, and present-day sexually transgressive and opportunistic ënu as representations of queer women in Taiwan (difficult to categorize and recognize in contemporary high literary terms or dominant ideology). The connective tissue is woven in the representation of their sexuality, and in its readings as both constitutive yet simultaneously critical of (rather than simply denigrating and denying) their particular gender-class trajectories and sexual practices. Perhaps reading Chen Xue and her ënu alongside Yuan Hongdao and his Qifa is one way to rethink yinfu as not merely the composite tropological object of misogynist representation but one whose assemblagelike body parts and sexual/market opportunism continue to resist and critique progressive intellectual appropriation and criticism (including my own). This is where political solidarity can become the intellectual and practical mediation or lining that allows for contact between the two, yinfu and ënu, as representations inhabiting at once different and coeval time and space, read here side by side. The figure of a feminist woman-intellectual reader, in reading and service to yinfu and ënu, shifts away from models of universal liberation (centripetal to the United States and Europe) as well as the historically authoritative position of the intellectual/literatus (centripetal to some culturalist and/or statist Chineseness) toward new interventions and struggling aggregation. This is how an examination of misogynist reading structures can then begin to excavate in the "past" (Yuan Hongdao's letters) and "present" (Chen Xue's short stories) sensual/sexual sentiments in reading and writing that are lines of flight from the strictures of modern democratic bipolar gender dominance.

I have indicated in the above the multiple contexts that have served as fulcrum to the major concerns of this book. Let me now go through each of the eight chapters in turn. In chapter 1, the "modern" egalitarian and individualist sexual ideology of major twentieth-century scholarly studies and interpretations of JPM are reviewed and analyzed. Symptomatically—however otherwise researched, erudite, and sophisticated the scholarship—most studies reproduce a consistent gendered logic.

Chapter 2 examines the transformations of the mental world of the literati of the mid- to late Wanli period, reading in detail the prefaces of Li Zhi and Jin Shengtan for the SHZ in order to establish the shifts in concerns vis-à-vis an increasingly distant imperial bureaucracy, and an increasingly vibrant and ever-present urban market in fictional books. This shift of focus, from imperial service to market management, parallels the expansion of a "public" space that had hereto been envisaged and represented as "private"—that is, having little to do with bureaucratic and official service to the imperial state. The rise and commercialization of such a non-state-service-oriented "public" space marks the beginning of new discursive battlegrounds, defining and negotiating new subjects of representation, consumption, and ownership. The Wanli proponents of minor literary forms include among them famous and influential admirers of the SHZ (JPM's previous shorter life) along with the first readers of a manuscript version of JPM, the earliest recorders to date of JPM's appearance.

Chapter 3 reads some of these earliest records of readings. One of these readings (Yuan Hongdao's) makes a telling comparison. This comparison holds the key, I suggest, to understanding some of the embedded cultural meanings of a new fascinating cultural object. The reading of JPM is through such a comparison subliminally articulated with what has been called the "shamanistic substratum" of popular fictional forms.[23] This articulation retrieves for all those who have the necessary cultural capital or knowledge a *structure of reading* that correlates illness, melancholy, and everyday consumption, in a rhetoric evoking Taoist hygienic regimes of the body and its preservation. The problem then becomes one of distinction, or internal stratification within a reading public that at the time ranged from elite readers—the cream of the Wanli crop of imperial examinees—to overreaching and newly wealthy provincial clerks and even bond servants. Sensual/sexual consumption presents a terrain par excellence for struggles *between men* as to what can and should be consumed by whom, in what circumstances and forms, and for whose good and what kind of benefit? Aestheticization is one answer to the problem since an aestheticized erotics can serve to both distinguish between users (readers) and between modalities of use (ways of reading, whether exhortational or prohibitive, gluttonous or refined).

In chapter 4, I take a closer look at one instance of such aestheticization as reading strategy by analyzing Zhang Zhupo's prefaces and how-to-read listings for "his" JPM. In arguing specifically against a "pornographic" reading of JPM, and promoting an ethical, filial even, alternative reading, Zhang Zhupo produces both the moral (pornographic) subject and his pornographic (immoral, antimoral) "other"—Pan Jinlian, a yinfu for all ages.

Part 2 is made up of successive and sequential interventionist readings of JPM. The first sequence, in chapter 5, is the preliminary "seduction." Textual seduction works through a staging of an eroticized battle between a martial-warrior hero and a tiger. This is then juxtaposed to the same hero pitted against an adulterous and licentious sister-in-law, as representative yinfu.

The second series of narrative moments, read in chapter 6, are those of fascination. Textual fascination is produced in pictorial setups and a narrative paralleling of a concubine-yinfu hanging from her feet, with her vagina as receptacle for plums and penises; wives, concubines, and bondmaids in pairs on a swing in the garden; and finally a bond servant's wife, the most recent favorite of the master, hanging from the rafter in her room. Bondage imagery is for women whose familial and sexual place is that of bondmaid, concubine, or bond servant's wife. Bond servants abound at this particular moment and place (the late Ming Jiangnan period) via a commercial urban economy whereby they are sometimes able to overreach their sociofamilial base status to become sexual/market opportunists and wielders of an insecure wealth and intimate power.

In chapter 7, I read the tropes whereby bondmaid-concubines are made over into "obscene things"—a cat, dog's piss, but also the master's urine are all associated with the yinfu in such a way as to show up the contaminating powers of intimate domestic and sexual appendages. This particularly abjecting narrative sequence finales with the antifilial master reduced to livestock (thus of a less-than-human(e) order)—befitting one who played his extensions, dependents, and appendages to excess, yet also marking the revenge of the feline/female.

Chapter 8 offers a retake on Zhang Zhupo in light of recent literary developments in Taiwan. The appearance of lesbian erotic stories and queer fiction in 1990s Taiwan has elicited both formal responses from the literary establishment, readings as prefaces and criticism in major literary journals, and the informal ever-extending discussions on the Internet, especially among the various gay, lesbian, and queer discussion boards. I juxtapose Zhang Zhupo's reading of JPM with Yang Zhao's preface to Chen Xue's collection of short stories, *Enu Shu*, and find the continuing problematizing of the representation of female sexuality from self-claimed "representatives" of the literary field. But whereas Zhang Zhupo evinces a desiring and highly ambivalent relation with his textual objects, Yang Zhao's relation is both more condescending and prescriptive. This is not surprising in view of the new social and political forces at work in Taiwan at the moment, when democratizing momentum is fast transforming into a reticent policing of social and sexual dissidents. In siding with historical yinfu and contemporary ënu, this study proposes a counterethic of reading that would forge dissident erotic relations alongside and away from hegemonic male-female modalities of desiring, reading, and writing.

 PART ONE: PRACTICES

CHAPTER 1

Jin-ology

I submit that what the Chinese of today mean by "the love between man and woman" is still entirely bestial desire of the flesh (shouxing de rouyu). What should be done today, is on the one hand to forcefully eliminate such books as JPM, and on the other hand, to actively translate elegant works of romance and desire. Perhaps fifty years later, there may be some hope of a change in mores. These types of books [such as JPM], even if one were to regard them as literature, have no value. Why? An important element in literature is the aesthetic affect. And what is the aesthetic affect you get from reading JPM?
—Hu Shi, "Da Qian Xuantong shu"

In an essay recounting a personal history of his study of JPM, Zhang Yuanfen, one of the foremost Jin-ology (jin xue) scholars in China, writes of how the fact that he has a "feminine" name has resulted in rumors about him to the effect that "a woman who studies the JPM cannot be a good woman."[1] At about the same time in the United States, in a comparative work on desire in Chinese and French fiction with a section on JPM, author Tonglin Lu dedicates the book to her parents while apologizing for the indecency of this "gift."[2] In a Chinese-speaking context, and in the context of the study of Chinese literature and history in English, subjects of study connoting or somehow linked to sexual desire are, despite academic garb, not respectable. It is this halo of indecency that my study seeks to explore. JPM as book and constellation of myths have been tenaciously guarded as a "male" territory. The implicit gender and sexual politics in its twentieth-century readings need to be made explicit and analyzed for their implications.

The question that has haunted almost all twentieth-century interpretations of JPM—whether in China, Taiwan, Hong Kong, or the United States—has been: Is JPM an obscene book (yinshu) or not? Such a query presumes, just as it hopes to establish, a "naturally" or "essentially" indecent book. Only if this question could be answered conclusively, could the book be safely categorized and read accordingly. If obscene, then perhaps the book could be relegated to the realms of the trivial and incidental, instead of taking up a space between the inconsequential and truly important, marking the line between the two as porous and thereby portentous. The problem was that the book had once been included among the top four vernacular must-reads on the lists of renowned literati of the late Ming period. Moreover, in the twentieth century, these literati had come to be seen as harbingers of a distinctly "modern" ("Chinese") sensibility. Theirs seemed a taste both native and translatable into twentieth-century bourgeois bon vivant terms. What had they seen or read in this work that made it one of the four "great" works? How was it that by the early twentieth century, it seemed irreparably coarse and vulgar, long-winded and lewd?

The question of obscenity recurs in different forms in almost all the literary interpretations of JPM.[3] In attempting to actualize "obscenity" in the text, two mutually exclusive categories have arisen: one literary therefore not (truly) obscene, and another obscene therefore necessarily common and base. Invariably, the "obscene" in such a reckoning refers to the narrative's excessive and excessively detailed representation of sex and women (sex as for the most part women) as desirable, and hence personally, hygienically, and politically destructive. Insofar as these excessive details found both the literary and obscene, the claim to the high literary repudiates the concretely or literally "obscene" at the risk of being haunted by the return of that which it sought to expel. The more systematic and coherent the interpretation, the greater the force of the return.[4]

The force of the return is in part facilitated by a misogynist (and often eroto-phobic as well) structure of reading in which the reader-critic participates and is then reinscribed to the extent that he/she reads the "obscene" as not obscene at all. Be it a moral lesson on how not to cultivate the self (Andrew Plaks, *The Four Masterworks of the Ming Novel*), an illustration of a Chinese philosophy of human baseness (David Roy, *The Plum in the Golden Vase*), a celebration of a humanist individualist instinct (C. T. Hsia, *The Classic Chinese Novel*), an exposure of the evils of late Ming social and sexual mores (Huang Lin), or an incidental fashion of late Ming times (Lu Xun, *A Brief History of Chinese Fiction*), such readings regard the obscene as metaphysically useful or sociohistorically informative. It is only on these accounts that otherwise censorable parts are readable and acceptable. Neither the stakes nor effects of such metaphysical lessons or sociological information are questioned. What are the stakes, and what are the cumulative effects, at the levels of the literary, social or psychophysiological? One effect is to affirm that JPM is paradoxically obscene and not obscene at all since with the correct reading, it would yield its higher (ethical, philosophical, historical, or literary) message. At stake in positing such a paradox are the institutional and personal authority commanded by one's status as a "professional" member of academe, continuous with and succeeding to the position of erstwhile literatus, rather than just being any reader. Whereas "any" reader might succumb to (by believing in) the literal sex and literally sex-crazed women, a professional reader cannot avow to such a level of reading. Nor can the professional reader-critic account for the literal reader's persistence through at least three hundred years of "popular" readings, except perhaps as an inherent lack of training and knowledge. The assumption that remains constant from Zhang Zhupo in the early Qing period (late seventeenth century) to the present, in this line of argument, is that such readers "wrong" the narrative in being unable to recognize and realize its difference from common pornographic materials. This tactic of reading saves the now safely literary text and its knowledgeable (community of) reader-critics (erstwhile literati). It leaves aside the question of the nonetheless excessive detailing of sex and those innumerable readers transfixed in the wrong way.

It is the literally draining emplotting of women, and sex with women (often but not exclusively female bond servants) and male bond servants, that founds the metonymic networks of (male-literatus) personal and (imperial) sociopolitical meanings articulated in the narrative. Such a network further enables a masculine "structure of feeling" (in Raymond William's term) that is shared by both scholarly and nonscholarly opinion.[5] This, then, is the structure of misogyny that has gone undetected because it has repeatedly been considered incidental through at least three centuries of readings. The historical mapping of some of the better-known readings of JPM, alongside my excessive reading of JPM's textual processes as a misogynist, eroto-phobic sexual subjection, will together discover the extent to which the obscene, moral, and literary-aesthetic are mutually imbricated. The enduring obscene force emanated by JPM is this very imbrication.

In this chapter, I will first situate the institutional and historical frame within which questions concerning a politics of reading practices arise and signify. I will then reread relevant parts of selected major scholarly studies of JPM in the twentieth century in Chinese and English (in the fields of Chinese literary studies in China, Taiwan, Hong Kong, and the United States). Here, to begin with, I demonstrate how twentieth-century readings in Chinese of the representation of sex and women (nüse) in JPM have remained within the paradigmatic readings set up in the early 1920s by Lu Xun and Hu Shi. Such readings are unable to account for the representation of sex and women in a contextualized and contextualizing manner, whether within one text, between different recensions of JPM, or between text and sociohistorical context.

Second, this inability is partly conditioned by a (constructed) sense of "phantasmatic recognition" of a "modern" (male) subjectivity, or seemingly "recognizable" structures of feeling and reading in specific late Ming discourses on the part of certain intellectuals in the 1920s and 1930s. It is the historical and disciplinary or institutional context of such a fantasmatic recognition and this uncanny sense of recognition that dually ground diverse critics' readings of and reactions to sex in JPM. A reconstruction of an earlier indigenous Chinese "modernity" in terms of literary and emotional individualist precursors (late Ming–early Qing forebears of a "modern" male Chinese sensibility and taste) produces a culturally and politically useful or necessary sense of elite continuity. It is this largely invented "continuity" of the subject (male and literatus) that obscures the apprehension of the historicity of representations of sex and women in JPM. In other words, in the construction of an "authentically" Chinese modern male reading and writing subject whose precursor is projected as the late Ming individualist literatus, sex and gender ideologies are silently reproduced as attendant shadows. That there is a history to sex and gender representation is as conveniently forgotten as is the recent history of colonial encounters as partially determining and necessitating a reappraisal of the late Ming moment, and some of its cultural and philosophical thematics.

The final section will selectively review those readings in Chinese and English that have contributed to the gender and sexual politics that mediate the reception and circulation of JPM today. Such a review is necessarily bounded by the question it seeks to ask. In this case, scholarly studies that have been and continue to be of paramount importance, not least to this very project, nevertheless show a tendency to read gender and sex in JPM in a commonsense light, unlike almost every other aspect of the text—as if the representation of such familiar and familial matters as intimacy, gender, and sexuality had no history, no context other than "our" own in the present.

I do not deal with readings of JPM in Manchu, Korean, Japanese, Vietnamese, French, or German. Given the continuing impact of translations of JPM in, for example, Korean and Japanese, a comparative study of JPM in non-Chinese translations for differential inter-Asian cultural effects would be the necessary follow-up to the present work.

*Phantasmatic Recognitions*

When Lin Yutang writes for an English-reading audience in the United States in the 1930s that "in speaking of a scholar, *the Chinese* generally distinguish between a man's scholarship, conduct, and taste, or discernment," he was writing at a peculiar historical moment when what it meant to be at once "Chinese" and "modern" seemed to urgently need reformulation. Rather than jettisoning the entire history and culture of which he was heir, Lin chose to mediate that history and culture to an English-speaking audience. In the process of mediation, he "invented" a modern Chinese literatus, or a cultured Chinese male subject in translation. This process of mediation wherein a learned (what Lin terms "scholarship"), ethical ("conduct"), and above all aesthetically refined ("taste" or "discernment") male subject is formed, and wherein one can find distilled specific moments and elements of "Chinese" cultural history, merits a study on its own. What is particularly relevant in Lin Yutang's program of the "Chinese scholar as an aesthete" is his reification of a discourse about and attitude toward things and life that he then translates as paradigmatically "Chinese" and "refined-cultivated" at once. As has already been noted and studied, this discourse and attitude is largely a recuperation and selective translation of certain literati—men of letters in the widest and highest sense—of the late Ming moment.[6] Coincidentally, this same moment and these same figures have, in the history of Chinese thought in mainly sinology in the United States, also figured as preeminently "liberal" or "individualist" thinkers, iconoclastic and heterodox, approximating a quasi-romantic rebellious topoi.[7]

The ideological convergence of these two interpretative trends seems no accident—with Lin Yutang as the anticommunist "native" mediator producing in his English essays and translations the mirage of a quintessentially aesthetic and Confucian "liberal humanist," and the U.S. academic research that also produces a libertarian subject and/of discourse in late Ming China—in a concerted effort to show that "liberalism" is innate and natural in even so "different" a history and culture as "the Chinese case."[8]

But this is to stray somewhat from the topic of this chapter, although it indirectly indicates how the study of the late Ming is relevant or has in fact been "made" relevant to concerns of the present—namely, how to "naturalize" modernity and modern subjectivity in histories and cultures that did not produce it in the forms that make it recognizable (in today's world and the English ideo-lect). I would suggest that Lin Yutang in a populist sense and academic research on the "liberal self" in a more restricted institutional space have both been concerned with a discursive production of just such a modern Chinese subject. Interestingly enough, this subject is modern in a manner that is seen to originate in the late Ming, while being articulated through an aesthetic-philosophical discourse that is also deeply ethnic- and cultural-nationalist. I would add that this modern subject and subjectivity is furthermore gendered and of particular sexual tendencies. That is to say that Lin Yutang and academic discourses on late Ming thought together reproduce a specific sexualized male positionality in their diverse writings.

This is how a masculine structure of feeling and reading becomes an integral part of the historical formation of modern Chinese literatus as social status and psychophysiological subject: as both construct and perception of early-twentieth-century Chinese intellectuals. Lin Yutang specifically refers to the late Ming as a founding moment and the writers of the late Ming–early Qing as particularly close to the heart-mind of an early-twentieth-century Chinese (as opposed to Western/Anglo-European) elite aesthete-literatus.[9] What are the conditions for this affinity—of reading and writing, thinking and feeling, actions even—such as to be perceived as parallel to and originating in the literati-gentry urban material culture of a late Ming Jiangnan?

If certain figures and discourses of the late Ming period have been successfully recuperated for modernizing projects, what are the historical and cultural conditions of discourse that make such projects possible? How do emergent fields of cultural practice, amid the growth of a book market in

Jiangnan urban centers in the last decades of the Ming era, help to construct a "new" cultural subject? A subject that is at the same time both a "custodian of Classical truths" and "professional writer"?[10] Someone who reads and writes as a gatekeeper and mediator, someone who traffics in not just correct knowledge but tasteful "understanding"?

The recognition of an affinity between the inner life and cultural expressions of an elite group of literati in the seventeenth (Ming-Qing transition) and early twentieth centuries questions at least two aspects of modernity. One is the shared matrix (between present-day readers of Chinese texts and seventeenth-century readers) of a Chinese print culture that began at least in the eleventh century, and that only by the late twentieth century was beginning to be profoundly transformed by new computer technology. This in itself would necessitate the rethinking of how localized print cultures constitute one aspect of a Chinese print modernity. A second, more vexed issue is that of the historical point of rupture between a universal (Eurocentric) modernity, and a supposedly premodern (or non-Western-industrial-capitalist) culture and subjectivity. The positing of a radical rupture between modern and premodern as occurring sometime around 1911 reproduces the epistemological frame of the republican revolutionaries as historical "truth." It also reproduces as radical discontinuity what is as much a product as it is a symptom of a colonial subjection (in Chinese).

The modern/premodern binary that has inhered in much twentieth-century study of Chinese history and literature in English, as well as in many otherwise disparate and conflicting Chinese views of a pre-1911 literature and sensibility, is a convenient misconception. It allows for a definition of modernity that serves the purposes of a Eurocentric sense of modernity as a regional historical phenomenon whose significance is global and universal. At the same time, a generation of Chinese intellectuals thereby achieved a convenient shoring up of a psychically and politically necessary sense of radical rupture from a "feudal past." The two positions together produce a modern/premodern China as disciplinary frame and historical structure that underlies the fields of both sinology and early modern European culture. Sinology in the United States comprises the historical, textual, archaeological, geographic, literary, and folkloric study of "premodern" China (in the singular), and this is symptomatic of the problem. By contrast, "modern" China (likewise often in the singular, recapitulating a political nation-state as entity) is mostly the object of study of such supposedly modern disciplines as anthropology, sociology, political science, comparative literature, and cultural studies.

To put it in the most reductive terms, the production of a two-part temporal structure for a nonetheless homogenized China is at least in part a residual of early-twentieth-century colonial knowledge formation. This formation was at one point crucial for reproducing historically and epistemologically Eurocentric knowledge-production as the only "correct" knowledge of and for a modern self and present. Other possible modernities and trajectories thereof are then analyzed in negative terms, with the presupposition that some inherent "stagnating" or "static" element structurally prevented their development along the lines of an Euro-Anglo modernity and industrialization. As a result, China is yet another great, ancient civilization alongside the Greek, Hindu, and Egyptian, all of which somehow have too little (or too much, depending on which side one wishes to root for) to do with their present-day problematic incarnations.

One of the implications of such a view is a sometimes willed refusal to recognize what Raymond Williams has termed "residual" cultural formations in contemporary Chinese cultural formations.[11] These cultural formations and, as I shall show, specific structures of reading need to be understood not only in their synchronic but their diachronic dimensions. Such formations and structures have historically specific configurations and social as well as psychophysiological functions. The dual tracing of both their historical transformations and their social and individual usages at a particular moment and place would contribute to the understanding of particular cultural mechanisms of transmission and the power processes at stake therein.

This is where a comparative perspective may yet be useful—not in the sense of whether tragedy is or is not "universal," which really means whether it is or is not found in its European definition in "other" histories and modes; nor whether the novel is great in China, or not so great, with again the unspoken European modern novel as litmus test. Rather, it may be helpful in trying to think through questions of the production and consumption, the writing and reading, of distinct cultural forms at a specific moment in historical time within a matrix that is comparable, or thinkable dialogically. One matrix is the commercial print culture that in Europe at least, has already been acknowledged and is now being studied as one of the formative conditions of a (Anglo-European in origin, global in effect) modern subjectivity. As readers and writers, we live and think— we read and write—within the parameters of that technology, even if these same parameters are quickly being eroded, dislodged, and reformulated with computer technology.

A comparative perspective that takes into account the shared matrix wherein a "global" modernity is produced—urbanization, commercialization, print culture—may serve to redress the imbalance in English of stubbornly Eurocentric notions of fictional forms and development. The mirage of "similarities" and "differences" that strike a reader of so-called classical Chinese fiction and the Western novel are not reducible to a case of "seeing double," nor are they entirely the product of U.S. academic imperialism. Much more fruitfully, they may be seen as determined by comparable changes in modes of cultural production (print technology), and the relations between the producers of culture, their socioeconomic context, and consumers of their products. Vernacular fictional forms in Chinese and the allegedly modern subject that these fictions engender have begun to be studied. Poststructuralist deconstructive and new historicist studies have sought to and perhaps have succeeded in toppling the myth of a universal transcendental humanist subject of modernist discourses; regrounding this subject and formation processes, showing "his" embeddedness and inextricability from particular (neither universal nor transcendental) historical, social, political, and economic milieus, as well as "his" gender, sexuality, race, and class specificities. Other and alternative subjects and subjectivities have also emerged—out of histories that can no longer be considered singular or total, and in contemporary writings from positions of diverse marginality and alterity. Yet, "the" modern subject is still largely understood as a product of a European renaissance, enlightenment, and industrialization that migrated elsewhere through colonialism.

Furthermore, to return to the study of pre-republican Chinese literature, in both Chinese and English scholarly studies, the "myth" of a radical rupture around 1911 with the demise of the Qing dynasty maintains. This myth is the effect and product of a collaborative enterprise: between, on the one hand, a generation of intellectuals who had a vested interest in producing a modern Chinese writing to go with what they saw as a radically new body politic and, on the other hand, scholars who are sympathetic to or have acquiesced to such efforts at establishing a radical break with a "very" nonmodern past. The institutional shape of sinology in English reproduces this split—with modern Chinese literature and history beginning sometime in the nineteenth century at the earliest, as if contact with an imperialist West somehow inaugurates for all "other" locales the ascertainable beginnings of a bona fide modernity. Not surprisingly, this myth of a modernity of solely Anglo-European origin and configuration is sustained from the "outside" of sinology by studies of print culture in early England and Europe that relegate contemporaneous and comparable developments in print technology and dissemination in Ming China or Korea to the briefest parenthetical aside. Ignorance is at least partially accountable for a persistently Eurocentric understanding of the possible historical dimensions and contours of a twentieth-century "hybrid-modern" subjectivity in such non-Western geopolitical locations as Hong Kong and Taipei. Colonial and postcolonial history is formative of that subjectivity, but what of structural formations that arise prior to and have continued into the present—in however deformed and renewed configurations?

The effects of such a notion of rupture as the start of modernity for the study of Chinese vernacular narratives are at once explained and exemplified in C. T. Hsia's seminal *The Classic Chinese Novel*. Writing in the early 1960s in the United States, Hsia aims to provide, in his words, "critical interpretations" of six classic Chinese novels. In the introduction to the book, he gives an account of how vernacular Chinese fictional forms have fared since the republican revolution of 1911. According to Hsia, by the end of the Qing dynasty in the late nineteenth century, "enlightened scholars and journalists had become concerned with the social influence of popular literature and, in particular, of the novel."[12] This led to a call for "new fiction"—that is, fiction aimed at inculcating in the masses the new (modern, Western) ideas that would "[prepare] the Chinese people to face the modern world." Subsequently, the May Fourth writers registered this same dissatisfaction with the entire corpus of "old fiction," only with more ambivalence and a conscious attempt, at least on the part of Hu Shi, to salvage a few from the debris. Hsia explains this ambivalence of an entire generation of readers of old fiction in the following revealing terms:

> One could say that like Hu Shi, they were very fond of traditional Chinese fiction in their early youth, but once exposed to Western fiction, they could only acknowledge, implicitly if not explicitly, the greater technical proficiency of the latter along with its far greater moral seriousness.[13]

And Hsia concludes,

> Though as a rule exceptions are made of the greater novels, usually including the six to be discussed here, modern scholars and writers of the pre-Communist period are generally agreed that the traditional novel as a whole is profoundly disappointing. This feeling was at first inseparable

from a sense of national shame which they shared, but it soon matured into an honest recognition of the artistic inferiority of the old Chinese novel in comparison with the Western novel.[14]

It seems that Hsia may have been inadvertently speaking not just of Hu Shi's generation but even to some extent of his own, and his own ambivalence—equally obvious throughout Hsia's book. This ambivalence and the terms with which Hsia explains it are symptomatic. The trajectory of reading that Hsia describes is simultaneously a coming of age through an encounter with the "West" as modern political and military power, and Western fiction as embodiment and representative of that superiority. Both are, in the perception of the converted colonized, inherently imbued with "greater technical proficiency" and "greater moral seriousness," which together make up "artistic superiority." This is to say that this ambivalence—and the "critical" perspective it sustains—is a function of the historical moment and location that inform judgment, reading, and interpretation. Thus, Hsia is more prone to note the "militant nationalism" of what seems to him Mao Tse-tung's uncritical affirmation of old fiction as "national forms" of literature. Whereas Hsia's belief in "a modern preference for honesty and sophistication in literary understanding" goes unquestioned.[15] Modernity is equated with a biological maturity, not simply for individuals but for nations and culture.

> A student of the traditional Chinese novel who has been at all exposed to Western fiction is sooner or later struck by the sharp contrast between the majority of unrewarding works composing that genre and a number of titles which . . . possess enough compensating excellences to appeal to the adult intelligence. . . .
> Whatever the critical fashion in Communist China, it seems to me self-evident that we cannot accord the Chinese novel full critical justice unless, with all our due awareness of its special characteristics that can only be fully understood in historical terms, we are prepared to examine it against the Western novel.[16]

The Western novel in its unchallengeable superiority transcends its historical specificities, whereas Chinese (old) fiction can only be read, on the one hand, as cultural remnants of a history that is already past (in this sense, it very much resembles the art of native peoples in museums, which are neither allowed to evolve "into" the present nor assimilable without the apparatus of specialist academic knowledge).[17] Curiously, such a statement might almost be read as a resonant allegory of the geopolitical field. On the other hand, to be accorded full critical justice, Chinese fiction must be read against the Western novel, and here, "critical" in effect stands in for both "modern" and "Western." Ideology resides only within the texts read, with their writers and readers of premodern times, and finally also in a militantly nationalist Maoist China; the only thing that seems ideology free is Hsia's own book's modern critical (liberal humanist) cosmopolitan outlook. Hsia's book, fascinating as it is, is no less a product of its moment and place, and as such, more an account that mediates for an English academic readership of the 1960s in the United States a Chinese fiction that seems continuously in need of qualifications in order to measure up to so-called modern standards of reading.

From the perspective of the late 1990s, it is too easy perhaps to detect in Hsia's account an underlying devaluation of Chinese prose fiction that may be seen as continuing a "traditional" literati denigration for this least respectable of forms. Yet this "inherited" implicit denigration is further abetted by a new sense of the intrinsic inferiority of the genre. Thus, in conjecturing on the writer of JPM, Hsia refers to one of the candidates, a well-known dramatist of Ming Wanli:

> A noted playwright, Hsu Wei would have been familiar with the type of popular songs introduced in Jin Ping Mei, though one may question whether his eccentric genius *could have fathered a book of such low culture and ordinary mentality.* But quite apart from internal evidence, there is very little likelihood that the author could have been a leading intellectual of his time.[18]

Hsia's reading of Chinese old prose fiction as being the work of "low" and "popular" culture, aimed at readers who are not the elite of their time, allows him to register a contempt that masks itself as a critical judgment.

Two decades later, in a monumental work on Chinese prose fiction, Andrew Plaks responds to Hsia's interpretations and damning judgment. *The Four Masterworks of the Ming Novel,* of encyclopedic proportions and intent, signals a decisive paradigm shift in sinological work on Ming-Qing fiction, begun with Robert Hegel's *The Novel in Seventeenth-Century China.*

*Masterworks* shows up the lack of basis for Hsia's reading of Chinese prose fiction of the Ming dynasty by emphasizing the need for contextualization. In the introduction, Plaks offers a sweeping account of the "political, economic, social, intellectual, cultural, and literary history" within and against which background "the four masterworks" are to be read. At the same time, he explains how it is from the perspective of comparative literature that he is able to cohere his readings of all four works as "ironic" texts—the products of a mode of consciousness that are comparable to modern Western "ironic" works of fiction. He also notes how this comparative frame is further justified by the "globalization" that marks both late Ming China and Renaissance Europe. Finally, Plaks specifically writes of the usefulness of "inspiration and guidance from the traditional Chinese commentaries . . . [whose] excesses and idiosyncrasies . . . have often barred [their insights] from the serious study of the Ming novel in recent times."[19]

The triadic stress—first, on a contextualized understanding of prose fiction in Ming China; second, on the globalization that would warrant thinking across disciplinary and imperial boundaries; and third, on the importance of contemporaneous readings of this fiction for "reconstructing . . . what these books may have meant to their immediate audiences, the literati readers of the sixteenth and seventeenth centuries"—constitutes a paradigm shift in the study of Chinese prose fiction in English.[20] These points also serve to refute Hsia's equivocal judgments of this same fiction as written for and read (and preferred) only by the lowly, or in one's green youth.

In contextualizing prose fiction in the latter half of Ming China, though, Plaks foregrounds the correspondences between intellectual history—that is, the history of ideas—and the rise and culmination of prose fiction in their "definitive" forms as embodied in "the four masterworks."[21] Moreover, he explicitly cautions against connecting the "publishing boom" of the sixteenth century to the rise of new genres of fiction: "It is misleading to associate our masterworks of vernacular fiction with this development . . . [since] many of the earliest known editions of all four works are relatively fine printings, apparently expensive and meant for only limited circulation."[22]

The emphasis on the correspondences between a history of ideas and the rise of vernacular prose fictional genre, along with a de-emphasis on the material conditions (in terms of technologies of cheap reproduction, standardization, and dissemination), in fact the very medium that makes possible both intellectual history and prose fiction, would seem somewhat puzzling if it did not simultaneously serve another important thesis of the book.

> These remarks on self-consciousness, alienation, and the like may perhaps smack of the intellectual presumptions of contemporary sensibility. But we can anchor them more securely in sixteenth-century Chinese thought

Jin-ology 15

by recalling that the central concern of the intellectual life of Ming thinkers of all persuasions was the attainment of a degree of cultivation of the social and moral self revolving around a core of individual consciousness. This focus on self-cultivation enables me to bring my readings of these masterworks of the Ming "novel" into meaningful comparative perspective with the greatest examples of the European novel, since it, too, from Sterne and Fielding to Joyce and Mann, has been preoccupied with much the same exploration of the boundaries and substance of the self.[23]

In correcting Hsia's negative evaluation of Chinese fiction vis-à-vis the European novel, Plaks goes to the other extreme. He seems determined to view these four masterworks as the coherent—internally, ideologically—and formally consistent work of "masters," individual artists in the post-Renaissance sense of the word (namely, Sterne, Fielding, Joyce, and Mann). A comparative perspective, despite an extremely suggestive gesture toward the material and technological conditions of its possibility (fifteenth- and sixteenth-century global circulation of silver that have effects for both Europe and Ming China, and contemporaneous printing booms in both regions, centering especially in urban market towns on an unprecedented scale), becomes in *Masterworks* a primarily formal exercise in the rhetorical uses of irony as paradigmatic fictional device. To a certain extent, like Hsia's earlier equivocations, this is likewise a function of a historical and literary moment. Shades of a new critical formalism, and the ensconcing of the liberal humanist subject as autonomous and transcendent artist at the heart of the book's readings, may be discerned in Plaks's reappraisal of the four masterworks.

For *Masterworks*, the literary work represents (reflects) in an albeit sophisticated and complex manner the creative genius of the literati who wrote it.[24] This, then, is how the central intellectual concerns of Ming life may be seen to illuminate the masterworks of prose fiction of this period. A primarily formalist interpretative apparatus will not allow for questions of the material conditions of a cultural form, however; nor for questions of the power effects and subjective affects obtaining in these forms; nor of the subjectivities they produce, more than reflect. By this I do not mean to impute that literati were not the writers and readers of prose fiction in Ming Wanli. Rather, given the fact that literati in increasing numbers and with great fervor engaged in fiction writing, editing, rewriting, and printing, what was in it (this heretofore disdained, and still in Ming Wanli disclaimed and disreputable even, activity) for them? What new structures of feeling and reading did these new forms of writing engender? What kind of work did these fictions do, socially, politically, economically, and psychically? If the transmission of literary traditions was supposedly modernized with the advent of print technology, the transmission of literary authority was "institutionalized" at least with the first imperial examinations in Tang China, and literati production of culture—however leisurely, dilettantish, or disinterested—does not transcend institutional or personal relations of power and interest.

In the last decade, studies in Ming fiction and history have begun to explore questions of literati representations of virtuous women, and how these reproduce vicariously prurient discursive effects (Katherine Carlitz); how the editing and anthologizing of "Yuan" drama in Ming Jiajing and Wanli has created a genre and an aesthetics, as well as technologies of reading that displace bodies with voice, gender with ethics (Patricia Sieber); how successive editions of Yuan drama register a shift in vernacular usage that may be a function of literati attempts to homogenize a written vernacular (Kimberly Besio); how the representation of women in Ming-Qing fictions shores up male anxieties of a feminized masculinity (Maram Epstein, Keith McMahon, and Martin Huang); how local elite interactions with Buddhist temples reproduced and redistributed local lines of power and resources (Timothy Brook); how a discourse of connoisseurship in Ming Wanli registers an increasingly commodified (elite) relation to art and art objects (Craig Clunas); and how generational discursive shifts among literati in Suzhou from Ming Jiajing through Wanli may yield traces of the subjective processes of a rapidly increasing urbanization, commodification, mercantilism, and boom in print culture (Tsao Jr-lien).

Macro- and microstudies like these allow us to more concretely and materially reconstruct the fantasmatic recognition that Andrew Plaks had already indicated in *Masterworks*. Such a recognition can surely no longer be seen as in Plak's words "smacking of the intellectual presumptions of contemporary sensibility" since a small but significant part of what constitutes "contemporary sensibility" in a Han Chinese cultural time/space is informed by and forged in a medium—book culture—some of whose gender and sexual configurations and patterns of consumption were crucially molded in Ming Jiajing and Wanli. Indeed, this is so much so that the discourses produced during the Ming-Qing transition have been resurrected and reappropriated in the twentieth century as "quintessentially" Chinese (Lin Yutang), cultivated and civilized, and "modern" individualist (Hsia and W. T. de Bary). These attempts differ from recent (late-twentieth-century) scholarly efforts at a textual archaeology or reconstruction of Ming subjectivities and modes of cultural reproduction in that the former contribute to an already mythic and homogeneous ethnic-imperial (now national-statist) identity that is signified variously as "Chinese" and "traditional." In so doing, these discourses can be seen as responding to and extending a centripetal urge for the unity and continuity of historical and cultural transmissions. By contrast, recent research has questioned or lead to our questioning of these weighty categories and identities, in seeking to understand how these and other affective signs (of fixed ethnic or gender and sexual formations) of the "past" continue to be produced and circulated, sometimes in forms difficult to apprehend in its "present" historical and contextual dimensions.

## JPM in the Twentieth Century

### BESTIAL DESIRES: HU SHI AND LU XUN ON THE JPM

Hu Shi (1891–1962) and Lu Xun (1881–1936) are the two major figures who, together then separately, set up the frame within which a "modern" re-evaluation of Chinese xiaoshuo, or a vernacular narrative fiction, could be made.[25] The two knew each other, and some of Lu Xun's views in his *A Brief History of Chinese Fiction* (1925) refer to Hu Shi's earlier findings.[26] Due in part to their subsequently divergent political trajectories, however, Lu Xun became the founding father of an orthodox Chinese marxist view of vernacular prose fiction (present-day Chinese scholars continue to cite his brief and sometimes elusive comments as authorizing pretext). Whereas Hu Shi's mode of a hybrid philological-historical textual reconstruction with "modern" evaluations has had more influence and authority in Taiwan (in 1958, he "returned" from exile in the United States to become the president of the Academia Sinica in Taipei).

Significantly, in his philological studies of classical xiaoshuo and his prefaces for new editions of "old" vernacular prose fiction, the one work that Hu Shi does *not* study is JPM. In a letter responding to Qian Xuantong and Chen Duxiu, he explains the reason for this omission.[27]

> As for your and Mr. Duxiu's account of JPM, I cannot agree. I submit that what the Chinese of today mean by "the love between man and woman" is still entirely the bestial desire of the flesh [shouxing de rouyu]. What should be done today is, on the one hand, to forcefully eliminate such books

as JPM, and on the other hand, to actively translate elegant works of romance and desire. Perhaps fifty years later, there may be some hope of a change in mores. These types of books [such as the JPM], even if one were to regard them as literature, have no value. Why? An important element in literature is the aesthetic affect. And what is the aesthetic affect you get from reading JPM?[28]

Qian Xuantong replied that

> all the xiaoshuo of China prior to today ought to recede to a [secondary] place in history. As of today, if one is to speak of xiaoshuo of value, the first thing to do is to translate, and the second to write [them] anew. Do you agree?[29]

In Hu Shi's view, JPM cannot be considered "literature" because as a representation of "the love between man and woman" (that is, sex and sexuality), it is too "bestial." Implicit in this purportedly aesthetic devaluation of the narrative's representation of male-female sexual relations is a nationalist, class-based, evolutionary view of gender relations and sexuality. The models for emulation and comparison are to be found in *translated* "elegant works of romance and desire." We can only surmise what works Hu Shi might have had in mind here: for correctly modern love between a man and woman, he probably meant Anglo-European novels of domesticity detailing and negotiating class and gender imperatives, constructing modern lives and feelings.[30] But in the historical context of Hu Shi's attempt to scientifically reevaluate the Chinese classical vernacular fiction according to modern values, these elegant works of romance and desire become the invisible criteria against which Chinese vernacular narratives along with the gender relations and sexuality these represent are measured and found dismally wanting, manifestly not-yet-human (civil)—that is, not yet modern, not yet middle class, not yet colonial.

Lu Xun's reading of JPM in *A Brief History of Chinese Fiction* is more contextualized as it seeks to explain in sociohistorical terms what Lu Xun refers to as "private subjects and lascivious passages."

> If we look at JPM from the point of view of literary language and imagery, it is a portrayal of worldly sensibility in a way that penetrates to the heart of sentimental hypocrisies. Because it was written near the end of the Ming at a moment of general chaos, the words are bitter and harsh. Yet there are also frequent intervals wherein private subjects and lascivious

passages are broached. These have been focused on to the exclusion of all else by later readers, and have thus earned it an evil reputation as an "obscene book." But at the time, this was actually in fashion....

Nonetheless, the writer of JPM was such a great writer that despite the inclusion of obscenities, other excellent parts [of the narrative] remain [untouched]; whereas lesser works [in its wake] focused entirely on copulation, and dealt with such abnormal sentiments, as if [their characters were] maniacal.[31]

According to Lu Xun, later readers and lesser works are responsible for JPM's unfortunate reputation: the one in selectively reading the narrative for its salacious parts only; the other for dealing with a subject that is actually only incidental to JPM. Therefore, despite its reputation, JPM is to be considered a great work of "worldly sensibility," inaugurating the generic line of Chinese domestic fiction that would eventually culminate in the *Hong Lou Meng* in the mid-Qing period.

Lu Xun's reading has determined the logic and terms of almost six decades of scholarship in China on JPM. Most notable is the reiteration in diverse forms of the "yes, but" or "despite, still" logic in subsequent arguments for the importance of JPM as an encyclopedic masterpiece, whose value from the literary, social, historical, economic, political, folkloric, and so forth point of view cannot be underestimated. Hu Shi's reading, on the other hand, may be seen as initiating the standard response of a "Chinese" liberal humanist modern (masculine) reading subject at a colonial historical juncture: a disavowal in the psychoanalytic sense.[32] JPM as representation of Ming domestic relations in all their ugly (nonaesthetic) polygamous and sexual detail cannot be salvaged for a "new" national literary canon.

The form and ideology, and sexual politics, of Hu Shi and Lu Xun's readings become the two founding paradigms for twentieth-century scholarly studies of JPM in Chinese. As a result, scholarly readings of JPM have, as one critic self-reflexively puts it, been more hypocritical than most readings by a "common reader": they (institutionally) cannot and (psychoanalytically) will not account for the "pounding heart" and "sweaty palms" experienced in or recorded as part of the process of reading.[33] Such readings have also, in their de facto denouncing (the Lu Xun paradigm) or ignoring (the Hu Shi paradigm) of sex and its representation in JPM, paradoxically rendered centrally meaningful that which they would have as incidental to the text. More pertinent to my study is how this determination to excise or ignore JPM's representation of gender politics and sexualities has actually served to maintain and reinforce an elitist authority in the study of a popular vernacular tradition. Where scholars differ from the "later readers" that Lu Xun faults for JPM's bad name, then, is only in how they do not avow to sweaty palms and pounding hearts, or only do so in biographical asides, not scholarly monographs. This difference authorizes and grounds readings or interpretations that claim a radical break from the pre-twentieth-century past, yet reformulate in "scientific" terms a politics of sexuality and affect that is homologous to those of literati readers such as Zhang Zhupo of the Qing Kangxi era.

ANCIENT FILTH: ZHENG ZHENDUO, WU HAN, AND LI XIFAN

In the 1930s, following in the wake of Lu Xun's reevaluation of vernacular classical narratives, Zheng Zhenduo and Wu Han set the tone for the serious treatment of JPM by their focus on the dual questions of authorship and the establishing of the book's period of writing. At the same time, both also explicitly addressed the question of "why such a famous book should include so many descriptions of sexual life," and "why it had come to be known as a 'dirty book'?"[34]

For Wu Han, JPM is a realist narrative (xiaoshuo), a realistic portrayal of Ming Wanli times and affairs. "[JPM] takes hold of one corner of [Wanli] society, and with a critical brush, it lays bare the linkage between the merchant class and bureaucratic powers of that time, as well as their ugly life."[35] Ugly is one way of aesthetically devaluing the sexual, as Hu Shi's letters have already shown. "Critical brush," on the other hand, valorizes the book and authorizes its scholarly reading. Nonetheless, ugliness seems inextricably intertwined with the book's greatness, its "wholly fearless baring of the perversity of Chinese society."

> JPM is a disreputable [bu mingyu] narrative; historically, readers have agreed that it is a representative "dirty book." Nobody would be willing to publicly admit that he is reading JPM....
>
> Yet, how can JPM only be seen as a "dirty book"? Its greatness is even greater than that of *Shuihu Zhuan*, *Xiyou Ji*, *San Guo*, all of which pale in comparison. What is reflected in JPM is a real Chinese society. And this society even today seems to not yet have become past....
>
> Excepting for its obscene descriptions, JPM is really a great and good book. We could put it this way: that it so exhaustively represents in minute detail that "fin de siècle" society. A society whose roots are still alive....
> Truly, in this great book, unclean descriptions are too many; they are like

flies in summer, numerous and difficult to get rid of. These descriptions are often strong, sufficiently so to make youths seduced to the extent of losing their souls. A healthy, new society really cannot allow for "dirty books" like this, just as the eye cannot suffer a needle in it.[36]

Zheng Zhenduo is in a quandary. On the one hand, he seems to follow Lu Xun's view of a great work marred by an unjust reputation and excisable obscene parts. On the other hand, shades of Hu Shi appear in his ambivalence toward the latter: what if these ignominious passages are so numerous and/or powerful (seductive) that they in effect contaminate and stand in for the whole—as they certainly do in the popular imaginary? The entire book is to a "healthy, new society" like a needle in one's eye. But the real power and danger of these "obscene parts" is how they seem to represent an aspect of a "real Chinese society" that has survived the revolution, and continues into the present ("and this society even today seems to not yet have become past"). It is precisely in the face of a similar recognition (which will be discussed later) that Hu Shi decides that works such as these must be consigned to oblivion. Likewise, Zheng Zhenduo's doubts about the narrative are transposed to the present state of Chinese society (again, an implicit non-Chinese modernity hovers in the background).

> Is it that Chinese society has evolved too slowly, too little? Or is it that the author of JPM has as it were entered the very bones of this society in his portrayal, in such a way that it [the portrayal] cannot be washed clean? Who can give us a clear judgment? A society as decadent and ancient as this one truly does not deserve to survive. Perhaps the time will come when the blood of youths will wash clean these disgusting caked remnants of ancient filth?[37]

JPM's obscene parts have become a projection and distillation of some "decadent and ancient" aspect of Chinese society and familial/sexual relations. In its metonymic (obscene representations numerous as "flies in summer") and metaphoric (for what is like putrid rotting fruit in a post-revolution Chinese society) significations, the pejorative meanings of the text's representation of sexual and gender relations are overdetermined, not analyzed.

In 1957, the interpretation of JPM took another turn. In a polemical response to an attempt to place JPM as the first major work of a Chinese social realist prose fiction, Li Xifan declares that it is SHZ rather than JPM that deserves the honor of being considered an inaugural work. The reason JPM cannot be seen as "originating" social realism lies in a fundamental ambiguity: JPM's sympathetic portrayal of what its author can only have intended as critique.

> But from the point of view of the work's objective effect, JPM is not so much "laying bare the evil totality of feudal society" as it is, through its artistic form, reflecting the author's semiconscious appreciation of those degenerate, decadent, and ugly things. Toward Ximen Qing, there is no doubt that, subjectively, the author's view [of him] is negative. Yet in concrete descriptions, the author is clearly attracted to his [Ximen's] degenerate life, sometimes to the point of forgetting the monstrous face of this bully, to stand by his side. . . . This contradictory attitude toward a character often results in the author's being trapped in a state of continuous confusion. Sympathy and fiery anger at the so-called "representation of women who are abused by the bully" are not at all visible in the aesthetic brushwork of the writer. So entranced is he in caressingly describing their [these women's] sexual life.[38]

For Li Xifan, the work's "artistic form" betrays its author's "semiconscious" sympathies, contradicting his critique of a degenerate bully. The focus of reading has shifted from a problematic text to a questionable authorial intention. "Because the author reveals in himself this ugly and evil thought and sensibility, and drowns himself in this dirty mud pit, he lacks a clear critical attitude toward ugly and degenerate life, and even semiconsciously aestheticizes it."[39] Alongside the greater sophistication of reading the ideology of a formal aesthetics is Li Xifan's passionate denunciation of the author's reveling in a too-well-executed mud pit. (Such a vehemence is interestingly shared by a startling number of otherwise scholarly denunciations of JPM's "dirt"—as if to emphasize the reader's dissociation from at least that part of the text read.)

Li Xifan's attempt to clarify the relation between a formal aesthetics of the narrative and a moral lapse on the part of its "creator" is most significant. Li Xifan reads this unethical aesthetics as the genesis of an entire subsequent decadent line of fictional development.[40] In redefining a Chinese social realism for the vernacular prose narrative, Li Xifan in effect delineates the moral parameters of the fictional representation of sex and women. More important, he establishes the gendered and sexual nature of that morality. What is immoral in JPM is not its objects of representation but rather the writing subject's affective investment in these objects. And the measure of such affective or emotional investment may be gauged through an analysis of formal and aesthetic aspects that simultaneously constitute JPM's claim to fictional innovation. For Li Xifan, the point is whether such a concession (to JPM's fictional innovations) is at all possible without at the same time condoning the unspeakably ugly. But precisely what is ugly for Li Xifan is never concretely detailed in the analysis (with the exception of the suggestive reference to the author's caressing attitude toward certain details of female sexual life). Li Xifan writes as if analysis itself might reproduce the immoral affective power of obscene narrative parts. These narrative parts seem to constitute nonanalyzable, nonassimilable kernels of affect that can only be "safely" treated (as in one recent study) with statistics and percentages.[41]

So objectionable were these obscene parts deemed by 1964 that JPM was (again) banned in China as "pornographic," withdrawn from public consumption and publication, and censored from all textbooks. From 1965 to 1978, not one piece of criticism on JPM seems to have been published.[42] Writing of the political difficulties of his intellectual "involvement" with JPM, Ning Zongyi recalls how "because of various reasons, the entire chapter on JPM was censored" (by himself) from a brief history of Chinese fiction published in 1979. Not until 1986, during a talk at the Second National Jin Ping Mei conference in Xuzhou could Ning Zongyi bring up for critique this story of self-censorship.[43]

The political nature of sex and morality as well as the "real" political effects of the symbolic are thus not merely a structural master-narrative within JPM but have throughout the history of its four hundred years of dissemination determined the terms and valence of its reception, publication, circulation, and readings. It is not an exaggeration to say that the politics of sex constitute a founding, though continuously displaced or disavowed aspect of a history of JPM's readings. JPM was banned in Qing Kangxi 26 (1687) for being an obscene story.[44] Yet in 1964, JPM's alleged obscenity rendered it ideologically unacceptable, and it was completely scrapped from literary history and scholarly attention—this time in seemingly different Chinese marxist literary terms. Continuity inheres not in some essential (obscene) JPM that has remained unchanged through the ages but rather in JPM as a powerful signifier of sex and sexualized women, as well as the perceived obscenity of a connection between sex, sexual desire, and base women. There is perhaps also continuity in the easy displacement of political moral fervor onto always already obscene things. How might one begin to understand the duration and tenacity of such a signifying complex? How might one understand the revival, at certain historical moments and in specific places, of textual and symbolic (re)encodings of sexual subjections—"ancient filth" difficult to apprehend?

### THE 1980S: HUANG LIN AND CHEN DONGYOU

In 1980, the first book-length study of JPM in China since 1940 appeared, as did fifteen articles in various journals, compared to five the previous year and none from 1965 to 1978. By 1984, several scholarly books on JPM were published, including a collection of the more influential JPM essays from the 1920s to the 1980s edited by Xu Shuofang and Liu Hui (Lun Jin Ping Mei), Cai Guoliang's Jin Ping Mei Kaozheng yu Yanjiu (an evidential study of the popular practices in JPM), and Zhang Yuanfen's Jin Ping Mei Xinzheng (establishing Jia Sanjin as the writer of JPM). Both Cai and Zhang reiterate the importance of studying JPM as a "realist" work, and Zhang further writes, "Whether reader or critic, none should nitpick the small evils of JPM, and forget its great realist accomplishments."[45]

But it is Huang Lin who, in an article published in 1985, confronted head on and sought to resolve both the questionable nitpicking and problematic "small evils." Only thus could JPM be revalued in its entirety, without having to concede that some parts simply could not be salvaged, however sophisticated the reader.

> In our national literary history, what is *Jin Ping Mei Cihua*'s most significant quality? I say: exposure [*pulu*]. It tears apart the veils of truth, beauty, and good that covers the world, and in a totalizing, concentrated, and penetrating way, exposes to direct sunlight the upper and lower, inside and outside of, human evil. This is how it shocks its readers to stand up and curse against, while hoping to change this reality. Moreover, for a relatively long period of time, it remained a mirror whereby people may know this society. Even in the thirties of this [twentieth] century, Mr. Zheng Zhenduo emphasized, "The society [portrayed] in JPM is not yet dead; its people are still alive among us." . . . This explains how "exposure" functions as the foremost value in JPM.[46]

Huang Lin's is a first attempt (since Zhang Zhupo of the Qing Kangxi era) to publicly (in published form) advance a totalizing interpretation of JPM that would account for its obscenity in positive terms. His article aims to rebut two prominent lines of thinking: the influential view advanced by Li Xifan in 1957 in which JPM's sole positivity is that of difference from and therefore showing up as less positive its contemporary heroic narratives of "common rebels" (SHZ); and the prevailing view where JPM is faulted for being entirely without "positive characters," without "light," and its author without "principles and ideals," or any clear sentiment of love or hate toward what he depicts in such detail.[47] Huang Lin, on the other hand, maintains that JPM must be evaluated not against narratives like SHZ or Xiyou Ji but rather as the first of its own line of narrative progeny: the first narrative of exposure through evoking sentiments of disgust by concretely detailed representation rather than moralistic interpolations. Huang Lin is claiming that JPM is, and remains, an exemplary narrative of exposure in terms of its aesthetic and affective effect on the (erstwhile and contemporary) reader.

In stressing the effect of reading on the reader, and the affective dimension of this effect, Huang Lin recapitulates Zhang Zhupo's argument for JPM as not an obscene book. But whereas Zhang was forced (ideologically and historically) to recast obscenity as a positive though "bitter filiality," Huang reformulates obscenity as a function of an implicit but devastating critique through (its) exposure techniques.

Thus, Huang contends, JPM's author does not believe in the essential evil of human nature (xing e lun), as some have advanced, but rather subscribes to a view of humanity's susceptibility to evil.

In short, what the author of JPM Cihua critiques is not what he perceived as human nature but rather the weaknesses of human nature—that is, their penchant for excessive desires. Here, of the four excesses—wine, sex, money, and anger—it is especially the desire for sex/sensualities (qingse) that the author considered the greatest seduction, and therefore the greatest danger for human nature.[48]

Yet how is this particular yet general human nature constituted, constructed even, not just in JPM as textual process but in its nearly four hundred years of readers' sociohistorically differently situated readings? Is this human nature gendered? Why might a narrative warning against the dangers of a male desire for sex (with mostly women whose sexuality kills) be deemed enough to ground, emotionally and epistemologically, an exposé or critique of particular familial-social and political-economic evils for all human nature?

If as Huang Lin proposes it is precisely the literary value and force of a narrative such as JPM to induce in the reader a shock that will make "him" stand up for change, the *composition* of that "shock" must be further, and much more closely, read and analyzed. One must also ask how that shock is different from, yet similar to, Zhang Zhupo's injunctions to his reader of JPM when Zhang Zhupo wrote,

> The reader of JPM should keep a spittoon handy in order to have something to bang on. . . .
> The reader of JPM should keep a sword ready to hand so that he can hack about him to relieve his indignation. . . .
> The reader of JPM should hang a bright mirror in front of himself so that he can see himself fully revealed.[49]

The three injunctions quoted here from Zhang Zhupo's "Dufa" (How to read) listing in his edition of JPM are sequentially significant. They enjoin the immediate release of aggressive force (the spittoon to bang on, the sword with which to hack about) that is envisioned as provoked by the narrative. Simultaneously, there is the ready examination of self (in a mirror) so that besides righteous anger and frustration, no other suspect mood emerges. But the literary meanings and social uses of this variation on the neo-Confucian stricture of *shendu* (wariness of self in solitude), and its relation to the solitude of *reading* (an obscene book no less), would necessitate a closer study of JPM in the context of Zhang Zhupo's work. For Huang Lin, by comparison, the shock value of JPM has to do with a collective sense of history (rather than Zhang's focus on a personal ethics), one's realization of and alienation from a mode of collective and historical life that is now deemed decadent and obsolete. The shock of one's reading, then, comes from a forced recognition that is simultaneously ideally the beginning of a salutary alienation as well as critique.

In 1988, with the publication in China of Chen Dongyou's *A Cultural Study of Jin Ping Mei*, the study of the book's obscenity entered a new phase, though not entirely breaking from the previous models of reading sex. In his introduction to a new Taiwan edition of the book published in 1991, Chen calls for a renewed macroperspective of the text—a perspective that would read JPM as a fictional crystallization of a Grand Canal socioeconomy that had by the fifteenth century made the cities along the canal the most wealthy and populated of Ming China.[50] The Grand Canal was first completed in the Sui period with Loyang as its center, its northernmost point is in what is now southwest Beijing, while reaching Hangzhou in the southeast. Two thousand, seven hundred kilometers in length, the Grand Canal had by the Tang dynasty become the empire's primary military, political, and economic lifeline. By Ming Wanli 6 (1578), not only were the major commercial centers and activities of the empire concentrated along the banks of the Grand Canal but a quarter of the empire's commercial taxation would come from the southern Zhili province, with the canal as its central line of communication.[51] Chen's claim is that JPM cannot be analyzed without taking into account the context of the conflicting economies and ideologies between an increasingly sophisticated urban commercialism along the canal area and the surrounding rural agricultural society. This geopolitical conflict of economies and ideologies lies at the heart of the contradictions that have been, according to Chen, misread as JPM's ideological flaw: the simultaneously sympathetic and exposing/punitive representation of such merchant antiheroes as Ximen Qing. The context for this narrative equivocation is precisely the uneasy coexistence of an urban mercantilism alongside a rural agricultural ethical and economic-political structure. Finally, Chen Dongyou criticizes previous JPM scholarship's inability to break from Lu Xun's explanatory logic in regard to JPM's allegedly obscene passages. "To explain the representation of sex between men and women in the work simply by the term 'fashion of the times' is too superficial; such an explanation is not grounded in the specificity of a cultural economic account of [a] human worldview."[52]

But when it comes to reading sex in JPM, Chen does not analyze the sexual representation in the book in relation to a Ming Wanli Grand Canal cultural economy. Perplexingly, he first quantifies the percentage of sex to other topics of representation in JPM.[53] Chen then goes on to enumerate what distinguishes these passages that have been censored in most modern editions of the work: "The sex that is presented in JPM is most often shaded by a markedly one-sided abusive usage [*wannong*] [of the object], and most of these are of men sexually abusing women."[54] It is abusive, Chen contends, to the extent that it is not based on sentiment (*qing*) and is merely a function of Ximen Qing's economic prowess. Chen's observation here can be related to the perspective wherefrom sex is narrated in JPM—an analytic point comparable to the "voyeurism" put forward by Katherine Carlitz and Andrew Plaks (as discussed below). It can also be seen as reformulating Hu Shi's criticism of "bestial desire of the flesh" in so-called Chinese terms as lacking in the proper (modern) "love," "feeling," "sentiment," translated here as *qing*.

Whereas Hu Shi had in mind the "elegant works of romance and desire" of the West, Chen's second point juxtaposes a passage from JPM with one from D. H. Lawrence's *Lady Chatterley's Lover* and then with a description of orgasmic physiology from Havelock Ellis. He concludes that JPM's representation of sex is closer to Ellis's than Lawrence's.

> The fine detailing [of sex] in JPM is a purely objective, mechanical detailing; its truth is a stereotypical, photographic truth, and neither an artistic finesse nor an artistic truth.[55]

But what does Chen mean by "artistic finesse" and "truth"?

> There is quite a bit of the description of sex in *Lady Chatterley's Lover* . . . but the author uses a subjective style to finely describe the protagonist's internal emotions in the moment of having sex. The author is not an observer but rather is an actor of the experiential school [of acting]. He uses his entire heart-mind and body to experience the protagonist's feelings, and sex becomes merely a medium, a bridge, a stage, [and thus] through sex, the entire soul of the copulating couple (or that of one party) is revealed.[56]

In contradiction to his own claim that JPM can and must only be understood within the context of a Grand Canal economic-material-cultural perspective, representations of sex in JPM (and not any other aspect) are singled out for a negative comparison with *Lady Chatterley's Lover*.[57] JPM's representation of sex is deficient not because it is narrated with too much authorial investment to qualify as critique or exposure but rather the opposite. In comparison with Lawrence's and Ellis's passages, JPM's representation is disturbingly closer to a clinical, objectifying description of sexual activity and physiological responses than a penetrating portrayal of the subjective affects of sexual activity from within its actor-agents. By juxtaposing Anglo-European modernist novelistic representations of subjective sexual affect with JPM's detailed narration of practices of sex, the latter could only be read as insufficiently "true" art, unable to move a modern reader.

Interestingly, the narration of sex is the only part of the text that Chen demands be modern in the sense of invoking an identificatory reading. The inherent contradiction of reading all of the narrative as historically and culturally embedded, except for its passages depicting sexual acts, can be read as reproducing the ideology of some transhistorical private-personal realm that is sexuality (whose ideal mode, perhaps not surprisingly, resides in Lawrence rather than JPM). Simultaneously, it could also signify the critic's being moved in a way that, felt as the wrong kind of sex, can now be disavowed or displaced in a new way. Instead of simply saying "let us translate" (as Hu Shi did), one can more specifically turn to Lawrence on sex in a much more recognized and recognizable high literary and love-bound mode. This indexes another shift, from an unspeakable and historically residual sense of the strong seductive powers of JPM's obscene parts, such as can be read in Zheng Zhenduo and Li Xifan, to desiring formations "in Chinese" in the model of Lawrentian subjects and narratives. A JPM once read as demanding sword and spittoon (Zhang Zhupo), or later, as precipitating the shock of historical recognition of ineradicable and ancient moral perversion (Huang Lin), can thus now be "scientifically" read as drably clinical, with little if any powers at all—at least not the kind of aesthetic power seen to reside in the normative subjective representations of desire and sex by a D. H. Lawrence.

While claiming to achieve an "objective," nonmoralistic analysis and evaluation of obscene passages in JPM, Chen Dongyou actually continues to devalue these. Chen refutes the ethicalized readings of sex in previous JPM scholarship, yet his own reading posits a universalist "scientism," following which JPM's representation of sex is first quantified, then evaluated against other samples of the "same" kind of descriptions. In rightly calling for the necessity of taking into account the reader-critic's own reproduction of precisely those ethical and moral structures that inform all of JPM, and that would result in the reader-critic's merely repeating what the narrative represents, Chen nevertheless replaces an "internal" ethical structure with an "external" aesthetic-scientific apparatus that is at least as decontextualizing.[58]

## TAIWAN AND HONG KONG: SUN SHUYU'S
### THE ART OF JIN PING MEI

I shall now turn to a more lengthy response to Li Xifan's debunking of JPM written five years before Huang Lin's article, published in Taipei, and disseminated primarily in Taiwan and Hong Kong. Sun Shuyu's *The Art of Jin Ping Mei* (1978) is the first of its kind: a small book written not just for academic readers but targeted at a mass audience, and providing a detailed, comprehensive reading of JPM in primarily New Critical terms, with a quasi-Buddhist twist.[59] Sun avers that JPM is not a book for everyone—certainly not for the young and hot-blooded. But mature readers will be able to appreciate the message hidden by the narrative's often flawed and distinctly premodern surface.[60] How so?

> As for Pan Jinlian, the writer has developed to the full her desires and passion, so that finally the reader understands how horrible is the jealous anger and sentiments of desire in a person's heart. As for Ximen Qing,

that bad man continuously reviled by the readers of SHZ, the writer has rewritten him in such a way that on closer perusal, we find he is actually drawn in our likeness—so much so that mainland critics like Li Xifan ... castigate the writer for making a bad man into a good one. But has the writer ever said anything positive about him? All he has done is to let us see how natural are the actions of this so-called "bad man," so much so that had we ordinary people the opportunity and guts, we too would act the same way. For one is born with desires; one is not born with a disciplinary ethics. The writer also tells us how "normal" Ximen is in loving his children, his wife and concubines, and his friends. This way, we completely lose our sense of superiority, and are able to understand how these innate and natural sentiments cannot save man from evil karma.[61]

Sun Shuyu's model of reading is New Critical in its evaluation of the text with little recourse to the historical and material conditions of writing and reading. Rather, the narrative is a great work of art precisely to the degree that it transcends the specific conditions that make it possible and meaningful. Thus, its greatness is at once an intrinsic part of the text, yet only fully recoverable with a mature and sensitive reader. Such a (superior) reader will be able to detect the normal and natural qualities of Ximen without unnecessary defensiveness, and will moreover empathize and identify with Ximen Qing, reading (him)self into the narrative, turning the narrative into a mirror, in order to then gain ethical insight and Buddhist enlightenment.

For Sun Shuyu, a primary marker of JPM's greatness, its quintessentially modern quality, is the irony that he identifies as characterizing the multiple perspectives whereby the writer represents his subject.[62] Ironic perspective is what transforms a Buddhist cliché about the karmic retributions of human desires into a moving and modern narrative of everyman's plight in this world. "Irony" is also what gives JPM its aesthetic value and critical currency. Yet Sun Shuyu is at some pains to translate this irony into Chinese, and he does so by means of many examples and phrases that mean something like a "nonunity of surface and lining" (biaoli bui). This is not to say that because the term is not "originally" Chinese it is therefore untranslatable, or untransposable in a Chinese-speaking context. What I do want to draw attention to is Sun Shuyu's use of irony as a critically valorizing term. Irony displaces any historical context for explaining the production of forms of meanings with a rhetorical context of U.S. New Critical provenance.[63] It seems hardly coincidental that while Sun Shuyu is recuperating the literary-critical value of JPM in terms of its irony in a reading that is disseminated in Taiwan and Hong Kong, Huang Lin should formulate a narrative theory of "exposure" whereby JPM might likewise be reinstated, but in terms of ideological enlightenment. Each is contributing to the reinstating of JPM as a "classic" worth serious scholarly attention in terms that are relevant to both the institutions (Chinese academia versus an academia in Hong Kong and Taiwan) and geopolitical situations wherein they write. I point this out not to invalidate their claims but to demystify the authority and "objectivity" with which such scholarly readings are very much invested, and nowhere deemed more necessary than in Jin-ology.

For both Sun Shuyu and Huang Lin, the authority that had previously resided in the text (therefore Hu Shi's need to more or less deny any value in JPM, and Lu Xun's concession that it is the first realist representation of social mores and worldly sensibility) is now located in the author-writer-creator who is endowed with transcendental talents and intentions only recoverable by the "right" reader-critic. Thus, the authority of "re-creating" aesthetic-literary meaning now belongs to the institutionally trained reader-critic.[64] The text is rescued from both undeserved ignominy and readers who are not able to appreciate its aesthetic-literary values. The reader-critic must mediate the reception of the book as art in an age of mass (improperly schooled) readers.[65]

In Sun's book, the thorny questions of JPM's obscenity and its representation of sexual acts are relegated to a long footnote. Sun Shuyu reiterates what Zhang Zhupo had affirmed three hundred years ago: JPM is not an obscene book since the "right" reading would not only fail to titillate but would, in fact, achieve a cleansing effect. "Representations of sexual acts comprise less than 1 percent of the book, and to readers who know [how to read], these sections are neither the most delightful nor the most important. . . . [A]n abridged version of JPM is nonetheless a satisfyingly complete read."[66] In his conclusion, Sun Shuyu invokes both the writer of JPM as a "writer's writer" and the reader as ideally a reader who has attained a certain level of expertise in reading (*you chengdu de duzhe*).[67] The one of course warrants, indeed necessitates, the other.

The effects of such a recourse to a specialized form of knowledge (the writer as professional author; the reader as trained expert) serves to offset this particular fictional narrative's disrepute as an obscene book. The work is thus not only "saved" for a new market of readers—the nonspecialists who might read Sun's introductory work[68]—but saved in terms that simultaneously install the reader-critic as specialist of an otherwise misunderstood author-writer and his fictional masterpiece. Moreover, this misunderstanding involves a sexual prurience that belongs neither to the text nor the author-writer but rather to that of ignorant readers. These readers misapprehend the work and do it an injustice; for them, an abridged version would work just as well. Especially interesting is how Sun (like Chen Dongyou a decade later) quantifies the objectionable sexual components of the text: these constitute "less than 1 percent" and therefore are not worthy of more than a footnote. It is as if the neat categorizing of representations and their precise calculation would yield the percentage of (libidinal-creative) investment on the part of its "creator"—the smaller the investment, the greater the relative unimportance of such passages, and the more successful the scholar's efforts at debunking misguided charges of obscenity.

Obscenity lies not in the text but with its dissemination in print, and its reception by readers who began to worry about that dissemination and how to authoritatively mediate, manage, and control it. It is not the text that is inherently pornographic but the ensuing battle over how (not) to read it that produces "its" pornographic reputation. Pornography is the product of an intensive moral economy redeployed at a crucial moment of a promiscuous proliferation of fictional genres in print. To assert that JPM is essentially obscene is not very different from saying that it is essentially a masterpiece that has been largely misunderstood as obscene by the majority of its readers and nonreaders. Both assertions dehistoricize the text, and remove it from the history of its contradictory and discontinuous readings — a history that has shaped its particular form and meanings as precisely a borderline text, and one that is extremely useful for and indicative of shifts in ideological and institutional realignments in literary fields in China and Chinese literary studies in the United States in the twentieth century. Overt political censorship (such as that in China in the 1950s) is as, if not more productive of critical discourse than the implicit self-censorship of a liberal yet prudish ideology (in Taiwan, for example).

SAVORY AND UNSAVORY ASPECTS:
C. T. HSIA AND ANDREW PLAKS

The scholarship in English on JPM has, earlier than that in Chinese, begun to break out of the disavowal/displacement paradigm set up by Hu Shi and Lu Xun regarding how to interpret representations of sex and women in JPM. Despite the framing disparagement of JPM as a book of "low culture and ordinary mentality," a phrase whose specific reference has never been clarified, Hsia is in *The Classic Chinese Novel* (1968) not as squeamish over sex in JPM as might have been expected.[69] Thus, he writes of the author-writer:

> Superficially, he is the stern moralist who seizes every opportunity to condemn adultery and debauchery, but the very fact that he takes so many pains to describe the sexual act belies the attitude of moral censure. While a dry, slangy, and at times almost clinical style suffices for most of the shorter passages, in the more elaborate accounts of coition the author relishes its every detail . . . with a kind of dispassionate lyricism which seems to imply that, while the participants may otherwise disgust us, the act itself, the performing organs, and the human bodies themselves are beautiful sights to contemplate. . . . [O]n the whole, the sexual act when performed to the mutual pleasure of the partners is never entirely robbed of its human meaning, and for the many frustrated women characters it remains the sole redeeming event in their dull captive existence.[70]

Hsia goes on to bemoan the fact of modern expurgated editions. These leave out an uninhibitedly pleasurable representation of sex that is at the same time "quite sensitive to the pain of sexual frustration."[71] Clearly, for Hsia, the weaknesses of JPM are ones that arise from structural and thematic comparison with exemplars of European novels—a lack of generic consistency, a distinct hybridity of composition ("the novel is almost a poetic anthology within a narrative framework"), and an authorial indulgence of ingenuity at the expense of creative discipline ("his inordinate passion for inserting extraneous material into his work").[72] Whereas its strengths are those aspects that for Hsia evince a "personal commitment" to individualist and humanist ideals that are framed in terms of an unresolved conflict between "conventional morality and the instinctive self."[73]

Part of what allows for a relatively positive assessment of the representation of sex in JPM is Hsia's schema of ideological and formal tension between social mores and instinctual individualism that redeems the otherwise "primitive" fictional forms of late Ming narratives. This tension is what makes them modern (progenitors of modern subjects, that is, Western individualism) as well as critically laudable (they are in this sense rightly seen as precursors of a more truly modern Chinese fiction). Yet it is precisely this distinction between "morally disgusting characters" and "pleasurable/aestheticized writing" that had since Zhang Zhupo puzzled and irritated reader-critics who had wanted to read JPM as a serious, consistent masterwork, whether in Confucian or New Critical terms. Hsia's teleology of a humanist individualism at the heart of classical Chinese fiction permits him to reverse the indictment: the morally disgusting characters who become agents in pleasurable and "well-written" sexual acts are the product of an author-writer who "seems incapable of resolving the contradictions in his own thinking." This author-writer's mind is "nothing if not common as he by turns appeals to one or another of the popular prejudices."[74] What is especially relevant is how in Hsia's reading, the "commonness" of the author-writer's mind permits recognition of a certain pleasure in the writing (and reading) of sex that would otherwise either be denied or displaced onto an aesthetics of writing.

Only by establishing a safe distance—that of a class-based cultural contempt—can the reader-critic acknowledge (the book's and his own) pleasure in the representation of sex in JPM, without incurring the danger of somehow being implicated in that pleasure. And in the case of Hsia's reading, this safety is doubly ensured through reading that textual pleasure as registering a humanist impulse, as championing the cause of the instinctual life of the individual. (Incidentally, this is also what founds Sun Shuyu's interpretation of the life energy at the root of what for him is a veritable realist masterpiece). But is not this pleasure gendered masculine? Is it not gendered in the sense that pleasures represented and taken in the reading are conditioned by, depend on, and produce specific (culturally) "masculine" (rather than biologically male) sexual dispositions that are simultaneously inextricable from the historicity of (re)writings and readings of JPM? This gender and sexual disposition, however, disappears in readings that fail to take into account its workings at the levels of both textual productions and "critical" readings. Not surprisingly, noncritical or nonprofessional readings tend to be less defensive of a gender particularity and more open to a sexual politics as inseparable from any reading of such an erotic and erotized book (a subject that I will return to later). Again, authority is at stake. The authority of a professional reader-critic rests largely on institutionally determined paradigms that in order to be authoritative, must present themselves as either literary and aesthetic (thus reasserting the autonomy of art as a field and the conjunctive authority of its specialists) or transcendent and universal (thus appealing to a transhistorical view of a shared humanity and its values).

Nonetheless, it is intriguing to note how twentieth-century critic-readers seeking some ideal modernity in sexual representations characterize JPM negatively as "bestial," "clinical," and "low" in culture. All would seem to negatively agree on a certain unreadability of sexual representation in JPM, its aesthetic and functional unusefulness from a reading position subtended by a viewpoint looking toward the present and future (of some Chinese humankind). Yet the question remains: How is one to understand or read against the grain of time what too easily gets read as clinical and bestial, dehumanized and nonhuman, in a seemingly "realist" narrative of that most "humane" of domains, the familial-domestic space of intimacy?

Plaks's *Masterworks* (1987) — in its historically, politically, and intellectually contextualized readings of the four masterworks of sixteenth-century Ming China — may be seen as implicitly arguing against Hsia's contention that classic Chinese fiction is structurally and generically inferior to its Western counterpart. More specifically, in Plaks's reading and interpretation of JPM in order to show the narrative's "high degree of textual control often astounding not only for its own time and place, but for the artistry of the novel in general," representations of sex can no longer either be exempt from authorial responsibility (as a "fashion of the times"), relegated to a dismissive footnote, or celebrated as a positive if contradictory sign of some instinctive individualist streak.[75] Authorial control of the text being the premise, whatever sex there is (and again, there is not as much as is reputed) must be seen as part of the overall design, which is in Plaks's reading consistently ironic and neo-Confucian. In strong contrast to Hsia's qualified affirmation of sexual pleasure, Plaks's reading of sex in JPM registers primarily unpleasure (he does, however, concede to very few moments in the text of "something resembling warm affection, mutual pleasure, or at least honest desire").

> In order to refute the view of *Jin Ping Mei* as no more than a positive or negative exploration of sexual behavior in general, or at least that of one jolly fellow in particular, it will be necessary at this point to take a careful look at the passages of erotic description that loom so large in the impression of the book for most readers over the past four centuries. . . . In attempting to come to terms with the function of these erotic passages, we must recognize, first, that in terms of sheer quantity they do not occupy as large a space as many readers — perhaps guilty of the type of reading insinuated by Zhang Zhupo — have felt. In fact, the total number of passages of true extended erotic description is fairly limited, to the extent that a thorough student can easily recall nearly all of the major examples. . . . This point is especially notable since, as we know, the sixteenth century in China was a time of considerable publication of erotic fiction. . . . Thus, any restraint the author shows in this regard — the reputation of the novel notwithstanding — must be viewed as a deliberate artistic choice.
>
> The real question we have to consider, therefore, is the quality rather than the quantity of the sexual description in the novel. Granted, this is

> a matter of personal sensibility, but I would hazard to say that in the entire vast narrative of *Jin Ping Mei* the number of scenes depicting erotic experience in sympathetic terms are no more than a handful, and those that could by any stretch of the imagination be taken as a glorification of the sex act, of the sort modern apologists of pornography might seek here are practically nonexistent. . . . [I]n virtually every other instance it can be demonstrated that, in one way or another, the author deliberately withholds the potential pleasure he has led the reader to eagerly await, so as to ultimately deny or deflate the sort of vicarious release that some pornography pretends to offer.[76]

In an attempt to prove JPM a narrative evincing the highest degree of a postromantic authorial control and design, Plaks formulates a theory of the representation of sex as reflecting aesthetic choice and (moral) restraint. If the author-writer is the controlling figure, sole guarantor of meaning and value, the reader-critic is his counterpart in realizing the aesthetic potential of the text. (Note how in both this and other critics' writings, there is a gendered, and to a degree eroticized, subtext wherein the text is a "female" "body" and serves as the medium of some sort of intellectual and aesthetic exchange "between men.")[77] In a sense, the reader-critic displaces the author-writer and speaks as if in his position, reenacting his intellectual and philosophical creative process. There is a rapprochement of these two positions, an almost seamless identificatory desire between the reader-critic and the author-writer. The former ventriloquizes the latter.[78] The problem with taking on the authority of the author-writer, though, is that the reader-critic simultaneously reproduces what can only be narrative effects and affects—the products of a certain form and combinations of narrative sequences, and the emotions therein invoked and orchestrated. Such effects and affects are then deemed "artistic," and therefore positively valuable and meaningful.

This is most clearly the case in Plaks's extended reading of one particular "figural recurrence" in JPM—the recurrence of the figure of Pan Jinlian "riding" her sexual partners to death. The ultimate licentious woman sexually wastes her hapless victims, and the reader, in Plaks's reading, can only be horrified.

> The key question for us here is, again, the *quality* of the sexual behavior that is shown. On this score we find the strongest evidence against the view of *Jin Ping Mei* as a work of pleasurable pornography. In order to establish this

> point beyond doubt, it will be necessary to dwell in considerable detail on some of the more unsavory aspects of the sexual behavior presented in the book, for which I beg the reader's indulgence.
>
> First, we should note that the vast majority of the sexual connections in the novel are the expression of illegitimate unions. . . . The roster of unsavory sexual relations depicted in the novel must also include the several examples of homosexuality presented. . . . Moving on to the actually detailed descriptions of heterosexual practices, we may note the special care taken by the author to inform the reader of the particular predilections of Ximen Qing's principal partners. . . . Here the use of the principle of figural recurrence: first setting up a pattern then plumbing it for significance, comes into full play. The clearest instance of this is the repeated description of Pan Jinlian's predilection for mounting her sexual partner. . . . [B]y the time we arrive at chapter 79, the image of Jinlian astride Ximen Qing's limp body emerges with full horror as nothing more or less than that of a vampire, relentlessly draining away his life essence. . . . We have just seen the very strong implication of sexual murder in the final image of Pan Jinlian as succubus, and this is only the final realization of a long chain of hints in the text (even before the cruel murder of Wu Da, Jinlian had already drained the vitality of Zhang Dahu), which eventually leads to the fulfillment of Ximen Qing's own pledge in chapter 5: "If I betray your love, may I end up just like Wu Da."[79]

The problem is not so much that Plaks should describe the representation of sex in JPM in terms of its quality—in short, that the "bad sex" proves that this is not a work of "pleasurable pornography." Rather, despite enjoining an ironic reading of JPM, Plaks has ironically failed to read Ximen Qing's sex with Pan Jinlian as precisely made to do the literary work of devaluing Pan Jinlian and construing her in the figure of a woman with insatiable "unsavory" and quite "particular predilections." In thus mistaking the referent for the sign, reading Pan Jinlian's "mounting [of] her sexual partner" as leading to sexual murder, rather than as a *narrative* stringing up of Pan Jinlian using her own feet wrappings (her "pleasures"; see chapter 4) or as a *narrative indictment of the succubus*, Plaks substitutes narrative effect for an analysis of representation. More seriously, structural ethical-aesthetic elements that work in terms of the text's gender and sexual politics rise to the status of a general truth.

The distancing tactic of Plaks's reading is the inverse of Hsia's reading of sex in JPM. Whereas the latter was enabled precisely by a belief in the "low culture" of the narrative's possible author(s) to allow for a certain uninhibited and therefore commendable "instinctual" pleasure, as if the author's "relishing its every detail" could only be the function of some déclassé nonaesthetic drive. On the contrary, Plaks's reading establishes every narrative detail as the result of a controlling, highly acculturated aesthetic principle, and thus cannot countenance any element or reading that might escape such control. Authorial intention and aesthetic irony permits and produces, in such a reading, a safely disengaging distance wherefrom the reader-critic may at arm's length read distasteful representations. In Plaks's view, relishing could only be a symptom of either sloppy or pornographic reading.[80]

Still, one must wonder at the affective powers of representations that elicit such diametrically opposed readings as Hsia's and Plaks's. How might readings such as these two work together—to produce not the "same" representation of sex in JPM but rather a consistent ideological effect in terms of readerly consumption? How is an authorial (and readerly) relishing of detail (Hsia) coextensive with the radical textual erasure, deracination even, of that sprout of relish and pleasure (Plaks)? What if both are the twin aspects of a brotherly narrative fantasy—a fantasy realized and concretized in readings such as these two, however academic and objectivist?

AN EXORCISTIC RITE FOR THE VOYEUR:
DAVID ROY, VICTORIA CASS, AND KATHERINE CARLITZ

In the introduction to the first volume of his translation of JPM (*The Plum in the Golden Vase or Chin P'ing Mei*), David Roy reads the entire text as an embodiment of the philosophy of Xunzi of the third century B.C.E.

> My reading of the novel has persuaded me that the implied author adheres to an uncompromising version of Xunzi's particular brand of orthodox Confucianism. . . . Xunzi is most famous for his enunciation that, although everyone has the capacity for goodness, human nature is basically evil and, if allowed to find expression without the conscious molding and restraint of ritual, is certain to lead the individual disastrously astray. That the implied author of the JPM endorses this view should be apparent to even the most superficial reader.[81]

The inherent evil in this version of human nature is then systematically worked out in the narrative through, particularly and especially, representations of sex.

> I believe that it was never any part of the author's intent to celebrate the pleasures of sex and that the sexual acts that he explicitly describes, and which have won the novel such notoriety, are intended, in fact, to express in the most powerful metaphor available to him the author's contempt for the sort of persons who indulge in them. The spheres of sexual, economic, and political aggrandizement are symbolically correlated in the novel in such a way that the calculated shock value of the sexual descriptions spills over into the other realms and colors the reader's response to them.[82]

The representation of sex becomes an extended metaphor for an authorial denigration of not just human nature but human nature in its sexual aspects and expression. The degree and detail of depictions of sexual activity is then in direct correlation to that of authorial indictment.

This may seem like yet another tactic for keeping narrative sex at arm's length, whereby it becomes nothing more or less than an elaborate, multi-leveled metaphor for economic and political excess. But in Roy's reading, there is an important emphasis on the centrality of sex and sexuality as controlling metaphors. It is Roy's dual concern with an implied individual author-creator, on the one hand, and the work's ideological and structural coherence (as an illustration of Xunzi's philosophy in Ming Wanli), on the other, that prevents him from asking what exactly constitutes the "shock value" of the narrative's sexual representations: On what kind of a scale, how measured, and to what category of subject? As for this shock value "[spilling] over into the other realms and [coloring] the reader's response to them," one would also have to ask: What about different readers' responses to these representations of sex? Can these responses be uniform and unchanging through four centuries, disregarding gender and sexual disposition, ethnicity, or geographic and economic situations? If a certain kind of reader is being projected in Roy's reading, it seems necessary to specify what kind and how that reader is constituted.

In another section of his introduction, Roy states,

> In view of the prominent role of sexual imagery in the novel and the immediate cause of Hsi-men Ch'ing's [Ximen Qing's] death, it is not surprising that [the] narrative shape itself should be subtly suggestive of the cycle of tumescence and detumescence.[83]

Where Plaks writes of an ungendered "body" of text, Roy metaphorizes the temporal dimension of this narrative body in the shape of an erotically aroused phallus whose swelling and postclimactic "detumescence" are then to be taken as yet another sign of "the author's conscious artistry."[84] Accurate and significant as this may be in describing the temporal trajectory of a certain textual physiology, such a reading also recalls the scholarly tendency to engender and/or sexualize this particular textual body in ways that sometimes exactly coincide with what the critics have set out to pinpoint as "bad (sex)." The representation of gendered and sexualized bodies interacting in the text are not reducible to either deletable textual excess, mere functions of an ethical didacticism, or even metaphors for social and economic decadence; instead they tend to spill over, as Roy puts it, into the very writings and readings that seek to enact scholarly containment of textual effect and affect.

Interestingly, in Victoria Cass's earlier study of JPM, there is a reading of sexual representation that avoids the dual poles of either negation or affirmation. Especially relevant is her suggestion that the eroticism of the narrative must be read in the context of the celebrations of the Lantern Festival.[85]

> The sense of the Lantern Festival as . . . an elaborate *exorcistic rite* is a useful metaphor for the novel's central view of eroticism. As the novel attests to the dangerousness of eros, so it implies the necessity of an immersion in eros.[86]

By reading eroticism as symbolically and structurally parallel to the exorcistic ritual celebrations of the Lantern Festival, Cass is able to posit sexual representations as a narrative site for the playing out of just those social and psychic, gendered and sexual forces that are ritually unleashed for more effective personal incorporation and public appropriative usages.[87] My readings (in part 2) of the narrative processes that contribute to the formation of a structural misogynist subjection describe how an exorcism of a particular form of male-female desire is at stake—an exorcism achieved through the fantasmatic staging of that desire in the figures of licentious women.

But in order for the staging of that desire to work its effects on the reader, to ensnare the reader as it were into a sequential narrative enactment of desire and its ultimate exorcism, there would have to be a function of the text that would position the reader for maximum investment without identification (with, for example, Ximen Qing). Katherine Carlitz suggests in *The Rhetoric of Chin P'ing Mei* a crucial point that is also taken up in Plaks's reading of the text in *Masterworks*.[88]

> Certain readers of Chin p'ing mei have, however, sensed an inconsistency between the obvious corruption surrounding sexual activity in the novel, and the apparent relish with which that activity is sometimes described. ... [T]he two attitudes are not necessarily inconsistent. ... The author of Chin p'ing mei ... communicates the illicit nature of Chin p'ing mei's sexual encounters by making us voyeurs: in clandestine company with P'an Chin-lien [Pan Jinlian], Ying Po-chueh [Ying Bojue] or various little boys, we watch these encounters through keyholes, we listen through walls. These other characters catch us in the act of watching Hsi-men Ch'ing [Ximen Qing] and his various partners, thus exposing our own frailties, demonstrating that the reader has as great a need for self-cultivation as do any of the characters in the novel.[89]

The passive pleasure of a voyeuristic imaging/reading is the mediation whereby a reader may partake of sexual pleasure, yet not pay for it—whether materially (excepting for the price of the book) or physiologically (unless metaphysiologically in the mode of Roy's textual tumescence and detumescence). This is the vicarious (virtual) sex of an early print culture. It had in its day as astonishing and disturbing an effect as computer sex had in the early 1990s in the United States and Taiwan, to name just two places of its as-yet-uncontrolled dissemination (see chapter 2). Coupled with a passive voyeuristic pleasure of the text is, however, the morally sadistic sexual punishment of lascivious women and men through a narrative emplotment that ensures they all die fitting deaths for their excesses. These are the two vectors of one narrative structure, and in my view, accomplish not so much a philosophical enlightenment as a metatextual exercise in misogynist emotional divestment.

That there is an economy of sex was a commonplace of Ming Wanli, when handbooks of sexual hygiene were to be found among the books of most literati.[90] As Carlitz writes,

> [This] notion of sexual economy, of getting and spending, ... is fundamental both to the role of sex in Chin p'ing mei and to the role of women in the traditional characterization of the "bad last ruler." Women are, potentially, instruments of dangerous disorder, and they are also sexually enervating. ... A principle aim of sexual hygiene is to avoid "overspending" on the part of the male who needed to nourish himself through sexual activity, rather than destroying himself. This notion of expenditure makes an equation between money and semen, physical resources and financial resources, a natural one.[91]

The equation is "naturalized" precisely via such popular discourses as narrative fiction. The place and function of a woman in this sexual economy is especially significant, though. Clearly, this sexual economy was developed with a (literate and potentially literatus) masculine subject as its central concern, with a woman being both the object and medium whereby male self-nourishment is attained. The danger, of course, lies in the possibility that the object should turn into an active agent, getting her sexual nourishment at the male's expense. Whereas manuals and compilations on sexual hygiene were directed toward guiding the projected male reader through a conservationist sexual regime, I will argue that the narrative of JPM works in conjunction with such discourses, but to a different effect. JPM does not proffer a sexual regimen to be followed; rather and more important, it reformulates preexisting structures of misogynist and eroto-phobic feeling into a narrative of (his/her) sexual desire and its consummation in ugly deaths—for the women who embody it and the men who do not resist it.[92]

At a textual level, JPM is a misogynist sexual fantasy that ultimately works for a projected masculine reading subject to divest from what is initially presented as seductive and fascinating. But this communal masculinist fantasy has—in its fine details, its hybrid forms, its polysemic discourses, and the sheer cumulative weight of a history of its readings—achieved a "truth" effect that necessitates further analysis. One of the questions that I ask is how this truth effect has evolved and crystallized to such an extent that the representation of women and sex in JPM have become that which is merely incidental to the narrative, and at the same time, what paradoxically founds it. Women and sex are continuously read as peripheral yet central to JPM's literary and/or philosophical message (of enlightenment, inverted self-cultivation, exposure). Yet such readings repeat the structural and emotional interchangeability of women and sex (with women and boys) as representation in the text. This interchangeability works to facilitate a reader's emotional investment/divestment—a narrative process that culminates in an emptying of sexual affect as the ultimate realization of the unity or oneness of sexual desire and emptiness.[93]

## BREAKING THE MOLD

A more recent evaluative work assessing the contributions of JPM to an aesthetics of narrative fiction, written by a team comprising both established and younger-generation JPM scholars in China, was published in 1992.[94] Here, one finally encounters a break in Chinese scholarship from reading JPM with sex in brackets or JPM as entirely built on an erotics that must then be accounted for in pseudoscientific terms. In both Bu Jian's comparison of JPM with its unambiguously great dramatic contemporary Mudan Ting, or The Peony Pavilion, and Zhang Guofu's short essay "Women and Sex in JPM," and JPM as "fiction of moral education in the form of the fu," there is a departure from the usual scholarly defensiveness against the book's reputation and an attempt to ask new interpretative questions.

Pu Jian reads JPM's fictional treatment of sexual desire against the Mudan Ting's dramatic presentation of the "same" problematic.[95] This is a step as much toward a more particularly contextualized understanding of how JPM was produced and read in Ming Wanli, as toward a deeper understanding of how sexual desire is paradigmatically thematized in the two "founding" works of their respective genres: JPM for the extended fictional narrative of an erotic sensibility, and Mudan Ting for the dramatic fiction of a romantic sensibility.

Zhang Guofu's states in no uncertain terms that women are the foremost "negatively marked figures" in JPM.[96] This very succinctly establishes the difference and distance between a projected authorial intention (which is how the question of character and figuration had heretofore been posed in Chinese criticism), and the ideological effects of a narrative fiction as text. Thus, Zhang Guofu is able to read the "women" in JPM as legitimately struggling for power and survival by whatever means necessary, with sex and sexuality their primary and perhaps only weapon of choice. Although still operating along the lines of fictional representation as reflecting an external social reality, Zhang Guofu is nevertheless able to go beyond author-identification and a masculinist moral judgment. Pan Jinlian can no longer be read in terms of whether or not she is "a ruthless and depraved adulteress and murderer."[97] Rather, she is rendered in terms of the strategies whereby she may gain power and "self-worth" in a situation that is socially and domestically stacked against her.[98]

More significantly, Zhang Guofu finds the aesthetics of the narrative to be primarily determined on moral grounds. Thus,

> the fiction's depiction of each woman's sexual activities, its frequency, degree, and the sexual techniques attributed to each woman, are all consistent with the author's moral judgment [of each]. That is to say, in depicting sex, who and how, and how many times, all are decided by Xiao Xiao Sheng's [the author's] ruler of moral "distribution."[99]

This distributive method is then applied: first, to the logic of social hierarchy; second, to a Confucian ritualist ethics; and third and last, to the extent of personal self-discipline. Pan Jinlian would then clearly be the most "licentious" since she is not only one of the lowest by birth but also in her status as sixth concubine, and finally, in her total lack of virtuous self-restraint in such matters as greed for personal, symbolic, and sexual gains. She wants it all—therefore her portrait as the most licentious woman in the history of Chinese fiction.[100] Thus, whereas Plaks writes of the "particular [sexual] predilections" of Ximen Qing's partners as rhetorical and thematic functions that might—through a vicarious participatory reading process that alternately titillates and deflates with the accent on the latter of course—finally educate the reader in the dangers of sexual excess, Zhang Guofu is able to desist from either awarding the author or his work any transcendent educative meaning, and reads sex and women's sexuality in JPM as narrative deployments for maximum moral aesthetic effect.[101]

To reiterate an important point, Zhang Guofu's analysis of how sexuality is more a function of JPM's mainly moral project rather than an inherent essential component of the text to be reified as either outrageous or wonderful is salutary in its demystification effects. Such an analysis also implicitly agrees with one of the assertions of this book: that obscenity in the text and generations of readings has more to do with a misogynist morality that is shared in varying and different degrees by the text and readers alike. Neither authorial intention nor textual essence imparts obscenity to the text. Rather, the latter is the joint product of complicit textual and reading processes.

CHAPTER 2

The Manic Preface:
Jin Shengtan's (1608–1661)
Shuihu zhuan

As a commoner, [I] have not the power to prohibit men of the world to write, and have simply retrieved one text [SHZ] from the hands of pig herders and bond servants, and have [re]arranged it in orderly sections. This will [not prohibit men from writing but will] prevent those who have not yet written books from [ever] daring to write, and will exterminate in one day all the books already written. This is how Shengtan's [my] contribution to the clearing up of the world will prove even more marvelous than the fires of the Qin [that burned all the books].
—Jin Shengtan, Quanji

If witticisms surprise their author no less than their audience, and impress as much by their retrospective necessity as by their novelty, the reason is that the *trouvaille* appears as the simple unearthing, at once accidental and irresistible, of a buried possibility. It is because subjects do not, strictly speaking, know what they are doing [writing] that what they do [write] has more meaning than they know.
—Pierre Bourdieu, *Outline of a Theory of Practice*

Contrary to what still seems to hold as "truth" in Eurocentric accounts of writing and print, Europe is not the only place where, in the sixteenth century, there was "created a market in which thought could be bought, sold and exchanged."[1] An extremely "dynamic market for books" existed in the urban centers of late-sixteenth to early-seventeenth-century Ming China. This chapter is concerned with the ways in which a market for commercial books, a discourse on authenticity and authority in two instances of late Ming editorial and reading practice, and reading strategies promoting an ethico-aesthetic consumption of "popular" texts link with and reciprocally define each other. Articulating these linkages will help us to understand some of the ways and terms in which one late Ming wenren was able to construct an alternative field of cultural power and "create" works of empirewide dissemination and influence.

In his *Traditional Chinese Fiction and Fiction Commentary*, David Rolston identifies three stages of fiction commentaries.[2] The first stage is in the last decades of the sixteenth century (Wanli), the second stage is in the first quarter of the seventeenth century (Wanli through Chongzhen), and finally, the third and critical stage is in the last two-thirds of the seventeenth century (late Ming through Qing Kangxi). In the first stage, "commercial motives dominated," and the commentaries are "quite rudimentary and generally uninspired." The second stage is "when the market was flooded with bogus Li Zhi commentaries" that "spend more time attacking their texts than praising them," while the third stage includes Jin Shengtan and Zhang Zhupo, "who were really commentator-editors, however they publicly denied it."[3]

The question, then, is what are some of the conditions for this shift? Do these conditions range from commercially motivated yet uninspiring commentaries, through a period of pirated commentary editions attributed to famous names—commentaries that (still) tended to belittle their object texts—to finally a period of the proliferation of aesthetic-ethical commentaries that leave their commentator-editor-*writer's* imprint on the fiction of later times? For Jin Shengtan is surely as much coproducer of SHZ as it is known, talked about, and dramatized on television by the late twentieth century, as was the "writer" or "writers" before he got to the text. Furthermore, as I shall try to show, whether or not intentionally, Jin Shengtan in effect reenvisioned and expanded the field of his endeavors. Yet he was enabled and indirectly instigated to do so by (market) forces that in a previous stage or moment, still tended to evoke ambivalence in their workings and products—so much so, in fact, that those who did engage in commentating on published editions of fiction could only do so in a spirit of engaging in trivial work while denigrating the text commented on.[4] I will suggest that counterintuitively, a close comparison of prefatorial materials by second-

and third-stage commentators (Li Zhi and Jin Shengtan) show up in relief market forces as shadows cast by Jin Shengtan's "megalomania."[5] The figures in Jin's writing that crystallize and signify shifting material conditions for a magisterial authorial persona in commentating are at least partially produced by what at this time had become invisible or difficult to discern — that is, commercial motivations or market forces.

Whereas Li Zhi theorized a political ethics of reading SHZ that is grounded in a discourse stressing *authenticity*, Jin Shengtan agrees with Li Zhi that SHZ is a classical fiction, yet goes on to elaborate on how the text's "classicalness" and transmittability—in short, its discursive *authority*—lies not in a political ethics but rather a *fictional aesthetics*. Such a rhetorical shift represents the effects of an imperial examination culture in the throes of a print renaissance; when debased cultural forms such as vernacular fiction could be articulated to the flourishing culture of examination self-help texts, and textual exegeses are made commercially viable and intellectually entertaining.[6] Such a shift may well be reconstrued as inaugurating something resembling modern fictional criticism.[7] Its practitioners can then be reframed as the earliest theorists of a Chinese fictional canon. I shall argue instead that small rhetorical flourishes that attain the status of buzzwords be reread for their contextual significations. In advancing a quasi-theory of fiction when presenting his edition of SHZ, Jin Shengtan was in fact responding to and reformulating contemporary print market practices. His prefaces to SHZ, when compared to Li Zhi's, evince a greater and more nuanced sense of a market in books, as well as an editor-commentator's potential and future place in a commodified textual culture. Sophisticated and quasi-modern aesthetic approaches to fiction are thus an effect and function of a reciprocal relation between contemporary editorial and exegetical practices, and the print culture that is its material condition. Hence, the prefacing and reading tactics of different market editions of a popular fiction by two of the best-known late Ming figures express a changing sense of and continually shifting negotiations with an expanding market in fiction.[8]

Ming Wanli (1573–1620) through Chongzhen (1628–1645) was a period of great flux and change in the fields of Jiangnan literati (wenren) endeavours.[9] These changes had partly to do with the increased alienation of an entire class of wenren from the orthodox ladder of ascent through imperial examinations and bureaucratic service.[10] Disaffected wenren publicly aired their contempt for the examination system and how a utilitarian education was producing profit-minded literati unworthy of the name. For the first time, this publicizing of a prosaic "personal" discontent was propagated through the very medium whereby wenren had always sought to distinguish themselves—that is, writing. More significantly, many Jiangnan wenren in the late Ming period who could write (and according to some detractors, even those who couldn't) could in this era get his written products in print: as a compiler of examination cram books; as an editor of literary anthologies; as a dilettante poet or hack essayist; or as a collector, an editor, an annotator, or a writer of drama and fiction. A writer, once established on the market for books in print, could take on a variety of nonorthodox roles and practices.[11] The multifaceted careers of Chen Jiru (1558–1639), Feng Menglong (1574–1646), Ling Mengchu (1580–1644), and Li Yu (1611–1680) are cases in point. For those few leading figures in the late Wanli Jiangnan literary field such as Li Zhi (1527–1602) and Yuan Hungdao (1568–1610), empirewide urban renown in print would even lead to contemporary forged publications under their best-selling names.[12]

This chapter takes as its point of departure the widely acknowledged though less-well-documented urban "printing boom" in the Jiangnan region in the last five decades of the Ming dynasty, from around 1600 to 1644.[13] Beginning to be studied since the late 1980s are the sociopolitical (objective) and psychophysiological (subjective) effects of a Chinese commercial print culture from the Sung era through the twentieth century. Susan Cherniack's "Book Culture and Textual Transmission in Sung China" is extremely suggestive in how it links what she several times calls the "explosion of books" in late Sung to problems of transmission and power in the institutionalization of a hegemonic Confucian corpus of texts and directions of thought. According to Cherniack, book culture, the proliferation of books in print, and the shift from a preprint culture to a print culture constitute destabilizing forces in the transmission of orthodoxy and canonical texts.[14] What her study indicates, and to some extent lays the groundwork for, is further questioning concerning the subject of this destabilization. What are the effects of print culture on a literati subjectivity that is positioned paradoxically as both transmitter and (potential) author within and of "this culture of ours"?[15] How does print culture affect, through the various stages of its history from the Sung to the Qing, a likewise shifting subjectivity in its increasingly heterogeneous producers and consumers? What is its role in the institutionalization of an autonomous literati culture as a public field of belletristic endeavor?[16]

If the Sung may be seen as inaugurating not just book culture but, to some extent, aspects of modern print culture consciousness—such as the introspective turn that is materially and psychologically encouraged as well as conditioned by silent reading alone—modern "Western" notions of authorship and intellectual property also seem recognizable in, for example, Zhu Xi's decision to maintain authorial control in print by buying the blocks of his text that an official was on the verge of putting to print.[17] Nevertheless, how specific readings of texts, and actions taken to control texts by both imperial and personal authority, are to be interpreted must await further study that could sufficiently contextualize and particularize these questions for each given historical moment.[18]

If as Dorothy Ko writes, Wanli Jiangnan was the moment and place when "books became firmly linked with profit, in both the economic and moral sense, in the minds of readers and publishers," then what about the innumerable writers, anthologizers, compilers, and commentators?[19] What went on in their minds? How was the linkage between books, material and/or symbolic profit, and the urban marketplace where the relations between the two materialize present in their writings? This is the question I ask in this chapter, via a juxtapositioning of Li Zhi's editorial preface to the 1610 Rongyu Tang edition of SHZ with Jin Shengtan's three prefaces (the last of which is dated 1641; I shall focus on the first two) to his 1644 "abridged" seventy-one *hui* edition of SHZ. I suggest that in the several generations separating these two *wenren*—both of whom were major figures in the late Ming field of nonorthodox writings—an expanding print culture, perceived negatively as an excess of books in print on the market for new cultural commodities, produces distinct situational shifts that inform the editorial concerns and reading tactics of Li Zhi and Jin Shengtan. Li Zhi reads SHZ as potentially addressing the emperor and his ministers, thereby positioning himself as a loyal yet critical reader within the physical and geopolitical empire of the Ming in a moment of internal imperial crisis. In contrast, Jin Shengtan's reading of SHZ, written and published in the midst of both internal and external threats (peasant rebels and Manchu forces as well as an economic depression) formulates what I shall call a *textual empire* whose contours are not geographic but rather consist of discrete vernacular texts that merit transmission via corrective readings and rewritings (reprintings).[20] I maintain that the envisioning of such a textual empire is, as it were, the positive imprint of a negatively perceived book market that had exceeded bureaucratic and literati control—in Chen Longzheng's (1585–1645) words, a place where "books are not books, [and] reading is not reading [*shu ji fei shu du yi fei du*]."[21] The struggle over—and rearticulation of—social, symbolic, and ideological authority in newly "public" literary domains (genres) had become the central concern of ambitious and talented fiction editors and commentators.²²

In explaining both the success and ultimate failure of Li Zicheng's rebellion in the 1630s and 1640s, James Parsons notes the "fragmentation of gentry power." He attributes the latter to the disappearance of "great gentry clans with firmly grounded regional power."²³ Cynthia Brokaw, on the other hand, quotes Mori Masao in describing a gentry that had become by the early Qing "essentially private in nature," indicating reduced engagement with local state or bureaucratic services. By the late Ming, with the rise in absentee landlordism and the demographic move to urban centers, the gentry had already begun surrendering "the initiative for local government" and demonstrably lacked "interest in the welfare of their local communities."²⁴ Dorothy Ko, furthermore, stresses how family publishing (*jiake*) "constituted one facet of a general trend toward privatization in Chinese life in the Ming Qing period, when the family became the locus of a host of formerly 'public' activities."²⁵ I will contend that Jin Shengtan's (invisible) "textual empire" is a personal invention yet "public" extension of this "privatization" ("private" as opposed and relative to "bureaucratic" service) and "fragmentation" that marks gentry and literati print productions in late Ming Jiangnan especially. This, in turn, is linked to how "private" cultural practices had by the late Ming period and in the Jiangnan region especially become reformulated as sites of public ostentation and social competition.²⁶

*Book Printing and the Literary Market*

Histories of Chinese printing agree that printing in the Ming period surpassed the Yuan and Sung eras in quantity, albeit with some reservations as to the quality of the printed product. A well-known saying goes, "When the Ming [started] printing books [therein was] the destruction of books" ("*mingren keshu er shuwang*"). Numerous Qing bibliophiles have likewise registered their contempt for the error-ridden cheap editions and cut-and-paste products of the notorious late Ming *minke* or Fujian print shops.²⁷ Even contemporary, well-known cultural figures from the Ming Jiajing (1522–1567) to the Ming Chongzhen periods have noted their disapproval of current printing practices. In a collection of notes first printed in the mid-Jiajing, Lang Ying (1487–1566)—an "author, bibliophile, and connoisseur of antiques"²⁸—writes under an entry titled "On Books,"

Our dynasty has enjoyed peace for a long while, and ancient books have mostly been recovered; this is a great fortune. It is too bad that this should be marred by the bookshops of Fujian. These bookshops have only profit as their aim, and every time they chance on the good books printed in various provinces, should these books be expensive, the Fujian bookshops will immediately reprint them. The number of *juan* and table of contents will be exactly the same, but the contents [of the book] will be greatly diminished without anyone knowing, thus one book can be sold for the price of half a book, and people fight to buy it. . . . Alas, when the fires of the Qin burned and the Six Classics were left incomplete, [that was the work of] the political exigencies of the time [*shi*]. Today it is profit [*li*] that causes ancient books to be incomplete. Those that are [responsible for] this culture [of ours] ought to advise the Emperor to set up an office in charge of this matter, just as there used to be in ancient times. Those in office in Fujian could learn more about this situation and punish the culprits.[29]

The problem as Lang Ying puts it is unparalleled in the history of books. Lang Ying evokes the Qin emperor's notorious book burning as the only comparable precedent to what he sees as a similar destruction happening in his own times. Cut-and-paste pirating tactics had made Fujian printing practices analogous to book burning in their destruction of a symbolic and material wholeness of some originary copy. Incomplete books were now the result of mean profit rather than political exigencies. The profit to be made in a book market for cheap reprints ("one book can be sold for the price of half a book, and people fight to buy it") was clearly irresistible to the proliferating print shops (*fangke*) in the Jiangnan region of the late Ming period. Lang Ying deplores these profit-motivated printing practices, and by implication, the commercial values that the pirated books both express and camouflage.

Lang Ying figures a commercial printing of books as a lesser (because nonpolitical) mode of book burning. Nearly a century later, this same figure of speech would reappear not just to incriminate an expanding print market but to articulate a proper field of ambition and endeavor for the literati aspiring to a textual rather than political reputation (*ming*). The crucial difference between a scholar at large of Lang Ying's station and generation, and one of Jin Shengtan's times and talents, are for the purposes of this chapter, that the latter engaged in a mixture of editing, commentating, and anthologizing in addition to writing—all of which together comprise his

The Manic Preface   53

"works." Jin Shengtan was thus much more deeply engaged than Lang Ying in activities that formed a part of the print culture and book market of his times. Jin Shengtan was not an exception. As of the Wanli, many of the most renowned literati in the Jiangnan region had a hand in editing and printing (Chen Jiru, Feng Menglong, and so on).

Contemporary accounts of Ming printing have dismissed the comparison Lang Ying sets up between an excessive output of printed books with Qin book burning.[30] I suggest instead that Lang's rhetorical tactic was an accurate expression of his generation's conceptualization of books, printing, and the scholar's relation to these two as yet clearly demarcated fields. The printing of books had not yet (for Lang Ying) markedly begun to impinge on the writing of books. Editing had not quite transposed itself into an alternate form of writing. As of late Wanli, however, when prefacing and editing had begun to be considered a form of writing and "authoring," when editing and anthologizing might have constituted a major part of one's "works" or "oeuvres," then a conspicuous market in books and its connection to one's writings had to be (tortuously) reconceived. Thus, the figure of book burning (fen shu) metaphorized into its apparent opposite — that is, bookmaking (zuo shu), which as a term signifies and conflates editing, commentating, and printing. This paradoxical double figure of book burning and/as bookmaking is then developed for maximum cultural and commercial meaning and profit within the context outlined above — that is, in the first two of Jin Shengtan's three lengthy prefaces to his best-selling (edition of) SHZ, printed in 1644.

At least three aspects in Jiajing to Wanli (1522–1619) printing developments are relevant to the formation of a literary market and commercialized editing-publishing field.[31] The cost of printing in the Ming was significantly reduced around the beginning of the Jiajing reign (1522) due to a change in font. The new "craftsman-style" (jiangti) enabled an increase in both woodblock cutters and output of printed texts.[32] Then there was the "rediscovery" of the taoban technique, which reputedly first used in the Yuan period (fourteenth century), had by the late Wanli era been improved on by several commercial publishers to such an extent as to produce books in up to five different colors.[33] Taoban was used in printing illustrated editions, and elaborate luxury productions that differentiated between text and commentaries by various writers — a practice originating in classical exegeses, but by the late Wanli, in the printing of multicolored editions of anthologies, turned into a form of conspicuous consumption.[34] Finally, the prosperous Jiangnan region witnessed a phenomenal increase in private (personal or familial) publishing activity, *sike* or *jiake* (this is in addition to official publishing, *guanke*, on the one hand, and commercial publishing, *fangke*, on the other) as of the Jiajing (1522–1567).[35] The most active periods seem to be during the Jiajing (1522–1567), Wanli (1573–1620), and Chongzhen (1628–1645) reigns. Among the private publishers in Jiangnan of the Wanli and Chongzhen are the following names of empirewide renown: Chen Jiru (Wanli *chusheng*), Dong Qichang (Wanli 17 *jinshi*), Jiao Hong (Wanli 17 jinshi), and Feng Menglong (Chongzhen *gongsheng*), who publishes under both his name and that of his studio, Mo Han Zhai.[36]

Private publishers tended to put out orthodox and canonical works (*zhengjing zhengshi*), new anthologies of the Tang and Sung poets, or the more serious works of their literati friends and associates. Commercial printing houses or *fangke*, by comparison, were increasingly publishing works for urban consumption, including encyclopedias, almanacs, eight-legged essay cram books, and drama and fiction with prefaces, commentaries, and illustrations, some even in color.[37] Yet there was a crossing of the fine line between these two sectors of nonofficial printing by certain literati figures. In Wanli 27 (1599), Jiao Hong published his edition (*Jiao Hong kanben*) of a collection of Ming biographies anthologized by his famous friend Li Zhi—namely, *Cang Shu* (68 juan) and *Xu Cang Shu* (27 juan).[38] In this same period, Li Zhi's name appears (as part of the title and as the commentator) on at least eleven editions of drama and fiction, and as the anthologizer-editor of a collection of his younger contemporary and friend Yuan Hungdao's essays.[39] Five of these titles, including *Li Zhowu piping Zhongyi Shuihu zhuan*, are editions printed by the Hangzhou bookshop Rongyu Tang. Clearly, Li Zhi was both in demand as a writer of "serious" works printed by a private publisher and friend, and the alleged commentator of new editions of drama and fiction printed by commercial printing houses. This popularity *in print* attests to the currency and market value of "Li Zhi"—less as a writer and more as a name (with cultural weight or capital), not the person but rather the commodified persona—on the market for books in Ming Wanli.[40]

To recapitulate, Ming Wanli and Chongzhen are periods rightly described as high points in a late Ming printing boom. This is recorded in the notational writings of the literati of these times, often in negative or at least highly ambivalent terms. That Li Zhi's name is associated in print not simply with philosophical writings, essays, and so on but also with the editing and commentating of drama and fictional works obviously evidences the "syncretism" of his reading habits; the oft-mentioned interest of late Ming literati in popular genres; and the eclectic nonofficial nature of Li Zhi's activities and associations, epitomizing the iconoclastic wenren of this age.[41] For the purposes of this chapter, however, I wish to emphasize the signifying, circulatory, and disseminating power of Li Zhi's *name* as a sign or marker with a speculatable exchange value. Without the potential of such a value, there would not be the various commentated editions of drama and fiction from the hand of a nobody (purportedly named Ye Zhou), circulating in the name of the infamous Li Zhi.[42] In a sense, this is a commercial tactic that is all too familiar: a brand-name sells, the real thing or not. On the other hand, once such a name is established in print, chances are that its very controversial, marginal, or contested nature may well ensure both circulation in the present and transmission into the future. I am not saying that Li Zhi the person knew he was making it big by writing what ought to be burned. But I am suggesting that by the time Jin Shengtan prefaces and comments at great length on *his* rewritten SHZ, what Li Zhi elsewhere critiques as "the way of the market"[43] of the Wanli had crystallized into a distinct way of reading, a new literary practice, generating an at once market-oriented and market-resistant prefatory discourse. This is what necessitates a rereading and comparison of Li's and Jin's prefaces to SHZ since there occurs within and between them significant differences in their representations of the relations between the writer/reader, the text, and a changed and changing empire. A "way of the market" impinges on and transforms these relations.

*Where Have All the Real Men Gone?*

In his study of Yuan Hungdao and the Gongan school, Chou Chih-P'ing writes of the importance of Li Zhi as a precursor, personal friend, and teacher of the Gongan brothers.[44] Given Li Zhi's emphasis on "the childlike mind" and "spontaneity in writing," Chou ponders the seeming inconsistency of what he terms a "pragmatic" rather than "expressive" bent in Li Zhi's reading of SHZ. "The preface to *The Water Margin of Loyalty and Righteousness* [SHZ] illustrates that the aesthetic qualities of the novel were completely ignored, while its social and political value were strongly affirmed."[45] Chou goes on to ask whether such a pragmatic reading contradicts Li Zhi's "individualistic and expressive remarks on literature." The answer for Chou is no, since "recognizing the social and political functions of a novel is quite different from regarding literature as nothing but a vehicle for promoting Confucian teachings." Chou finally notes how this "theoretical mixture of pragmatic and expressive viewpoints" also characterizes Yuan Hungdao's later comments on JPM.[46]

Chou's question is directed by his attempt to explain Li Zhi's reading of one fictional text (SHZ) in light of Li's historically relativist or evolutionary view of literature.[47] How could one who so penetratingly argues for the timeliness of modern forms (drama, fiction) relapse into a sociopolitical/pragmatic rather than an aesthetic/expressive view of fiction when prefacing a contemporary narrative text?

There is both a disjunction and virtual presence that is crucial to understanding the terms with which Li Zhi read SHZ, and the very different terms with which Jin Shengtan would read the "same" text some forty years later. The virtual presence is that of a market for fiction, while the disjunction is one of time and generation. In the forty years that separate Li's and Jin's prefaces, the conditions for the reading and prefacing of fiction changed to the extent that an aestheticized consumption of fiction became not just possible but necessary, not yet for Li Zhi but certainly for Jin Shengtan. Without a thriving market for fiction, an aesthetic of fiction would be not thinkable, neither necessary nor profitable. Only with an aesthetics of a literary product could one convincingly establish the latter's seemingly noncontingent (to time, place, and material conditions of production) differential value. Aestheticization *authorizes* new cultural forms as reified objets d'art for scholarly study and connoisseur appreciation, while veiling from view (actively forgetting) their simultaneous presence as products on a market (the source of a potential *inauthenticity*). As a *literary* process and institution, aestheticization invents the autonomy of cultural forms vis-à-vis social and economic production and circulation contexts. Through the formulation of a more aesthetic than political ethics of reading fiction, fiction becomes incorporated within a privatized (that is, nonbureaucratic) new public domain of literati cultural work (Jin Shengtan). Yet at the same time, the nonmercantile and even antimercantile quality of such a private arena must be asserted—precisely through the articulation of aesthetic principles of writing and reading that are posited as "organic" (transhistorical and therefore noncontingent on material conditions of the present)—to ensure distinction from commercial cultural products and run-of-the-mill consumers.[48]

Li Zhi was born in Jiajing 6 (1527), and detoured through officialdom before becoming an "iconoclast" writer and thinker in his fifties in the Wanli era ("before I was fifty I was like a dog barking as other dogs barked"). *Fenshu*, a collection of his writings, was first published in 1590, *Cangshu* was published in 1599, and a collection of his posthumous writings, *Xu Cangshu*, came out in print in 1609. Jin Shengtan was born in the late Wanli (c. 1610), never made it to officialdom, and probably did not want to, instead making a life for himself as a commentator, editor, and writer all in one, as well as a charismatic lecturer on the side. His edition of SHZ was printed in 1644 (with a preface dated 1641). From 1644 to 1660, he edited and commentated ten published works, including *Xixiang Ji*, an anthology of Tang writing, and a collection of model examination essays (*shiwen*). Only after his death were his noneditorial writings published and listed by his cousin Jin Chang as *nei shu* (the inner books). He is nonetheless primarily known for his edition of SHZ; in fact, this edition was so popular as to eclipse most of the other editions then in print.

The disjunction, then, is between a Jiajing generation literatus whose activities included official duties, the rejection of officialdom, and extensive travel and writing; and on the other side, a late Wanli-born literatus whose major intellectual activities consisted of editing, anthologizing, and commentating works already in print. That Jin Shengtan has been characterized more often as either a "writer" or "critic" by twentieth-century scholars rather than the editor-commentator-anthologizer-writer-critic that he surely was, says more about the subsequent professionalization of these various aspects of the production of books as well as how these different activities became increasingly differentiated socially and symbolically. To stress Jin as a writer or critic is to emphasize his "original contribution." To stress that this contribution took the form of editing, rewriting, anthologizing, and commentating, demystifies its "originary" value.

I am not arguing against Jin's "originality." I am saying that the form it took—the prefaces and commentaries, cuts and selections—and a "new" self-consciousness concerning that form constitute a large part of that originality. Jin Shengtan implemented both a new mode of creating written and published oeuvres, and also a new way of conceptualizing it. The extent of his difference, and its implications, is most apparent when read alongside an earlier, far more "established" writer's preface to the same fictional text—that is, Li Zhi's preface to SHZ.

Li Zhi's preface articulates an ethical affect of reading. Through such a reading, projected readers—certain subjects and positionalities of reading—will be imbued with a more effective and ethical political knowledge. What is notable is how Li Zhi assumes an alienation from the imperial power (in the authors who are compared to the sages of antiquity), justifies this alienation, identifies with it, and simultaneously theorizes it as valuable and productive. What (authorial) alienation produces are fictional embodiments of a rage that when correctly read, will both attenuate the writing subject's psychosomatic illness and provide a preventive lesson for imperial personnel management.

> The Grand Historian says both *Shuinan* [*The difficulty of persuasion*] and *Gufen* [*A loner's anger*] are the works of wise men and sages in a fit of rage.[49] Therefore, the sages of antiquity did not write when not in a rage. To write without rage is like trembling without being cold, to groan without being sick. One could still write, yet what would there be to read? SHZ is a work of rage. Since the weakening of the Song, disorder has resulted in the wisest men in the lowest position, while despicable men have been elevated to positions of power. Gradually, the eastern and northern barbarians came to be at the top while men from the middle plains are at the bottom. . . . The two authors [of SHZ] physically lived in the Yuan, but their hearts were with the Song, and despite being born in the Yuan, were actually enraged by the events of the Song; that is why, enraged at the two [Song] emperors held hostage in the north [Jin], they wrote of the conquering of northern Liao so as to release that rage. Again, it is their rage at the compromised comfort of the move to the south that explains the writing of the destruction of the southern *Fangla*, which alleviates that rage. And who are they who enable this release of rage? They are the bandits [*qiangren*] who have gathered at the Water Margin. It is impossible to not see them as [embodying] loyalty and Righteousness. That is why the two authors wrote the records of the Water Margin, and named it "loyalty and righteousness [at/of the Water Margin]." As for why [those who have] loyalty and righteousness have all repaired to the Water Margin, the reasons are apparent. And as to why each and every one of them is [the embodiment of] loyalty and fraternal righteousness, how this has come about, is also clear. Today, it seems the principle that [men of] small virtues rule [men of] great virtues, and [men of] small wisdom rule [men of] great wisdom. . . . This is like the use of [those with] little force to subjugate, and to have those with greater force the subjugated, how could the latter let themselves be taken without resistance? This [situation] will inevitably force all the men of great force and great virtues in the empire to the edges of the empire, to the Water Margin. . . . This is why those who rule an empire/country must read this record. Once they read this, all [who have] loyalty and righteousness will not be at the Water Margin, but rather at the sides of the emperor/ruler. Wise prime ministers must

read it, for once they read it, [those who have] loyalty and righteousness will no longer be at the Water Margin, but will be at the court. Military advisers at the capital and generals at the frontiers likewise must read this. Once they do, [men of] loyalty and righteousness will no longer be at the Water Margin, but rather will be among those chosen to protect the heartland. Otherwise, such men will not be at the court, by the emperor's side, or in the cities of the kingdom. Where will they be? They will be at the Water Margin. And that is why this record is a record of rage.⁵⁰

The rage of SHZ is that of its two authors, who specifically wrote from a position of double disempowerment—at once ethico-political and ethnic. Since Song times, not only were the morally corrupt in power—which in itself was sufficient explanation for the demise of the Song empire—but this had directly led to the takeover by non-Han barbarians of the north. The result, according to Li Zhi, was a rage that could only be expressed and (symbolically) avenged in the narrative conquest and destruction of barbarian enemies beyond both the northern and southern frontiers. The fictional agents of the two authors' rage at and revenge against their historical situation are the 108 heroes of Liangshan, all of whom are characterized by Li Zhi as being embodiments of true loyalty and righteousness in a corrupt age. Li Zhi reads into the two authors' motivation for writing, their identification with and projection onto the brigand heroes of a previous Song moment, the authors' own rage at occupying a temporally disjunctive yet analogous position (to the brigands) in the Yuan. It is at this point that two historical moments read as equally corrupt are conflated with a third—Li Zhi's own moment in the present: "Today, it seems the principle that [men of] small virtues rule [men of] great virtues, and [men of] small wisdom rule [men of] great wisdom." In a sudden shift from the narrative and its dual temporality—explicitly Song but implicating Yuan—from rhetorically asking why the true loyal subjects are brigands at the margins of the empire, Li Zhi brings up the present and how a reversal of values has "today" attained the status of "principle." This is what the world has come to, Li Zhi seems to be saying, and is it any wonder that in such a world, the authentically great and good should all turn into thieves at the borders of the land, at the edges of forsaken waters? It is this third moment, a Ming Wanli one, that accounts for Li Zhi's final injunction that those occupying certain positionalities must above all read SHZ if they are to bring (back) to the center of political power those who should be, but are not, there. These positionalities are tellingly listed in order of power and significance. First is the emperor and ruler, then the prime minister, and finally the military advisers and generals. The affective powers of SHZ are such that by merely reading it, these subjects in power will be emotively enlightened as to how to bring to their sides those who by moral right should be there.

By indicating the relevance for "today" of correctly identifying the Song-Yuan rage at the heart of SHZ, Li Zhi has perhaps given voice to "his" rage, or at least the rage of those in his time who feel and see themselves, amid "inauthentic" values and subjects, alienated in their "authenticity" and clearly marginal to political power. Theirs is not a position that can redress this wrong and prevent the demise of the Ming empire; rather, they are the ones who will if not write an authenticating enraged text, at least read such a one as SHZ with a vindicating self-recognition (in accordance with SHZ's narrative logic of heroes being forced into brigandry and exile, or *guanbi minfan, bi shang liangshan*).

In asserting the loyalty and righteousness of the book, and its heroes as embodiments of the authors' righteous rage, Li Zhi in effect justifies political alienation, incriminating the ruler, prime minister, and military advisers—in short, all those in political power who have failed to distinguish between the authentic and inauthentic. But how is one to understand this alignment of alienation with an authenticating affect, as if alienation were tantamount to ethical and affective authenticity?

Li Zhi's was not the only reading of SHZ in the Wanli in this vein. An earlier preface by Wang Daokun (1525–1593) to another edition (*Zhong yi Shuihu zhuan*, Wanli 17) advances a similar notion.

> I have gone back to the sources [for why the 108 have turned to brigandry] and [find] they have either been faulted by their officers for minor misdoings, or are wronged by mediocre officials and have no way of proving their innocence. They see through the evil ministers at the emperor's side, [yet can only] beat their breasts in rage, furthermore knowing to discriminate between the civilized and barbarians . . . [T]hat is why they finally congregate in the mountains outside of the towns. Although they steal money and goods, they do not kidnap women and children; they will only harm the wicked, and will not hurt good and innocent people. They incant and harbor a righteous energy; they are one hundred in number but one in heart.[51]

Both of Li Zhi's points on the ethical and ethnic "correctness" of the brigands are made here, though in less categorical terms, as if needing to persuade both reader and self. In a later (date uncertain) preface to yet another

The Manic Preface 61

edition (the Bao Han Lou edition, *Zhong yi Shuihu quan zhuan*), however, a certain Wuhu laoren (Old Man of the Five Lakes) writes what could almost be read as an addendum to Li Zhi's preface.

> Between heaven and earth, it is difficult to find the authentic [*zhen*] man, and the authentic book also is rarely met with. Only with the authentic man can one momentarily [experience] an authentic person and an authentic friend [*zhiji*]; only with authentic books can there be in the million years hence an authentic field of endeavor [*shiye*], authentic belles lettres [*wenzhang*]. Even so, this man need not necessarily be the likes of King Wen, King Zhou, Confucius, or Mencius, for those who are courageous and love to fight [*haoyong douhen*] may also have an authentic spirit [*zhen qi*]. Nor does a book need to be one of the classics of antiquity, for works of a derisive and angry [*xixiao numa*] bent may also achieve authenticity [*zhen jing*]. . . . Alas, that I cannot meet in person the likes of Song Jiang and his men, at least I am able to meet them in spirit. In today's world what man does not pretend to scholarship, or masquerade as a famous literatus [*mingshi*], or brag about knightly qualities, in order to line his own pockets and oppress the innocent in the role of mediator and with cohorts to help out. Such men are intimate with those in office so as to confuse [others] regarding their public status; they are benevolent to the townspeople so that the latter will believe in the righteousness of their doings; [they have transformed] this great wide world into a truly despicable and execrable world. Where is the virile blood [*xuexing*] of these men, where have loyalty and righteousness repaired to? These are men that have surely never read SHZ.[52]

Wuhu laoren (Old Man of the Five Lakes) is writing along recognizably Wanli lines of thinking. Although he does argue for the true spirit residing in men surely not of the usual literati stamp (in high office or of well-known sagehood) "who are courageous and love to fight," he also parallels the rarity of authentic men to that of authentic books. He then delineates in angry detail the many ways in which in this age, men fake scholarliness, sagehood, talent, courage, and so on. Even if he finds execrable how men of today have learned to market themselves, he also finds this situation exactly parallel to the market in books, where authenticity can no longer be seen to reside in what merely looks and sells like the real thing. To the contrary, by making such a comparison, the Old Man is calling for authenticity in genres and modes of writing that used to be devalued and marginalized, and to a large extent, probably still were despite their being championed by the likes of Li Kaixian, Li Zhi, and himself.

In identifying directly with the characters represented in SHZ, and the book itself as an undervalued genre of writing, neither of these prefaces or readings is as sophisticated as Li Zhi's. Li prefigured the tortured contentions of a later generations' readings of fiction in identifying not with the representation but the affect that propels and informs it, the rage that authenticates a skewed and skewing narrative. But importantly, both of these prefaces share Li Zhi's preoccupation with authenticity as an endangered quality in the commodification of men and books. The danger comes from a surfeit of inauthentic impersonations on the political and symbolic market for men. Authentic men are increasingly to be found among the socially marginal, even the ostracized and alienated. Thus the linkage between the political alienation that Li Zhi presumes and the ethical as well as ethnic authenticity that justifies it.

### Jin Shengtan's SHZ: A Prohibitive Text

Thirty years after Li Zhi's preface was published, Jin Shengtan's three long prefaces to his own copiously commentaried, rewritten, and restructured version of SHZ appeared in print. The first two of these will be the focus in this chapter. In his prefaces, Jin seems to be writing indirectly against precisely Li Zhi's proposal that SHZ is a text by, for, and about loyal and righteous subjects. Jin's edition became, by all accounts, the definitive version of the narrative in question, much as Zhang Zhupo's version has long been the best-known, if not the only known JPM in circulation until the twentieth century.[53]

I will first read the second preface, where Jin discourses at length on how *The Water Margin* (SHZ) has been entirely misnamed and misread—as a narrative about preeminently loyal and righteous subjects in the guise of bandit-heroes. What Jin Shengtan perceives as a willfully pernicious misnaming of both text and subject seems directed against Li Zhi's earlier preface, where the latter "rectifies" a title that was by then already in fairly wide circulation: *The Loyal and Righteous [at the] Water Margin* (or, *Zhongyi Shuihu zhuan*). Li Zhi's preface justifies this title through articulating an ethical affect of reading. Jin Shengtan, writing in 1641 (the date of the third preface), adamantly refutes any claims for the narrative as one whose subject could be termed loyal and righteous.

In observing things one should examine their names, in judging persons one should discern their will. When Shi Naian recorded the story of Song Jiang and named this book *The Water Margin*, the utmost evil and rebellion [were relegated to the water margin and] not in the same place as the Middle Kingdom. Yet, some disorderly ruffian of a later age went and mistakenly added "loyalty and righteous" to its title. Alas, how could loyalty and righteousness be at the water margin? Loyalty [*zhong*] is that utmost virtue whereby one serves one's ruler, whereas righteousness [*yi*] are the great measures whereby one leads those beneath one, to serve one's ruler with loyalty and to use those beneath one righteously; that is what befits a prime minister. . . . As for what Naian meant in speaking of "the water margin," the king's empire is bordered by waters, and that which is on the outer side of these waters, and which is at a great distance [from the empire] is "the water margin." And that which must be kept at a great distance, are the evil things [*xiong wu*] of the empire, those who all under heaven would together strike at, as well as the bad things [*e wu*] of the empire, those who all under heaven would together reject. If one were to place the loyal and righteous at *The Water Margin*, are we then to take the loyal and righteous as evil and bad? And if at *The Water Margin* are the loyal and righteous, are there none then in the entire country? For [if] the ruler is nonetheless the ruler, and the ministers are nonetheless ministers, how could there be no loyal and righteous [men] in the empire? To say this [that the loyal and righteous are all at *The Water Margin*] is to incriminate the ministers, yet it would be difficult not to implicate one's ruler as well. [If fathers] are still fathers, and sons are still sons, how can it be that there are no loyal and righteous [men] in families? Although [such a title] speaks only of incriminating the sons, yet it would be difficult not to implicate the fathers. This is why whosoever terms *The Water Margin* a loyal and righteous narrative, that man must harbor toward his emperor-father a heart that is resentful and contrary [*dui*], which point must not remain unexamined. One must reflect on why Song Jiang and company, 108 in all, should have ended up at the water margin? When these men were young, they all had the disposition of tigers and leopards, and when they came of age, they all committed acts of murder and banditry, after which they became convicted felons at large, and at death, they are all thieves who have initiated rebellions. If a king were to arise and have them all killed, then thousands and more would be happy at their deaths. How is it that [in the narrative] they should finally fortuitously survive punishment by death of the Song dynasty? And if those 108 men should survive the

Song's punishment, might there not be hundreds of thousands more of such men who will think of trying these same actions in later ages? Naian worried about this, therefore he vigorously penned this record and titled it *The Water Margin*, by which he meant to say that even should these 108 men escape from personal deaths, they would certainly not escape from their fated [fictional] exile [to the water margin] after their [historical] deaths, and this is the will of the superior man [who was their author]. Those who mistakenly give this narrative the name of "loyalty and righteousness" are they not taking [a narrative] that is meant to be prohibitive for one of exhortation [*jiang wei jie zhe er fan jiang wei quan ye*]?[54]

Jin Shengtan identifies two crucial misreadings on the part of past readers (such as Li Zhi) of SHZ. The first level is generic. It mistakes a prohibitive narrative for an exhortational one.[55] The outcome of such a misreading is high treason since it is tantamount to an ethical, political, and affective transgression against the ruler (father) and country (state/family). An exhortational reading would condone and identify with insubordination by reproducing in the reader the identical affect (resentment) that the 108 hero-bandits, and indeed the text itself, are seen to embody.

A corrective reading such as Jin Shengtan's ensures distinction between these two modes. In contrast, a wrongheaded reading like Li Zhi's muddles the fine line separating the prohibitive and exhortational, mistaking the former for the latter, reading rage (exhortation) in the place of punishment (prohibition).

What further distinguishes these two models of reading is the projected situation of the author/writer, an imaginary political and cultural context of writing. Exhortation arises from rage long held back, a rage that is transfigured into writing. Thus, Li Zhi averred that the authors of SHZ are loyal and righteous subjects denied political station and service. Their writing is a transmutation of political service, and in Li Zhi's reading, addresses the center of political power. In a sense, Li Zhi reads fiction as a function of politics. Jin Shengtan disagrees. In his "How to Read *The Fifth Book of Genius*," which follows his three prefaces, he writes on the situation of this particular "genius" (*caizi*):

> When reading a book the first thing to be taken into account is the state of mind of the author when he wrote it. For example, the *Shiji* [*Records of the historian*] was the product of Sima Qian's [born 145 B.C.E.] bellyful of stored-up resentment. Therefore he poured [his emotion] into the writing of the collective biographies of the knights-errant and the moneymak-

ers. . . . The *Shuihu zhuan*, on the other hand, is a different matter. Its author, Shi Naian, had no bellyful of stored-up resentment he needed to let out. Well-fed, warm, and without anything else to do, carefree at heart, he spread out paper and picked up a brush, selected a topic [timu], and then wrote out his fine thoughts and polished phrases [jinshin xioukou]. Therefore his judgments do not go against those of the sages. People of later times were unaware of this and went so far as to add the characters for "loyal" [zhong] and "righteous" [yi] to the title and considered its writing to be similar to Sima Qian's writing of the *Shiji* to express his resentment [fafen zhushu]. This is precisely what ought not to be done.[56]

But the misreading is not Li Zhi's. It is rather a function of both the disjunction (in time and generation) and virtual presence (of a market in cultural persons and books) that produces, in Jin Shengtan's prefaces, a new conception and representation of writing and "making books." It is as if Jin Shengtan were projecting the author/writer (now no longer dual, as in Li Zhi's preface, but single and singular) as a dilettante writer of the sort he himself might have been, or could aspire to be. The author-writer is thus represented not as alienated from or frustrated in political service to the king and empire, enraged at the impersonators in power. Instead, he is represented as the gentleman of leisure, the aesthete and connoisseur, one who does not miss government service but rather lays claim to *cultural authority and distinction*. From the studies of Craig Clunas and Wanyi Chen, it is apparent that this "new" type sought distinction in all manner of cultural activities, not just writing.[57] In the process, of course, new cultural modes of production and new genres of writing such as editing and commentating fiction also came to be redefined. (By the twentieth century, these new modes of writing and authorship would be formally canonized as early modern fictional criticism and theory.)

The crucial change is from writing and reading as a sociopolitical function with an attendant topoi of *authenticity* to commentating and editing fictional works (redefined as writing) as a distinct aesthetic field of endeavor, a textual and textualized empire, where the topoi shifts to *authority in writing*. This is a shift with many more aspects than I am able to deal with here. Nevertheless, let me reiterate the degree to which such a shift in a distinct positionality of writing and reading is discernible in juxtaposing these prefaces.

Both Li Zhi and Jin Shengtan valorize a text already in circulation, and apparently popular across the dividing line of those with degrees and those without. For Li Zhi, the value stems from the text as embodiment of affect—of rage. This authenticating affect ensures its exhortational effect vis-à-vis reading subjects in political power (the emperor, his ministers). In this reading, the text and its representation of marginal brigand-heroes circulate between a small circle at the top of a political hierarchy and a few real/good men. The latter are alienated but loyal and righteous subjects who are or have been misplaced. The text mediates their rage and speaks for them to those in positions of power (in the circle of power). The implications of such a reading are dual. It has the democratic potential of empowering whosoever (in later ages) should feel rage at the margins of the empire. It is this potential that provokes Jin Shengtan to retort, "If those 108 men should survive punishment by death . . . might there not be hundreds of thousands more of such men . . . in later ages?" Second, by incriminating the extensions of a centripetal structure of power, Li Zhi's model of reading implicates the very center of symbolic power. Again in the words of Jin, "Although such a title speaks only of incriminating the sons, yet it would be difficult not to implicate the fathers."

In response, Jin Shengtan advances a more convoluted, somewhat contradictory, though also quite different scenario for the production of good writing, its circulation and transmission. SHZ is not the virtual "fit of rage" of an alienated political subject but rather the "tapestried heart-thoughts and embroidered mouth-phrases" of a consummate *writer* in a moment of leisure. It is the product of a *literary* mediation: the tapestry and embroidery of *literary technique* as opposed to the immediate outpouring of some authenticating emotion. What is at stake is no longer the differentiation between good and bad, authentic and inauthentic subjects, which constitutes a form of reading and knowledge necessary in the official bureaucratic realm. What is at stake now is the distinction between good and bad writing, or transmittable and untransmittable texts. Furthermore, whereas the distinction between good and bad, authentic and inauthentic subjects served the purpose of a political lesson in imperial personnel management (Li Zhi), the distinction between good and bad writing, writing that is or is not imbued with the correct authority—the ethico-aesthetics of reading prose lodged at the heart of Jin Shengtan's preface and enterprise—will instead become an exercise in the preparation for *cultural* service in a (transhistorical?) textual empire.

When and how are political subjects in representation (the writer, the brigand-heroes, the reader) deposed—displaced by writing, aesthetic techniques of writing, and "technologies of reading," or in short, an entire spectrum of textual functions?[58] When does fictional (xiaoshuo) representation begin to see itself as such? One partial answer (and there are others) would be when there are mirrors—or in this case, a market—where the material forms of such representation are singular yet at the same time (infinitely) multiplied. To repeat the words of Chen Longzheng, "In this age, printed books [keben] have run amock, [so that] books are not books, reading not reading, both have become an obstruction to cultivation of the self [fan wei xiu shen zhi lei], and are greatly to be detested."[59] For Jin Shengtan, writing (fiction) is foregrounded precisely at a moment when books are faced with a fate worse than extermination—that is, indiscriminate duplication. Reading is problematized to the extent that the line between books and nonbooks needs redrawing. Thus, aestheticization or an aesthetic/textual approach to writing is at least partly a function of the increased commodification of books, reading, and knowledge in the last decades of the Ming dynasty.

*Book Burning and Bookmaking*

This brings us to Jin Shengtan's first preface, wherein he develops an elaborate justification for his own reading/writing in an age filled, in his opinion, with indiscriminate (unauthorized and so worse than inauthentic) writings in print.

> The origins of the making of books may be traced to how the sages of antiquity shared in the sentiments of the people and came up with the principles for ruling. The making of books began with knotting rope, and peaked in the writing of the six classics. Those who held tablet and brush in hand were all in the status/position of the sage, and possessed the virtue of that status. To be in the position of a sage is to have its powers/authority, to possess the virtues of a sage, is to know the reasons and origins [of things]. To have that authority and to know the reasons [of things] is to write because it is fitting, and to write because one cannot not write.[60]

Jin Shengtan begins by establishing the hallowed origins of writing and books. Books are the embodiment of an organic (hierarchical) relation between the learned and ruled, and commemorate that relation through their (the books') codification of the rules that govern that relation ("the principles for ruling"). He then goes on to assert how the very occupying of the position of a sage ensures the authority (*quan*) and virtue (*de*) that go with that position. Writing is both fitting and obligatory to one occupying such a position—an embodied disposition as it were; at the same time, it is a prerogative and sign of one's distinction from and mediation between the positions above (the ruler) and below (the ruled).

> If Zhongni [Confucius] was not willing to give over to the courtiers [*zhuhou*] the authority to write books, how could he have been willing to give over the authority to write to commoners. That is why [I say] the writing of books is the affair of the sage. One who is not a sage and who writes, that man ought to be killed, and his book, burned. . . . Why? He who is not a sage and writes a book, his book breaks with the way, and he who is not the son of heaven and writes a book, his book breaks with [the codes for] ruling [the empire]. To break with the way and the [codes for] ruling is a perverted discourse [*hengyi*]. Perverted discourses, how can these not be burned? One who writes perverted discourse, how can he not be killed? . . . As for the first emperor's burning of not just books but the classics of the sages as well, [that shows] he had the authority but not actually the virtue, and not having the virtue, he did not know the reasons/principles [of things], and not knowing the reasons/principles, he burned all [the books]. To have burned even the classics [*shengjing*], that is the First Emperor's error [*zui*]; to have burned books, that is the First Emperor's great work. Alas, with the rise of the Han dynasty, there was a seeking for books that had survived [the burning]. At the time, many of the officials at court submitted [to the emperor] books and were therefore able to obtain promotion. That is how it came about that men of ambition from the four corners of the empire all claimed to have books, and the number of books submitted all of [a] sudden increased to even greater numbers than before the burning of books. Today, from antiquity to the present, people only know the great destruction of the burning of books, [so] how could they know of the even greater harm of seeking after books? When books are burned, there will no longer be books under heaven. That is how the books of the sages will be preserved. When books are sought after, there will be [too many] books under heaven, and that is how the books of the sages will perish. To burn books is to prohibit [*jin*] the writing of books by all men under heaven; to seek after books is to license [*zong*] the writing of books [*zuo shu*] by all men under heaven. As for giving license to all under heaven to write books, what [kinds of] books will not come of this?[61]

The symbolic significance of the First Emperor's book burning lies in its (negative) consecration of a quasi-sacred social and political power of writing and books; writing and books as the manifestations of a "natural" virtue and authority of, respectively, the sage and emperor. According to Jin Shengtan, the one flaw in the first emperor's burning of books arises from the latter's insufficient virtue, and therefore an attendant inability to discern between classics and mere books. (Later in the preface, Jin Shengtan will refer specifically to sishu, or "personal" books, written for "private perusal" and consumed in "private.") Only classics merit preservation and transmission. All other books ought to be burned; indeed, they must be burned if the classics are to be preserved. The emperor's burning of *all* books, in turn, led to the Han court's seeking after books. According to Jin Shengtan, this is the actual "originary" moment of an excess in books that has attained unimaginable proportions in the present (Ming Chongzhen).

> As for the books of today, they are such as Cang Di could not have foreseen when he invented writing, nor could they have been foreseen by the First Emperor when he ordered the burning of all books. Truly, to have [the authors] all killed would not be sufficient to protect the innocent, nor would burning all [the books] be sufficient to destroy all these traces. The Han's seeking after books is at the source, is to be faulted for beginning this criminal state of affairs. That is why [I say] that the crime of burning books is great, but that of seeking after books is even greater. The crime of burning books lies in also burning the classics of the sages [shengjing], . . . the crime of seeking out books lies in the circulation of personal books [sishu]. . . .
>
> As for the books of Zhuang Zhou, Qu Ping, Ma Qian, Du Fu, Shi Naian, and Dong Jieyuan, all of these are books produced [in that moment] when the heart ceases to beat and the vital energy is exhausted [xinjue qijin], and one's face is like that of a dead man; then and only then one's talent circulates before and behind to become [congeal into] a book. . . . Only then can one know that when the ancients wrote books, it was certainly not haphazardly. Yet men of [today's] world still will not examine themselves and take the measure of their [lack of] power, and thereupon cease writing. Such men truly are not even worth killing, and their books not worth burning. As a commoner, [I] have not the power to prohibit men of the world to write, and have simply retrieved one text [SHZ] from the hands of pig herders and slaves, and have [re]arranged it in orderly sections. This

will [not prohibit men from writing but will] prevent those who have not yet written books from [ever] daring to write, and will exterminate in one day all the books already written. This is how Shengtan's [my] contribution to the clearing up of the world will prove even more marvelous than the fires of the Qin [that burned all the books]. This is why [I have] in this first preface outlined the rise and destruction of classics past and present.[62]

Jin Shengtan's presentation of "the rise and destruction of classics past and present [*gujin jingshu xingfei*]" juxtaposes three moments (Qin book burning, Han book seeking, and late Ming book printing) whose temporal discontinuity and technological differences in bookmaking must not (and cannot yet) register. Qin book burning and Han book seeking can then signify on two levels at once: as "history" and "homology." History or the past provides Jin with a causal explanation for today's excess in books. It also installs a homological frame wherein a Han triadic relation—the court's book seeking, the myriad "men of ambition from the four corners of the empire [who] all claimed to have books," and finally, as a result, books in "even greater numbers than before the burning of books"—is remapped onto the present situation in which Jin himself is writing. These two levels of meaning serve to both hide and reveal Jin's quandary. Jin's situation is that of a "commoner" who claims compulsion to an attenuated form of writing ("arrangement" of a sagely text in orderly sections, or editing) that will yet accomplish marvels—firing up the world's bookish excess and scaring off would-be pretenders to fame in writing. Note Jin's extreme belittling of his writerly work and the equally extreme aggrandizing of the potential for contribution of his small endeavors. There is surely more than polite rhetoric at work here.

I have quoted Jin Shengtan's first preface extensively to, in part, emphasize the inordinate length of his three prefaces, as well as the terms and sequence of thought in which he authorizes his work—the commentating, editing, and rewriting of an "unorthodox" text. Authorization, rather than the authenticity of Li Zhi's generation and positionality of writing, has become the question and what's at stake.[63] The authority to write (to author books) and whence it derives is acutely problematized when there is, as Jin puts it, an unlicensed proliferation of indiscriminate writings and books not subject to the control of the court but perhaps even inadvertently encouraged by the court (the Han seeking after books, the Ming edict on nontaxation of books).[64] In Jin's hyperbolic view, the writers of these books should die for writing excess and their books burned, if burning were not too strong a measure for such worthless things.

The resentment (for surely it is resentment) in this harangue is not with the imperial power that has not recognized a writer's loyalty and righteousness, and thus given him a fitting office. The resentment in this preface is against a world filled with unimaginable quantities and kinds of books, such as the ancients could never have foreseen. How is one "writer," an inordinately talented commoner no less, to distinguish his work from all of these "books"? How can this book claim distinction, value, and contribution among all the others in the world? Jin Shengtan's answer is to commentate in such a way as to "save" one book from the indiscriminate heap, and more specifically, to rescue it from intellectually untrained and socially unacceptable hands. Jin Shengtan is hyper-conscious of his lack of an imperially delegated authority (quan)—that is, position—whereby he might prohibit most men to write. At the same time, his certainty of his de, or sagely virtue as a form of symbolic power, authorizes his writing in the attenuated forms of prefacing, editing, and commentating. He thus envisages his writing as a commoner with de the only permissible kind in a world glutted with nonauthorized (not from the brush of one with official authority) and unethical (without de) books. He further claims, hyperbolically of course, that his writing will prove as effective as book burning in "exterminat[ing] in one day all the books already written [*yizuo zhi shu, yi dan jin fei*]."

In this sense, Qin book burning becomes nothing less (or more) than an extended metaphor, figuring the manner in which one talented commoner's book (Jin Shengtan's SHZ) will outshine and outsell, by its ethical and aesthetic merits, all other books on the market.

There is a paradoxical twist in Jin's figurative usage of book burning that does not (yet) occur in Lang Ying's notation on how Qin book burning had left the classics incomplete in the same way that Fujian bookshops in the Jiajing had mangled books for profit:

> One book can be sold for the price of half a book, and people fight to buy it. . . . Alas, when the fires of the Qin burned and the Six Classics were left incomplete, [that was the work of] the political exigencies of the time [*shi*]. Today it is profit [*li*] that causes ancient books to be incomplete.[65]

If Qin book burning could be excused for the destruction of the (originary) classics only on the grounds of political expediency, there is no excusing the destruction of books effected by the market-oriented Fujian book printers. Lang Ying parallels the devastation of the two (ancient book burning and contemporary book printing) to foreground the destruction of books that has become a cliché of late Ming book culture, and also to note how even in destruction one must differentiate between a political motivation and degraded profit making.

Jin Shengtan turns this parallel on its head. Qin book burning is to be commended for exterminating all but that which by right of authorization (quan) and virtue (de) is transmittable to posterity. And that is exactly what Jin Shengtan claims to do in inhabiting the role of rewriter—that is, editor, prefacer, commentator, and expurgator of SHZ. In an age of the indiscriminate reduplication of books, only aggressive editing as a form of book burning could ensure the transmission of the appropriate texts. The paradox is how Jin Shengtan's editing is formulated as simultaneously a bookmaking (zuoshu) *and* book burning (fenshu). Prefacing and editing are thereby redefined as the most sagely of practices, a form of hallowed writing in a (printing wise) sacrilegious age. At the same time, the social and economic context of a book market out of elite/imperial control is figured through an extended and verbose rumination on the necessity for contemporary book burning—that is, aggressive editing.

I propose that it is Jin Shengtan's inhabiting a position (commoner or *shuren*), place (Suzhou), and time (Chongzhen era) when bookmaking could be and certainly was for others like him at once an "obsession" and a livelihood, a means of symbolic distinction and work—in short, a cultural practice with an evolving built-in sense of a market in books—that partially explains what some have considered a "megalomanic" prefatorial style.[66] Only thus could Jin's book have it both ways: as, on the one hand, symbolic-political and cultural-ethical capital (quan and de) for the writing/reading subject, and on the other, competitive commodity on the market for new fiction. The tactic is to reconfigure the former domain sufficiently to both encompass and overshadow the latter function.[67]

In Jin Shengtan's final injunctions to his target readers (in "How to Read *The Fifth Book of Genius*"), symbolic capital, social distinction, and "the way of the market" finally fuse to map a new territory for textual endeavors.

> Formerly when young people read SHZ they learned many irrelevant matters from it. Although the punctuation and commentary of my edition is only rough and incomplete, after the young people read it, they will have learned many literary devices. They will not only know that there are nu-

merous literary devices in SHZ, [but] they will also be able to detect even the literary devices in the *Zhanguo Ce* and the *Shiji*.

The SHZ is, after all, only a work of fiction. Young people are anxious to read it. Once they have read it, unexpectedly it will cause them to learn a number of literary methods.

Once young people have learned these literary methods, they will want to read without stopping such works as the *Zhanguo Ce* and the *Shiji*. The benefit of SHZ to young people is great.

Formerly SHZ was read even by peddlers and yamen runners. Although not a word has been added or subtracted in this version, it is not destined for petty people. Only those with refined thoughts and feelings can appreciate it.[68]

If it continues to be perceived as irrelevant to the study of the classics, to one's ambition to be good and great, and to one's excelling in the examinations, then neither the reading nor editing of fiction can be justified. Jin Shengtan recasts SHZ as a youth's primer wherein is laid out in the most concrete, gory, and attractive detail just those lessons in the craft of examination essay writing that every male youth must learn. (In the third preface he remembers how at ten, the classics would put him to sleep, whereas SHZ kept him awake and made him learn.) Jin Shengtan's SHZ is a youth classic. "The benefit of SHZ to young people is great." (Remember, he will also edit an anthology of shiwen, or model examination essays, for cramming purposes.)

Jin Shengtan concedes the minor status of fiction, but argues a pragmatic view of its usefulness. It is pleasurable and easy to read, therefore attracting both the right and wrong sort of readers. Jin's work is to ensure its "user-friendliness" for the right readers: young male inheritors to "this culture of ours." Jin's edition will thus (hopefully) be too *specialized*, pedagogically oriented as it is, for former readers such as peddlers and yamen runners to appreciate.

These are the terms with which Jin Shengtan establishes his edition's value as a youth textbook (symbolic capital), its function of differentiating between the refined and vulgar (social distinction), and its target and ideal reader population (the way of the market)—young aspirers to textual specialization as cultural refinement instead of the vulgar semiliterate readers (that have given fiction its bad name). In effect, a new territory of cultural work has been mapped and given proprietary meaning: the editing of fiction as tutelage of young literati in the making, as a means of guarding the gates to "our" cultural/textual empire, and incidentally perhaps, as a way of life (the beginnings of market specialization rather than bureaucratic professionalism).

*The Way of the Marketplace*

> Although I do not dare claim myself to be one who has made great contributions to this culture of ours [*siwen zhi gongchen*], I have approximated the bit of clay sufficient to guard a pass, or so put by the East Han general Wei Xiao, whose presence singly guaranteed the guarding of the Hangu Guan border mountain pass [*fengguan zhi wanni*].[69]

These are the final lines of Jin Shengtan's first preface. This "culture of ours" is likened to an empire besieged. Jin Shengtan is not, in such times, the statesman who will contribute to the empire by the usual means such as writing-authoring. Rather, his function is figured as the military contribution of a general singly guarding that crucial weak point at the borders of a *textual* empire. SHZ is that socially and symbolically borderline text. If it can be saved, so can the empire's future generations. What lies outside that pass, beyond this text? It is the hordes of barbaric, unedited books (in an urban marketplace) that threaten to infiltrate "our" cultural space and heritage, that pass for the authentic and ethical, and confuse those who have not yet been initiated into distinguishing between the refined and vulgar in reading.

Who counts as the unspoken, the understood "we" in "this culture of ours [*siwen*]"? This was crucially (and once again) at stake in the last decades of the Ming. It was at stake not so much perhaps in the political space of governing—someone like Jin Shengtan would never serve in government; instead he would align himself symbolically through editorial work with imperial pedagogical service—but rather in the new fields of discourse, in the fertile field of editorial works on writings ranging from popular fictional forms to examination essays (anything but the classics, almost). It was at stake precisely in the widespread "private," "personal," or "familial" writing, editing, collating, and printing of books (Jin Shengtan's *sishu*, late Ming *sike*), and of course, in the parallel phenomenon of the attribution of books written or edited by "nobodies" to famous names.

In claiming for himself and his "works" the status of gatekeeper of a threatened textual empire as well as transmitter of pretexts to the classics for the true inheritors, Jin Shengtan pits the market against itself, so to speak, and wins out. His market sense is evidenced in a rhetoric that seeks at once to transcend, critique, *and* capitalize on market effects. Hyperbole and talent together assure that Jin Shengtan's works will be transmitted through the ages, and his SHZ reprinted and read as if it were the only SHZ worth reading.

Several generations earlier, in the context of a market in cultivated men, Li Zhi had already critiqued the way of the market and claimed to transcend it, but did not devise a rhetoric (bookmaking as book burning) and mode of writing-authoring (prefacing and commentating) that ultimately made the most of its own ambiguities and contradictions in an emergent market in fictional books. Nonetheless, he was not entirely exempt from some "market" effects, such as the various commentaried editions of fiction and drama attributed to his name, and perhaps even the naming of his books (*Fenshu*, or *Book for Burning*).

> The friendship [jiao] that is difficult, is difficult to sever. That which is easy, is easily severed. Why is this? Because the world is filled with friendships forged along the principles of the urban marketplace [*shidao zhi jiao*]. For that which is of the urban marketplace, how can it be treated as [an authentic] friendship, and how can it be faulted for its easy severance? This sort of friendship [jiao] is merely a form of exchange [*jiao yi*], a form of circulation [*jiao tung*]. That is why those who associate for the sake of [self-]interest [li], are estranged when that interest ends. Those who associate for the sake of [the other's] influence [shi], become enemies when that influence is gone; intimate in the morning and strangers by evening, that is to be expected. Only the gentleman [junzi] is above concerns of influence and power, and seeks the advice of those of like disposition [tongzhi]. Only then does friendship become difficult. . . .
>
> One who is a sage should have the wherewithal [huo, virtue, wealth] of a sage, and not be a sage and merchant at the same time. My only quarrel is with the scholar of today who claims to be a sage yet possesses the know-how of the marketplace [*ju shijin zhi huo*]. He is a sage by day, yet the [true] descendants of the Han will see him as having abducted the throne, like Wang Mang, and kill him. He does business on the sly, but the young hangabouts will see him as a thief and hold him in custody. Not only will he die at the hands of true men of wisdom, [but] he will also be imprisoned in the marketplace, [and] he is a hundred thousand times worse off than those who are really of the market. I don't know what class of men he might be said to belong to.[70]

Li Zhi's quarrel is with a new breed of men who are neither scholars nor urban merchant types, yet act as if they are both. These men are socially unclassifiable and ethically corrupt. They are outwardly learned and inwardly followers of the market way. Li Zhi is, in fact, describing a type that arises from changed material and social conditions, a parvenu subject whose practices include cultural and symbolic production (the way of learning and sagehood) yet in an exchangeable, profitable form. These scholars possess not the virtue of a sage but the know-how of the marketplace.

Yet that which is the distinctive possession (huo or virtue) of the scholar-sage is also the know-how of the merchant (huo). It is as if the very market use to which the learning of the sage (*shenren xuewen*) had been put by inauthentic scholar-merchants had inadvertently peeled off to show the commodity aspect of both knowledge and learning.

The way of an urban marketplace, its principles and practices, was a material presence and social force (divisive and cohesive at once) in Jiangnan Wanli through Chongzhen. This chapter suggests that it is not merely a backdrop against which distinct cultural modes of production and particular forms of writing and practices of reading emerged. The prefacing and reading tactics of different editions of one "best-selling" fiction by two well-known late Ming figures evince an evolving consciousness of, and dialogue with, a market in fiction. These prefaces also indicate the traces of a distinct shift toward greater "autonomy" (vis-à-vis bureaucratic service or the political field) and an accompanying market sophistry from the Wanli through Chongzhen periods. Jin Shengtan's ethico-aesthetics of fiction is, from this viewpoint, a strategic countering of market "democratization"—how his edition differs from the commonplace—while at the same time articulating a "new" class of young, rather than déclassé, reading subjects. This is an ingenious market tactic, a deployment of market know-how, and whereas Li Zhi identifies and deplores such market know-how in a market for men in his generation, by the Chongzhen and notably in Jin's prefaces, a *book* market know-how is a built-in disposition, and can no longer serve to mark the difference between an ethical and unethical manipulation of a commodified state of books, print, and knowledge (learning).

In effect, the symbolic and cultural value (as a form of capital) of fictional editorial practices is much increased through Jin's ethico-aesthetic project as a form of (market) specialization. This project is also a function of social distinction, permitting both practitioners (editor-writers) and consumers (readers) to differentiate themselves from those who do not know enough to purchase and read *this* edition. These two aspects of Jin Shengtan's editorial practices will, in turn, affect market formation. One thus witnesses the virtual monopoly of Jin's edition through the Qing to, arguably, the present; concomitantly, Jin's interpretations have become an indivisible part of a corpus of SHZ-related idées reçues; finally, fictional commentaries à la Jin Shengtan such as Zhang Zhupo's on JPM (1695) attest to Jin's lasting influence on the new "genre" of commentaried editions of fiction. Given the conjuncture of time (Ming Chongzhen), place (the Jiangnan urban marketplace with its flourishing print trade), and person (a talented literatus at large), it is then no accident that Jin Shengtan should have envisioned his bookmaking as comparable to the First Emperor's book burning in its effects on an emergent fictional literary field, a vernacular textual empire.

I have in this chapter, in a limited manner, established the generational differences as well as corresponding rhetorical shifts and prefacing strategies between two commentators and readers of SHZ in the Wanli and Chongzhen, respectively. Such shifts, I suggest, must be understood as informed by changed conditions in an urban market for books—books concerning and arising from concerns about everyday life and the time-space of leisure that had, by the late Ming in the Jiangnan, become the focus of a major discursive consideration.[71] The interrelations between a writing subject, the market in books (fiction), and specific prefatorial topoi (authenticity, authority) have been the primary focus of this chapter on Li Zhi and Jin Shengtan on SHZ. I have noted a thematic development from Li Zhi's concern with authenticity to Jin Shengtan's preoccupation with discursive authority. The former emphasizes and must be read in the context of the positionality of a literati subject's estranged relation to, amounting perhaps to an alienation from, the imperial state and bureaucratic service to the state. Whereas Jin Shengtan stresses a writing and reading positionality that faces not the central government but a (translocal) decentralized market of books along with the "unauthorized" (lacking in virtue and authority) personas and books populating, indeed glutting, that suddenly magnified new "public" space. The magnitude of this market may be inversely (as in a mirror) surmised from this positionality's attitude and style of writing: the megalomania of Jin Shengtan's writerly voice is a sign and an affect of the expansiveness of the market to which he addresses himself and his works.[72]

Jin Shengtan's reading of SHZ as prohibitive rather than exhortational must likewise be linked to an expanded market in fiction. This newly differentiated aesthetic-ethical mode of reading, however, as well as its linkages to the particular space-time and varied pursuits of a life of leisure and material wealth, will be examined in the following chapter, with a return in time to the generation between that of Li Zhi and Jin Shengtan, and the discovery of an excessively marvelous manuscript. The prohibitive mode of reading, I shall contend, is a function of an aestheticization that indexes the increased commodification of writing, culture, and an elite discourse on melancholy and its narrative cure in Wanli Jiangnan.

CHAPTER 3

A Cure for Melancholy:
Yuan Hongdao (1568–1610)
and Qifa (Seven Stimuli)

I love beautiful women.
You have bad health.
—Yuan Hongdao, *Yuan Zhonglang Quanji*

Of the seven feelings natural to mankind, melancholy is the most intractable.
—Preface to JPMC

On Cherishing Illness

Yuan Hongdao (juren 1588, jinshi 1592) was the second of the three famous Yuan brothers of Gongan, in the Huguang prefecture.[1] The brothers' ancestors had been of military stock, but "their grandfather began turning the attention of the clan to books."[2] This "attention . . . to books" was to have proverbial and phenomenal social returns in Yuan Hongdao's generation. The three brothers were not only among the "cream" of the Wanli crop of jinshi, the most renowned of their generation, but also of paramount importance in their associations with the most culturally significant men of their day.[3] Their circle of close friends and associates included Li Zhi (1527–1602, juren 1552), who had by 1581 forsaken bureaucracy (politics) and left his family (domesticity) to pursue an "independent" thinker's "individualistic" liberation.[4] Among their friends was also Dong Qichang (1555–1636, jinshi 1589), the period's most "celebrated practitioner and theoretician" of painting and calligraphy, and the primary figure in the late Ming debate over the redefinition of the canon in art history as well as the significance and place of Song versus Yuan art in that canon.[5] More important for this discussion, the manuscript copy of JPM that Yuan was reading in 1596 (Wanli 24) was borrowed from Dong Qichang. Of the three Yuan brothers, the eldest, Yuan Zongdao (1560–1600, juren 1579, jinshi 1586), was most closely associated with Dong Qichang, while Yuan Hongdao was decisively influenced and also admired by Li Zhi—who Yuan Hongdao had personally visited twice in Huang An in the late 1580s.

Literary history records Yuan Hongdao as leader of the Gongan school of literature, advocating against the former and later seven masters of literature, and especially the latter's call for a return to a traditional formalist poetic (on imitation of Han and Tang poets).[6] For the Archaic school, the history of literature was characterized by a gradual deterioration, and the only way to return to the glories of an ancient past was to apply oneself to the study and imitation of ancient models—that is, the prose of the western Han and poetry of the high Tang periods. Yuan Hongdao, on the other hand, extending Li Zhi's notions of historicity and relativity to literature, expounded the autonomy of dynastic periods, writing to the effect that "since dynasties rise and fall, the standards [of literature] do not remain unchanged. It is inexhaustible mutation that makes literature so valuable. Therefore [literature of different periods] should not be judged in terms of superiority and inferiority."[7] Thus, the point of contention between the Archaists and the Yuan brothers was not that the ancients produced unparalleled poetry but how to best emulate ancient excellence. As Chi-p'ing Chou puts it, "For the Archaist Masters, 'antiquity' was not only a valuable quality but also an attainable one—through an imitative approach. Antiquity remained a valuable quality for the Yuan brothers, but it was not attainable, and certainly not through an imitative approach."[8] What Yuan Hongdao did believe possible was the emulation of the "independent spirit" of the Tang poets, specifically in how the latter sought to distinguish themselves from the literature preceding them.[9]

The question in Yuan's provocative call for a reevaluation of literary history, in terms of its institutional (and institutionalizing) effects, can be restated as follows: How can one establish one's difference, not simply vis-à-vis a specific point and model (of poetry and poetic) in the past, with whose spirit rather than letter one identifies, but through simultaneously constructing a literary lineage and affiliation from the vantage point and given the parameters of one's own poetic practices? The question is one of both aligning one's poetic practices to a newly defined or created "antiquity" (canonical legitimation) and distinguishing this poetry, its "new spirit" and effects, from prior and contemporaneous competing poetic practices (the later seven masters, the Archaist school). I am not imputing intention on the part of the major proponents of this literary circle. Instead, the effects (as evidenced in literary histories, for example) of their practices and criticism permits a retrospective analysis of the ways and terms in which their writings produced the "Gongan" phenomenon. One way was to reconfigure the field of poetry writing and reading so as to define one's own position as well as identity in the present through one's (positive) relation to an idealized and redefined past (valorizing Su Shi of the Song, rather than Tu Fu of the Tang), and one's (negative) relation to a competitive recent past and present.

To recognize the canon-forming function of a poetic discourse is not to discount the importance of specific topoi in the reconfiguration of a field of discourse. In the case of the Gongan school and Yuan Hongdao, to "uniquely express [one's] personality and innate sensibility without being restrained by convention and form" (*du shu xingling bu ju getao*), as most-often-quoted dictum of this "School of Innate Sensibility" (*xingling pai*), may be considered just such a topos.[10] Obviously, Yuan did not think to "define" what he meant; that task would be left to scholars and literati who, through their differing reconstitutions, would place Yuan in the appropriate or necessary contexts for their arguments (late Ming degeneracy, early modern individualism, and so on). This point has already been judiciously noted.[11] What interests me, however, is one instance and figure of writing whereby Yuan seems to concretize a poet-writer's emotions and the corresponding situation wherefrom these arise. In this instance that is also a figure of writing, illness and melancholy are the dual privileged state of one's body and emotions, in relation to an undiscussed healthy and content body and mind. Literariness (*wen*) arises not as a function of literary competence (learning) but is instead forged in the matrix of an emotion-situation (melancholy-illness) that can neither be forced nor pretended.

In the preface to Tao Xiaoruo's (Tao Ruozeng, Wanli 16 juren)[12] *Zhenzhong Yi* (*Sounds emitted while sick in bed*), Yuan Hongdao writes:

> Those who [a situation] forces into a cry do not choose their sound. It is not that theirs is not [musical] sound. When melancholy touches the mouth, there is [something] more than [that sound/music produced by] choice. Those in antiquity who made poetry [wei feng zhe] largely came from the ranks of grieving men and lovelorn women [laoren sifu]. It is not that grieving men and lovelorn women had more art [zao] than scholars and literati [xueshitaifu]. Melancholy does not come on the latter yet their writing is ornate [wen shen]. When the one who speaks is not sincere, those who listen cannot be moved. . . . The most important element is that the emotion is true [qingzhen] and that the diction is straightforward [yuzhi]. Thus there are times when [the poetry of] laboring men and lonely women [is] superior to [that of] scholars and literati—just as the groanings of illness are more pleasing [kuai] than the sounds of everyday [health]. It is not that illness produces [literary] writing [wen] but that the feelings/emotions of illness are sufficient for [literary] writing. Nor is it that all feelings/emotions in illness are writing; rather, the writings of illness make no pretense [jiashi, or false ornamentation]. This is why the man who is enlightened cherishes illness [tongren guibing].[13]

Reflecting and writing on the occasion of a friend's work that had been composed during an illness, Yuan is moved to compare the groanings of illness to an art (poetry, writing) whose artistry (motive force) lies in the material and physio-psychological conditions of its producer and production. Ancient poetry could move the listener/reader, Yuan states, but nowadays this quality has been lost because poets have the tools but no force, rhetoric but few emotions. In order to reproduce what had been in antiquity a common state (the pains of laboring men and lovelorn women forced into sound), one must "value" homologous situations in the present (Wanli Jiangnan). This is one way of producing an authentic writing that will affect one's reader. Contemporary writing is not affective because it is largely the product of the wrong emotion-situation matrix. Thus, poets of today will experience in a situation that approximates the grief and loneliness of poetic subjects in antiquity, the genuine suffering that gives rise to an authentic writing. In illness, poetry would be as if wrenched from the body; a veritable transcription of melancholy, whose art/literariness would be manifest in its power to move.

> My friend Tao Xiaoruo is talented in poetic composition; during his illness he casually jotted whatever came to him in metered verse. There is nothing more melancholic than illness. . . . Thus, there are times when

[the songs of] grieving men and lovelorn women are superior to [the poetry of] scholars and literati, and oftentimes that which comes from groanings is more pleasing than everyday [sounds].[14]

The parallel construction whereby Yuan formulates his comparison allows the phrase to signify on two levels—literal and figurative—at once. Literally, the book of poetry Yuan is prefacing is a product of "groanings" when ill. Yuan lauds not the talent, nor the product, and certainly not technique but rather the circumstances and mood of its composition. This and nothing else guarantees its "sincerity," its power to move. It is genuine "melancholia" (as anyone who has ever been ill could attest, Yuan seems to be saying). On the other hand, the groanings of a (this) Wanli poet is sequentially parallel and comparable to the grieving men and lonely women (who metonymically represent genuine song) in the preceding phrase; moreover, the latter are oftentimes more superior than scholar-literati (of today).

Hence, Tao Xiaoruo and those who share or know his melancholic disposition are, like the grieving men and lonely women of old, superior to the many scholar-literati of the present who fake it. At this moment, in Ming Wanli, illness and melancholia serve to manifest *and* approximate an idealized state of "grieving men and lovelorn women" of a homogenized past. The difference evoked yet suspended in Yuan's paralleling of the two (Ming Wanli melancholic poets versus ancient commoners, grieving men, and lovelorn women) lies in their respective situation within a family-state continuum (as in the binomial *guo-jia*) and vis-à-vis the central axes of power. Grieving men and lovelorn women of a faraway past did not choose exile or abandonment—thus the inherent pathos of their compelling laments (*po er hu zhe bu ze sheng*). Located in a contrasting temporality and space, discontented and frustrated men of talent (retired or nonofficial literati, local rather than governmental scholars at large in a wealthy urban milieu) in Ming Wanli must, paradoxically, (over)value the occasional "illness" above everyday health if they are to write compelling poetry. As such, poetic subjects of the past embodied a continuity (totality) of experience and time, and therefore of melancholic force, that is not immediately reproducible in a present temporality no longer experienced and represented (by its poetic subjects) as continuous. Yuan represents this disjunctive temporality as a split *within* the ranks of contemporary poets (scholars-literati)—between, on the one hand, those who reside in the everyday, are not "sick" yet "groan" in pretense, and on the other hand, the few who are genuinely talented, sick, and melancholic, and who inscribe this distinguishing mental-physical disposition in poetry and writing.

The once experientially continuous state of exile and abandonment along with its attendant melancholy is thereby transposed into a function of poetic (and social) distinction. At the same time, what had been conceived of as involuntary—and therefore spontaneous and compelling—is transformed into a valorized and even willed uncommon, not-ordinary material and psychic situation. In other words, political and sentimental "exile" (of the past) is rendered into the everyday and commonsense, even somewhat trivial figure of illness and/as melancholia; this noneverydayness is then stressed precisely to counteract its banality. It is as if the political-sentimental continuum could only be embodied, in a Ming Wanli moment, as a personal-physio-psychological disjunctive.

The everyday, trivial, commonsense, small and personal, quasi-public "private" as figure and value (of writing) relative to the "public-official-political" space of antiquity is precisely what marks the discursive bent of (some) Wanli literati-scholars in a dual sense. For not only is this how Yuan Hongdao represents his, and his circle's, defining difference from other scholar-literati-poets both preceding and contemporaneous to them; it is also how they have been represented (albeit in polarized terms) in the writings of Qing literati, and twentieth-century literati and academic scholars. At the negative pole, one reads of the threat of such a poetic (of illness?) for the "health" of the empire (Gu Yenwu, Wang Fuzhi); how concessions to a vulgar and facile emotionalism have precipitated the demise of the empire. By the early republican era, in contrast, the same rhetoric and moment are read as repositories of a nationalist "modern individualism," and even mythologized as a quintessentially *Chinese* aesthetics of the everyday.[15]

By Ming Wanli, an ideology of a "liberatory" emphasis on individuality and emotions had become the vogue. This was a function of the populist synthesis of Buddhist, Taoist, and neo-Confucianist discourses in the teachings of the Wang Yangming school, with Li Zhi represented as its most extreme or radical product. Yet this was also a function of the inefficacy of court politics, which by the Wanli had become an arena too dangerous and uncertain to venture into if one were in the position of scholar-official, ideologically and institutionally trained to mediate a formal and correct political power. It was both dangerous and uncertain at least partly because of one's structural counterposition, at the Ming Wanli court, to the alliance of "evil" eunuchs and "bad" ministers, with the latter alliance resulting in a catastrophic maximization of "intimate" political power.[16]

Contrasting with a potentially perilous situation at court (for the ambitious literati-official) was the wealth and relative distance from imperial court politics of urban cities in the Jiangnan. Here, literati-officials in "retirement," or nonofficial literati who had never made it past the local examinations (some, such as Dong Qichang's close friend Chen Jiru, would then simply choose "retirement" for life), could congregate and form alternative venues of literary fame (in print, on the book market), while cultivating the refined pursuits of a leisurely and gentlemanly life (Yuan Hongdao)—mixing with the urban crowd, setting the fashion for the day (Chen Jiru), and living like local kings (Wang Zhideng), or living as the impoverished but honored guests of the innumerable urban nouveau riche with cultural aspirations (Tu Long).[17] Some would start their own publishing houses (Chen Jiru, Li Yu), or become quasi-professional editors, rewriters and compilers for commercial publishers (Feng Menglong, Xue Gang). With the increase in and expansion of urban centers as a matrix for an enlarged "public" culture and consumption, the accumulation of symbolic capital—that is, the pursuit of ming, or fame (Yuan Hongdao, Zhong Xing)—could be diverted from political-bureaucratic service and redirected in local and transregional literary and cultural pursuits.[18] What had previously been considered as belonging to a "private" sphere of nonbureaucratic works had by the late Ming, through expanding commercialization and increased commodification, become an enlarged urban "public" sphere of cultural and social competition.

John Meskill's study of the ambivalent and changing attitudes toward wealth and consumption in late Ming Jiangnan shows the extent to which a money economy and the commodification of all aspects of everyday life had become the focus of concern of local elites.[19] Craig Clunas has furthermore analyzed how this concern was crystallized in a new aesthetic, as opposed to economic, garden culture. Clunas argues for a distinct discursive shift "away from the 'good' realm of production, of natural increase and natural profit through the ownership of land, and towards the problematic realm of consumption, excess, and luxury."[20] Wealth and consumption had by the late Ming, and especially in the Jiangnan region, emerged as a riveting "public" interest (above official-bureaucratic concerns), a new field of competition, and an affective, aesthetic-ethical, and social problem. Such at least are the implications of late Ming discourses on garden culture and the literary consumption of new cultural objects. These discourses trace the emergence of a discriminating subject: gendered male, literatus, talented and propertied, without official position, but with a shadowy counterpart against whom he is defined and seeks to differentiate himself—that is, non-scholarly commoners, merchants, and even bond servants who at this historic moment and region came to possess the material conditions to aspire to taste and distinction.[21]

Let us now return to Yuan's remarks on how illness must be especially valued in such times. The pursuit of fame (ming) is the unacknowledged constant that connects the scholar-literati who pretend to an ill they do not feel and those who are ill. What differentiates these two groups are the meanings of their will to fame.[22] The distinction, then, lies between those whose groans merely accumulate a political-bureaucratic symbolic capital, and those who "groan" in the sincere expression of an illness that is represented as homologous to the exile/abandonment of men and women of antiquity. Illness is Ming Wanli's version of political exile and sentimental abandonment. But not all illnesses count; nor all melancholy arising from illness. Rather illness and melancholy are necessary pretexts to an affective writing without pretense. As such, they guarantee the "sincerity" (cheng) or "authenticity" (zhen) of the latter.

If illness or bing, as a situational-emotional matrix beyond one's choice or control, is valorized as a necessary pretext for good poetry, then obsession or pi may be seen as another such pretext (contiguous to bing) for a genuine connoisseurship or knowledge of seemingly trivial objects.[23] Thus, in Yuan's "Notes on Vase Flower Arrangement," he defines the true "lover of things" (hao shi zhe) by naming a mythico-historical few, then goes on to generally categorize the many who are lacking, and therefore of hateful countenance and vulgar preoccupation:

> I have observed that all the people in the world who have no taste in repartee and whose countenance is detestable are people without obsessions [pi]. If they really had an obsession, they would immerse and drown themselves in it, giving their lives to it. How, then, would they have time for such matters as money, servants, officials, and commerce?[24]

The sequence of exposition is significant in delineating an embedded context for and counterposition to Yuan's enumeration of exemplary "obsessives" or connoisseurs (of the past). The embedded context is obviously the present moment and place of writing, to which Yuan does not even need to directly refer but implies when he writes of "my observations" of the tasteless and ugly of this world. The problem with these many who lack taste is their lack of an obsession.

In his study of the Yuan brothers, Chou translates pi as "hobby," yet explains that for Yuan "it was more an obsession than a hobby," that it "was not simply a hobby or pastime, but actually the focus of one's life."[25] Although perhaps not accurate in its rendering of the aesthetic and physio-psychological dimensions of pi, "hobby" I think aptly renders a social and temporal aspect of Yuan's, and Ming Wanli, pi in general. According to Yuan's observation of his contemporaries, those who lack taste in conversation and are not pleasing to the eye lack an obsession that would *divert and refine* an attention otherwise vulgarized in the pursuit of "money, servants, officialdom, commerce."[26] The aesthetically correct object of pursuit diverts precious and talented energies, and just as important, refines them. Conversely, the social milieu and practices (urban wealth, commercial consumption, print trade, fashion) that have produced the very space/time of "leisure" in Ming Wanli—whose everyday practices Yuan seeks to aestheticize in what could be called a witty manual for the aspiring[27]—these can only be indexed and implicitly denigrated. Money, servants, officialdom, and commerce cannot be made into "embodiments" of one's superior qi—all the more so since one's qi finds itself embedded in precisely such crass material surroundings and desires. Horses, tea, stones, and cleanliness, however arbitrary and banal as they may seem, can imprint one's exceptional qualities. In privileging the haphazard objects of talented men's obsessive attentions rather than either the life of an ascetic recluse or imperial service in the bureaucracy, Yuan Hongdao has been interpreted as inverting the hierarchies of literati practices (that is certainly one effect of such an aestheticizing discourse, thus the characterization of such writings as having contributed to the fall of the empire). But he is also, in effect, shoring up innate talent and authoritative superiority in an aesthetic and discursive consumption of a selective list of everyday objects—all obtaining from a Jiangnan literati's life in leisure. One Ming Wanli answer, then, to a situation-emotional matrix that will produce good poetry, interesting conversation, and an attractive mien is: illness, and an everyday obsessive practice diverted, indeed, de-invested from public life, whether official or commercial.

Illness is to be valued insofar as and to the extent that it guarantees authenticity of emotion, which in turn is the source of good taste (tasteful obsessions). Melancholy, on the other hand, is a by-product that can be transcended, suffered, or lightly dispelled in the tasteful consumption of the appropriate objects.[28] Thus, the proposing of an aesthetic and prophylactic mode of consumption—a mode of consumption evidenced in the records of readings of a (or several?) JPM in the Wanli. I will now turn to these readings and analyze them for how *reading* as one modality of elite consumption of new urban objects is recast for contemporary privatized usage with a new social or "public" function. Such a structure of reading mediates the dual concerns for a personal preservation-cultivation (the care of the self, hygienic and moral) and social distinction (aesthetics/symbolic capital).

*A Narrative Cure*

The earliest recorded mention of JPM in print is a letter written in 1596 (Wanli 24) by Yuan Hongdao addressed to Dong Qichang asking for the latter part of the manuscript of JPM, the first half of which Dong had lent to Yuan.

> A month ago, Tao Wangling [Wanli 20 jinshi] happened to be visiting; we had five days of exhilarating conversation, after which we took a boat and journeyed to the five lakes, and viewed the most awesome sights of the seventy-two mountains. On returning from our trip, we talked about the ends of heaven and earth that we had nearly attained, [and thus] my illness was somewhat alleviated [*bingmo weizhi shaoque*]. The only regret was that you were not of our company. Where did you obtain *Jin Ping Mei*? Glancing through it while leaning against a pillow, its pages emit an erotic haze [*yunxia manzhi*]; it is greatly superior to Mei Sheng's *Qifa*. Where is the latter part? After you have had it copied, where can I exchange this part for the rest? Please let me know.[29]

A pleasant visit from a friend; a trip by boat through splendid mountain-ringed lakes; an illness temporarily alleviated. Yuan Hongdao's opening lines frame the request that is casually led up to—the object of his letter to Dong Qichang. The frame merits repeating, for it serves as both detour to and oblique inversion of the request that ends the letter. Thus, at the center of the letter are Yuan's three foremost preoccupations: his illness (physical discomfort and mental boredom), that which has provided a much-needed respite (a trip; a manuscript), and the possible continuation of cure and pleasure (Dong's missed presence; the missing latter half of the manuscript). The first half of the letter presents how a friend's visit has resulted in conversations and a trip that have partially cured the writer, whereupon the writer adroitly turns to the friend that was *missed*, and an equally *missed* second part of a pleasurable manuscript, casually perused while lying (presumably ill) in bed.

"Where did you obtain *Jin Ping Mei*?"—the question that immediately and significantly follows the phrase declaring how much Dong was missed in the present company, in its metonymic shift from Dong to Dong's manuscript, belies the "casual tone" of the letter.[30] This "repetition" carries with it an urgency that is underlined by a final request for explicit instructions as to how to obtain what Dong must have in his possession, but had not yet passed on. The question Yuan's letter poses, then, is not so much "Where did you get it" but rather "Where and how can I get the rest of it?" The urgency of Yuan's request, on the other hand, arises from and is represented in his letter through a specific context (also a pretext) and a telling comparison. The context is (personal) illness, wherein the manuscript is parallel in function to salubrious company and sights. Nevertheless, the comparison establishes the parameters whereby the meanings of this curative function may be at once indexed and reproduced (produced anew for a contemporary use, as in the putting of new wine in old bottles, as if a formal repetition could reproduce a taste or an effect of a process that is temporally and spatially different and unrepeatable).

What and how could it signify, to implicate the reading (consumption) of a manuscript (new cultural object) with fascinating erotic properties in the cure (well-being) of one's person? What sort of a cure did Yuan represent in evoking at this particular juncture, in the context of this request, Mei Sheng's *Qifa*? Through what modality of an assimilative reading process might JPM become a *Qifa* for the particular time/place, positions, and modes of Yuan's reading? How were subsequent readers compelled to respond to the implicit valorization in Yuan's comparison, and invoke it either as *authorization* for their own reading (Xie Zhaozhe, 1616?) or to warn against an influential but dangerous overvaluation that could *authorize* the wrong readings/readers (Li Rihua 1615; Yuan Zongdao 1614)?[31]

I shall deal with these questions in turn, but first a detour through a symptomatic reading of Yuan Hongdao's comparison. In his book-length study of the Yuan brothers, Chou devotes an entire subsection on Yuan Hongdao's "interest in novels."[32] This interest was one perhaps influenced by Yuan's quasi-mentor Li Zhi—not the first but certainly the most well-known advocate of the ethico-political viability of contemporary minor vernacular fiction. It was an interest shared and indeed capitalized on, professionalized even, by such younger contemporaries as Feng Menglong (1574–1646) and Ling Mengchu (1580–1644). Chou's question is: Was Yuan's particular interest based on a "poetic" or "aesthetics" of the "novel" (an emergent extended vernacular narrative form)? Did Yuan's various comments on JPM amount to a narrative poetic? Chou concludes "that his [Yuan's] motives for speaking highly of novels [JPM and SHZ] were based more on didacticism and a certain kind of sensualism and curiosity, rather than on appreciation of their literary excellence." As for the comparison Yuan makes, Chou states that this is "what deserves attention in this [Yuan's] letter." The comparison, according to Chou, yields the following:

> There is literally nothing in common between Qifa and the JPM. Not only do they belong to different genres, but they are also addressed to completely different audiences. Qifa was addressed to the Prince of Chu, or to rulers in general, while the JPM was addressed to the general reading public. . . . Therefore the comparison made by Yuan Hongdao was by no means based on their form, structure, or even literary excellence. . . . Yuan Hongdao's comparison between the JPM and Qifa makes sense only if his comparison is based on thematic grounds and refers to the didactic purposes of these two works. In other words, Yuan Hongdao believed that the JPM was not merely an erotic novel, but a book containing moral teachings, and that there were serious meanings hidden behind the vivid descriptions of love-making.[33]

Chou's reading and conclusion takes for granted what has in recent studies of the late Ming begun to be questioned—that is, the processes whereby new vernacular cultural forms in print are transformed into new "literary" genres with authorizing genealogies and distinctive filiations, putting them on a par with already established works and genres (Laura Hua Wu's study of Jin Shengtan, for example). I have also argued that the evolving of an aesthetics of extended narratives must be seen in conjunction with increasingly active nonbureaucratic literati interest in the market in fictional books. In Li Zhi and Yuan Hongdao's generation of readers, a fully developed and *autonomous* aesthetics of narrative did not—could not—yet appear, just as the market in both short and extended fiction was still in the 1590s a relatively new place for literati investment and self-representation. Li and Yuan stand out as champions of debased fictional genres in modern literary histories precisely to the degree that these genres had not yet emerged as an "independent" field of literati endeavor *in their writings*. This was to change quite rapidly within the next few decades, culminating in Jin Shengtan's declaration of a new writing-editing positionality as guardian of the gates of an emergent aesthetic and ethical new "genre" of fiction (see chapter 2). Thus, Yuan can only be faulted for not "commenting" on JPM according to an aesthetics of a genre (Chou's "novel," or extended narrative in prose-verse) on the ahistorical assumption that "aesthetics" transcends temporal specificity and power processes. As a proponent of the most influential poetic of his day,[34] and one who was situated at the acme of scholarly-official achievements in his time, Yuan was probably not sufficiently interested in or motivated to formulate a fictional aesthetics (unlike Jin Shengtan or Zhang Zhupo, neither of whom gained the jinshi degree; see chapters 2 and 4). Yuan Hongdao had a surplus of cultural capital, which he deployed in advertising a dangerously enticing new toy whose safe use was guaranteed by precisely this surplus capital, not considered available to all.[35]

Yuan was clearly eager to eye the rest of a remarkable manuscript whose pages emitted a curative "erotic haze."

In his letter to Dong Qichang, Yuan is less concerned with justifying his pleasure in reading the manuscript narrative at hand (as the "didactic" model of reading would have it) than with representing *an embodied process of reading* that I shall characterize as "modal"—of or relating to structure rather than substance, and articulated to affect, in this case, melancholy, or *youyu*—thus encapsulating in his seemingly offhand comparison a modality of reading.[36] This modality of reading invokes and produces not a category of texts but a gendered and socially specific relation of consumption to erotic textual objects.[37]

To repeat Chou's question: "On what basis . . . would Yuan Hongdao say that 'the JPM . . . is far superior to . . . *Qifa*'?" My tentative answer: on the basis of the homologous effects of two nonidentical yet comparable modalities of reading. Yuan is indicating, by making such a comparison, a *structure of reading* that can and does ultimately become, with repeated and successive retrieval, an aesthetic-ethical form of consumption—of any obscene textual object.[38]

I agree with Chou that Yuan's comparison is of signal importance. Chou states that Yuan's lauding of "novels" is based "more on didacticism and a certain kind of sensualism and curiosity," but sensualism and curiosity remain unexamined in Chou's account.[39] I suggest that the implicit "didacticism" in the comparison is an effect of the particular modality of reading invoked with *Qifa*, and that it is rather Yuan's sensuality and curiosity that needs further analysis. How do these sentiments work, and to what psychic and social effects, within this modality of reading? The sequential thematics of Yuan's letter to Dong contextualize Yuan's perusal of a portion of JPM with, on the one hand, illness and an attendant melancholia, and on the other hand, the pleasurable if temporary "cure" provided by the presence of a friend, mountains, lakes, and part of a wondrous manuscript. How are these analogous? How do good company, a trip through splendid mountainous scenery, and dipping (reading, *lueguan*) through part of a manuscript work their cure?

Mei Sheng's Qifa

> The Heir Apparent of Chu was ill, and a visitor from Wu came to inquire after his health. "I have heard," he said, "that your Royal Highness's precious body has not been well. Has there been any relief?" The Heir Apparent replied: "I feel weak. I respectfully thank you for your concern." The visitor continued:
>
> "At present the whole world is at peace / The Four Quarters are in harmony / Your Highness now has a full life before you / But in my opinion / You have long been addicted to comforts and pleasures / Day and night you never stop / Evil Ether has invaded you / Congested in your chest / Listless and without a will of your own / You sigh and suffer from hangovers / Troubled and frightened / You find no sleep when you lie down / You hear things where there is no noise / And detest the sound of human voices / Your vital spirits disperse and scatter / And all the hundred diseases develop / Hearing and sight are blurred and dimmed / Joy and anger become unpredictable / If the illness lasts long without being stopped / Your great life will be ruined.
>
> Isn't that Your Royal Highness's condition?" The Heir Apparent replied: "I respectfully thank you for your concern. Owing to our sovereign's strength, though the symptoms appear from time to time, my illness has not gone to that extent." "Nowadays," the visitor said,
>
> "The young men of the best families / Invariably live in palaces, reside in sheltered quarters / With protective nurses within / And magisterial tutors without / There is no chance for social mingling / Drinks and foods are pleasantly flavored, sweet and crisp / Meat and wine are fat and strong / Clothes are of many kinds and plentiful, light yet warm / Melting hot, sweltering and scorching.
>
> "Even one who had the firmness of metal or stone would melt and dissolve, break and disintegrate under these circumstances. How much more one built around sinews and bones! Therefore it is said: He who gives in to the desires of ear and eye, who indulges in the comforts of body and limbs, will hurt the harmony of blood and vessels. Indeed, going by chariot and coming by sedan chair has been called 'an omen of paraly-

sis.' Secluded apartments and cool palaces have been called 'go-betweens of chills and fevers.' Gleaming teeth and moth-like eyebrows have been called 'axes that cut vitality.' Sweet, crisp, fat, strong food and wine have been called 'drugs that rot the intestines.' At present Your Royal Highness's complexion is pale, your four limbs are numb, your sinews and bones are disintegrating, your blood vessels are enlarged, your hands and feet are inert. Girls from Yue serve you in front, beauties from Qi wait on you in back. Always coming and going from one amusement and feast to another, yielding to pleasures in secluded rooms and private apartments—this is swallowing poison voluntarily, and playing with the claws and teeth of wild beasts. The consequences are deep and far-reaching. Indefinitely putting up with the congestion and not stopping [such practices]. Even if you had Bian Que as a physician and Wu Xian as a shaman, what could be accomplished? Now in the case of an illness like Your Royal Highness's, the only proper thing to do is to have gentlemen outstanding in this age for their broad experience and retentive memory seize the opportune moment to speak to you of the things they know, to reform your thoughts and change your views, constantly at your side, helpers like the wings of a bird. Then neither the joy of immersion in pleasures nor the idea of colossal licentiousness nor the intention of idle indulgence will be able to reach you." "All right," said the Heir Apparent, "when my illness is gone, I propose to do what you have said." "Now," said the visitor, "Your Royal Highness's illness can be cured without drugs, acupuncture, or cauterization. It can be dispelled by the persuasive force of essential words and marvelous doctrines. Don't you want to hear them?" "Yes," replied the Heir Apparent, "I would like to hear them."[40]

I have quoted above the entire introductory section to *Qifa*, or the *Seven Stimuli*. The "seven stimuli" (or "arousals," *fa*[41]) that follow are: the saddest music in the world, the most delicious food, the finest horses, the most extravagant sight-seeing and luxurious banqueting with live entertainment, the most spirited hunting, viewing the miraculous bore of the Winding River, and finally, the wise and magical words of experts in philosophy and the occult arts. These seven stimuli are enumerated sequentially for cumulative aesthetic and hygienic effect in alternating prose and verse, with the seventh stimulus serving as a climactic conclusion to this example of early *fu*, or prose poem (also translated as rhyme prose, poetic essay, poetic description, or rhapsody).[42] The introduction sets the scene and "places" the principal players: the heir to the kingdom is ill, and a visitor (an itinerant persuader/court poet?) comes to inquire after his health. The prose poem takes the form of a question-and-answer session between a sick prince and a visitor-poet with persuasive-curative powers. The visitor begins by proffering a diagnosis: "You have long been addicted to comforts and pleasures / Day and night you never stop / Evil Ether has invaded you / Congested in your chest / Listless and without a will of your own / You sigh and suffer from hangovers / Troubled and frightened / You find no sleep when you lie down." He then goes on to state that the cause is clear: "Nowadays . . . [t]he young men of the best families / Invariably live in palaces, reside in sheltered quarters / . . . Drinks and foods are pleasantly flavored, sweet and crisp / Meat and wine are fat and strong / . . . Therefore it is said: He who gives in to the desires of ear and eye, who indulges in the comforts of body and limbs, will hurt the harmony of blood and vessels." But the visitor brings with him the appropriate cure.

The prince's illness is physio-psychological.[43] His insomnia, delusions, anxiety, depression, melancholy, and deteriorating sight and hearing are all taken by the visitor to be manifestations of a life of excessive comfort and pleasure. The visitor finds the prince's illness a direct consequence of his material and social situation: surrounded by nurses and tutors, consuming rich foods and wines—these would dissolve and break even metal and stone, not to mention sinews and bones. "Desires of ear and eye" (*ermu zhi yu*) and "comforts of body and limbs" (*zhiti zhi an*) have so enfeebled the prince's psyche and physique that "Evil Ether" (*xieqi*) had infiltrated his torso and congested into a physical and psychic blockage or malaise. It is this physio-psychological congestion that the visitor claims to be able to cure, miraculously, with persuasive words (*shuei er qu*).

Persuasion in this case works through "word magic," and may be seen as a virtual "psychotherapy," with the visitor seducing and fascinating his listener by conjuring up vision after vision, fantasy after fantasy, in a cumulative sequence of extraordinary sensual and intellectual pleasures.[44] This is a gradual drawing out of evil ether with poetically conjured (representations of) poisonous drugs (*duyao*) that are evil ether's topsoil in the male physique and psyche. Seduction and fascination through incantatory language and vision work in that order: first seduction, then fascination—thus the importance of *sequence*, or as Dore Levy puts it, the principle and logic of enumeration.[45] This sequence advances toward a prognosticated end.

> The visitor said: "Let us do this for Your Royal Highness: We will present to you experts in philosophy and the occult arts, distinguished and wise,

men such as Zhuangzi and Weimou, Yang Zhu and Mozi, Bian Juan and Zhan He. Let them discuss the subtle mysteries of the world and discriminate between true and false in the myriad phenomena. Confucius and Laozi will display their teachings for you to view. With Mencius moderating the discussion, the chances of error will be less than one in ten thousand. These surely are the most essential words and the most marvelous doctrines in the world. Doesn't Your Royal Highness want to hear them?" Thereupon the Heir Apparent, supporting himself on a low table, rose and said: "My mind has been cleared as if I had just heard the words of the sages and wise men." In a turbid flow, perspiration issued [*nianran hanchu*]. With a sudden outburst, the illness ended.[46]

The cure is effected through the sweat-inducing properties of seven successive and cumulative fantasy formations. The visitor enwraps his listener in fantasy after fantasy, to finally force out or purge from the prince's body the congestion that is illness. In the introductory section, the visitor promises to cure without resorting to physics, to (force the malignant congestion) out by means of (persuasive) speech (*shuei er chu*). By the end of the last stimulus, the prince is for the first time roused to stand and notes a sudden clearing up of the mind (*huanhu ruo yi ting shengren bianshi zhi yan*), as if he had just heard the words of the sages and itinerant persuaders. Then perspiration issues in a flow (*nianran hanchu*) and terminates the illness. The not-quite, but-almost-simultaneous clearing up of the mind (huanhu) and cleansing out of the body (nianran hanchu) are attributed to an "as if"— as if the prince had just heard the words of sages and persuaders. This is another level of "fantasy" or "make-believe," a literary tour de force, crucial to the efficacy of the cure. The sixth stimulus in effect function on two levels at once: as both simulation of and preparation for the "words of sages and itinerant persuaders." When practiced as a cure for a depressive illness, fantasy formations (dangerously?) become as aesthetically and hygienically satisfactory or affective as the twice-deferred moral and political teachings of sages.

The two deferrals or postponements of the ethical teachings of sages occur at the beginning and end of the prose poem. In the introduction, following the visitor's delineation of symptoms and cause, the visitor utters the first of a two-part prognosis:

"Now in the case of an illness like your Royal Highness's, the only proper thing to do is to have gentlemen outstanding in this age [*yishi zhi junzi*] for their broad experience and retentive memory seize the opportune moment to speak to you of the things they know, to reform your thoughts and change your views [*biandu yiyi*], constantly at your side, so as to be wings to a bird [*yiwei yuyi*]. Then neither the joy of immersion in pleasures nor the idea of colossal licentiousness nor the intention of idle indulgence will be able to reach you." "All right," said the Heir Apparent, "when my illness is gone, I propose to do what you have said."[47]

The proper thing in the case of an illness like the prince's is to gather at his side outstanding gentlemen of the day so as to, with their "essential words and marvelous doctrines" [*yaoyen miaodao*], transform the prince's practices and thinking (biandu yiyi). The prince accepts this proposal for the future: "when my illness is gone." It is at this moment—of the visit and in the poem—that the visitor *inserts* the entire sequence of his essential words and marvelous doctrines (though not claimed as such) whose persuasive force, plus the final invocation of the wise men of the past, will together accomplish the cure. The dispelling of the cure will then allow the prince's putting into practice the visitor's initial advice: the gathering of outstanding men (like the visitor himself perhaps) around him (the prince) as long-term preventive medicine.

Thus, the visitor's own "cure" is remedial. It is supplementary and secondary to a more efficacious long-term preventive regime, consisting of the presence and teachings of sages and wise men who duplicate the symbolic power and discourse of the names (Yang Zhu, Mozi, Confucius, Mencius, and so on) evoked in the last stimulus. This presence, however, can only be deferred due to the tenacity of the prince's affliction. In its (the wise men's ethical discourse) place, and arguably mimicking the efficacy of its ethical and symbolic powers, the visitor perforce incants an arousing sequence of poetic visions. These visions ultimately work in the manner of a seduction and fascination, an enthrallment in sensualities whose effect will be measured by the extent to which the prince is moved (physically and mentally) by and through a last nonvoluptuous (de-cathecting) stimulus.

A slippage occurs when prognosis of a future long-term preventive regime is displaced (in effect) by a gradual yet drastic enactment of a cure on the spot. Or, when the presence and discourse of sages and wise men (their essential words and marvelous doctrines) is evoked in the very beginning only to be deferred to the last. And then, to be yet again postponed in the last stimulus, in an enumeration of contemporary embodiments of illustrious names of the past, as the final fantasy of seven fantastic situations: the visitor now invites the likes of "Zhuangzi and Weimou, Yang Zhu and Mozi, Bian Juan and Zhan He" plus "Confucius and Laozi," with Mencius as moderator, to present themselves to the prince in order to discourse on "the subtle mysteries of the world and discriminate between true and false in the myriad phenomena." Mysteries and distinctions are elided as the visitor concludes, "These surely are the most essential words and the most marvelous doctrines in the world"; wouldn't you (the prince) now like to hear them? Whereupon the prince rises from his seat, speaks, sweats, and is cured.

The prose poem outlays the cure as a vortex, enwrapping its sick subject within, beginning with the foretelling of a long-term preventive regimen and ending with an invocation of the start of such a regimen. Thus, the visitor's last question—Wouldn't you like to hear *their* essential words and marvelous doctrines?—refers back to what he (the visitor) had proposed from the outset, but which the prince's condition had forestalled, forcing the visitor to techniques not of enlightenment but arousal (stimulus). The difference is not oppositional; rather, arousal works to prepare the ground (the prince's body-mind) for a future teaching and enlightenment that are not part of this particular quasi-shock-therapy, spiral-shaped cure. There is an alignment of purpose, but a difference in technique and strategy—in language, genre, and structure—between these two parts of what ethically constitutes one cure.

In a sense, the visitor stages his own position and performance as mediator (poet-shaman) whose verbal visions (text) are both a pretext to and themselves embodiments of a *yaoyen miaodao* (essential words and marvelous doctrines) whose aesthetic and hygienic properties are conceived of as differently efficacious, but temporally and ethically articulated to the yaoyan miaodao of sagelike contemporary wise men. This is quite aptly, as Hans Frankel phrases it, not an enlightening but an "*exorcising fu.*"[48] An exorcism of the evil forces (material and erotic sensualities) entrapping the prince's body *and* thoughts must be effected *before* more lasting defenses against desires of the ears and eyes, as well as comforts of the limbs and body, may set to work with their moral suasion (the teachings of wise men of the past). Exorcism works through a psychophysiological process whereby a sequence of fantasies (imaginary sensualities) seduce and fascinate—arousing and stimulating (fa), simulating desire—to a climactic and likewise imaginary or poetic abject state that is twice represented. The first time, a physical fear and abjection are enacted through the enumeration of a fantastically violent bore (the sixth stimulus). The second time, an intellectual and ethical subjection completes the cure, and then prepares for the next stage of long-term preventive enlightenment.

*The Bore at the Winding River*

The visitor said: "Let us do this: on the fifteenth day of the eighth month, you go, accompanied by nobles, friends, and relatives from afar, to view the bore of the Winding River at Guangling. When you arrive, before you behold the bore itself, just seeing how far the water's power extends is fearsome enough to terrify you. Viewing its overtaking, its pulling up, its stirring up, its converging, its washing—even one who has in his mind a general conception of the phenomenon and the ability to articulate it in words, really cannot give a detailed sequential account of it. . . .

The rapid flow descends downstream / Nobody knows where it stops / Now it splits into many winding flows / Suddenly it twists and proceeds upstream without returning / It goes to the Vermilion Bank and vanishes in the distance / Inside you feel empty, upset, and exhausted / In the evening it disperses and starts again in the morning / In your heart you keep and hold it / Thereupon it bathes the breast / Washes the five organs / Cleanses hands and feet / Rinses the hair and teeth / It does away with indolence / Purges impurities / Clears up suspicions and doubts / Sharpens ears and eyes.

At this time, though men have chronic illnesses and lingering diseases, this will straighten hunchbacks, make the lame get up, open the eyes of the blind, and unlock the ears of the deaf as they observe. How much more is this true of those who only suffer from minor mental upsets and excessive eating and drinking! Therefore it is written: 'It clears up dullness and resolves delusions without any difficulty.'" The Heir Apparent said: "Good, but what kind of phenomenon/force is the bore [*ranze tao he qi zai*]? The visitor said: "This is not recorded; but I have heard my teacher say, There are three things about it that seem supernatural/divine but are not:

A sudden thunder is heard a hundred miles / The river's water flows upstream / As does the sea's rising tide / The mountains give forth clouds and take them back / Day and night without ceasing / The water flows in fullness with rapid speed / It gushes up and the bore begins / When it first begins / The drops come down in a vast descent / Like snowy egrets swooping down / A little farther on / It's splendid, towering, and bright / Like pale-silk chariots with white horses and canopies spread like clouds /

It's as jumbled as the piled baggage of the Three Armies / When it swells at the sides, rising on top / It glides like a light command chariot directing the troops / Six dragons harnessed to the chariot / Take orders from the Great White River God / Halting and rushing on, always high / Front and rear, always joined / Lofty and tall / Freely expanding at the sides / Billows flowing over each other / A fortress many-layered and strong / A mixed multitude, like army columns / Booming and crashing / Crushing and gushing / Absolutely irresistible / As you observe its two edges / They stir with wrath / In vast agitation / Striking above, rolling below / Like brave warriors / Rushing out angry and fearless / Trampling cliffs and bursting across fords / Filling every bend and cove / Flooding shores and rising above sandbanks / Whoever meets it dies / Whoever opposes it is destroyed / . . . There is no time for the birds to fly away / For the fish to turn around / For the beasts to run off / Helter-skelter / The billows swell and spread like clouds / Rush upon the southern hills / Strike in the rear at the northern shore / Topple hillocks and mounds / Flatten the western embankment / Perilously steep they rise / And collapse the sloping banks / Not until the foe is drowned do they halt / Striking and pushing the roil and roll / Swelling and rising they splash and dash / Perverse and cruel in the extreme [*hengbao zhi ji*] / Fish and turtle lose their powers / Upside down and topsy-turvy / Out of balance and control / They float and crawl along / The magical phenomena and miracles [*shenwu guaiyi*] / Cannot be told in full / They only make one stumble in giddy perplexity and fright.

This is the most miraculous and extraordinary sight in the world. Can Your Royal Highness force yourself to rise and view it?" The Heir Apparent said: "I'm sick, I can't."⁴⁹

Halfway through the fifth stimulus (the one preceding this quotation), which encapsulates the enthralled aggressivity (the fascination phase of the cure) of the hunter's chase (in "the most spirited of all hunts") through imperial parks, when "sweat flows / saliva drips" (*hanliu mozhui*) and "the hunted flee and cower in distress," the prince had shown "a sign of vitality" that first appeared as qi on his forehead, which slowly "increased and rose, filling almost his whole face." The visitor, seeing the look of pleasure (*yue se*) on the prince's face, continued detailing the fantastic hunt and concluded that "this surely is something Your Royal Highness would enjoy." For the first time, the prince is stimulated to reply, "I would like very much to go along. I only fear it would inconvenience my courtiers." And the text notes: "But he was beginning to look better."[50] It is at this crucial point (the arousal of spirit, color, desire) that the visitor begins the sixth, longest, most powerful stimulus.

Having gone through the stages of seduction, music, food, banqueting, and women to the first signs of arousal following the visitor's fascinating representation of the most spirited hunt, the prince had in effect passed from a phantasmic consumption of pleasures (music, food, women, and wine) to an equally phantasmic enthrallment in and enactment of a hunter's aggressive and competitive chase, and its prizewinning outcome. How, at this point, could the arousal of the prince's spirit-energy (qi), accumulated from such pleasurable and enervating fantasies, be put to curative use?

The answer lies in the visitor's long-winded answer to the prince's question: "What kind of force [qi] is the bore" that it can work such medicinal wonders as you, the visitor, claim? The sixth stimulus rehearses in minor key the movement of the entire prose poetic (account of a) cure. The visitor "knows" of a place whose phenomenal waters will cure diseases through direct immersion or, as in this case, even the power of its representation (although the visitor begins the representation by denying the very possibility of representation).

But to repeat the prince's question, What sort of force does one confront here? Whence does the bore derive its cleansing, purgative, healing powers? The bore works similarly as divinities (supernatural powers), but is not in itself divine (*sishen er fei*), says the visitor. It kills whoever it meets, and maims whoever opposes it (*yuzhe si, dangzhe huai*); it rears up and advances like an army, attacking, killing, and maiming like warriors; its deafening roar confounds and confuses; it is so swift that neither bird, beast, nor fish can escape its overswell; its final crash to the earth topples, flattens, and collapses, striking the ground; drowning its foe, it is "perverse and cruel in the extreme" (*hengbao zhi ji*). Subjected to (even the representation of) such a violent spectacle, man is reduced to limping and stumbling (away) in fright—an abject state. Here is a physio-psychological humbling that will not just counteract the preceding (desiring) arousal of a victorious hunter's chase and kill (in the sixth stimulus). Rather it aligns, indeed transmutes, a hunter's pleasure in killing to the equal (perhaps greater) pleasure of drowning, being overpowered and cleansed visually, sensually, bodily, from the inside out and outside in, by a death wave (the bore).

In the beginning, "you feel empty, upset, and exhausted / In the evening it disperses and starts again in the morning [*molisan er fashu*] / In your heart you keep and hold it [the bore] / Thereupon it bathes the breast / Washes the five organs" and so on. Cleanses hands and feet / Rinses the hair and teeth / It does away with indolence / Purges impurities / Clears up suspicions and doubts / Sharpens ears and eyes." In that one night of emptiness, before the morning's arousal—this is the time/place of the bore's miraculous cure.

The *Seven Stimuli* (*Qifa*) is a textual representation of a dialogue that seemingly chants the process of the singular cure for princely melancholia and delusions. Enthrallment to excessive desires and pleasures is topos as well as paradoxical means of ablation. This is a fu that represents both the subject's (prince's) succumbing to and extrication from a physio-psychological malaise that arises from his addiction to inordinate desires (*zong yu*) of the eyes, ears, limbs, and body. Can it be said, then, to "tame the erotic and the sensual by including them as part of a general plenitude?"[51] Perhaps representation, whether in the visitor's speech or the text that is this fu as we know it, always already entails the "taming" (rendering assimilable and useful) of its "objects," however dangerous and poisonous ("this is swallowing poison voluntarily, and playing with the claws and teeth of [a] wild beast," says the visitor of the prince's situation).[52] The beautiful and seductive things and phenomena whereby the prince's attention is captured, and which are then strategically turned to poetic/exorcistic use, or on another level, the process (the prose poem, the fu of "curing" excess desire as a form of malaise (without speech but not without groans) with desire as poetic language (speech, rhetoric)—both are a taming of obscene objects or excessive desires; an incorporation of unethical practices into an ethico-poetic order and language. Nonetheless, different modalities of taming may be distinguished, and perhaps the dominant line of fu (and its descendants) problematizes enchantment through disenchantment embodied in the figure of an ambivalently seductive divine lady.[53] Whereas another minor "filiation" (a shadier one), an already (by the Ming) residual structure of reading, is alluded to when Yuan Hongdao writes of reading his JPM alongside the *Seven Stimuli* (of prior readings and memory). One difference lies in the major or upright path toward enlightenment (the lyrical will to self-represent) in contrast with a minor, circumambulating route through abjection (the prosaic tendency toward a self-abnegation)—as reading processes that traverse different "genres" or literary categories. The former leads to a gentle resignation (feminization); the latter to a virile renewal.

If melancholy (*yu*) is the underbelly of a late Ming exuberant qing, then the fu of an abject cure of the body-spirit is the twisted tail of the fu of enlightened disenchantment. This fu seduces and fascinates not to enlighten but abject. Immersion in and incorporation of pleasing things and phenomena induce the necessary state of arousal for a final, exorcistic dispelling of evil ether and/as sweat (body fluid). Of course, the role and position of a mediating poet-shaman is crucial—since he stands in the (framing and authorizing) place of the discourse of (all) sages of old—who not only administers the final cure (the seventh stimulus) but will manage its future efficacy (the introductory prognosis; enlightenment as postcure regime).

The *Seven Stimuli* does not represent sublimated desire (passion/love) and its enlightenment; rather, it seems more preoccupied with *metastasizing* problematic desires (*ermu zhi yu ziti zhi an*)—its duplicitous forms, pernicious objects, and attendant ills. Metastasis in this case involves violent procedures. The military vocabulary in both *Qifa* and in this reading of *Qifa* are not accidental. Invasion must be countered with attack from within and a dispelling that combines extermination with expelling—in short, an exorcism.[54] Thus, material and sensual desires must be represented in such a way as to present the problem (the enemies without/within), its cause (their hold on the subject), and its dislocation (expulsion from the subject in corporeal form). At the same time, an aesthetic-ethical practice of language (prose poetry, fu) both delineates the process and success of the metastasizing cure, and on another level, itself becomes a *figure*, an embedded structure of reading, invoking and yoking together the metastases of desires and a cure for melancholia.

Yet precisely insofar as *Qifa* both tells the story of the visitor's cure of his prince and is the poet's prose poem or fu telling that story—the folding in on itself of the story and the poem detailing it produce readings that refuse to differentiate between inner and outer folds, which readings therefore pronounce both story and poem contaminated by the evil ethers that are supposed to inhabit the prince's body and thoughts. Thus, although in principle neither prince nor prose poem may be disbelieved (both occupy an exalted and powerful position—the one politically, the other culturally and symbolically as initiator and exemplar of its own subgenre), paradoxically, both become subject to doubt on ethical grounds. The prose poem is all the more questionable for having very few willing to record on perusal the sudden breaking into a cleansing sweat. In his definitive work of "literary categorization" and criticism, however, Liu Xie judges the poet to be above suspicion, but the work itself as beyond the saving powers of even an extraordinary literary beauty. Of course, it may actually be just this beauty that incriminates and contaminates beyond repair.

In Liu Xie's (c. C.E. 465–522) sixth-century *The Literary Mind and the Carving of*

*Dragons*, which together with Xiao Tong's (C.E. 501–531) *Wen Xuan* "establish" the early literary field and its obligatory readings, the *Seven Stimuli* is categorized a "miscellaneous writing" (*za wen*) with an ethically compromised aesthetics.

> Since the writing of *Qifa*, many have followed in Mei's footsteps. A look at this initiating attempt of Mei's will convince us that it is truly outstanding, indeed a work of great beauty. . . . In general, they [*Qifa* and its emulators] all describe palaces and hunting in the grand style. They are concerned with outlandish costumes and exotic food, describing with extreme dexterity the most seductive and fascinating of songs and women [*ji gumei zhi shengse*]. These delicious conceptions move one's bones and marrows [*ganyi yao gusui*], their voluptuous verse touches one's very soul [*yanci dong hunshi*]. Although they begin with the lascivious and the excessive, they conclude with the upright. But for every remonstration there are a hundred encouragements, which tendency is not easily reversible [*ran fengyi quan bai shi bu zifan*]. . . . The only piece that speaks of ancient worthies, basing its thought on Confucian principles, is the *Qi Su*; although it is not outstanding in its literary [*wen*] quality, the ideas [*yi*] it contains are truly lofty and profound.[55]

Despite, or rather because of, *Qifa*'s and its "visitor's" "dexterity" with language, the process and success of the cure, and its moral prognosis and finale (peopled with "ancient worthies"), Liu Xie pronounces not just the *Seven Stimuli* but all (except one) following in its *Seven*-part structured footsteps to be beautiful enough yet lacking in uprightness. The crux of the problem is, in Liu Xie's formulation, a *disposition* of the work that is realized in its reading—all the more dangerous in its being nearly impossible to counteract; that is, its tendency to encourage and entice (*quanyou*) far more than to remonstrate and prevent. Such a disposition, however literary and enchanting, can only be considered as a works that belongs to the "branches of the belles lettres, inferior pieces produced in times of leisure [*wenzhang zhi zhipai xiayu zhi mozao*]"[56]—in other words, the branches rather than trunk of one literary tree, trivial objects of play rather than the fruit of serious ethical thought.

In thus explicitly placing Mei Sheng's *Qifa* and its entire "clan" of followers on the margins among the "uncategorizables" of the family of good writings, Liu Xie projects writing as reproducing a social and ethical order where seriousness is measured by the distance and infrequency of a piece of writing's *discursive* contacts with *shiyu*, or sensual desires. To directly address the problem of sensual desire, to further claim and tell a cure—as the visitor from Wu does in *Qifa*—is to dangerously overstep the boundaries of the admissible in good writing and ethical speech. The visitor's audacity is in alleging that a poetic sequencing of sensualities will initiate a two-part cure for one's material and sensual pleasures (*yanchen zhi le*) and melancholia, with ethical enlightenment a promised yet deferred future presence. This is to speak (the visitor) and write (*Qifa*) of what Confucius (one of the sages whose presence brings about the prince's speech and sweat) considered better left beyond either speech or writing. "The subjects on which the master did not talk, were—extraordinary things, feats of strength, disorder, and spiritual operations [*zi bu yu guai li luan shen*]."⁵⁷ One recalls the visitor's disclaimer, when he begins to discourse on the seventh stimulus, "the most miraculous [*gui*] and extraordinary [*guai*] sight in the world [*ci tianxia guaiyi guei guan ye*]," that there are three things about this miraculous vision that "seem supernatural but are not [*si shen er fei zhe san*]." They are not supernatural, or spiritual operations, in how the vision operates on one's sentiment *and* body organs as literally and figuratively a force that although not to be rendered in so many words, "makes one stumble in giddy perplexity and fright [*shenwu guaiyi bu ke shengyan zhi shi ren bo yan*]."⁵⁸ The vision works on and reconstitutes the body as well as emotions in a way that facilitates an exorcism and cure signaled, and completed, in the evocation of the names of wise men and sages along with their teachings (the seventh stimulus).

Importantly, *Qifa* represents a specific sociohistorical conditioning of the prince's illness—a conditioning or context that is inextricable from the aesthetico-hygienics of its cure. The two are reciprocally organized so as to maximize the effects of the cure. This, Liu Xie notes in passing, "[Mei] begins with the perverse but concludes with the proper [*shixie mozheng*]; his purpose was to give warning to one who was brought up in ease [*suoyi jie gaoliang zhi zi ye*]."⁵⁹ This fu was intended, he avers, for princely melancholia, and only thus can the precedence and overwhelming presence of perversity over the proper be understood. The political power, material consumption, and cultural capital of a princely position necessitate and legitimize otherwise, and ultimately, improper language and measures on the part of the visitor-poet, whose double is then Mei Sheng, the writer of this fu. Liu Xie, then, is able to laud Mei Sheng's talent while denigrating its product. Mei is master of an "exquisite phraseology" (*qin yan*), the richness of his language rivals the patterns of clouds (*yuci yungou*), its grand beauty startles like a sudden gust of wind (*kuali fenghai*). But such works as *Qifa* are "inferior pieces" produced in trivial moments of leisure.[60]

Excessive sensual and material consumption (in leisure) are the inherent dangers in a *princely* situation; these inevitably lead to illness and melancholy. The curing of princely illness and melancholy through literary and linguistic excess and exorcism, however aesthetically executed, can only be evaluated as on a par with and sharing in the dangers of its purported aim and subject. The *Seven Stimuli*, like the prince's illness and melancholy whose cure it enumerates and effects, is therefore a product both of and detailing excessive material and literary consumption (the desires of the ear and eye on two levels, formal and thematic), and marking, if not quite advocating, the exclusive and exclusionary time/space of a *princely* leisure and condition (comforts and pleasures of body and limbs).

*An Obscene Book for Everyman's Melancholy*

Wanli Jiangnan was the place and time of material, rhetorical, and fictional princely comforts and desires, although this time was dangerously and unethically enjoyed by parvenu subjects (Ximen Qing as the not-quite-literate, newly rich merchant with no family, no past, and no future whose social and political power is bought via the military with silver and punished with an overdose of *se*, or excessive sensualities).[61] The space/time of leisure along with its attendant comforts of the body and limbs, and myriad desires of the eyes and ears, were now presumably within the reach of not just the hereditary emperor and princely families but prominent local families, well-connected regional officials, literati who had learned the art of marketing the self (see chapter 2), and urban merchants, even bond servants, who had made it big and begun to amass cultural capital. Yet the problem of everyday and cultural consumption was heightened. In particular, it was heightened with the appearance of an apparently new manuscript, obscene in its minute detailing of a startlingly and recognizably "contemporary" and excessive everyday life and the "small" (clearly nongentlemanly) people populating that life. Whose life of degenerate luxury did it represent, as a pleasure/lesson for whom? And with what vicarious and/or resentful sentiment? Whose book was it, and how was it ascertained, by what rights or forms of (new) knowledge, distinctive strategies of reading?

I suggest that for Yuan Hongdao, perusing part of a manuscript version of a JPM recalls *Qifa* in how the latter constitutes an immersion into and exorcism of the pleasures and desires of a space/time of leisure. To the extent that Qifa both thematizes and formally incants a cure for melancholy and illness resulting from social ennui and physical comforts, JPM achieves a similar cure for a sociohistorically distinct and different subject. This is at a moment when illness is valorized as distinguishing one's poetic groanings as the expression of truly felt melancholy, and arises perhaps less from princely ennui than sociopolitical disaffection. The cure in the form of an extended narrative that includes both prose and poetry though in a "contemporary" debased linguistic medium (the language of licentious women and adulterers; popular songs of the day) seems homologous to the cure achieved by an exorcistic fu—Qifa. JPM not only narrates seductive and fascinating contemporary "illness" (money and sex, wine and passion) and its "cure" or punishment (death by depletion); it formally enacts a sequential illness-cure regimen that simultaneously establishes a select circle of readers able to invoke the appropriate modal of reading. Just as illness and melancholy are functions (and discursive forms) of social and literary distinction, so too are regimens of cure and hygienic self-preservation. Without Qifa in mind and body, one might well go the ignominious way of the merchant-parvenu and his "half-human half-object" women in JPM. With Qifa in mind and body, one is aesthetically and ethically enabled to achieve the metastases of text and desires necessary for a prophylactic reading.

This is precisely the point of the second of the three prefaces to JPMC.[62] This preface directly responds to Yuan's reference and comparison thirty years after Yuan's letter to Dong (attesting to the circulation and influence of Yuan's approval).

> The Jin Ping Mei is an obscene book [hui shu]. In praising it as highly as he did, Yuan Hongdao was merely giving indirect expression to his own discontent, not bestowing his approbation on the Jin Ping Mei. Nevertheless, the author did have intentions of his own that were prohibitive [jie] rather than exhortational [quan]. . . . So effective is his delineation that we cannot but break into a sweat as we read. Thus, his intentions are prohibitive rather than hortatory. . . . My friend Chu Xiaoxiu once accompanied a young man to a banquet at which live entertainment was provided. When the point came in the play at which the Hegemon-King feasted at night the young man drooled with admiration, saying, "How can the life of a real man be anything but this?" "The fact is," responded Xiaoxiu, "that it is only by way of contrast with the denouement at Wujiang that the dramatist has inserted this scene." Those present who overheard this re-

mark sighed at the prescience of his comment. Only those who grasp the significance of this statement [story] should be permitted to read the *Jin Ping Mei*. Otherwise, Yuan Hongdao may be accused of having been a flagrant instigator of venery [*dao xuan*]. The people of this world must be exhorted not to follow in the footsteps of Ximen Qing.⁶³

The Pearl-Juggler of Eastern Wu has no doubts: JPMC is an obscene thing whose reading/consumption ought to be restricted. The restriction, however, does not extend to those who break out into a sweat, and those who drool with envy and admiration, as long as these same subjects simultaneously apprehend the *aesthetic/ethical sequence*, the formal logic, undergirding the text-as-enactment and thus protecting the knowledgeable consumer. Rather than signs of a prurient desire, sweating and drooling in such a modal of reading can be transformed, metaphorized into a therapeutic discharge beneficial to a basic regimen of accumulation and retention. Embedded within this figure of sweating and drooling as one reads is a "cure" à la *Qifa*. Desire is used against itself—less in producing detachment or disenchantment, as in inducing a minor physical and psychic discharge, an exorcism through the flow of metonym bodily fluids (sweat and saliva rather than the more intensive semen).⁶⁴

But alongside and possibly preceding the question of the restriction of readership is the question of distinction, or distinguishing among reader-groups. What has been conjectured to be the earliest preface to JPMC records the division of readers into three groups. These three groups comprise the uppermost few of sagelike quality, a broader elite well versed in the classics, and a third greater number whose reading abilities are roughly equal to those of a "three-foot-tall lad." JPMC, avers this particular prefacer, was composed with the *pleasure and edification* of this last vast number in mind. These men too suffer from melancholy. Theirs is not the melancholy of their betters but may nonetheless lead to illness. This less exalted suffering can, the prefacer assures us, be cured by JPMC.

> Of the seven feelings natural to mankind, melancholy is the most intractable. For such men of superior wisdom as may occasionally appear in the natural course of evolution, the fogs and ice that melancholy engenders disperse and splinter of their own accord, so there is no need to speak of such as these. Even those of lesser endowment know how to dispel melancholy with the aid of reason [*li*] so that it may be prevented from encumbering them. Among the many who fall short of this, however, who have been unable to achieve enlightenment in their hearts, and who

do not have access to the riches of the classic tradition to alleviate their melancholy, those who escape its infection are few. It is in consideration of this fact that my friend, the Scoffing Scholar, has poured the accumulated wisdom of a lifetime into the composition of this work, consisting of one hundred chapters in all. . . . As for this story, although it may be couched in the everyday language of the marketplace or the idle chatter of the boudoir, even a three-foot-tall lad can derive as much pleasure from it as he would if he were enabled to suck the nectar of Heaven or pluck the tusk of leviathan, so easy is it for him to understand.[65]

Of the three classes of men envisaged in the first preface to JPMC, the third class is the target readership. For these men, melancholy is intractable because they do not have the ethical and intellectual/aesthetic resources of the first two classes. This new category of men suffer from melancholy and can afford to buy books, but may not have the appropriate training to call on Qifa for a prophylactic reading. Still, JPM is adequate in itself to the task of dispelling such third-class melancholy. Its language is such as will sustain the interest of a three-foot-tall lad while its thematics will show how "when joy reaches its zenith, it gives birth to sorrow." So enticing are the details of the birth of sorrow that the reader will "be beguiled into forgetting his melancholy with a smile." Clearly, this preface is less concerned with restricting the readership of JPM, or restricting its benefits to a more distinguished group, as with the "marketing" of JPM as everyman's antidote to an everyday melancholy. The market niche and target readership of this new cultural product is, for this preface at least, less a class of connoisseurs than it is the larger number of potential reader-consumers who are not connoisseurs, do not necessarily know the classics, and are semiliterate (in terms of classical education), and yet could benefit from a narrative that purportedly seduces as it cures.

Taken together (as they are printed in JPMC), these two prefaces evince a triadic concern and market strategy. On the one hand, the earliest reader(s), as prefacer(s) of a text about to be circulated at large, envisaged its target readers as *commoners*—urbanites possibly whose social status is uncertain and unspecified, and whose (classical) education may be incomplete, but who apparently have the necessary buying and reading power for this particular text. Their potential as readers arises from an affective condition that is posited as shared among all categories of men—an affective condition (melancholy) that is curiously and sensually specifically articulated to this narrative in both manuscript and textual form in the Wanli. On the other hand, just as Yuan Hongdao may be seen as disseminating a discourse on the social distinctions obtaining in illnesses, melancholy, and obsessions, so too do (a greater number of) the earliest readers of this text (namely, the second preface, the colophon, Li Rihua, Xie Zhaozhe, Xue Gang) worry about its populist and popularizing potential, its indiscriminate and indiscriminately *pleasurable* consumption ("even a three-foot-tall lad can derive as much pleasure from it"). This danger is then countered on two fronts. First, through a discourse framing the text and defending a priori against potential "abuse." Thus the colophon by Nian Gong: "The ignorant go so far as to regard this as an obscene book. In so doing, not only do they fail to comprehend the author's purpose but they also unjustly repudiate the intentions of those who would disseminate it." Nian Gong absolves at once authorial intention, preface materials, and the printing of the book. But if danger lies in the ignorance of the reader, it also—and more seriously—lies in the failure to distinguish among the elect. Here one returns to the second preface. This *is* an obscene book, only if one fails to read it as *a book*—that is, an aesthetic/ethical object sequentially arranged for maximal "obscene/purgative" effect. In order to ensure its being consumed as such a literary albeit obscene object, it must come with the proper "credentials": prefaces, editing, and commentaries providing it with the appropriate textual affines. Therefore, a secondary discourse arises, detailing the ways toward a safe reading, for those who may not carry it with them, as Yuan Hongdao happily did.

*All Who Can Read*

Yuan Hongdao's "missing" the latter part of a marvelous new manuscript (c. Wanli 24, 1596) proved to be for the next twenty years (up to c. Wanli 44, 1616) the central reference point for nearly all the written records extant that note knowledge of JPM. His younger brother Yuan Zhongdao writes in *Youju Feilu* how he had seen half the narrative while staying with Yuan Hongdao in Zhenzhou (Wanli 25–26). Yuan Zhongdao had, however, first heard of the narrative from Dong Qichang, who recommended it as one of the very best of recent xiaoshuo. After having perused a part of it, Yuan Zhongdao remembers how when Dong spoke to him of this narrative, Dong had said that he'd determined to burn it. Yuan Zhongdao continues,

> Recalling this [comment of Dong's] today, [I think] there is no need to burn it, nor is there any need to recommend it. Let it be. Burn it, and

there would still be those who will keep it; this is not something the forces of men can abolish. To recommend SHZ is to advocate brigandry, this book advocates licentiousness. Those who have the teachings of the sages at heart, why should they claim this [narrative] as a new marvel, thereby astounding the stupid and harming the mores?[66]

Yuan Zhongdao implicitly disagrees with Yuan Hongdao, judging his brother imprudent in "recommending" a book that he now conveniently remembers Dong Qichang mentioning as fit only for burning. Yuan Zhongdao favors a neutral attitude. Let it be, so that it will not attract more interest than it deserves, he thinks. In fact, Yuan Zhongdao is precisely noting and worrying about the additional value attributed to a book once "those who have the teachings of the sages at heart" begin to write about it, to advertise its marvels in print. He is, in effect, trying to counteract Yuan Hongdao's recommendation by remarking how another cultural authority, one from whom Yuan Hongdao had gotten the manuscript in the first place, had advised that it be burned.

If Yuan Zhongdao considers JPM something to be read but not written about or discussed for fear of increasing its commercial and popular value, Xie Zhaozhe (jinshi Wanli 20, same class as Yuan Hongdao), in a note on JPM in the *Collected Works from Little Grass Studio* (*Xiaocao Zhai Wenji*), seems to guardedly agree out of a similar concern that it might fall into the wrong hands.

> This book surely must not fall into the hands of pedantic scholars and vulgar men! . . . Although some may deride me for advocating licentiousness, I dare not say [whether I am or not]. Yet, even Confucius did not delete the licentious airs of Zheng and Wei, [for such texts are] what Cai Yong could not do without in his rooms.[67]

Xie Zhaozhe is straightforward about how the book must be kept away from the inferior classes of men that include the lowest in taste and knowledge among the scholar-gentries (*baoru*), and those who have mastered reading as well as writing and aspire to a culture that is *not* theirs (*sushi*). These classes of men are a contemporary (perverting and pervertible) outgrowth—such men will harm the books that fall into their hands.[68]

The beneficial, medicinal even, qualities of books and writing—especially the strange, rare, and different (*yi shu*)—incidentally remain a focal point of concern half a century later in Li Yu's *Xianqing ouji* (*Casual expressions of idle feeling*, 1671) in a section on illness and its seven medicinal cures (*liao* bing). The fourth medicinal cure is labeled as "that which was never before seen in one's life . . . as medicine." In this little essay, Li Yu expounds on the beneficial qualities of objects never before *seen or possessed*.

> That which was never before seen in one's life can be taken as medicine. To want what one has never possessed is a desire all men have. This is like [the feeling of] men of letters [wenshi] toward marvelous and strange books [yi shu]; military men toward a precious sword; the drunkard toward famous wine; the beauty toward exquisite ornament. They will all give their all, emotionally, and will not be afraid of any difficulty, in order to have and be with the desired object. They will look for these objects everywhere. To allow these persons to see these objects, to find these especially under difficult conditions, this is the technique whereby to manage and control [jianu] the patient. . . . As for marvelous and strange books, these are not necessarily subtle works and secret volumes, hidden within broken-down walls. Rather, all new books, those never before seen, are marvelous and strange books. For example, Chen Lin's xi and the writings of Mei Sheng. These are medicines that have been tried by those before us. Strange and marvelous writings communicate with the gods, and when ghosts and demons are confronted with these, they are obstructed. What I mean by "men of letters" [wenren] does not necessarily refer only to those with talent [but] rather all who are literate, who can read, can use books as medicine.[69]

In contrast to Yuan Hongdao, Li Yu never made it past the provincial level exams and was beset by poverty for most of his prolific life. He engaged in writing, printing, and bookselling, and kept his own troupe of actresses to perform his plays.[70] In this passage, however, there is clearly a structure of reading and feeling that is seen to inhere in the reading of particular books and writings—new books and strange writings—that work in a parallel manner to the writings of Mei Sheng in the past. While Mei Sheng's writings are seen to provide a structure of reading that has worked in the past, new works will forge new structures that will work in the present and future. Li Yu seems less interested in distinguishing among the literate of his day (between the true and false, the talented and not-so-talented). Rather, he is more concerned with the medicinal properties of *new* books, books never before seen, which may act in the same manner as medicinal works of old such as Mei Sheng's.

More than half a century earlier, Yuan Hongdao was charmed into forgetting illness and melancholy by a new marvelous manuscript on a par, in his eyes, with the best of the ancients (Mei Sheng's *Qifa*), noting this fact nonchalantly in a letter. Li Yu, on the other hand, in a series of essays listing and enumerating the concerns and tasteful manner of usages of a connoisseur's life in leisure, is purposefully articulating the medicinal properties of *new objects* on a market in books in which he, as an owner of a bookstore, was in much greater proximity than the likes of Yuan Hongdao in the Wanli. If Yuan may be characterized as advertising a new object through the fame of his name as well as the empirewide circulation of his letters and essays, then, Li is selling all new books and objects that may fit each consumer's needs, notwithstanding the consumer's cultural/class qualifications. Yuan's nonchalant records of reading JPM gave rise to a spate of reactive comments—more or less all worried that his enthusiasm would have a *magnifying effect* on the value of the manuscript in question. In Shen Defu's well-known note on JPM, he says, "As for this kind of book, someone will surely print it, and yet once in print it will reach all the family and houses [of the empire]; this will do harm to people's feelings and thoughts [*huai ren xinshu*]."[71] The magnifying effect of Yuan's cultural capital in pointing to this new manuscript as a good read is thus parallel to, and a byproduct of, the magnifying effect of an empirewide market in books. Yet by Li Yu's time, the value itself of new books and objects must be *magnified or enhanced* through a specialized discourse, simultaneously aesthetic and hygienic, or medicinal. The focus of a discourse on distinction has shifted from the consumer to the object. Hence the necessity, for one so poor and undistinguished as Zhang Zhupo, to distinguish and make a name for himself through editing and commenting on, therefore attaching himself to, an already infamous book. JPM as an insufficiently aesthetic yet fully commercial and enticing object is a prime candidate for a reading that will produce it as an aesthetic-ethical antidote to and displacement of excessive sex and sensual practices.

The representation and problematization of sensualities (in a family of writing that does not encourage such representation, and must qualify its every occurrence) is, in part, a refraction of a sociohistorical conjuncture where and when subjects of writing (the visitor-poet) and reading (the melancholy prince) had become obsessed with the materiality—in other words, abundance, color, beauty (se), richness, consumption—of everyday life and its leisure spatiotemporality. *Qifa* may be said to represent an obsession amounting to addiction in princely quarters and on an imperial scale, for the alleviation of an imperial boredom and melancholia. I claim that the appearance and reading of JPM circa 1596 could be seen as proffering a similar cure for a sociopolitically differently positioned, though "still" melancholic writing-reading subject.

The cure is constituted through a structure of feeling activated by a specific modality of reading. Such a reading would permit a reader to be pleasured as if for his own good, with the pleasure arising from what seems no different from mundane immoral sensualities, but with an important difference. These pleasures of reading are structured and sequenced à la *Qifa* so that they simulate sensualities in a prearranged, or high literary, representation. This representation will effect, with the right "mediation" (either one's own literary capital, or the instructions of one who possesses that capital in the form of marginal commentaries and prefatorial how-to-reads), the necessary cure—that is, (temporary) liquidation of boredom and metastases of desire through a virtual (never actual) immersion in various everyday sensualities. This cure can only succeed if it ultimately reinstates the subject to the power (ethical and aesthetic) that is contiguous with his position in the social and cultural space wherein these structures of feeling and reading are operative.

I am suggesting a position of reading that is reproduced in the structures of reading that inhabit given texts—facilitating yet not determining their disposition toward a particular modality of reading. Yuan Hongdao's comparison of JPM with *Qifa* thus establishes three elements that are crucial to the future "fate" of this then-new cultural object: its use value as cultural object, its particular place in the literary "line" or canon, and the modality of its consumption (how to read it in order to obtain the maximal pleasure and benefit). These three elements simultaneously function to advertise, legitimate, and provide a new textual object with a suitable classical alibi.

CHAPTER 4

Tears of Ressentiment:
Zhang Zhupo's (1670–1698)
Jin Ping Mei

The sword [dao] of a military man, and the brush [bi] of the gentleman of letters, both are tools for killing. That a sword can kill, everyone knows. That the brush can kill, not everyone knows this. . . . As for killing with a brush, in comparison with killing with a sword, its speed and violence is one hundred times greater [than the latter].
—Li Yu, Xianqing ouji

I read JPM, in its three main seventeenth-century versions, as a discursive crystallization of various strands of a late Ming misogyny.[1] In this chapter, misogyny will refer particularly to an early modern Han-Chinese narrative misogyny—that is, the process and products of a late Ming–early Qing ethical and aesthetic narrativization of male fear of, and fascination with, the desire for women (hao nüse). Narration functions in this case as the primary mode of representation, and an ethical and aesthetic telos, as a structuring principle, or the moral bone that will make the animal upright and humane and the writing properly ethical and literary.[2] The process whereby a narrative becomes both ethical and aesthetic resulted in JPM's paradigmatic stories of the social and sexual relations of gendered bodies in a polygamous domestic space. Nearly four hundred years later, it continues to work its powers on the cultural imaginary of a "modern" Chinese-speaking world. Contemporary reactivations, in appropriating and reconfiguring parts of JPM's gender and sexual vision, have yet to be traced through, for example, analyses of the dramatic and filmic retellings of this story of, as Zhang Zhupo terms it, "adulterous men and lascivious women . . . pimps and whores."

One of the issues that prompted this study is the social effects and subjective affects of a widely circulated text—a text circulated in the present not so much in its material form of a one-hundred hui narrative but rather as sign, denoting pornographic representations of excessively (that is, aggressively) sexual women.

JPM's earliest printed edition (JPMC) appeared in the Wanli (1573–1619) reign of the Ming and includes a preface dated 1618.[3] Another extant edition, *Xinke Xiouxiang Piping Jin Ping Mei* (hereafter XXPJPM) was published during the Chongzhen reign, while Zhang Zhupo's commentated text, based on a version of the Chungzhen edition, was printed in 1695 and subsequently became "the most widely disseminated . . . [and] influential" of all the extant editions.[4] But to speak of commentated text is to misrepresent Zhang Zhupo's project. His interpretations and evaluative essays, pre-hui notations, and marginal comments together produce an "other" JPM, much more literary and somewhat less erotic. In effect, Zhang Zhupo "reads/writes" his JPM—his reading being a mode of rewriting that passes itself off as mere reading.[5]

I use "read/write" to stress the degree to which at that historical juncture, reading—in the form of editing, collating, and commentating (*pingdian*), became a mode of rewriting and framing that oftentimes went so far as to produce another version of a text (as in the famous case of Jin Shengtan's truncated yet definitive SHZ).[6] Extended narratives like SHZ and JPM already are, to use Patricia Sieber's formulation for late Ming Yuan *zaju*, sedimented cultural products in their complex layering and redeployment of different genres of writing (song, drama, historical anecdotes).[7] The literati or scholarly urge to provide prefaces and exegetical notations that valorize, but also in some cases cleanse a text of "impurities," cohere its ideological valence, and reinscribe it as "literary," all served to make a vernacular and vulgar genre more like "literature" in a classical sense, assimilating it into the space of symbolic capital and literati cultural hegemony.[8]

How, then, was JPM read/written in the late Ming–early Qing (seventeenth-century) conjuncture, amid a cultural and political revaluation of popular writings and sentiment? In the late Ming, political resentment was already in place, with large numbers of disaffected literati turning away from the examination system (usually after having failed numerous tries at the provincial level) to pursue other possibilities for success and recognition of their talent (see chapters 2 and 3). Political resentment is the structure of feeling that T'ien Ju-K'ang names "frustration" and "anxiety" in his study of Ming-Qing ethics, and that he links to this period's literati's vicariously fulfilling discourses that effectively "created" and continuously reproduced the cult of widowhood.[9] Not only does T'ien find a phenomenal rise in the numbers of virtuous widows committing ritual suicide from the Wanli period on; he also notes how these acts are morally and discursively valorized through the writing and compiling of anthologies of virtuous widows and the recording of their model deaths in local histories.

In her pathbreaking study of stories of women's virtue written during this period, Katherine Carlitz examines the incongruence between the didactic aims of such narratives and the almost passionate attention to details of the maiming and disposing of women's body parts in these writings. Interestingly, she finds that although these stories were framed so as to control (the writer/reader's?) "desire for women; by the end of the dynasty, there is a noticeable shift . . . from desire conceived [of] as negative to intense emotion (including sexual) desire conceived [of] as positive. . . . [A]t the same time, we see women reduced . . . from powerful emblem[s] of loyalty to object[s] of connoisseurship."[10]

Intellectual historians have charted the flourishing in the late Ming into the Ming-Qing transition of a discourse on precisely this intense emotion or sentiment (qing), whose "liberatory" effects range from what Hsu Pi-ching terms the "emancipation of self from the shackles of cultural puritanism," to a proliferation of writings anthologizing, editing, and commentating on previously contemptible vernacular fiction and drama.[11] "Liberation" has to be, in this context, carefully examined and qualified; whose liberation, whose gains, what kind of gains, and at what expense? As Carlitz's findings suggest, whereas intense emotion is authenticated and valorized, it is simultaneously redefined, and appropriated to *new* discursive and social uses.[12]

How can a microreading, a reading in detail of JPM in its various recensions, discover the textual strategies that constitute part of a process of subjection, sexual and political, of an "ideal" reader? I suggest that the text and its mythologies produce an ideal or projected reader in a structure of reading that is both a textual process and a cultural mythology. Together, these then produce a gender- and sexuality-specific reading positionality that may be partially archaeologically retrieved in its historicity, as it partakes in various late Ming discourses that have contributed to the making up of a "modern" aestheticized man of letters in Chinese.

In this chapter, I read in detail some of the strategies at work in Zhang Zhupo's reading of JPM, specifically as elucidated in his prefaces to his commentated edition of JPM. His strategies enable what might be termed a fraternal exchange between the text and its reader/writer. That there is material profit in the reading, editing, and commentating of vernacular texts is obvious—thus Zhang Zhupo's caveat that he "is not doing this for fame" but "for a bit of money in order to live."[13] Yet is there any other profit to be gained besides one's living? Does not the reference to "merely making a living" from a certain occupation just as easily disclaim other investments in the project? What returns are projected, beyond immediate relief from economic straits, in terms of cultural and symbolic capital? And more subjectively, what about much less visible, but no less ideological profit—that is, emotional and/or libidinal gain?

I reread Zhang Zhupo's "Idle Musings," "The Number One Marvelous Book is Not an Obscene Book," "Embittered Filiality," and the 108 items of his "How to Read [JPM]" in order to understand the meanings and function of *yuan*, or ressentiment, in his implicit theory of fictional literature. What is at stake in the triangular articulation of *yuanru* (the resenting Confucian), *yinfu* (lascivious women), and *wenfa* (literary codification) in Zhang Zhupo's reading/writing of JPM? And where do gender and sex enter this triangulation? Zhang Zhupo's tears of ressentiment are sociopolitically gendered, I argue; furthermore, the shedding of tears is, for Zhang Zhupo at least, occasioned by a narrative instance of filial piety supplanting, though not eradicating, sexual desire for bad women. For male desire continues to be implicated, not merely in each narrative instance of its displacement (with filial sentiment) but more in the ethico-aesthetic strategies whereby it seems erased time and again from textual object and reading subject.

*A Narrative of Ressentiment*

> Anyone who says JPM is an obscene book has only taken the trouble to read the obscene passages. I read this book exactly as though it were a work by Sima Qian. . . .

> The JPM is characterized by an air of resentful indignation, but then its author is certainly a reincarnation of Sima Qian [who was wrongfully castrated]. . . .
> The story begins with Meng Yulou playing the guitar [puns with "to sigh with resentment"] and concludes with Han Aijie carrying her guitar [puns with "to harbor resentment"]. This is because the author had a bellyful of outraged tears but no place to shed them. Therefore, he created JPM as an outlet for his tears.[14]

In 1695, the thirty-fourth year of the Kangxi reign, approximately a century following the first mention of JPM, Zhang Zhupo, a literatus who by that time had failed the provincial examinations four times, wrote while residing in Suzhou extensive commentaries on JPM in less than a month.[15] His prefaces, pre-hui exegeses, and marginal notations were printed together with the text that same year, to be disseminated as the *Zhang Zhupo ben*, or Zhang Zhupo's JPM, as in Jin Shengtan's SHZ. The commentator's published version had, if not quite superseded the narrative text, effectively inlaid his readings to the narrative—so much so that one might well call it a rewriting. The narrative text now comes with a lining that changes the texture, moral value, and ideological configuration of the textual body, to which it clings like a second skin.[16]

Zhang Zhupo claims to both "find" in and reinscribe into "his" JPM, *yuan* or ressentiment. This is resentment with an added temporal axis, a sense of time having passed between the suffering that gives rise to *yuan*, and the (later) literary expression of this re-sentiment—in short, the literary revisiting of a past sentiment.[17] Yuan is compounded with the long frustration of immediate relief from suffering, the foiling of any possibility for revenge. It is thus an emotion that has aged and, in the process, soured; Zhang Zhupo names it "to harbor sourness and nurse resentment [*hansuan baoyuan*]."[18]

In his study of Nietzschean ressentiment, Richard Sugarman writes that "when the desire for revenge is stymied its expression is altered but its intention remains the same, thereby venting its affects in effigy." Furthermore, "the structure of entire political orders . . . can prefigure the likely emergence of '*ressentiment*.' . . . [P]olitical '*ressentiment*' is not necessarily a function of economic class or the system of governing. . . . It is . . . a function of the discrepancy between social status and factual political power."[19]

As I have already mentioned, the frustration that has been variously examined as the source of governmental inefficiency if not sabotage by contemporaries in the late Ming–early Qing transition, and by recent scholars as that which propels the discursive and social cult of widow suicides, can be read as a form of political ressentiment.[20] It remains to be seen how a sociopolitical sentiment may be, in one narrative instance, discursively rearticulated to serve both social and psychic ends; and how in the process, a virile and moral male subject is reaffirmed through "venting in effigy" the ressentiment that will inoculate him from a contaminating desire, figured as female, feminine and feminizing (yin), and obscene (yin).

When Zhang Zhupo writes that (his) JPM begins and ends with figures that signify yuan, it is no accident that these figures are (base) women playing musical instruments.[21] After all, women have served since the Han as tropes through which an entire tradition of literati-poets figured their (uncertain) place in the polity.[22] And women playing musical instruments further connote the tradition of song and poetry, wherein idealized, passive, pining, and languishing female figures embody the male scholar-official's unspeakable longing for an erring/errant emperor (guiyuan shi). Within this tradition, yuan is a distinctly "feminine" sentiment, modulated in the register of a virtuous erotic, articulated through a "masculine" authorial voice and position. In JPM there are few such figures, either of pining, silent women, or of absent, longed-for patron-emperors. Rather, yuan is a founding sentiment for JPM by Zhang Zhupo through the figure of Sima Qian, whose political castration and imprisonment produced an inaugural work of history.[23] What is constituted in Zhang Zhupo's appropriation of yuan?[24] Are Zhang Zhupo's tears a sign of erotic virtue, conflating the eroticism already present in the lyrical tradition of yuan with the righteously moral-political resentment of a Sima Qian? Will resentment then produce, and vindicate, Zhang Zhupo's reading/writing of a compromised and compromising JPM?

In a prefatory essay titled "Zhupo's Idle Musings," Zhang Zhupo begins with a foundational question:

> As for JPM, why was this book written? I say, these are the defiled words of a humane man of ambition [renren zhishi], a man of filial and brotherly piety [xiaozi tidi] who lived in the wrong times, and could neither ask justice of heaven, nor speak of his wrongs to mankind. Filled with indignant resentment and unshed tears, he wrote these defiled words as an outlet for his resentment ... and because he could not ultimately fulfill his ambitions, the more poisonous his words, the greater the sorrowing of his

heart. This is what is called "to harbor sourness and nurse resentment" [hansuan baoyuan].[25]

What Zhang Zhupo seems to be saying is, yes, these words are poisonous and defiled, contaminated and contaminating (yudu), yet I (Zhang Zhupo) read in them the great resentment and sorrowings of a virtuous man.[26] The interest of Zhang Zhupo's reading is not so much the curiously familiar logic whereby authorial intentions, and virtuous suffering for that matter, are seen as determining (and authenticating) the ultimate "meaning" of a text. Rather, on another level, a slippage occurs (and recurs) between Zhang Zhupo, writer of the preface, and the author of this narrative of ressentiment whose feelings and thoughts are, in the course of the essay, inhabited by Zhang, rendered as if they were his own syntactically and semantically.[27]

> When resentment [yuanhen] deepens without one's being able to speak/spit it, fermenting day after day, high as the sky, wide as the blue sea, when will I ever be able to forget! Face awash in tears, pierced heart shedding tears of blood, even were this enemy to be excoriated a hundred times, it would be to no avail. Such sourness as this, every single moment of it, fermented over a thousand years, will not spoil. . . . The author in his ambition would not stoop to a revengeful act but instead takes his revenge in the finely wrought words of a hundred chapters; who could say the sharpness of a knifelike brush would not kill once and for all! This explains JPM.[28]

Yuan here is the ressentiment that accumulates over time, accentuating and deepening one's sense of suffering, making it imperious that an outlet be found (in/through writing), and with that outlet, an object(s) at which to direct the revenge that had been kept from its "originary" enemy. Zhang Zhupo's reading of the motivations for the writing of JPM, for its foundational sentiment, installs the moral character of its protagonist (the figure of the long-suffering author). It is his (the author's) virtue that ensures the probity of Zhang Zhupo's own project—that is, saving JPM from readings that defile it. This virtue is, however, in an unlikely echo of its Latin forebear (virtus), simultaneously invested with "virile" qualities, in signifying a "manly" rather than "womanly" subject. This is obvious in the reference to the author as a person of filial and *brotherly* piety; and even more apparent in his being the reincarnation of a *wrongfully castrated* grand historian, Sima Qian.

The figure of Sima Qian, previously invoked in Jin Shengtan's rewriting of the SHZ to legitimize and valorize Jin's own project as well as its object-text, provides the prototype for the author with whom Zhang Zhupo so identifies. This author's suffering and resentment speaks passionately through Zhang Zhupo's writing, while Sima Qian's castration, political imprisonment, and subsequent historical writings provide a priori justification for the groanings of a purported late Ming literatus (the author). By figuring the author of JPM as a late Ming Sima Qian, Zhang Zhupo is able to reconfigure his (the author's, but also his own, by extension and identification) political ressentiment as a yuanhen that is at once political and moral/sexual—political in motivation, and moral/sexual in effect. The "resentful indignation" (fenmen) that fills the textual space of JPM materializes, at least in Zhang Zhupo's reading of it, as "the bellyful of outraged tears" that the author could not shed, but that would, in the belly of the text as it were, "sour" the narrative with a corrective morality.[29]

> The author was unfortunate to have experienced this tragedy [shen zao qi nan]. He can neither spit it, nor swallow it, nor can he scratch it, and wailing is of no use, thus he uses this [writing] to relieve himself [zixie]. His ambitions sadden, his heart is pitiful.[30]

Zhang Zhupo attempts here to read/write the subjective experience of a figurative castration. Ostensibly speaking of Wang Shizhen (1526–1590), who was rumored to have authored JPM so as to avenge the unjust killing of his father by Yan Song, then chief minister (in 1559), Zhang Zhupo suggests that the tragedy the subject experiences in his person (shen) becomes manifest as a pervasive, insistent disease.[31] This disease is foreign to one's constitution, since one cannot swallow it, but it also resists easy ejection, since one cannot spit it. It is furthermore ineffable and unspeakable, as one can neither scratch nor scream. The only way one may relieve oneself of this excessively uneasy state is to write. The crucial question is then: What of? What kind of writing will bring relief?

> In JPM, the author devotes serious attention to the description [zheng jing xie] of six women. . . . The full treatment is reserved for Li Ping'er and Pan Jinlian. But again, he describes Li Ping'er by what he does not say about her, which is to say, he describes her while keeping his focus elsewhere. This is because the focus of his description is always on Pan Jinlian. Because he always concentrates on Pan Jinlian, it is no wonder that she emerges as the most vicious of all his characters. Such indeed is the awesome power of the writer's brush. . . .

As for Lady Lin, what incalculable resentment must the author have had in his heart to pour it all on Pan Jinlian. Not only does he kill and dismember her, even the household where she got her start in life, and the persons who taught her, even they must be put to death before [the author can feel] relief.[32]

Such is the power of reading/writing a narrative that details the obscenities as well as the eventual outcome of and retribution for such obscenities in a finely moral/aesthetic parading of a succession of yinfu, or lascivious women, in all guises: Pan Jinlian as prototype, the ultimate castrating-murdering vamp; Li Ping'er as Jinlian's rival, a compassionate maternal-whore; Song Huilian as Pan Jinlian's double and nemesis; Chunmei as Pan Jinlian's maid and extension/continuation; Wang Liu'er as Song Huilian's successor; and Lady Lin as a highly placed, sociopolitically powerful yinfu.

"If the author had not had intense feelings he would never have written this book."[33] Yes, but what receptacles did he devise for appropriate self-relief (zixie)? And how were these receptacles made fitting for the program?

The subjective, personalized experience of ressentiment, as Zhang Zhupo reads/writes it, recalls the throes of, strangely enough, JPM's ambivalent treatment of Wu Song's and Li An's inadmissible desire for seductive women in the figures of Pan Jinlian and Chunmei. This desire (hao nüse) is—the moment it arises in the male subject both inside and outside the narrative (Wu Song and his reader)—externalized to the extent that it is narrated as consistently passive and (non)responsive to an active "other" figure of seduction, Pan Jinlian and Chunmei (via her nurse, who she sends to Li An). Wu Song's entanglement with Pan Jinlian parallels, in SHZ, his heroic fight with and killing of a formidable tiger (see chapter 5). His revulsion at and resistance to Pan Jinlian's seductive advances are narrated with as much gusto as the technical virtuosity of Wu Song's combat with the tiger. Revulsion and resistance are also seen as reaffirming his virility insofar as it is an ethical one—a virility whose founding principle is homosocial honor (yi), or a fraternal code that sublimates homoeroticism and denies male-female erotic desire. This is what happens, both intertextually and at the extratextual level. In SHZ, and more ambivalently so in JPMC, Wu Song is unmoved and unresponsive. Yet one reads of the violence with which he pushes her off (from himself) then throws away the infamous half-drunk cup of wine she offers him (as in: "If you'll drink of my leavings, it'll be as if you've had a bit of me").

Finally, there is the moral sadism in the reading/writing of each step of his eventual disemboweling of Pan Jinlian (Zhang Zhupo counts the recurrence of "knives" in this bit of masterly narration) ostensibly for having murdered his brother, but also more subliminally, a repetition of that earlier "pushing" (of her body) and "throwing" (of her cup and its remnants), only this time for "real" with a knife.[34] Violence is tainted with sexual desire; as much desire as was in Pan's seduction scene, which gave rise to Wu Song's (and the text's) punitive and sacrificial killing of Pan Jinlian. The reader/writer (as realized in the commentaries for this episode of both Jin Shengtan and Zhang Zhupo, in their respective versions of SHZ and JPM) colludes in the denial of any moral/sexual desire in the male figure (and by extension, the male reader who identifies with this heroic figure). This denial grounds itself in the externalization and projection of desire onto the figure of an actively seductive yinfu, who must then be literarily killed, doubly killed, for seduction (she is sexual therefore nonvirtuous), but more crucially, for inducing impossible and improper desire.

The above is not a digression since the ejection of an inexpressible corporeal unease (desire)—and the literary work that is the product of a successful ejection—is at the crux of Zhang Zhupo's identificatory reading of the author and his invocation of Sima Qian to figure that identification. There is a parallel, a homology, between Zhang Zhupo's reading of authorial intentions, in the style of a Sima Qian, and generations of male readers' collusion with JPM's textual and moral sadism. Likewise, the latter were enabled, through reading, to rehearse a three-step process of the rousing of desire in the self, a denial of that desire, and the projection of that desire onto figures of yinfu in the narrative, with the added pleasure of punishing these figures for the initial moment of arousal. So, too, Zhang Zhupo claims for the author (and himself) the arousal of a frustrated desire for political revenge, through wrongs committed against the virile and virtuous self-body (figurative castration); the turning sour of that unspeakable ressentiment; and the search for an appropriate outlet for that unquenchable ressentiment so as to vent itself "in effigy." The effigies in this case are yinfu, coinciding with those that presumably interest more "vulgar" readers. Relief obtains through the transmutation of ressentiment (affect) into writing; of a murderous revenge held back, then redirected to become the literary killing and defiling, with words, of lascivious women, Pan Jinlian and their like.

## Filial Piety, Sexual Desire, and Literary Pleasures

That which is most true [zhen] under heaven are the Five Constant Relations [lunchang]; the most false [jia], are wealth and beauty [caise]. Of the Five Relations, the relation between ruler and official, friends, and husband and wife can be forged. But as for the relations between father and son, and between brothers, like water that flows from one source, branches that grow from one trunk, each branch and tributary is the product of heavenly will. That there can actually be false fathers [jiafu], false sons [jiazi], false older brothers [jiaxiung], false younger brothers [jiadi], and their likes! Alas, if even this can be falsified, what cannot be falsified? . . . How tragic, that sensual desires [shiyu] should lead to fascination [mi] with wealth and beauty [caise], which in turn will lead to effects of cold and heat [lengre], which then will cause the disordering of true and false [zhenjia]. It is because of their false relations, wherein every servile urge is indulged, that those of us who are true have likewise been poisoned and contaminated [jie zao qi yudu].[35]

In this lengthy passage, Zhang Zhupo elaborates a Confucian ethics of sociofamilial relations against which the fictional enterprise of JPM must be read. He sets up the moral axes of true and false, or authentic and inauthentic, whereby sociofamilial relations and the self that becomes a subject within these parameters must be ethically evaluated and ontologically justified. His reading of JPM is, on one level, a remapping of fictional characters and narrative thematics within this moral frame, categorizing and listing the true and false subjects, the authentic and inauthentic relations. The result is an overwhelming outnumbering of the false and inauthentic, over the true and authentic. At this level, Zhang Zhupo's reading is a reading of the text as "actual events" (shishi), of the characters and incidents as representations of their counterparts in lived experience. But there is another equally important level of reading—a reading of the aesthetics, the literariness, of JPM—to which I will later turn. This second level of reading will prove paradoxical, problematizing Zhang's moral project. It will also elucidate the no-win sexual and textual position of yinfu. The position of yinfu in the text signifies a fundamental and eroticized immorality in the yin-nature of women. This position is simultaneously metonymically linked to a literary and erotic "beauty" (se), an aesthetic quality whose seductive techniques, like yinfu's yinhua, the obscene speech of lascivious women, must be detoxified for the appreciative consumption of the discriminating. The question is, How?

If there were no Li An, the sole example of a filial son, would this not be tantamount to the extinction of men of conscience? Observe how the author tells the tale of the mutual reliance of Li An and his mother to show him as a filial son who maintains his chastity as though it were jade and will let no injury befall the body that he has inherited from his parents, in contrast to the likes of Ximen Qing and Chen Jingji who are really inferior to pigs and dogs.[36]

The antidote to sensual desires gone wild is, for Zhang Zhupo, filial piety, read into JPM as the only redemptive feeling in a text filled with excessive desires. Subject to the latter are primarily "false" or otherwise compromised masculine figures: Ximen Qing, the false husband and father; Chen Jingji, the false son-in-law; Ying Bojue, the false friend; pigs and dogs in the guise of men. Filial piety is then the single sentiment that will rectify a text filled with adulterous men and licentious women.

For Zhang Zhupo, the episode that encapsulates an ideal masculinity, an ethical virility, in the figure of a filial son, Li An, occurs in the last hui of the narrative and takes up very little narrative space. Chunmei, last alive of the three main licentious women, is now the principal wife of a commandant in the military, and seeking a lover, she decides on Li An, a retainer in the household. She sends her son's governess to Li An one winter night with gifts of women's clothing and a fifty *liang* gold piece, ostensibly in gratitude for his having saved her life. The next morning, Li An returns home to his mother and shows her the clothing, whereupon she asks, "Where does this come from?" He tells her, and she bitterly exclaims,

> When Zhang Shen committed evil [had sex with the wife of his master], he was given a hundred beatings and killed. She's now given you this stuff. What's the meaning [of the gift?] I'm now over sixty, [and] ever since your father died, my eyes have only had you to look at [you've been my sole support]; if anything should happen, who would I rely on? Don't even go in tomorrow morning.[37]

Afraid that Chunmei would send someone for him, Li An's mother tells him to go to his uncle's to hide out for a while. "Being a filial son," Li An did as his mother told him; he packed a bag and left for his uncle's in Qing Zhou county.

The true (*zhen*) filial son, like the true brotherly brother (Wu Song), is one who is able to foil, resist, and sometimes even punish seduction. And yet, one reads in this anecdote a seemingly insignificant detail: the passing of a whole night before Li An returns home with the gifts—a night that is, in both the Chongzhen and Zhang Zhupo's JPM, filled with indecision and unease as an insomniac Li An paces his small room (*dang ye chou chu bu jue*).[38] What can he be thinking? What in these gifts can be so threatening or alluring? Like Wu Song at the beginning of JPM, Li An seems not untouched, his very indecision a sign of desire, of movement in the heart. It is this budding desire that his mother squashes, by reference to an even more imperious and certainly more legitimate need: her own—for a son who has become, since the death of his father, her only means of emotional and material support. Li An's possible succumbing to seduction is foreclosed: the disruptive wavering of sentiment redirected toward acquiescing to his mother's will. Sexual desire is doused with filial piety. Or filiality, itself a movement and direction of feeling, becomes the rectification of an erring desire; grafted onto desire, it is propelled by what had been an impure force.

There is a gap between Li An's silence (fraught with possible meanings—among them, the sprouting of an illicit desire) and his mother's speech, disciplinary in purpose and effect. In fact, the reinstating of morality in the text occurs in and through the speech of the mother. It also occurs in Zhang Zhupo's effusions over her words, in effect attempting to close that gap and hide its indeterminacy.

Thus, Zhang Zhupo the reader sentimentally reads the maternal words of entreaty: when the mother says, "My eyes have only had you to look at," Zhang is moved to respond: "Such plaintive sounds ... truly the tears and blood of a thousand years." And again at the end of the mother's speech, Zhang remarks that "the voice and words of a virtuous mother ... [are] sounds that move one tears [*ling ren luo lei*]."[39] This is a rare moment for Zhang Zhupo, as the single and singular instance of the "voice and words of a virtuous mother" in the entire JPM.

Having shown an example of Zhang Zhupo's literal reading of a "true" mother speaking to her "filial son" and saving him from the snares of one of the last yinfu in the narrative, let me now juxtapose his "authentic" sentimentality at, and recognition of, the power of maternal speech to move with his mediated, in effect much more distant and distancing reading of the obscene speech (yinhua) of lascivious women that sound forth throughout JPM.

> The author has put into the mouths of Pan Jinlian [concubine] and Wang Liu'er [wife of the underling who becomes the mistress of the master]

totally shameless and utterly unspeakable things, so intolerable that even Li Guijie and Zheng Aiyue [prostitutes] could never have brought themselves to say them. By so doing, the author expresses his profound condemnation of Ximen Qing, who is really less than human, for when he is exposed to such bestiality [*gouzhi*] he actually expresses a preference for it. It follows that when Wang Liu'er and Pan Jinlian both get a crack at him on the same day, it is the death of Ximen Qing.[40]

Zhang Zhupo neither repeats the yinhua of these yinfu nor tells of his immediate response to such obscene speech. Instead, his response is twice mediated. First, through the figure of Ximen Qing, who does respond, but in the wrong way, by becoming ensnared and fascinated by yinhua. Second, through the literary encoding of yinhua as a device whereby to emplot and incriminate (*shenzui*) false masculine figures such as Ximen Qing, who lack the morality that would produce an authentic virile masculinity (along with a filial self-preservation—that is, longevity—of the body-self inherited from one's parents).[41]

Let me stress here the distancing effect of such a doubly mediated reading of yinhua. Once yinhua becomes a fictional device, its power to move and seduce, which it clearly has within the narrative itself, is denied and erased. The only trace of its powers remain in Zhang's invective, "gouzhi," whose startling yet banal figuration of yinfu as dogs and pigs registers the negative sentiment with which the compound was inscribed. There is also the indictment of Ximen's "perverse preference" (*pian xizhi*) for such bestial language (yinhua), and more sinisterly, a concluding phrase referring to the outcome of such a perverse preference. If the seductive powers of yinhua are such as to be sidestepped even in the reading/writing of it, how much greater are the powers of (one's desire for) women's bodies, "when Wang Liu'er and Pan Jinlian one day both get their hands on him, Ximen dies"?

The implications are clear. How one reads concerns life and death. At the very least, reading produces either an authentic and ethical masculine subjectivity (which ought to go with a filial longevity), or it reveals one's subjection and proximity to a state of feminized animal immorality (an ugly death is the only fitting end). This is, of course, to crudely summarize Zhang Zhupo's reading of Ximen Qing's reading of the yinhua spoken to him. In Zhang Zhupo's reading, the obliteration of the powers of yinhua and yinfu is the result, effected through his reading of yinhua and yinfu as purely literary constructs. His reading drains these obscene figures and voices of the emotive powers they evoke, not in anyone but precisely in a reading subject and position whose only similarity to the likes of Ximen Qing is an equally vulnerable sexualized male/masculine disposition.

Thus, yinhua are not so much shameful (*wuchi*) in and of themselves, nor even in being mouthed by obscene figures in shameful contexts (yinfu in bed), but rather particularly in how they are made to function in Zhang Zhupo's reading of Ximen Qing's reading of yinhua as a textual product. Shame is the meaning produced when yinhua is read, paradoxically, as the encoding of a literary technique (wenfa) that Ximen Qing misreads, half-literate oaf that he is. These misreadings will then cost him his life.[42]

Ximen Qing "perversely prefers" a mode of speech, which he takes too literally, by which he is then ensnared. His is the position of the sailors who hear the sirens sing, unable to read the song as text and test, to see self and siren from a position of authorial control.

The paradox lies in Zhang Zhupo's double vision of the text he reads with such investment. He reads JPM simultaneously on two levels, along two seemingly parallel lines that eventually meet and produce one text, what he calls "his JPM." This is what I shall label Zhang Zhupo's "parallactic" model of reading; a parallax denoting, according to the *Oxford English Dictionary*, the mutual inclination of two lines meeting at an angle. The two lines of visionary rewriting converge to produce one, "unified" text.

These two lines, or points of departure, in Zhang Zhupo's reading are, first, his concern with an ethical authenticity (zhen/jia), which he reinscribes as a major axis in JPM. And second, his elucidation of an aesthetics of the text, which aesthetics comprises the literary codifications (wenfa) discernible only to a few discriminating literati souls (or heart-minds). Alongside a moral reading against inauthenticity and hypocrisy, against the perversion of a sociofamilial ethics in terms of narrative thematics and characters, one finds Zhang Zhupo elaborating a theory of reading as practice, of literary artwork as the joint production of a reading/writing process, and finally, of composition as evincing the highest degree of authorial control. Thus, "the literary quality of this book [JPM] is such that it seems, in passage after passage, to have stolen the creative powers of nature [*huagong*] itself."[43]

> If you read JPM as a description of actual events [shishi] you will be deceived by it. You must read it as a work of literature in order not to be deceived by it. . . .

> If one tries to take in large chunks of it [JPM] at a time it will seem as tasteless as chewing wax. The only thing one will be aware of is page after page of women's talk [man pian laopo shetou eryi], and one will be unable to see it for the marvelous work of literature [miaowen] that it is. If one is not concerned with it as a marvelous work of literature, but only anxious to read about the marvelous things [miaoshi] it contains, one deserves only contempt. . . .
>
> Now, if benighted readers should succeed in convincing the rest of society that this literary masterpiece should be regarded as an obscene book and kept out of sight, then the labors of the author who drained himself mentally and physically to create this masterpiece not only for his own benefit but also for that of the gifted writers of all time, would be undone by vulgar men and would prove to have been expended in vain. This is what is meant by saying that the reader does JPM an injury [incriminates it].[44]

The paradox lies in erotic duplicity morally reviled and yet simultaneously aesthetically valorized. Yinfu and yinhua are not what they seem, they cannot be taken at face value, their beauty hides filth—in short, theirs is a moral depravity. Those who read them incorrectly, who invest too much in such figments of (whose?) fantasy—both "internal" readers such as Ximen Qing, and "external" readers such as the vulgar men who (like Ximen Qing) incriminate the text—are even more contemptible. At the same time, the text is not what it seems, it cannot be taken at face value, its apparent filth hides beauty—in short, this text is ethically uncontaminated and incorruptible. But this is so only for those who know how to read, who refrain from any emotional entanglement with textual figures and "marvelous (obscene) things"—excepting affective investment in the authorial resentment reinscribed into the heart of an obscene narrative as filial piety; only these chosen few will reap the proper benefits.

In other words, what differentiates the latter mode of reading from "vulgar," Ximen-style, gluttonous reading is yuan (ressentiment, resentment). Ressentiment ensures one's correct investment in a mirroring condition of and in the text—the condition of yuan that is read and interpolated as the founding moment of great literary texts, from Sima Qian down. Ressentiment also shores up, inoculates, reading/writing, thereby forming and safeguarding an authentically—that is, ethically—virile masculinity in the position of reader/writer and author who together produce and create a "new" JPM.

The author achieves his effects with such supernatural skill that the twists and turns of the plot beguile the reader without permitting him to see [mi mu] where the golden needle has done its work.... Whenever I concentrate my attention on this kind of writing, following its every twist and turn and exploring its structure, I feel just as though I were discovering the extraordinary sights of the five sacred mountains and the three islands of the immortals. I can never tire of pleasures such as these.[45]

What are the benefits for the initiate in such a reading/writing? What profits in question are at stake? From this passage, at least, one reads of the inexhaustible mental pleasures (wo xin le ci, pu wei pi ye) of such a project. This is rendered in the suggestive comparison to a physical trip to a marvelous place, a mountainous region with rivers and islets whose topographical outlay is then the source of a psychic sensual pleasure, wherein (in a more literal rendition) "I immerse my self/heart [xixin qizhong], twisting and turning in tracing the comings and goings of each beginning and end."[46] These twists and turns also figure narrative entanglements, what Zhang refers to elsewhere as "marvelous things"—here again, the source of pleasure, but a pleasure significantly qualified, made ambivalent in Zhang Zhupo's use of "mimu." Mimu, according to both the Kangxi Zidian and Hanyu Dacidian, in this particular compound form denotes a blurring of the gaze due to sand, or some such minute foreign object, lodged in the eye; a misty (but also, in Zhang Zhupo's use of it, mystifying) teariness.[47] It is a condition that would prevent "clear" perception of the "golden needle" that would discover the fabulated nature of this vision.

As the passage quoted above indicates, the mental and visual pleasures in JPM read by Zhang Zhupo the virtuoso reader follow the identical contours as well as comings and goings of those marvelous things that ensnare, to ultimately kill, Ximen Qing within the text and vulgar readers like him outside the text. Their eyes are permanently blurred and teary, and they learn to like it, evidently unable to distinguish the dust in their eyes from the needlework of the text.[48]

Reading the same marvelous yet obscene things, both Zhang Zhupo and vulgar readers obtain identical mental sensual pleasure. But what heightens Zhang Zhupo's pleasure while at the same time intermixing pleasure with pain, the idle leisure of reading with the labor of writing, is the distinctly refined, even cultivated masochism of distinguishing in the exact moment and place of pleasure the sand that is to be picked from one's eye with a needle. The immediate and unrefined pleasure of a readerly consumption

Tears of Ressentiment  133

of miaoshi, yinfu, and yinhua must be instantly distanced and mediated through the refined pleasure-pain of a writerly labor, of reading as if one were oneself (the author) re-creating the text from its conception.[49]

> If you read JPM as a work of literature by the author, you will still be deceived by it. You must read it as though it were your own work in order not to be deceived by it.
>
> Though you should certainly read it as though it were your own work, it is even better to read it as a work that is still in its early planning stages. Only if you start with the assumption that you will have to work out every detail for yourself in order to avoid being deceived will you avoid being deceived.[50]

Picking the dust, those marvelous things (miaoshi), from one's eye with the needle (jinzhen) that threads these things into a piece of masterly writing (shengong guifu zhi bi)—this is how I would characterize Zhang Zhupo's project of reinscription, of reading/writing a moral agenda and aesthetic legitimization onto a sinuous (ququ zhezhe) text filled with "women's tongues" (laopo shetou) in more ways than one. In Zhang Zhupo's reading, there is a political gendering of the text as well as of its reading/writing, a gendering crucial to the vindication and reinstating of both author and reader/writer as ethical, virile males.

## Textual/Sexual Politics

I would now like to repeat a question asked at the start of this chapter, only this time, not to examine the subjective workings and psychic gains of Zhang Zhupo's reading/writing practice but rather to query its significance in terms of sociopolitical profits, and its implications for a cultural, textual, and sexual politics, insofar as these intersect with the larger project of the renewed subjection and legitimation of an endangered species. What is at stake in this triangular articulation of yuanru (the resenting Confucian), yinfu (lascivious women) and wenfa, or *wenjia zhi bifa* (literary codification, the brushwork of a literary master), the mediating third term?

One tentative answer is: the circulation and dissemination of the vernacular embodiments of a seemingly comprehensive record of "bad women" (bu liang fu).[51] Thus, the circulation of a "new" vernacular sexualized discourse on certain "women" and male desire for them (hao nüse), widely disseminated as books in print among men (scholar-officials, nonofficial scholars, and commoners too) and perhaps even some women.

Undergirding this circulation is the normative construction of a readerly subject gendered male, classified literati (whether or not official), through a classical cultivation that includes the consumption of (and identification with) "female figures" in poetry and prose. These normative reading/writing subjects viewed the greatly increased dissemination and popularity of vernacular fiction from around the Ming Jiajing (1522–1567) as increasingly problematic, yet at the same time materially and culturally profitable. As problematic must have been the rise of a reading "public" not limited to those whose subjection occurs via the institutions of examinations and officialdom, readers who were increasingly nouveau riche merchants, clerks, manager–bond servants and shopkeepers, prostitutes, concubines, gentry women, and tradeswomen.[52] All are more or less parvenu subjects who had *not* undergone the disciplinary tutelage and ideological indoctrination of a classical education prior to the taking of examinations. Such subjects would be unable to read in the correct way, where reading feeds into and parallels an ethico-political cultivation and subjection of the self.

Half a century earlier, Jin Shengtan, in his definitively rewritten and commentaried version of SHZ, proffers the following by way of concluding "How to Read *The Fifth Book of Genius*":

> Formerly SHZ was read even by peddlers and yamen runners. Although not a word has been added or subtracted in this version, it is not destined for petty people. Only those with refined thoughts and feelings can appreciate it.[53]

The missing term here is "women," which occurs alongside "petty people" (xiaoren) in the *Confucian Analects* to name the two categories of persons with whom the gentleman-literatus would always have difficulties. Zhang Zhupo, who referred to his own project on JPM as following in the footsteps of Jin Shengtan, fills in that missing term (just as JPM fills in, extensively and in harrowing detail, for the inadmissible male-female erotic desires of SHZ):

> JPM is a work that women should never be permitted to see. Nowadays, there are many men who read passages out loud to their wives or concubines while taking their pleasure with them inside the bed curtains. They do not realize that even among men, there are few who recognize the force of exhortation and admonition or respond appropriately to what they read. How many women are there who are capable of responding

appropriately to what they read? What would be the consequences if they were to imitate, however slightly, the things they read about? Its literary style [wenfa, bifa] are not such as could or should be studied by women. If they are well educated enough to do so, they should be encouraged to read the Zuozhuan, the Guoyu, the Shijing, and other classics and histories.⁵⁴

Needless to say, women are innately incapable of becoming the discriminating readers/writers who can appreciate such an admixture of the sexually repulsive and morally edifying exemplified in the masterpiece that is JPM. Whereas (almost) all men may aspire to learning how to read in such a way as to heed admonitions hidden amid the visual and sensual, not one woman could do so.⁵⁵ Zhang Zhupo significantly elides the reason for women's inherent deficiency vis-à-vis texts like JPM, noting only the dangers of their taking such a narrative literally, identifying with its "women" and doing as these yinfu do, becoming yinfu in the process. Even with the classical education that (some) women may undergo, tutored readings in classical texts cannot save them from the perils of reading JPM literally. Against a feminized and devalued model of reading based on identification and mimicry,⁵⁶ Zhang Zhupo posits an alternative model grounded in the ability to benefit ethically from a visually and sensually enticing, but morally and literally mediated, marvelous writing (miaowen). What prevents women from obtaining such benefits? The sociopolitical subjection that produces yuan in the mode of Sima Qian. A particular ressentiment, then, is at this conjuncture sociopolitically configured as a "male" sentiment and further redeployed in the production of a "literati's" vernacular genre.

Earlier and contemporary "allegorical" readings of JPM, to which Zhang Zhupo refers but discounts, may thus be seen as the ideological forerunners, in a differently complex manner, of Zhang Zhupo's reading/writing. These allegorical readings have read JPM as a fictional narrative recasting of a "historical" evaluation of the last bad emperors whose excesses bring down the family/state continuum. Such allegorical readings read (bad) men for (bad) women, moral for sexual, and empire for family—oftentimes, with a resulting erasure of the less powerful term in the structuring dichotomy. Yet the ever-present potential for just such an "allegorical" (historical) reading has simultaneously justified if not legitimated its improper "carrier" or vehicle. The signified does not ultimately transcend the signifier. Rather, it is the distinction between the two that is recurrently made to serve aesthetic and ethical along with simultaneously sociopolitical ends.

It is within such a tradition of readings that Zhang Zhupo is able to commend the virtuous and revile the depraved (in the narrative), as if he were not at the same time speaking of gender and sexuality, the accidental virtue of the one (men) and the immanent, naturalized depravity of the other (women). "Virtuous persons are not lacking in JPM, yet these are all men; there is not one good woman."[57] In this ethical-allegorical reading of an "obscene" narrative, a reader's (manly) virtue cannot but find itself morally reinvigorated through the perusal of women whose penchant for immorality and sensuality is repeatedly reread/rewritten as natural and innate.

> Egregious, indeed, is the yin nature of women. Although it can scarcely be said that there are no examples of chastity among them, yet they find it all too easy to abandon it [shishou zhe yi]. Everything depends on the sort of family instruction each woman receives. . . . This is a matter in which the head of a family cannot be too careful.[58]

From this and the preceding two passages quoted, at stake in the rereading-rewriting, indeed literary encoding of popular vernacular works such as SHZ and JPM is the reappropriation of the representation of violently virile homosocial heroes and transgressively sexual women into an expanding elite cultural space. At stake is not only the reader-conditions for discriminating perusal and circulation but also new material and psychic benefits. The emphasis, explicitly or implicitly stated in these readers/writers' own "Dufa" essays, is on how to edit, reread, rewrite, and commentate these texts in ways that would make them less palatable to "even" peddlers and yamen runners, not to mention women. The subtext of their project is to ensure that homosocial heroes (SHZ) and sexually transgressive women (JPM) continue to mediate the symbolic exchange between elite men—an exchange that reconfirms cultural and gender/sexual powers, while simultaneously venting fears of disempowerment on all fronts. In short, the upshot is to make of "obscene things" (yaoyin zhi wu) metaphors and literature for the safe as well as hygienic pleasure of generations of discriminating gentlemen-literati to come.

> The three characters of the title JPM [literally, "plum blossoms in a golden vase"] constitute a metaphor for the author's accomplishment. Although this book embodies so many of the beauties of spring, every blossom and every petal of which cost the author the creative powers of spring itself to evoke, these beauties should be placed in a golden vase where they can diffuse their fragrance in a cultivated environment and adorn the desks of

men of literary talent for all time. They must never be allowed to become the playthings of the rustic or the vulgar.[59]

### Fictional Disemboweling

Alienated from the structures of institutional power in greater numbers and more diversified status (shenfen) than ever before, some literati may have found a way to vent their yuan or political ressentiment "in effigy."[60] They can then have it both ways: on the one hand, serving up morality garnished with se, while with the other, consuming se in the form of a superlative morality. Thus, the tales and records of sensually virtuous widows, and at the other end of a discursive continuum, the fictional retellings of the gory, sexual deaths of vamps at the hands of virile heroes. The moral and gendered subjection of the "reader/writer" is at stake; this subjection is both problematized and assured through the textual consumption of figures of women, virtuous and admirable in self-mutilating fervor or repulsive in sexual excess.[61]

Fictional figures of wanton women may therefore be seen as the obverse, the turning inside out, of historical recordings of virtuous widows. Both serve to exemplify sexual and moral anxieties not "their" own but residing elsewhere, in the subjects who read/write such women into powerfully problematizing literary existence (so powerful, sometimes, that critical "disembowelings" must then be undertaken, as in the case of Zhang Zhupo). These are the two poles of a discursive continuum, the dual deployment of complicit textual strategies.

I also posit that the moral and literary evaluative reading/writing of JPM that Zhang Zhupo embarks on works according to a parallactic logic. His reading/writing is one in which investment in and profit from the object (the text) are measured from two different positions (that is, the sexual/moral and the textual/aesthetic). In effect, the identity, or sameness, of the object of scrutiny (the obscene text) and the teleology of the reading/writing project (an ethical-aesthetic trajectory) ensure while producing complementary and incremental ideological effects. The moral and literary become two sides of one textual body, whose rectification is then both the responsibility and privilege of a select few.

The task is all the more arduous in that the textual body in question is dangerously effeminate (one is tempted to say queer; see chapter 8) because it is filled with "women's tongues," yinhua in various forms and voices, but also because its texture is of such curvature—so winding, flowing, and shimmering—that it easily leads the reader astray, filling his eyes with erotic tears. Both (yinhua and textual texture) must be corrected, and this can only be done by injecting into the text, via reading/writing, line by line, hui by hui, explanations that will undo the text's dubiously base feminine nature, and instill a proper dose of ethical and virile antibodies. Li An and Wu Song, filial and brotherly heroes par excellence, would be the internal agents of textual inoculation, while Zhang Zhupo's own paradigmatic readings would serve as the extratextual dosage necessary for safe journeying through this fictional topography. There are no "women" in this text; rather, there are phantasmatic forms said to embody certain types and particular base classes of women, along with a fictional form and language regarded as threateningly unmanly, unethical, even animal.

The transitional period from the Ming to the Qing has long been associated with the proliferation of precisely such degenerate forms, mostly erotic texts, some seen as more didactic and others tending toward the celebratory. The implications of this chapter are that in fact, "pornographic" texts—that is, texts that could be read pornographically, with yinfu the dust in the reader's eye, wherefrom tears of eros, but also pain and disengagement—are a production of precisely such recuperatory readings as Zhang Zhupo's, rather than vice versa. That is to say, pornography does not precede the discourse (and widespread dissemination of a discourse in print) that names it (yin shu), that brings its workings to light, that theorizes its difference from a correctly cultivated and ethical recovering or rereading. Pornography is not, as Zhang Zhupo and readers like him would have it, in the "eyes" and heart-mind of the beholder. It is inextricable from the hegemonic morality that writes (against) it. The early modern period produced, among other things, what can only be called a pornographic morality—a morality that produces its pornographic others. My aim in this chapter has been, at least in part, to discover the complicity of a late-seventeenth-century (misogynist) moral and pornographic agenda; how the one gives rise to the other—but not, and this is important, as in the oft-mentioned "orientalist" (or "essentially" "Chinese") logic of a complementary duality where the final overall balancing of the two annuls whatever particular effects and negotiations of power are between and within the two, thus producing an illusory state of self-adjusting dichotomies. Rather, in and through Zhang Zhupo's reading and reinscription, morality naturalizes depravity as sexually feminine and socially base, while an aesthetics of literary codification mythifies (hardens into mythology) a feminized and base sexual immorality as "women." Both projects work simultaneously, yet not in any arbitrary or accidental fashion, on producing specific transhistorical and transregional figures and forms—fictional yinfu.

 PART TWO: INTERVENTION

CHAPTER 5

Seduction: Tiger and Yinfu

After killing a tiger, to suddenly kill a woman, ah, nothing is so ferocious as a tiger, nothing so exquisite as a woman, no two things could be more different.... After killing a tiger to suddenly kill a woman ... as I read [of the killing of the woman], I choke and gape and lose all color; this is truly more horrifying than the killing of a tiger.
—Jin Shengtan, *Jin Shengtan Quanji*

Glaring at her [Pan Jinlian], he [Wu Sung] said, "I am a heroic man [*nanzihan*], with teeth and hair, who stands with feet to the earth and head against the heavens, not a pig or a dog that would defile the mores of men and the principles of human relations. Saosao [wife of my elder brother] do not be so shameless and stoop to such indecency. If anything should happen, my fists shall not recognize the wife-of-my-brother that I see with my eyes. Never do this again."
—JPMC

SHZ is a narrative of a secular warrior ethos.[1] In this sense only, it follows on and can be considered a "commoner" or "debased" sequel of the *Sanguo Yanyi* (or *Romance of the Three Kingdoms*) as a hallowed historical tale of the king, wizard, and warriors. The warrior ethos of SHZ is, however, in crisis in a world filled with perfidious state officials, evil money-loving men, and adulterous women.² It is even more in crisis in the persons of the heroes or *haohan* (the good virile man) themselves as quasi-criminals, "forced to become Liang Shan rebels" against the will of the state. The mandate of heaven recorded on a stone tablet listing the names of the 108 is, as Jing Wang has shown, fictional and mythic apparatus to justify and ideologically contain the paradox of bandit-outlaws as embodiments of the heroic code; or alternatively, heroes in the guise of unleashed heavenly (evil) forces to go with as much as to fight against evil times.³ Yet the paradox of heroic yet evil, or morally ambivalent, men seems particularly suited as oblique ethical-political commentary on whatever times the narrative could be made into something allegorically resonant and controversial.⁴ In a sense, though, SHZ is precisely about this dilemma, or what happens when a warrior ethos, code of practice, and structure of sentiment is *not* and cannot be securely aligned and in service to the son of heaven, the head of state. What form of narrative and denouement would befit such an ethos embodied in "common men" rather than ideal historical figures of a more ancient past who might attain godlike proportions (as Guanyu of the *San Guo* does in the Qing)?⁵ What kinds of plot and figuration could transform the common man into a hero, the embodiment of the heroic code?

It is in the narration of an already secularized (no longer linked to state service) and thereby residual warrior ethos *in disjunction* with an imperial state (Sung and Ming) that SHZ represents heroes who adhere absolutely to the heroic code of righteous loyalty (yi) so as to ensure the cohesion of a (mythic) communal and quasi-biological brotherhood. Although not entirely a society without a state in which all members are undivided and chieftainship is primarily a matter of prestige rather than power, the Liang Shan brotherhood is in relation to the society from which it has or dreams of having escaped egalitarian and communal. As a brotherhood of "warriors" (bandits, rebels, and heroes), the cult of virility and war (martial prowess) that marks the heroes is accompanied by a hatred and fear of women evocative of that noted in Pierre Clastres's *Archeology of Violence*.⁶ This is a hatred and fear different from, though not unrelated to the refined and reticent misogyny-erotophobia of some late Ming–early Qing literati.

For SHZ, and the first ten chapters of JPMC, violence is to seduction as the tiger is to yinfu (the licentious woman).⁷ This is a narrative and sociopolitical regime where the hero's counterpart (and trial) is beast and beauty, the animal and the lustful woman. It is a narrative and sociopolitical timespace to be differentiated from the shading of beastlike beauty (Pan Jinlian) into commodity acquisition for the rogue (Ximen Qing) turned mercantile collector or urban conspicuous consumer. Thus, in JPMC, and even more in XXJPM, yinfu are no longer only or simply embodiments of life-threatening tigers and counterparts to heroes who ritually kill them off, but are becoming with each episode and edition more and more players and agents in an urban domestic world traversed with mercantilism. The shift from SHZ to JPM might then be characterized as the shift from a "debased" warrior ethos (which inaugurates the martial art genre of narrative and structure of sentiment) to the representation of a world of commodity exchange in intimate male-female and master–bond servant relations. That the two narratives are so closely linked (JPM evolving out of one episode in SHZ) reinforces a shared historical moment as matrix wherein two seemingly opposed and contrasting "worlds" coexisted—one perhaps already only memory, myth, or tale; the other on the rise, directed toward present and future.[8]

*Violence and Seduction*

Violence is to SHZ as seduction is to JPMC. A series of (hard) seductions, full of sex and death, demonstrating what Jean Baudrillard terms seduction's "reversible power," wherein each party takes up a challenge and plays it to the end.[9] The basic affinity of violence and seduction, the symbiotic relation of SHZ and JPM, is from the start clear. The beginning of JPMC rewrites a particularly seductive episode of its "brother" text. Wu Sung kills a tiger; this is a bloody duel between a hero and fate, a man and tiger, life and death. Wu Sung challenges fate, the tiger, and death by refusing to heed the warning of the wineshop keeper. In winning this duel, he accedes to the ranks of "super-virile-men" who will seduce and compel by the very aura such an act of suprahuman force and courage grants them. And the first who will succumb to his (natural, innate) seduction, who will dare to challenge Wu Sung's mythic power, will be his brother's wife, Pan Jinlian. Her infamous seduction of this hero is in effect merely a counterseduction, a rise to the challenge of his power, an attempt to retaliate in turn. She succeeds insofar as she finally "forces" him to kill her, albeit as sacrifice at the altar of his dead brother and his own desire (for her/to kill her).

The two modes—violence and seduction—both potentially deadly, are above all modes of narrative operation. The two narratives that deploy these two modes of operation attempt to enact through such deployment two kinds of "rites": initiation and exorcism. At stake in SHZ is an ethical, homosocial (and problematically homoerotic) bonding of and between men—a bonding endangered as much by the (new) logic of money and its possibilities of changed social relations based primarily on considerations of exchange, profit, and commerce, as by the seductions of licentious women, yinfu in various guises.[10] SHZ would seek to neutralize such threats (defend against them?) by the repetitious enactment of diverse scenarios of male bonding, with violence (between men, and between man and woman) the major mode of lubrication and cohesion. It is as if violence could at once sublimate and transpose the homoerotic and male-female tensions disavowed in this heroic text. As for JPM, it is precisely the lingering power of licentious women—a power that extends to beyond their deaths in discourse—that JPM would seek to exorcise once and for all in a seeming excess of the obscene and immoral.[11]

The pretext for seduction, in the case of the episode that inaugurates JPM, is another seduction, a failed one, and for this very reason highly significant in its "originary" text, SHZ. In SHZ, seduction signifies both the final testing of a hero (for Jin Shengtan, Wu Sung is even more heroic than those several heroes that came before him, not the least because of the conjunction of "meeting a tiger" and "meeting the sister-in-law") and a revelation of the nature of licentious women in general (again, if only according to Jin's constant exclamations on how "truly" the author has literally captured his yinfu). Pan Jinlian is, throughout SHZ episodes, simply "that woman," a pejorative generic term that stresses her "representative" status.[12] As such, Pan Jinlian would seem to be merely a code name for an operation—of a double seduction and its violent undoing or overturn.

Seduction is in this case a double operation—in two movements—wherein the second repeats the first, and is at the same time a return to as well as completion of the first. Thus, in SHZ, Wu Sung "meets" his sister-in-law just outside the door-curtain to her house and seduces her "naturally," on the spot, exonerated of "guilt" by a text that assumes the (seductive) power of its 108 heroes. Likewise, she later unwittingly knocks Ximen Qing on the head with a pole, when letting down the same door-curtain, thus seducing him. Both Pan Jinlian and Ximen Qing are seduced "at first sight," and both will rise to the challenge and try to counter a prior seduction with a consecutive one—this time by tactics and maneuvers somewhat similar (to each other's), but to very different effect.

SHZ, however, would hide these two "prior" seductions and highlight the ones following to such an extent that it would almost seem as if the latter stood on its own, unprovoked and thereby doubly guilty. This dissembling on the part of the text will be made all the smoother by an accumulation, a buildup of narrative effect achieved by a not-so-subtle shifting of narrative viewpoint, apparent only if one juxtaposes the two episodes (neatly narrated in two sequential chapters) of the tiger and adulteress.

In the SHZ version of the encounter with the tiger, the narration clearly focuses on the hero, rendering his actions, thoughts, exclamations, and physical reactions. The tiger is, in the process of this narration, the other, that in which the hero will see himself reflected in even greater heroism; first a rumor, then the "subject" of a wanted notice, the other is both absent and present to the hero and reader, titillating "us" with the possibility of its appearance. But even when it does "appear" from behind a clump of trees, where neither the hero nor reader could have known of its "presence," the tiger is subsumed and ancillary to the hero, both an extension and reflection whose death will simply constitute the "logical" completion of its nonbeing. For the tiger's death completes the hero; through death, the hero appropriates the other in an amplification and expansion of self; a renewal (rebirth?) of the self, at the price of some (any) other. The killing of the tiger and subsequent rewarding of the hero serve as a reaffirmation of homosocial bonding. Thus, Yanggu county (the socius) is released from the spell of terror and death (the tiger), and at the same time, by means of this sacrificial killing, reabsorbs within itself as hero the exceptional one who killed the plague of the county.

Shades of an unlikely Oedipus? Unlike the mythic hero of the "Western" past, this hero on proving himself is not (re)admitted, nor recognized as king, but made to work in the county as a banal local commandant (*dutou*) under the prefect. The hero is here subjected to the logic of a formation (patriarchal bureaucratic monarchy) that is already alienated from an imaginary "sacred" king-wizard-warrior brotherhood bonding, to which he would return—though only in the guise of having been coerced to do so. Hence, the escapades of the 108 "heroes" who, unable to survive within a debased socius, are forced to set up an alternative utopian communal brotherhood whose hierarchy is determined not arbitrarily and therefore unequally but by "natural" means, with the most powerful and cunning being the "natural" leaders, those with the most prestige rather than political power. Wu Sung has, at this point, yet to prove himself a member of this quasi-sacred brotherhood; he is still accepted as a member of profane society. In killing the tiger, he has merely proven his extraordinary physical powers—enough to be immediately awarded the post of commandant. In killing a woman, he would prove not only his physical but also his extraordinary moral prowess (asexual virility) in so absolute a way that even the society on which such a morality is partially based and within which it is delimited finds Wu Sung's ultimately too expensive an act. Yet when working for the prefect, Wu Sung is merely one subordinate among many with few distinguishing features (apart from his physical force and supramorality). When it becomes a question of honor (between brothers), his heroic attributes merely avenge honor at the expense of his superior's economic connections and benefits. Thus, in profane society as it is represented in SHZ, heroic honor and/as righteousness (that which enforces and sacralizes homosocial solidarity) cede to the monetary ties between the prefect and the local merchant-entrepreneur (Ximen Qing) and adulterer.

In the interlinear commentary to the line where Wu Sung thinks to himself (just before running into the tiger and after realizing the danger of trying to cross the mountain pass alone), "If I go back, he'll [the winekeeper] laugh at me, then I wouldn't be a hero, I can't go back," Jin Shengtan notes: "To weigh one's honor with one's life, is that not exceptional?"[13] What would be exceptional, and what Jin implies here, is the either/or logic of "honor or life," an ultimate and absolute statement wherein heroic honor is the only weight or value of a life, and the two are equalized in their ethical incommensurability. But Wu Sung, after a moment's reflection, or not thinking at all, says, "What the prick are you afraid of [to hell with fear]! Let's go up and see!"[14] If the moment of vacillation seemed fraught with meaning for the reader (Jin Shengtan, for one, seized on it to declare the hero supramoral for properly valuing honor), it could in another reading seem much less so for the hero and text (thus the necessity of additional writing between the lines?). Wu Sung's second thought may just as well be simply a will to take life by chance, to gamble life against honor. This would be a quite different logic and regime (valuation) of life (and meaning) from the one written in by Jin Shengtan. The latter operates at the level of morality, in terms of an honor that can transcend and transfigure life, for which life would be a vehicle. (In somewhat the same manner, writing between the lines, editing and rewriting SHZ allows for the transformation of the text from "popular" but commonplace to a model for writing and manhood). Whereas Wu Sung's second thought might at least as much be a throwing of the dice, a challenge to life as fate, with honor as fantastic surplus, an extra bonus, for having conquered life (in the exceptionally virile and shall I say mirroring form of the tiger, and later in the more threateningly feminine figure of the yinfu).

Yet it will be precisely Wu Sung's identification with this surplus moral value (in SHZ) that will lead to his further mythification, as well as his forced expulsion from a socius that can no longer afford such values but nevertheless must pretend to. For if it did not lay claim to this surplus and pretend or purport to produce it, if only in fictional form, the very basis on which this sociohistorical formation and mode of moral relational reproduction rest would collapse of itself.

Wu Sung's encounter with his adulteress sister-in-law (Pan Jinlian) is the necessary correlate to his meeting with the tiger. If the latter establishes his claim to heroic status on the basis of a superhuman physical power, the former must test his "moral" (sovereign) power—that is, the extent to which he will preserve and avenge the homosocial ties that constitute the basis of heroism (and a patrilineal socius). The moment she is introduced in SHZ, one reads of how because her husband was "short and squat and had such a squirmish figure, and did not know the ars erotica" (fengliu), Pan Jinlian is driven to adultery and develops a penchant for "stealing men" (touhan).[15] (Recall how the tiger suddenly appeared, and was "both famished and thirsty.") This leads to trouble, of course, and Wu Da is forced to move to Yanggu county just in time to bump into his brother Wu Sung, patrolling the streets of town as its new commandant (dutou), his "reward" for killing the tiger. Wu Da brings the hero home, where the hero meets Pan Jinlian and the second scene of reciprocal seduction unfolds.

Just before the scene, there is the following description of Wu Sung:

> Readers: Wu Da and Wu Sung are the two sons of one mother. Wu Sung is eight feet tall, and handsome besides; he has the bodily strength equivalent to thousands of stone—if it were not so, how could he have killed that fierce tiger? As for this Wu Da, he is not even five feet tall, ugly to boot, with a weird-looking head.[16]

In this seemingly straightforward piece of authorial discourse, the two brothers are described—but imbedded within this depiction and already in operation is the mechanism that will lead to Pan Jinlian's attempted seduction of Wu Sung. This mechanism is at once revealed and concealed in a moment of reflection on the part of the adulteress (note how in this chapter, reflexivity belongs solely to the one who is seen as initiating action—in this case, Pan Jinlian). Thus, when Wu Sung is alone upstairs with his sister-in-law while Wu Da goes out for wine and food,

> the woman looked at Wu Sung, and thought to herself, "Wu Sung and he are brothers of the same blood, one mother, yet he is so tall and big. If I

had married such a one, I would not have lived in vain! Just look at that 'three-inch mulberry-bark manikin' of mine, three parts human, seven parts ghost, what bad luck! According to Wu Sung, he actually killed that big animal; he must be very strong, and he says he hasn't married, [so] why not tell him to come and live here? Who would have thought this would be where my fate lies!" [17]

Wu Sung's body is clearly the focal point of both narrative description and the eye and desire of the adulteress: both are transfixed by this body and the material force, the power and violence, it embodies. The very sequence of thought is highly evocative in its (dis)connectedness: death—animal—strength—marriage/sex—fate. The eroticism of strength and violence, its association with death (the killing of the animal) and copulation (marriage), and even further, with the ultimate death of the subject ("this would be where my fate lies" ominously prefigures Pan Jinlian's violent death, like the tiger's—who she would almost seem to envy—both at the hands of Wu Sung), seem almost too obvious, but also dangerously contagious.

Jin Shengtan notes the connections in Pan's thought, shaking with laughter, in two lines more veiled than the text itself.[18] After "he must be very strong," Jin writes, "she thinks of his strength! *juedao* [what a laugh]." And following "to come and live here," Jin remarks, "these two phrases linked together, *juedao*!"[19] What is Jin Shengtan alluding to that can or need be neither spoken nor named, but in the act of pointing to it, causes him to erupt in sidesplitting laughter? Or perhaps it is precisely this very same "it" that erupts from him, almost as if he were seized by a fit, or *seized by her fit*, touched by her desire. One is reminded here of George Bataille's linking of eroticism to death and laughter, and of how "sexual turbulence ... always disturbs us, sometimes shatters us, and one of two things ensues: either it makes us laugh, or else it impels us to the violence of an embrace."[20] As Jin Shengtan roars with (voyeuristic? vicarious?) laughter, Pan Jinlian is impelled to seduce Wu Sung, who had already seduced her with the subliminal erotic violence of his body and (the rumor of) his killing of the tiger.

Hence the symbiosis of these two episodes (in SHZ): killing the tiger as foreplay to decapitating the adulteress, Pan Jinlian (and adulterer, Ximen Qing, but his head merely sets off hers—though it also serves the more important semantic function of making the hero's vengeance too costly); an escalation of violence and a move from animal sacrifice to the sacrifice of woman.[21]

The crucial difference between these two episodes can only be seen from the level of a certain textual logic. SHZ is, in one sense, about the production and preservation of social stability, but from the perspective of those who the social and its hegemonic ruling-managerial class (scholar-bureaucrats in alliance with the state) deem marginal and basely heterogeneous—"heroes" outlawed from a society wherein their code is no longer socioeconomically viable, yet nevertheless commanding great affective power.[22] The possibility of such a perspective is already a sign of the emergence of an alliance of such forces at the bottom (of society), and this would tally with the historical reality of the late Yuan and early Ming eras. Especially interesting is the way in which these largely base heterogeneous elements are, in the course of the narrative (of SHZ), assimilated by and into the homogeneous socius (from which they had been expelled) through a transfiguration and transvaluation of base/inferior into sovereign/superior heterogeneity. Thus, the central politico-thematic motif of SHZ simultaneously serves as justification and validation of a paradoxical hero/outlaw status—*bishang Liangshan* or "driven to join the Liangshan rebels"; in other words, "driven to revolt." The term "driven" would here signify irreconcilable contradictions vis-à-vis society, which forces these "representative" individuals outside a homogeneous society and together. The power configuration formed on the borders of society would threaten not the homogeneous society in which it has no place but the sovereign heterogeneous ruling segment at the top of the social hierarchical structure, whose legitimacy lies precisely in a sacralized "heterogeneity" from the commoner masses (*baixing*), whether by inherited title, heavenly fiat, or both. The scholar-bureaucrats, or those who administer by prerogatives moral and cultural, constitute the swiveling neck linking the heterogeneous (sacralized) head to a homogeneous (profane) body. SHZ produces in/as narrative a process whereby rebels (base, heterogeneous elements) and rebellion are transformed as well as revalorized into heroes of and in service to the state (in alignment with the hegemonic sector at the top). Because of their "ennobled" difference, such heroes come to embody the highest values of the society from which they had been excluded, and which they will now serve and preserve, if not dominate.[23]

Wu Sung is just such a hero-rebel. Thus when Wu Da bumps into Wu Sung as the latter is being paraded through the town, the former exclaims how he has both resented Wu Sung and missed him. Why resentment? Because, Wu Da says, you used to give me a lot of trouble with your daily drinking and fights—I never had a month's peace with all the occasions I was called into court on account of some trouble of yours.[24] Wu Sung is different from his brother, Wu Da the pastry seller, in a much wider sense than is indicated by their quite different appearance and "character." For Wu Sung is, in everyday life—or before he kills the tiger—a bum, a drunk, useless yet different in an otherwise useful and production-oriented agricultural society. Whereas Wu Da is one of the urban, small-time peddler-merchant types.

It is through killing the tiger that Wu Sung is recognized for what he has the (physical and ethical) power to be: no longer a heterogeneous bum at the bottom of society, but rather a sovereign element, still different, although in an elevated and superior sense. Refusing and executing his sister-in-law will accomplish his transfiguration. Wu Sung will then have proven his ethical/spiritual power in not only withstanding evil (in the banal figure of seductive woman) but in exorcising it from the socius.[25] Through this bloody act, he will have accomplished the subtextual initiation into the brotherhood of the 108 heroes of Liang Shan: by enacting his allegiance to the values of honor and loyalty, and by sacrificing two heads at the altar of these transhistorical quasi-religious values.[26]

In this way, meaning (honor/righteousness) is reestablished in SHZ, as is temporary stability and justice in Qingho county, after the beheading of the adulteress and sentencing of the hero-avenger. Both hero and adulteress have been as if expulsed from society, though the latter only in order to further work/steal in complicity with it, in its name, and on its behalf; while the former, the woman, seems gone for good.

Wu Sung the hero, rather than Ximen Qing the adulterer, is in this narrative of a residual warrior ethos the licentious woman's "real" counterpart, as the agent of her expulsion, the disciplinary master to her errant bond slavery, the seducer of her final seduction to death.

*Operation One*

I now turn from SHZ's warrior ethos to JPMC's urban mercantilism, or the story that postponed Pan Jinlian's "sacrificial beheading" to no good end—wherein some reader(s)/writer(s) was sufficiently intoxicated to rewrite her story sometime in the last hundred years of the Ming. The narrative is told not from the perspective of those who belong, by moral right, to the top/center (this would be the task of commentarial insertions, such as Zhang Zhupo's, and the righteous readings of twentieth-century critics), nor quite from the perspective of its base heterogeneous elements (familial bond servants and small-town prostitutes). Rather, it is more from the perspective of those who are in the middling sector, drunk on wealth trickling down, alternately fascinated and repulsed by it. One early reader conjectured that it reads like the daily records of some poor resenting teacher hired by a wealthy upstart family, whose revenge is transformed into the writing of this tale. This is then certainly not Pan Jinlian's, the licentious woman's, perspective but one that was fascinated and repelled by her cunning, speech, and ways and powers of opportunistic seduction.

The dual main "works" of SHZ comprise Wu Sung's killing of the tiger and his subsequent repudiation/sacrificial killing of his sister-in-law. Whereas in JPMC it comprises Pan Jinlian's (incomplete) seduction of Wu Sung and its reversal, Ximen Qing's seduction of Pan Jinlian.[27]

The first "seduction scene," infamous in SHZ and only slightly altered in JPMC, I will translate as literally as possible (from JPMC). Wu Sung had moved in with his brother and sister-in-law at the explicit invitation of the latter; only in the JPMC version does Wu Sung notice from the very beginning how "the woman was too enchanting, and kept his head down."[28] The hero is pensive, or he is self-disciplined. Yet Wu Sung's first reaction to Pan Jinlian's looks clearly acknowledges the latter's power of fascination—an acknowledgment that is at the same time a negation and refusal to respond.

A month after Wu Sung moved in, Pan Jinlian decided to put her plan (of seduction) into operation. The time is the eleventh lunar month; it has snowed for several days, and the world is clothed in silver and jade. On the appointed day, Pan Jinlian hurriedly sends off Wu Da, and asks her neighbor Wang Po (Dame Wang) to buy some wine and victuals for her; then she goes to Wu Sung's room and makes a fire, thinking the whole while to herself: "I will decidedly stir him up (*liaodou*) today; he's sure to be moved (*dongqing*)."

> The woman stood cold and alone under the blinds, and saw Wu Sung walking home in the snow. She pushed up the blinds, and smiling, said, "Shushu [young uncle], are you cold?" Wu Sung replied, "Thank you Saosao [wife of my elder brother] for your concern," entered the house, and took off his hat; the woman made as if to take it, but Wu Sung said, "No need for Saosao to take the trouble," brushed the snow off the hat himself, and hung it on the wall. He then unloosened his waistband, and taking off the outer vest of parrot-green silk, entered his room. "I waited all morning, why didn't Shushu come back for breakfast?" said the woman. Wu Sung replied, "An acquaintance invited me to breakfast, and just now another wanted me to go and have a drink, [but] I didn't feel like it and

came back instead." "Then please warm yourself by the fire," she said. "Yes, I will," whereupon he took off his boots and changed a pair of socks, put on warm slippers, picked up a stool, and came to sit by the fire.

The woman had earlier on told Yinger [Wu Da's young daughter by his first wife] to close and lock the front door, while she did likewise with the backdoor. She then brought some warm wine and food into the room, and put all on the table. Wu Sung asked, "Where is my brother?" "Your brother has gone out as usual to do his business. I will drink with Shushu," said she. Wu Sung then said, "Thank you Saosao, but I'll help myself." The woman also brought up a stool and sat near the fire. On the table were several dishes; the woman took a cup of wine, held it in her hand, and gazing at Wu Sung, said, "Shushu, please drink this wine." Wu Sung took the cup and drank it all. The woman poured another cup, saying, "Such cold weather, Shushu, why don't you drink a pair?" Wu Sung said, "Please help yourself," then took the cup and drank it straight off. He then poured a cup of wine [and] handed it to her; she took it and drank, then poured another cup and placed it in front of Wu Sung. Her bosom was partially uncovered and her hair half let down. She smiled ingratiatingly and said, "I hear that Shushu keeps a singing girl across from the town hall?" "Don't listen to such nonsense, Saosao, I was never that kind of person," said Wu Sung. "I don't believe it. Shushu's heart says one thing, his tongue another." "If Saosao doesn't believe me, go ask my brother." "Aya, what does he know? He lives as if in [a] drunken stupor; if he knew of such things, he wouldn't be selling baked cakes. Please drink another cup." And she poured another three, four cups for him. The woman too had drunk at least three cups, and the wine so warmed her desire, how could she control herself? Her passion like fire, she could only talk nonsense.

By this time, Wu Sung had begun to realize what was happening and kept his head down, refusing to respond to enticement [*doulan*]. The woman rose to warm more wine, and Wu Sung stayed in the room, stirring the fire with the poker. The woman soon came back, and with the bottle of warmed wine in one hand, she pinched his shoulder with the other, saying, "Shushu, aren't you cold, with so little on?" Wu Sung was already quite uncomfortable and made no answer. Seeing him silent, she snatched the poker and said, "Shushu, you don't know how to stir the fire. Let me stir it for you; once it becomes as hot as the bowl of fire, then it's fine." Wu Sung was by now more than half uneasy [*jiaozao*], but still remained silent. The woman took no heed of his restlessness, and throwing down the poker, poured a cup of wine [and] drank a mouthful, leaving more than half a cupful, and gazing at Wu Sung said, "If you have the heart, drink the half cup of wine I've left." Wu Sung snatched the cup and threw it on the floor, saying, "Saosao, don't be so shameless." At the same time, he pushed her so hard, she nearly fell. Glaring at her, he said, "I am a man, with teeth and hair, who stands with feet to the earth and head upholding the heavens, not a pig or a dog that would defile the mores of men and the ethics of human relations. Saosao, be not so shameless and [do not] stoop to such indecency. If anything should happen, my fists shall not recognize the Saosao that I see with my eyes. Never do this again." The woman's face turned crimson at being thus told off, and she called to Yinger to help clear up the table, all the while muttering, "I was only playing; it isn't worth being taken seriously. You wouldn't know a favor if you saw one."[29]

In this scene, seduction takes the form of ritual wine drinking; and the seductress performs the role of the establishment (or household) drink mate, one of whose duties is to accompany, urge, lubricate, and ornament the master-patron's drinking of wine. The master-patron never drinks alone, as it were, drinking itself being both a substance and function of dual power relations. When drinking, the adjunct-person (woman) is a never negligible "accompaniment" to the master-person's drinking (like peanuts), as one who serves, facilitates, and enhances by whatever means necessary the latter's pleasurable consumption (of wine or other comestibles). Wine is here the main object; the woman is the attendant object (part object, part subject). If there is a guest, then he is company of another register, of "equal" value as self, a potential opponent, one's equal and therefore one's rival in the challenge of sociality that drinking ritualizes. All three may be present: the host (master), the guest (honored person), and the (feminine) attendant-lubricant. For the host and his guest, the man and his rival-friend, the onus is both to outdrink the other and to cause him to outdrink himself; thus in the various games devised expressly for this ritual of wine drinking, there is the same seemingly senseless imperative to an excessive consumption of wine — it no longer matters by whom. Although he who drinks the most would seem to be the "winner" of this game, the one who temporarily reigns as most powerful in the circle of drinkers, no one who participates really "loses" in that all are drawn within the magic circle of excessive consumption and reciprocal loss/gain. The resulting orgiastic state of nonindividuating (homogenizing) drunkenness is sufficient to induce a temporary communal euphoria and effervescence. (It is partly for this reason that wine and food, without women, are so important in the brotherhood of SHZ.) In such a ritual, it is he who refuses to take part in shared consumption, or she who refuses to service that consumption, that is at once ostracized and outcast, perhaps even punished.[30]

It is within the rules of such an enchanted game that Pan Jinlian strategizes the seduction of her brother-in-law (who unknown to her, belongs to a nonurban world and ethos of consumption where women are the single taboo item). If the hero agrees to drink with her, to be served by only her (with no one else present), to drink from her hand and finally of her cup (of her remnants, her "waste"), he will have become subject of and to her game. He will have signaled a willingness to partake of her and other parts of her, to make of her his plaything, just as he had played with the tiger. Yet Wu Sung does more; a worthy adversary to the seductress, he is even more (than she) the crafty seducer. For in the certainty of his power (of seduction), he allows her to lead in the game (as a good hunter would his prey), following as if insensibly, until they reach the point of no return: consummation or complete reversal. Thus it is that in this scene, there is the operation of an incomplete seduction and its almost complete reversal.

The transgressive power of Pan Jinlian is that of a half-object become more than half-subject, of a "drink mate" who dares to incite and lead the ritual of drinking, of a woman (bondmaid and now wife to a lowly biscuit peddler) who plans and plays to the end the seduction of a "superman." The narrative voice of JPMC itself records the trajectory that accounts for Jinlian's dangerous propensity *not* to keep to her inferior place as wife to a lowly peddler; half a person to Wu Sung's larger-than-life status. "Now Wu Sung was a man of straightforward temperament and took this to be no more than his sister-in-law's cordiality. How could he have known that this woman had started her career as a serving maid and become adept at the art of playing up to others?"[31] *Guan huei xiao yier,* or habituated at the little touches that signal and entice in their message of intimate care—these are the techniques of servitude both necessary in one of Pan's gender and status, yet also dangerous in their potential ensnaring of the "true" subject of their cloy attentiveness. Finally, Pan Jinlian will remain trapped within the woman-sex-phobic narrative logic that created her, to ultimately be immolated at the altar of an honor she was from the first compelled and seduced to defile.

Seduction also operates as a mode of conversational intercourse. Thus, in the "to and fro" of the adversaries' conversation, the time-space specific to small-town seduction is composed. In this particular instance, however, it is destroyed by the hero's sudden reversal to monologic or heroic set speech: "I am a man" is a speech directed not so much to his opponent as to the readers. This bit of speech functions in much the same way as do the various narratorial interjections addressed directly to "readers." It is as if the hero must at this fraught and dangerous moment solicit the reader's full attention and identification, lest the reader has gone over unawares to the enemy, bewitched by the wiles and wine of the seductress. The narrator similarly intervenes in and interrupts the text, as if to warn the reader against becoming too entangled within the latter and, at the same time, as a half-serious declaration of authorial clearheadedness—I'm not deceived and I know what she's up to, but you out there, beware! Simultaneously, fully contrasted are the two time-spaces or regimes of value, knowledge, and consumption inhabited by the hero and his seductress. The latter is playful, and in her rebuttal even goes so far as to mock her opponent's refusal to play (as in, "You don't know how to play back, do you?"), thereby refusing to enter his world wherein she belongs among inhuman pigs and dogs who do not "know" the mores and ethics of man.

Nevertheless, the hero is seduced insofar as he cannot or does not act until the very last moment (consummation as the drinking of the dregs of her wine), when he is impelled to react against her decisive move. His enigmatic silences, brief responses, and what amounts to inaction up to that moment all constitute mere reactions that make him complicit, willy-nilly, to the inexorable movement of seduction. There is even, dare I say it, a slight degree of vicarious and hidden pleasure, which adds to the violence of his final (declarative) outburst and first action, as he pushes her away almost to the floor. Witness here the force of a retroactive guilt, supplement to denial and negation. He can no longer control himself, and must speak and act, as much to defend himself against himself as against her. One recognizes here the vehemence of morality on guard, both against its own hypocrisy and the game within which it sees itself, inverted yet nonetheless mirrored.

Alternatively, the hero has a sudden attack of acute moral panic—a function of the refusal to be seduced, while at the same time constantly seducing and seeking seduction. This would then be the source of that paroxysm of strength with which he killed the tiger, bare-fisted. In this case, the same fit cannot be likewise brought to consummation (death) since he can neither get drunk (with the tiger, so to speak, serving him wine) nor justifiably kill her right off as she is, after all, his sister-in-law and has only been caught playing with none other than himself. He must thus wait for his prey, to catch her in yet another act of seduction, with someone other than himself. Meanwhile, he succumbs to a burst of self-defending morality, in lieu of orgiastic killing, to assuage a moral thirst for blood.[32]

Instead of blood, then, there are half-revealed bodies: she, with her breast half uncovered, the little flesh exposed all the more enhanced by the clothing that sets it off and hints metonymically at its presence. Her hair disorderly and half down: this is an erotics of transgression; the suggestion of order disturbed, discipline unloosed, exciting more than total and simple disorder. There is also here an attention to detail and process important to any seduction: for seduction neither begins nor ends, but would go on like this, in small bite-size bits and halves. In this dual game, the hero plays his part as well, though with a nonchalance that would feign ignorance or disdain—yet for all that, not the less provocative. Indeed, Wu Sung starts undressing as soon as he enters the house. He begins with his boots, socks, and then the green vest. He has so little on, for winter, that she cannot resist touching him, pinching his shoulder, asking if he is cold: foremost on both their minds (for he understands and begins to be restive) as well as on the surface of the text is the presence of his body and perhaps hers.

There is also, at the same time, the orchestration of a crescendo of *shushu*'s (though translatable as "young uncle," when rendered into English it does not quite carry that peculiar note of "the child-object" captive and captivating within the sound of these two repeated syllables) as Jinlian seizes every single opportunity for speech to call him.[33] The sheer frequency and perhaps seductive power of this repeated evocation stands in for the relative absence (as yet) of her body. She is as vocal as she is textually invisible (except for that one line concerning half a breast and not-quite-disheveled hair). SHZ's austere commentator Jin Shengtan judiciously notes the shameless number of "uncles" she utters—thirty-nine in his SHZ version; while Zhang Zhupo less than a century later counts the ones in his edition of JPM—twenty-seven—the same number as in the JPMC version. These two commentators' obsessive attention to this detail of "naming" attests to the power of this particular naming's affect. There is beyond the "craft" of a writing that can so powerfully (re)construct a scene of seduction, an erotic tactics of "naming." This is a tactic, moreover, whose affect arises from the addressee's hearing his own sociosymbolic power—represented by and embodied in a title/name—evoked again and again in vertiginous repetition. It is a sort of auditory mirroring effect: instead of seeing and being fascinated by the image of himself in the other, the man hears his power echoed incessantly from the seeming depths of the other's desire for him.[34] To count these "desiring calls" would then amount to countering their fascination, breaking their mesmerizing spell. Wu Sung, however, counters with his own mode of counterseduction by turning the other cheek; hence he observes her charm and lowers his head, hears her call and turns a deaf ear—in effect goading her on.

Likewise, Ximen Qing will (later in the text) demand from his innumerable partners in sex that they call him "dada," avowing themselves abjectly his, as if fascinated by his power.

Operation Two

Exit Wu Sung, who has not only moved out of the house but has also left the town on an errand for the county magistrate. Enter the (other, second) seducer, full of irony and ease. He will not refuse to play; quite to the contrary, he will seize every opportunity, and in the absence of any, will create such situations as will impel full play to the death.

> One day in the third lunar month, the sun shone in springtime splendor. Jinlian dressed up prettily [and] could hardly wait for Wu Da to leave the house to take up her position behind the bamboo screen that hung over the front door. At about the time of his return, she would lower the screen and wait for him inside the house. That day something was fated to happen, and a man passed by the doorway at just that moment. Without coincidence there would be no story, and marriage is always predestined. The woman was holding the forked stick with which to let down the screen when a sudden gust of wind blew the stick from her grip so that it fell precisely onto the hat of a passerby. The woman anxiously smiled in apology, and noticed that the man was about twenty-five or twenty-six and cut quite a dashing figure. He wore a tasseled hat, golden filigree hairpins, a pair of jade rings inlaid with gold, a long green silk jacket, and on his feet, fine-soled shoes and socks of the purest white cotton. On his legs were jet drawnwork kneepads, and in his hand a gold-flecked Szechuan fan. All of this enhanced a figure like young Zhang's with the face of a Pan An, a delicious man, so romantic, who from beneath the blinds, threw me a look. The moment he was hit by the stick, the man stopped short and was about to loose his temper, when turning his head, he saw a beautiful and seductive woman. She had: hair in a bun as black as the raven's wings, brows arched clear and curved as the crescent moon, cold

*Seduction: Tiger and Yinfu* 159

and clean almond eyes, a fragrant cherry mouth, exquisitely straight jade nose, thickly rouged cheeks, a face round as a delicate silver bowl, a slender figure light and lissome as a flower, jade-white scallion-shoot fingers, a cuddlesome willow waist, a soft dough-white belly, tiny turned-up feet, fleshy breasts, fresh white limbs, and most of all, something squeazy-tight and creased-red and fresh-white and thickly-black, who can tell what it could be? The beauties of this woman were such that he could not look his full, and how was she adorned? . . .

On seeing her, the man half-dissolved, his anger flew off to the kingdom of Java, and he immediately put on a smiling countenance. The woman, knowing she was in the wrong, folded her hands before her and bowed to him deeply, saying, "The wind blew the pole from my hands and wrongly hit the gentleman. Please do not be angered." The man set his hat straight with one hand, bowed, and answered, "It's quite all right. Will the lady please not worry?" They were seen by the next-door tea shop neighbor, old woman Wang, who laughed and said, "Which gentleman is it, who should pass by this door? Well hit!" And the man laughed too and said, "Yes, it is my fault, I have offended, the lady must not be vexed." The woman answered, "The gentleman must not be angry." The man laughed again, pronounced a very loud "yes" [nuo], and said, "I would not dare," all the while fixing roguish eyes—used to flirtation in years of dalliance—on the woman's body. As he left, he turned his head and looked back seven, eight times before finally swaggering away, waving his fan. Thus the poem that says, "On a breezy fine day out for a walk / beneath the screen he chances on her timid charms / merely because, as he leaves, he gives her a meaningful glance / her heart's desires are aroused to commotion without end."[35]

The representation of seduction is like the choreographing of a pas de deux; it is a constant shifting of perspective so as to compose a flow of meaning filled to bursting with desire. There is nevertheless in this writing of a seduction a marked emphasis, a dominant perspective. The narrative tends toward the seducer's (the man's) point of view, to finally identify with him as the subject of the narration. This stress betrays the text's affiliations and "gender," so to speak: this is a gendered narrative, telling a man's tale, whose projected reader must likewise be male. (Recall Zhang Zhupo's instructions on how to read JPM: "JPM is a work that women should never be permitted to see. . . . How many women are there who are capable of responding appropriately to what they read? What would be the consequences if they were to imitate, however slightly, the things they read about? Its literary style are not such as could or should be studied by women."³⁶)

Note the importance in this section of writing of the eye and its gaze: the scene of this seduction turns on a series of looks (leading to anachronistic thoughts of a cinematic camera). The representation of seduction is structured as a series of looks: with the look comes a distinct being-looked-at-ness, a function of the power and potential violence of the former.³⁷ The first eye is the woman's, who sees the man; her pole had accidentally hit his head as he was passing by, and thus, she sees him from behind and "looks" at him, his every piece of clothing, including his socks, without however going beyond and beneath. Or rather, the narrative does not allow her to since from the previous scene with Wu Sung, it is clear that she could and did think and "look" from clothing to flesh. For the male object of the gaze, description, and language stop at clothing and ornaments, preserving a decorous invisibility of the male body, maintaining a discrete silence (as yet) on its "secrets." The second eye is the man's, who turning his head, perceives the woman, and in a very extended gaze, more than twice the length of the woman's "look," sees through her every piece of clothing, the narrative helping him to image and impel a (textual) striptease on the spot. It is as if she exuded a particular and permissive being-looked-at-ness that compels the looking eye to aggressive penetration and decomposition. For if the male body was, in the previous moment, still unseen and whole, the female body is now seen in a virtual lyric dismembering. Her figure is described from hair to foot, and from clothing to flesh back to clothing (the last part, in verse, is not quoted in this excerpt) with the logic of striptease: saving the "best" for last. Hence, the centripetal item/object of textual revelation must be the vagina, as good a guess as any.

This is represented in terms of colors and textures, evoking the sensation of the body part in a contiguous (nonpunctuated) set of four trisyllabic phrases, whose second and third syllables are identical, repeated onomatopoeic modifiers (*jiujiu, zouzou, xianxian, yinyin*) of the first term—the first denoting quality (jin or tight), and the other three, colors (red, white, and black). This particular line in a sense "climaxes" a penetrating description; it closes the first part of the male gaze on an ecstatic and extended sixteen-character phrase, the reading of which may leave the reader breathless (the phrases depicting other corporeal items at most numbering nine—for raven-black hair and crescent-moon eyebrows) or nearly so. This is a veritable climax of anticipatory pleasures, which language, in the glossolalia of repeated identical syllables, approximates by taking pleasure in its own sounds. Meaning, like the woman's body in its clothing and discrete wholeness, is an obstruction and a nuisance, and must be simultaneously preserved and destroyed—evoked only to be decomposed; mimicked in order to better assimilate and become—in a visual-textual consumption, a feast for the eyes and mind-heart. In a way, Pan Jinlian is reconstructed here for the first time (each such literary stripteases would enact this reconstruction of "woman," as if for the first time): from a variety of "name-objects"—raven, moon, almond, cherry, jade, flower, scallion, willow, and finally plain flesh—most of which are edible and quite worn with metaphoric use. "Woman" is at most a pastiche or collage, composed of the most mundane things. Yet this does not lessen the pleasure of consumption, or that of reading; woman is thus, if anything, made even more "feminine."

But there is a third eye to be reckoned with in this scene of full-fledged, small-town seduction: the eye of the witness, the voyeur, the one who withstands seduction by becoming and embodying its very function; the eye of old woman Wang, the tea seller, go-between, and meddler-in-affairs; the eye of the mediator, middleperson, broker, parasite. It is her gaze that will interrupt and disrupt the play between these two; her interjection breaks the spell between them as well as between the text and reader. The seducer wakes up and must leave; the writer/reader is as disinclined as he. Thus the breaking into poetry, as if prose could no longer sustain the weight of all this desiring-commotion.

This position of the third—the interceptor, mediator, parasite—of any dual sociosymbolic relation will be an important one in the text's working out (undoing) of seductive strategies. Parasitic tactics such as Wang Po's will ensure the interruption and disruption of meaningless dual play: turning the game into a triangular one, where the interceptor may gain whatever the outcome for the other two involved. The parasite has nothing to lose and merely plays with influence/power (capital) intercepted and stolen from one or the other of the two parties involved—without the dual parties' knowing, of course. The parasite plays always in the name of a "host" body, riding on its back, goading it along, pretending or aspiring to be its extension and instrument. The astute parasite will then alternate between two "hosts" making each believe the mediator is adding to his/her chances of winning. In JPM, as in any centripetal text/space, parasites abound and proliferate. Ximen Qing is the exemplary host body for any number and variation of parasitic agents, and Pan Jinlian quickly learns to play both positions (object and parasite-mediator) with consummate artistry at will.

Those women of inferior positions, half-object and half-human as they are seen to be, fail to do so at the risk of what little chance of survival they might otherwise have had in these particular centripetal texts/spaces.

The narrative logic, for all its centripetal force, thrives and can only be sustained through repeated parasitic interventions. Hence the nearly four chapters that go into the making of the successful seduction of Pan Jinlian by Ximen Qing. Without Wang Po's eyes that evaluate and capitalize, and words that enhance and ensnare, where would Ximen Qing and the likes of such small-time libertine-entrepreneurs be? At the same time, the presence of mediating and intercepting conduits-persons ensures a counter-centripetal narrative force, as well as the diversion and minor redistribution of resources (money, cloth, grains, and so on).

## Big Rats and Seductresses

> From the Jiajing and Longqing reigns [1522–1572] on, powerful and high-ranking houses have led the way in extravagance and excess. Those who wear ceremonial sashes and scholars' caps excel in craftiness and arrogance. Every day they give rise to strange stories; every year they start a hundred new enterprises. Herd boys and village elders wrangle at being "big rats"; girls in the fields and crones in the brush crave to be seductresses. The teaching of relationships has been wiped out; the constant force of morality is gone. Taking up my brush in the midst of this, I burst out between laughter and anger.[38]

In the last hundred years of the Ming dynasty, the morality that kept relationships in their hierarchical positions, and persons in their properly and reciprocally superior-inferior, parent-child, master–bond servant, men-women places, seemed to dissolve and erode in the midst of commercial wealth and its attendant consumption practices. It is in this kind of socio-economic matrix that the particular power of material seduction and erstwhile nonfetish objects of consumption appears suddenly enhanced and magnified, perhaps even enchanted.

JPM records this enchantment; in the eyes of the bygone hero who does not belong to this urban world, and whose warrior ethos marks a disjunctive time and space. In the eyes of a new breed of masters, libertine-rogues, and merchant-entrepreneurs, "orphans" (without the restraint and constraint of existing familial-social ties) driven to establishing and making the most of bureaucratic, commercial, and sexual connections, sometimes headily mixing all three (as in Ximen Qing's dalliance with Lady Lin).[39] In the eyes of a new breed of bond servants, more than servants or former bondwomen, the likes of Wang Po, Pan Jinlian, and Chunmei, some of whom have learned the art of capitalizing on their inferior status, perfecting techniques of servitude, to finally mediate and broker opportunistically between differential positions of power to ensure survival, even success. And in the eyes of the judgmental few, moralizers in the position of scholars at large, wanting no truck with any of the previous categories of persons, yet surrounded and perhaps daily fascinated by all of the above.

> Although Sungjiang has been called licentious and extravagant, we never before had the term "woman hanger-on" [nu bang xian]. From the time that Saleswoman Wu [Wu maibo] came on the scene and saw that the physician Gao Heqin had no offspring and rented herself out to beget a child with him, she became famous as a woman knight-errant. Families of wealth and official connections competed to invite her in. Wherever she went, the houses treated her as especially precious. On the pretext of being a trader, Wu made her daily living as a hanger-on in rich houses. She was skilled in making sexual devices and aphrodisiacs and leading people to indulge themselves in wine and wallow in pleasures. From this she accumulated an estate of several thousand taels. She came and went in sedan chairs and was called "Triple Wife" [san niangzi].[40]

CHAPTER 6

Red Shoes, Foot Bindings,
and the Swing

Do not covet things and be weakened by them. Do not get used to things and be controlled by them.
—Sun Chengen

All those who read this book should at this point reflect deeply on it, and they will find in a world of obscenities and desires the lessons of the ancient sages.
—ZZJPM

Why has the refined and subtle disciplinary-bondage, or disciplining the bondmaid-concubine sex of the Grape Arbor episode been so long ignored, gone undetected, or been dismissed with an unexamined "obscene"—if not for the secret edification and vicarious enjoyment of nearly four hundred years of cultivated and therefore superior readers/writers in complicity with its affects along with the semantics these reinforce? This is a narrative pleasure all the more effective in donning the mask of a punitive gender-class morality that both activates and justifies it. This is also how bondmaid-concubines are punished for familial maneuvering and sexual opportunism, via precisely the sex that constitutes their sole resource and recourse to power in the intimate politics of polygamous everyday life.

*Red Sleep Shoes*

One late spring night, Ximen Qing, having drunk and eaten with Pan Jinlian in her rooms, prepares to go to bed with her when suddenly he notices the gauze silk sleep shoes with red shoelaces she is wearing. "Ayia! How come you're wearing these shoes? They're ugly and strange to look at," he exclaims. "I have only one pair of red sleep shoes, one of which was soiled by that little slave who found it [in the garden]. Where am I to get another pair?" says she. "My child, tomorrow, sew another pair and wear them. Didn't you know, I—your da—wholeheartedly only like [those who] wear red shoes [or, likes to wear red shoes], looking [at them] my heart loves/desires."[1]

Ximen Qing's pronouncement is surely the most perfect statement of a subject's (scopophiliac) desire, its ambivalent wish for those who wear red shoes and to wear red shoes oneself, its powerlessness in relation to the object desired, and the gaze ("looking") that mediates and positions this imperative desire. The gaze signifies fascination: with red sleep shoes, and metonymically, the cloth-bandage that wraps the feet, and the bound feet that these "feet wraps" at once designate and hide. It is a fascination whose syntax, like the sentence that gives it voice, is peculiarly (simulating oral speech) fragmented and repetitious, almost without an object: I—wholeheartedly—like—wear red shoes—looking—heart—loves/desires.

And yet, the entire narrative of JPM could be said to rest on (to have its gaze more often than not fixed on) feet—the bound feet (or "golden lotus") of that most promiscuous of women, Pan Jinlian, whose name appears in the first character of the narrative's title (JPM). One recalls her first arranged meeting with Ximen Qing at her next-door neighbor Wang Po's, who expertly coaches Ximen on the crucial sequence, the ten steps, whereby to "ensnare" this female (*cier*). The last decisive move, according to Wang Po, is to accidentally cause his chopsticks to fall on the floor beside her feet, and before picking them up, to pinch her feet—her golden lotus. If she cries out for help, then all is done for; if not, "then she must be willing."[2] As it turns out, when Ximen Qing pinches her on the tip of her embroidered shoes, she begins to laugh and says, "Guanren, don't be rash. You've the heart; I'm willing too. Do you really mean to hook up (*gouda*) with me?"[3] Three years and eighteen chapters later, after Jinlian had already become Ximen's "fifth," during a feast celebrating the Lantern Festival at which the whole family is assembled—with all six wives, the daughter, and son-in-law—Jinlian again touches and is touched, this time by the rakish son-in-law, who in receiving a glass of wine from Jinlian's hand, is pinched on the back of the hand by Jinlian and, in return, kicks her foot. This time as well, Jinlian smiles and softly asks, "Strange-oily-mouth, what if your father-in-law should see?"[4]

The father-in-law doesn't, but someone else does—someone who had only recently entered the household, as the new wife that mistress Yueniang (the first wife) had purchased for the bond servant (*jia ren*) Laiwang, whose wife has just died of consumption. Yueniang had paid five taels of silver, two ensembles of clothing, four bolts of cloth, and several hair ornaments for this woman. This woman, who is delegated with the other bond servants' wives to work in the kitchen at the back, is incidentally also called "Jinlian," a name that Yueniang changes to "Huilian" to avoid embarrassing confusion with Pan Jinlian, or "Pan the fifth." Huilian not only shares Jinlian's name but is "two years younger than Jinlian," and moreover, "her feet are even smaller than Jinlian's."[5] She is clearly from the very first Pan Jinlian's narrative double, not only in sharing a name that must be disavowed but in closely repeating (with slight though significant differences), on a seemingly lower-class/status level, Pan's life story and disposition.

Song Huilian (or Jinlian) is the daughter of Song Ren the coffin maker and was first sold into Vice Prefect Cai's household as a bondmaid, but because she was considered a troublemaker ("she connived with her mistress in adultery") she is sold again, this time as wife to Jiang Cong the cook.[6] Jiang Cong is often called on to cook at the Ximen household, and this is how Laiwang hooked up with Jiang's wife. Later, when Jiang Cong is accidentally killed in a fight over money, his wife asks Lai Wang to have Ximen intervene for her (she is able to do so because of their liaison); as a result, the murderer is caught and her husband's death avenged. After this, Laiwang gets Yueniang to buy Huilian for him, without of course telling Yueniang the "whole" story. Huilian turns out to be clever and quick (shades of Jinlian again), coquettish and seductive, and once part of the Ximen household, soon begins to simulate the appearance and doings of Ximen's six wives, especially Meng Yulou (the fourth) and Pan Jinlian (the fifth): "[Huilian] would pad her hair comb extra high, fluff her hair very full, draw [curled hair onto] her temples extra long, and serving tea in the upper chambers, was caught in the eye of Ximen Qing."[7] Though it makes little sense in English, this is how the sentence literally reads in Chinese; I think this is important to note because the mode accentuates "catching her in the eye" as both metaphor for and prefiguring of the hook on that is to follow, planned and put into action by the only full-fledged "subject-person" of the household, Master Ximen Qing.

Huilian is Pan Jinlian's double, yes, but a slightly farcical one that is repeatedly overdrawn—hair too high, speech too quick and presumptuous, too apparently greedy for whatever she can get out of making it with the master of the house. In short, she oversteps her place (as anyone would, in her place, with enough cunning and wit); as a bond servant's wife and kitchenmaid, her place is even lower than that of the personal bondmaids of the wives. What the narrative seems to add to her account (and representation) is a certain overcompensation for this arbitrary social gap between her and the wives of Ximen Qing. This overcompensation produces a "subjective" depth (of psychological motivation: she is highly competitive and quick to emulate those who she aspires to, though given her lack of "breeding" she cannot but overdo). It also produces an "objective" (narrative) distancing effect (thus she can become, in turn and according to narrative needs, farcical or tragic, whereas Pan Jinlian is never either farcical or tragic, but always only too fascinating/frightening). It is as if the narrative simultaneously veils and emphasizes their proximity, their likeness. Both are born into the poverty that results in early bond servitude, and both are marked from the first by beauty and wit. And these latter qualities, at a particular moment in time and space, determine their superior "value" as human commodities as well as enhance their chances for self-marketing and self-advancement.

Soon after (noticing her), Ximen sends Laiwang off to Hangzhou with five hundred taels to buy a birthday gift—a splendid embroidered dragon robe—for Grand Preceptor Cai, plus clothing for the family; the trip would last at least a half year.[8] One afternoon, when Yueniang is attending a birthday party at the Qiao's, Ximen returns home slightly drunk, bumps into Huilian in the doorway, pulls her to him, and kisses her on the mouth, murmuring, "My child, if you do as I wish, you can have your pick of headdresses and clothing."[9] The woman does not say a word, pushes his hand away, and walks on straight ahead. Ximen then goes to Yueniang's rooms and has the latter's maid Yuxiao take a bolt of blue satin to Huilian with the following message: "Dad says that if you follow [his wishes] in this matter, whatever you want, dad'll buy for you. Today since *Niang* [mother] isn't home, [he] wants to meet with you. How do you feel about it?"[10] On hearing this, Huilian smiles without answering, then asks, "When will dad come, so I can wait for him in [my] room?" Yuxiao replies, "Dad says with all those guys [servants] watching, he can't come to this room, [so] he wants you to secretly go to the grotto beneath the rock mound [in the garden]; [since] nobody's there, it's a good place for a meeting."[11]

The "accidental" head-on collision sets up the sequence of moves that will eventually bring the master and bond servant's wife together for sex. Within this particular sequence (and here one can no longer speak of, nor find seduction, but rather a predetermined violation of exchange), the subject position is unambiguous and unchallengeable. For Huilian is Ximen's already, in name, body, and person, if not yet in sex. The doxa that seeks to deny and prohibit sexual contact between masters and slaves' wives is, in the words of the narrator addressing his "master-readers," founded precisely on the fear (of and for the subject as master of the household) of subsequent uncontrollability and disorder (within the subject and his household). Such a fear, with the fascination that borders it, would provoke as much as—perhaps more than—it inhibits; transgressions constitute not a denial of the taboo but rather its affirmation and completion.[12] Thus, the very ethics that regulate familial and sociopolitical relations in the name of loyalty and filiality, especially the latter in this case, mark the potential turning inside out or indeed mere literal extension of all such relations into the realm of incest. In the most extended sense of the term, JPM might be said to be about "incest," or its inverse value, filiality. The generational gap ordained between gendered bodies marked as superior and inferior in the social and familial spaces of intimacy become, in sexual exchange, annihilated. Disorder reigns.

One suddenly remembers how less than two years and ten chapters ago, Ximen bumped into Li Pinger, who by this time had become his sixth wife (fifth concubine). But that accidental meeting of two bodies in a doorway was quite different, not only in terms of the positions and relation of the two bodies that collide but in the outcome of the collision. Li Pinger was the wife of Ximen's neighbor (social equal, even superior) and "brother," Hua Zixu. Before that, she had been concubine to Minister Liang (Liang Zhongshu), and had been bought for Hua Zixu by his uncle, a eunuch (social marginal) at court (highly placed). Though the wife of the nephew, she was said to have been a favorite of the uncle until the latter's death (shades of impotent sexuality?). The eunuch had also bequeathed part of his fortune directly to her, leaving the rest to his nephew. Her value was thus to be calculated not only in terms of the succession of connections-relations through which she had "passed," among which she had circulated, accumulating with each different symbolic value and material resources. It was to be calculated also in terms of the body she herself possessed, pale and fleshy, and signifying the ultrafeminine as it was seen to be by Ximen when he suddenly bumped into her in the doorway of her home. He was "so struck [with her beauty], that his souls scattered beyond the skies," and he bowed deeply with his hand clasped before his chest (here was a beautiful woman with the added enhancement of power and wealth). "The woman acknowledged his bow, turned around, and went back indoors."[13] Yet she immediately sends out a bondmaid, who will act as her body-extension, while she stands behind the doorway with only her voice and a coyly half-revealed face to signify her presence. In this seduction-sequence, it is the woman who seduces actively, and initiates meetings and sex. This woman may do so since she has both power and money—as the wife of a eunuch's nephew and the onetime concubine of a minister. The stakes of this seduction will be high, however, inasmuch as it will eventually become a domestic game of four principal players (mother, son, concubine, and the father) and several bit players, all of who will die violently in a kind of relay of death (see chapter 7). But perhaps that is the outcome of all such play? A woman may win, but not for any duration enough to constitute anything more than anecdotes.[14]

One cold early spring night, while all the women of the house are drinking in Li Pinger's room, Ximen Qing returns home and arranges with Huilian to spend the entire night with her—hoping first to put her up in Pan Jinlian's rooms, then at Jinlian's refusal and suggestion, deciding to spend the night in the grotto beneath the rock mound in the garden. He then asks Jinlian to send her maid Qiuju to prepare the bedding for them beforehand. (Note once again the parallel "excess" sense of self, the pronounced agency—for one of bondmaid origins—in both Jinlian and Huilian. Huilian had actually expected the master to come to her rooms, the servants' quarters; Jinlian refuses to let her rooms be at the master's service.)

That Ximen and Huilian have not yet been able, after having met for sex several times, to find a place/space where they can legitimately spend the night and bed together, indicates not only the extent to which this particular relation (between the master of the house and his bond servant's wife) is spatially transgressive (no room can easily be made for her) but also the base marginality of Huilian in the household order of persons and things. For the division of space-time in the polygamous household is a matter of power and territoriality, and in one sense, for the subject-master, space orders or determines time. Hence, the first wife's rooms are located farthest in from the outside and are called the "upper" or "inner" chambers.

The second and third concubine's rooms are located to the first wife's left and right, and spatially indicate their "place" in the order of wives. Pan Jinlian and Li Pinger, the fifth and sixth concubines, occupy rooms nearest the outside gate, and belong to the "outer" and "front" part of the domicile. This last auxiliary and "excessive" luxurious addition is adjacent to the splendid garden (part of Ximen's bout of conspicuous consumption) built by Ximen Qing after having bought his neighbor's (Hua Zixu) house and land. In a sense, Pan and Li are territorially as well as symbolically nearest the "borders" of the household and most clearly "extravagant objects of consumption" like the garden, and the stories of how they "married in" and will eventually "leave" would seem to doubly reaffirm their precarious place and uncertain status. Each time Ximen returns from the outside, he will usually go to the first wife's upper chambers to change his clothing, eat and drink, and listen to her report of domestic affairs. He then chooses where he will sleep the night, an act that immediately becomes invested with meaning and power, and is the form whereby domestic politics and struggle is played out.

Wives and concubines are allotted at least rooms to call their own, wherein they are expected to put up and pleasure the master whenever he should so choose (he also has the "responsibility" to bed with one of them, once in a while, or so goes the theory). In contrast, prostitutes have their particular street in town, and "houses" and rooms that men with the money may "rent" for whatever period they should wish (although these too are distinguished according to wealth and clientele).[15] And even the wives of the small-time innkeeper or wine seller, in their small "independent" households, may take in lovers so long as their husbands are either away or willing to act the pimp.[16] Yet the bond servant's wife is territorially most vulnerable and marginal. Once she begins to have sex with the master-father, an intimacy of bodies that differentiates wives and certain favored maids from all other women within the compound, the fact that she is not any wife's maid (which would give sexual contact with the master a certain legitimacy and less potential power, since such contact is usually considered as adding to the interests/power of the wife in question) but a servant's wife marks her position as both too similar (as an inferior's "wife") and too "distant" from the master's wives for the latter's comfort and peace of mind.

Thus, when Pan Jinlian first dares to discover (again showing her agential will to power "inappropriate" for one who is not considered fully a person) Ximen Qing with Huilian in the grotto, Huilian hurriedly leaves on hearing the rustle of Pan's skirts outside—not without coming face to face with Jinlian in the doorway, flushing, and mumbling something about looking for Shutung, Ximen's boy attendant. Jinlian immediately confronts Ximen with her knowledge, putting the matter at its baldest: "We're [the wives] all available and waiting, and you [Huilian] have the gall to get in line! This old mother's eyes [I] just will not let it pass."[17] Pan Jinlian is half bluffing, of course, for she would never be so stupid as to think she (the part object/subject) could singly gain control or influence over Ximen's (the subject's) actions, but her best bet is to play the part of "the knowing third"—that is, the one who by becoming the third in this (and any) dual relation, transforms it into a triangular formation and is thereby able to maintain a certain partial leverage in that line-relation (between the "two"), which had almost succeeded in keeping her "outside." Ignorance would have meant powerlessness; to feign ignorance would be to forgo a mediating position of power, whereas the tactical revealing of knowledge is an oblique power that creates the space and position for future angling and maneuver. Huilian, as the "weakest" point of the triangle (the newcomer, the outsider), is at the greatest disadvantage, and ever since bumping into Jinlian outside the grotto (the new, less legitimate favorite caught by the old legitimate favorite), is especially conciliating to Jinlian, serving her as if she were the most important person in the household next to Ximen Qing—as she is, for Huilian at least.

Several weeks later (returning to that one cold early spring night), Ximen asks Jinlian to let him spend the night with Huilian in Jinlian's rooms. He is obviously refused; this would be ceding too much, with too little to gain. Jinlian instead proposes that they stay in the grotto, and sends her own maid to prepare the bedding and stove for them (a conciliatory move). She then proceeds, after making sure they have settled in for the night, to "take off her headdress and softly enter the garden, to listen to what they might say in private."[18] The glimmer of candlelight flickers through the window as Jinlian hears the laughing voice of the woman say to Ximen:

> "It's so cold, let's go to sleep—Why do you keep looking at my feet?—Haven't you ever seen ones so small?—I haven't got any shoe tops; who'll buy some for me?—I can only look at others sewing on their shoe tops, without being able to sew one for myself." Ximen replies, "My child, no matter, I'll buy you several shoe tops in as many colors tomorrow—Who would have thought your feet are even smaller than your fifth mother's." And the woman said, "Compare me to her! Yesterday I tried on a pair of

her shoes, and they even fit over my own—It's not really size that matters—as long as the pattern of the shoe looks nice." And Jinlian listening outside thought, the slave-whore, let me listen to what else she has to say. And she hears the woman ask Ximen, "Your fifth wife, how long have you [been] married [to] her? Was she a girl [virgin], or was it a second marriage?" "She's also a second timer." "No wonder she's such a know-it-all. So it's also a love match, a morning-dew marriage." And Jinlian hearing this outside was so angry her arms went limp and she couldn't move her feet, and said to herself, "If we let this slavish whore stay inside, she'll end up pushing us all down and out." And just as she was about to get angry and make a row then and there, she thought of how Ximen had a bad disposition and might bolster that whore's face, but if she were to restrain herself now, that woman might yet refuse, knowingly, to admit to anything. Bah, we'll leave a sign to let her know and speak to her tomorrow. Whereupon she went back to the garden gate, and taking a silver pin from her hair, used it to lock the door from the outside and angrily returned to her rooms.[19]

Small feet—shoe tops—your fifth mother's feet—know-it-alls (promiscuity?)—morning-dew marriages (temporary affairs). The overheard dialogue between Huilian and Ximen Qing provides, for both the one who listens outside and the ones who read (in secret?), a too meaningful trail of associations, the tracing of which will leave the eavesdropper paralyzed with anger and inhibited aggression (the release of which will only come after Huilian's death, with the cutting up of the shoe the latter had so wanted), and the reader, with perhaps the same paralysis and a more diffuse aggression—directed at once at eavesdropping women and promiscuous texts.

In inviting Ximen to look at her feet, and stressing their small size herself, Huilian is betting on what they will get for her: new shoes, other gifts, and hopefully the continued fascinated gaze of the master-subject (who has a wonderful penchant for golden lotuses). Placing her wager, she was certain of winning insofar as the other bettors were absent. She thought she was alone with the bank. But bound feet—and the parts of the body they stand in for—are valued in comparison with other bound feet, and Ximen the buyer-collector "reveals" himself in noting how these feet are even smaller than "your fifth mother's." In thus referring to Jinlian, he is of course indicating her generational advantage to Huilian, but this advantage has already been challenged, if not subverted, by his recognition of the latecomer's smaller bound feet. Huilian adroitly acknowledges this challenge, and even gains an edge, by pretending modesty, gesturing refusal—how can I, so lowly, compare with her, your wife?—only to be unable to withstand immediately pressing her advantage by mentioning how she had tried on Pan's shoes and how they had actually fit over her own (see, they really are too big for me). The resonances of this exchange seem too obvious. And in the (hidden) ears of Jinlian, they must have sounded insufferably presumptuous and taunting. The two (feet owners) are now on a level, in a potential duel as it were, with Ximen the arbiter/buyer/fetish consumer. Jinlian, who had previously so carefully and precariously maintained her advantage through knowing the secret between the two lovers, and strategically using this knowledge to subtly control both (Ximen always arranged his meetings with Huilian through Jinlian, and Huilian had to continuously kiss up to Jinlian in preemptive fear of her jealousy), now suddenly finds the tables turned and herself playing on a level with as well as against Huilian. There is also the humiliation of finding this out in a way that could only put her at further disadvantage. Jinlian is reduced to fuming, to a paralyzed silence, and vows to win the next bout—to the end.

Jinlian's first retaliation—a silver hairpin as a strategic sign of presence, and wager accepted—is meant solely for Huilian, since only she will heed this sign that is intended for her and signifies both warning and threat to a foe. Ximen is now firmly in the place of the ascendant third, the one who dominates/determines the value-position of the other two points of the triangle. The next morning, when Huilian finds the door locked on the outside and recognizes the hairpin as Jinlian's, she knows that she has been heard and must answer/pay for whatever she had thought so assuredly gained the night before.

But how and what had Huilian, temporarily at least, won? Not the attentions and gifts of Ximen Qing but rather a seemingly arbitrarily secured connecting line that, like a conveyor belt, assured an endless provision of all kinds of leftovers and sometimes even, with some maneuvering and luck, a substantial place for life (subject to the caprice and lifetime of the master, that is), or a concubine status. This had already happened with Jinlian, whose biscuit-peddling husband had only to be poisoned away, and the more difficult "heroic" brother-in-law enticed into murdering the wrong man (instead of succumbing to the snares of his sister-in-law) and exiled into hard labor. If Huilian was eager to ensure a relative continuity and stability of the connecting line, Jinlian, having already assured the permanence of the link, had now to ascertain its continued and, if possible, ever stronger effectivity. Such an effectivity was measured by the degree to which the object could subject the subject; or how an inferior positionality could, through a certain mode of linkage with a superior one, accede to the latter's power and parasitically wield it at second hand, perverting and reversing it, at (invisible) will. This tactic of utilizing a superior other's power, as if one were only part of the superior other (and this sentence reads strangely for it is written from the parasite's viewpoint, whereas that viewpoint is said not to exist, ought not exist), is termed "the art of maneuvering power" (quan shu) and is identified by Zhang Zhupo as the form of power at which Pan Jinlian excels (just as she excels at certain techniques of the bedchamber).[20] One is reminded here of the countless women-commodity-things, or eunuchs and other such problematically feminized villains of history, who were said to have been experts at quan shu, and begins to wonder whether this was not another means of naming and discrediting the playing with power by those in inferior positions, and whose power has therefore to be both explained and defamed.

The problem with quan shu is that it is no mere resistance of power, but an active using of it in the contrary, or reverse, direction. It is a sending it back along the same connecting line whence it came, except in such a way as to make the receiving point accept it *as if it were its own*. This is very near to the workings of seduction, or the seducing of the subject *by and through itself*, via each and any part-object. The inferior who resists without any return relay of power, twisting power to serve the nonperson "self," might also be the one who self-destructs, and whose self-destruction can and must then be read as a righteous accusation of an otherwise unaccusable superior position-person. Herein lies the difference between the comic tragedy of Huilian, who finally commits suicide and is to this day read as the bond servant who is ethical in a way that shames her superiors—thus embodying a "universal" lesson—and Jinlian, who is fascinating, dangerous, and profoundly executable, exorcisable.[21]

How is such a reversal of power activated? In this particular episode of the text, it is activated by the fascination of the subject with shoes and, by extension, bound feet, feet wraps (and if books could smell, I would wager for a certain kind of smell as well).[22]

What fascinates Ximen Qing are Huilian's feet, bound even smaller than Jinlian's. In gazing at and playing with these feet, Ximen Qing adds one more pair to his collection of diverse object-fetishes. The latter are all part-objects: their fascination for the subject lying in how they are at once linked to and separated from him, interlinked with his body, representing its bor-

*Red Shoes, Foot Bindings, and the Swing* 175

ders but also how these may be threatened and attacked/provoked only to be further extended and strengthened, repeatedly, with each "new" part-object of desire. Ximen Qing repeatedly seduces, or is fascinated by and collects/assimilates women—their bound feet in red sleep shoes—pretty young boys, and various curios as well as the most refined of foods. The discourse of this assimilation is represented as primarily visual and orgiastic (ecstatic); in the language of the text, he uses the same fascinated gaze to as if devour (a visual devouring—*guan wan*, or literally to "look at/play with") the repeated in/out movement of his penis in a succession of mouths, vaginas, and rectums along with the curios that he acquires.[23] What this "devouring-copulation-contemplation" affords him is a constantly desired sense of satisfaction, with an emphasis on the satiation and plenitude of this particular mode of happiness: each time "he felt a heart full of happiness."[24] The affect merely repeats the bodily effect: an assimilation (of a body part, food, or thing) that gives a sense of repletion and expansion. It is as if such a collecting subject-body could expand powerfully, indefinitely, excessively. The moral doxa that this transgressive "feasting" completes, and that in turn founds it—without which it would lose its very force of desire—is the ecstatic implosion/death of the bloated body/subject concerned.

On another level, the reader too would read/consume the text with as much avidity as Ximen devours his "things." Hence, as at least two commentators have recorded, the very title of the narrative would signify its being yet another thing for the collector-literati: plum blossoms in a golden vase—something only to be found in the connoisseur's book room and certainly not appreciable by the vulgar, least of all by women. For only the collector-literati is sufficiently equipped (with cultural capital) to discern the "truth" residing in such a profane and obscene "thing-text" (see chapter 4).

### The Swing

A swing is built, one fine spring day just before the Qing Ming Festival, in the large garden at the front of the Ximen compound, adjacent to the rooms of Pan Jinlian and Li Pinger. Henceforth, as the text narrates it, the women of the house (Yueniang, the five concubines, the daughter, and favored bondmaids) will play with this swing when the master is away.[25]

The swing is a game to be played, not alone but with others—the very playing of which will ascertain each player's sociosymbolic status and power as well as their interrelations. For only those few with the power of ownership (Ximen, Prefect Song, Grand Preceptor Cai, and so forth) can afford to play, while those who play with them, share in and are carriers of this power as its precious objects of consumption and reproduction. Thus Ximen will "play" at Chinese soccer with "professional players": the more or less destitute men, commoners and/or slaves, who go around the whorehouses looking for an appropriate master-subject with whom to play—or rather, around whom (and/or whose favorite prostitute) these men will play so as to provide pleasure and a suitably inferior contrast—a fake game, whose force is clearly centripetal and whose outcome certain from the outset. In return, these men are thrown some money and leave content.[26] But a swing is different; here is an object, mechanical and undifferentiating. It will not tell the pleasing and stabilizing "difference" between the women (as professional soccer players will) who swing but instead may well activate, in the accelerated movement of its mechanism, an accompanying vertigo and nausea for the lookers-on (readers included) if not the one swinging. It is another mode of fascination: that of the gaze being pinned down, fixed, by the rhythms of a moving object, the first stages of a light hypnosis and/or as loss of control.

Fascination, as textual strategy, is induced through the welding together of suspension and repetition—these two constituting the two poles between which the textual rhythm alternates and perceptibly accelerates. Without this pendulum movement, this interchange of rhythm, stasis, and boredom would ensue, and fascinated consumption-reading cease. In narrative terms, suspension is the "slowing down" of narration, or the writing of seemingly "irrelevant" details and "hallway" scenes (in between "rooms"), characters, and events—anything that would seem to momentarily suspend and distract one's interest and attention. But suspension is on the same continuum as cumulative, accelerating repetition; it can, at any moment, reverse gear into repetition and vice versa.[27]

Thus, the setting up of a swing in the garden and the gathering together of all the women (that matter) in the household—namely, the wives plus Jinlian's maid/accomplice Chunmei (the second character whose name is the last character of the title, JPM), and Huilian the "newcomer," who had so quickly moved from kitchen to upper/inner chambers, to play/swing in the garden with the wives. Of them all, only Jinlian laughs while swinging, irrepressibly, joyously, so hard that her body is bent double—and she slips, falling and almost making Meng Yulou (fourth "wife,"/third concubine, also called "Meng the Third"), who had been swinging with her, fall as well. Yueniang then delivers a lesson on the dangers of laughter and laughing for women, especially while swinging: look at what happened to Jinlian, and it happened to a neighbor's daughter with whom "I" had played as a girl; poor thing, she slipped and landed sitting astride the seat and was later sent back the next day of her marriage in shame because she was not a virgin—herein lies the danger of laughing while swinging. This is a little story with a moral, both at the level of the narrative and metanarrative. For the "writer" had signed himself (or themselves) the one who laughs; and the narrative was supposedly "named" after three women, one of whom laughs excessively, obscenely (Jinlian), while another seems often to cry (Li Pinger), and the third is perpetually, angrily resentful (Chunmei).

What makes Jinlian laugh? Perhaps it is the swing that carries her body off the ground and swings it rhythmically to and fro, as if in mockery of another kind of movement, with another body—the movement itself seeming a crossing and recrossing of invisible boundaries (of bodies, of territories). It is pleasure, of course: the pleasure of swinging standing up, above the heads of all present, and defying the constant danger of falling off, the centripetal pull of the firm ground. In laughing, Jinlian (as she is wont to do) dares to take pleasure from and in a situation where such pleasure is forbidden, except for those few who have the subject power/position to afford it; for whom in fact such pleasure is reserved, as with the "collecting," the buying up and accumulating, of land, women, and objects. In this text, and in such a world, women (all part subject-objects) had best not laugh at all, or may do so only when given the license, as in the guise of a professional prostitute, one who gives pleasure by assuming the form of pleasure in the body. This, finally, is the linkage between women's laughter and their hymen: one can only laugh once, and that one time will define one's value and "womanhood."

Of all the women who swing that day, only Jinlian laughs, Pinger is afraid, and Huilian shows herself to be a true "swinger." For Huilian can swing standing up by herself, needing none to accompany or push her. She quickly attains the highest limit and provides a memorable sight, with her scarlet bloomers and five-colored anklets showing and flying in the wind. The danger is that she is in no position for this nondependent pleasure. And in fearlessly enjoying the moment, she inadvertently (again and again) trespasses on others' (the wives') prerogatives. One of these "others," the only one to equal Huilian's daring on the swing, will—framed within a narrative logic in which both are doomed from the start—challenge her to a duel to the death.

(Incidentally, the modern Chinese verb for swinging [dang] is a homophone with the first character of the compound phrase "loose woman" [dang fu], thereby perhaps accidentally strengthening the association of "swinging" with a woman's [lack of] morals, and physical movement with ethical disorder. The one [movement] may lead to the other [disorder], but conversely, so could the latter arouse the former; thus failure to "cultivate" one's body, taming and breaking it in with discipline, may well give rise to a corresponding loosening, erring, and eventual dissolution of the heart-mind. That, at least, is what Zhang Zhupo notes with regard to the recreations of the women of the Ximen household: how can a first wife, the mother of the household, initiate unprofitable and nondisciplining play, and not only that, invite the son-in-law into his father's women's quarters to push them at swinging, precisely such an action as would induce the dangerous swaying of his heart-mind.[28] One is led to surmise, in reading Zhang's reading of this particular incident, on the concomitant swaying of a certain reader's heart-mind, set going by a reprehensible narrative filled with laughing, swinging, and who knows what else.)

Just as the women are swinging in the garden, who should return but Laiwang, Huilian's husband, who had been conveniently sent away to Hangzhou. It is his return that declenches the showdown between Jinlian and Huilian, played out in the alternation between modes of speech, each mode seeking to fascinate, confuse, and sway/influence.

The showdown proceeds in three rounds, with the first round set off by Laiwang, who, having learned from his mistress Xue'e (Ximen's least-favored third and most lowly wife, who had once been a bondmaid, and was neither beautiful nor witty) of Huilian's affair with Ximen, and Pan Jinlian's mediating role (putting them up in the garden and so on), in a drinking bout with the other servants, tells all:

> How Ximen took his wife in his absence, and how Yuxiao acted the pimp, and how they even took to spending entire nights together, put up by Pan Jinlian. They'd better not bump into me, for I'll strike him with a white knife, and pull it out red, and I might very well kill that Pan whore as well. I'll only die for it anyway; see if I don't do as I say. That whorish Pan, to think that when she killed her first husband, Wu Da, and her brother-in-law took the matter to court, who helped her out of trouble by going to Dongjing [the eastern capital]? Wu Song was sentenced to military service at the borders, and now she's on safe ground and enjoying herself; she'd actually incite my wife to take a lover. She and I are enemies for life.

They say, if you do it, then don't stop halfway. I'll tell her when I see her. Even the king can be hit, if you're willing to risk death.[29]

One of the other bond servants present, Laixing, who had long held a grudge against Laiwang for having been given the profitable errands that had previously been his (before Ximen had begun to notice Huilian), reports on his tirade to Pan Jinlian in the presence of Meng Yulou. "Yulou felt as if she'd suddenly been dipped in a basin of cold water, so shocked was she, while Jinlian flushed bright red and gnashed her silvery teeth."[30] She immediately tells Meng Yulou all about the liaison between Ximen and Huilian, exposing the illicit affair and explaining that she had no part in it, but had rather threatened to tell Yueniang and refused to put them up in her rooms. What she significantly fails to mention in her long, impassioned, and detailed retelling of events to Yulou is how she had eavesdropped on them, and how subsequently had been able to indirectly "blackmail" Huilian into subservience and fear. And just as she had previously maintained a complicit silence on the affair, certain of her power/leverage in it, so now she remains silent on that one point that would fill in precisely the extent to which she had been involved.

She will instead utilize this silence to combat Laiwang, who has now proven to be a greater threat to her position than his wife; for Huilian's danger lay only in her resemblance to Jinlian—a resemblance or "identicalness" that could, had Jinlian not "intervened," have resulted in the replacing of the one (foot) with the other. Huilian's feet were, after all, even smaller than the fifth mother's and her red sleep shoes almost identical, except for the negligible (vulgar) green thread with which they were sewn. By eavesdropping and letting Huilian know she knew, Jinlian had reasserted a crucial differentiating power factor: one whereby she would be able to maintain a certain ascendant and controlling influence on this relation between the master-subject and his "new" object of fascination. Jinlian had, at just the right moment, tapped their line and made profitable, discreet use of the information gained. But Laiwang's threat to Jinlian was of a different, more lethal kind. Being a male bond servant, and particularly one who knew all about her past (with the tirade, he had placed himself in the position of the eavesdropper, but one who was "using" the information heard indiscriminately), he was in a sense beyond her sphere of power and could only be "touched" (as in a duel with swords) through Ximen Qing, his master/father and now the lover of his wife. The game of three players had, with Laiwang's return, transformed into one of four: Laiwang had accidentally, drunkenly, initiated the "new" game by challenging Pan Jinlian, who he mistook to be the weakest adversary (Ximen was certainly too formidable, while Huilian—being at once Ximen's lover and his wife—was both too distant and too close to be attacked).

Jinlian's strategy—one that would prove fatal to Laiwang, but even more so to Huilian—was to pit Ximen against Laiwang (goading him to battle with great persuasion) and to become Ximen's internal strategist in the sense of proffering plans in his name, to her gain. She would become his sword (exhibiting the seeming malleability and changeability of the part-object), one that had taken over the offensive, while Huilian was thus "forced" into the position of Laiwang's defensive shield insofar as he was her husband and she was perforce that which automatically linked/opposed the two. On one level, then, there is an unequal fight between two men—the one with a weapon and the other with only a shield—and a flawed one at that; or the punishing of one man by another for daring to conceive of even challenging the latter and for being the husband/owner of the woman the latter wants/takes (for it is the right of a husband that Laiwang evokes in his tirade against his master/rival, forgetting momentarily or strategically that Ximen is his owner and master, therefore entitled to dispose *as he might wish* of him and his). On another level, there is a combat between two women, both the "same"; a combat in which two men are the "shadow warriors"—the one a king, the other a scapegoat. The loser must be the woman who thinks as much of having the king as of saving the scapegoat; the winner being she who in becoming partially king, identifies the scapegoat as such and devises a means of having him banned from the kingdom. Suddenly the stakes are clear: just as Pan Jinlian perceived a threat in one who was too "identical" to her, so Laiwang could only be scapegoated in order to avoid the simultaneous presence of two potential master-subjects. For in daring to resent the master/king's attention to his wife, and in revealing the secret of the master's concubine's bloody past, as well as the illicit origins of their relation, Laiwang not only trespasses on the master/subject's property but would claim a justice in doing so that belongs to master-subjects only and not at all to bond servants.

Thus, when Pan Jinlian tells Ximen Qing, acting the innocent bystander who gets hit by a deflected bullet (or one that was misaimed on purpose), she does so in such a way as to first incite him to anger (dropping a reference as to how if Ximen uses the man's wife, no wonder he'll borrow your concubine [Xue'e], and want to kill not only you but your wives as well). She then speaks of her own victimization by an appeal to her legitimacy and, by implication, his face/honor (what if I bear you children and they should later hear of how their mother has to thank *a slave* for saving her life? Think of the loss to *your face*, not to mention mine. I might as well die first). Ximen reacts immediately and gives Xue'e a whipping, confiscating all object-symbols of her status as a concubine as well as reducing her to kitchen(bond)maid status and work (the lot of the wives of bond servants). Having thus worked off/displaced his anger, he calls Huilian to him and is quickly persuaded by her of the reverse of Jinlian's story: that Laiwang had been framed by a jealous coworker and should be sent away on some far-off purchasing errand again, "so that once he's gone, it'll be more convenient for whenever dad wants to speak to me."³¹ The subtle and seducing reference works, of course, and Ximen happily decides to send Laiwang on the birthday-gift-bearing trip to Dongjing, the eastern capital.

Yet the pendulum swings back: Jinlian hears, again from Laixing, that Laiwang not only gets off unscathed but is to be rewarded with a trip to Dongjing, and fuming, goes directly to Ximen:

> Do as you want, since you won't listen to what I say but would rather listen to that slavish-whore woman's one-sided words, whatever she says. She only thinks of protecting her man. That slave has been threatening [you] for more than a day. He'll leave his wife to you, and take all the money and enjoy it somewhere far away, and he'll even look you in both eyes. Your part of the money doesn't matter, but what about the others' one thousand taels of silver? You'll have to pay it back, of course. I'm only telling you; you can do as you wish. Your wife's only thinking for you. This slave's been speaking out for some time now, and since you want his wife, you can't have him at home, but sending him off's no good either. If you let him stay home, you'll have to be constantly on guard, but if you send him off, and he uses your money, you won't be able to say a word. If you want his wife, the best thing is to get rid of him for good. . . . That way you won't have to worry, and she'll serve you with heart dead [she'll be completely yours].³²

[With a heart dead and feet on the ground.] The very phrase is used (even today) in the context of a complete, near-abject subjection and "loyalty-filiality." To have one's heart dead is to be devoid of the ability to desire; feet firmly grounded graphically suggests the inability to move, fly, and follow the objects of one's desire. Jinlian perceives in Ximen's about-face the strength of a desire that can only bear parasitic intervention that follows the grain, and will certainly resist anything that would control, curb, or change its course, or go against its grain. Accordingly, she changes her tactics and focuses on how to kill Laiwang riding on the wings of Ximen's desire for his (Laiwang's) wife.

Ximen again changes his mind, keeps Laiwang at home, and gives him six sacks of three hundred taels of silver each to open up shop at the front of the house. That night, an uproar in the upper/inner chambers awakens Laiwang and he rushes in with a baton to catch the intruder/thief—who turns out to be none other than himself. Thus is Laiwang framed and imprisoned with attempting to rob then murder his master (for the sacks were found to be filled with tin rather than silver taels). Huilian once again pleads for his innocence and release, suggesting that Ximen buy Laiwang another wife "since anyways, I'm no longer his."[33] She again offers herself (in exchange for Laiwang's safety), this time not for rent but for sale, with permanent right of usage. Ximen is once more hooked, and promises to get Laiwang freed and to install Huilian in rooms across from the compound, all to herself, with personal maids, just like a concubine-to-be.

This time, it is Meng Yulou who tells on Huilian (she was present when Laixing first reported Laiwang's tirade to Jinlian), inaugurating the third and final round of combat, and quite neatly completing the journey of tales told and retold, each time to a different end. For Meng Yulou's only concern is that a bond servant's wife not be added to their ranks (of wife and concubines) and be made "just like you and me; what effrontery, and big sister [Yueniang] won't even say a word."[34] And this time Jinlian vows that if Huilian is made into Ximen's seventh wife, "I'll write my name Pan backwards." She goes to Ximen and retells the case with a telling difference:

> If you let the slave out, then you can't have his wife, for then he'll have an excuse, and where will you put him, if you leave him in the house, neither meat nor vegetable, how is he to be treated? If you want to marry her, the slave's still around, but if she's to remain the slave's wife, you've spoiled her so she's always getting onto her betters' head and faces [stepping on our toes], and even if you were to buy another wife for that slave, you'll have his wife. And what if one day he comes in and sees the two of you together—is she to stand up or not? Not only will this become the joke of relatives and neighbors, even those in the family will no longer respect you. Since you want to do this sort of thing, don't be a worm that's afraid of getting its eyes muddy. Kill the slave off and you'll hold his wife in peace.[35]

Jinlian is not only a consummate and persuasive storyteller but the mode, language, and manner of her delivery constitute faultless examples of the "art of maneuvering power" (quan shu) from a position in which one has nothing and everything to lose, including one's life. In effect, quan shu is in this particular case a tactic of utilizing the powers that subject one in reverse mode, never entirely resisting the subject, but rather subjecting and manipulating him in such a way as to taste of one's own desires obliquely, at second or sometimes even third hand. It is the leaking of an excessive yet legitimate (fascistic) power, and the perverse growth it unceasingly feeds into, within which it finds itself mirrored, shrunken, twisted, and much more lethal. This has been dubbed a "feminine" tactics (yin mou), flowing as it does, barely perceptible, and within lines of masculine power, always in reverse, and perversely determining the issues without ever being held accountable. It is a parasitic mode of power that arises in regimes masculine, centripetal, and authoritarian; while unable to transform its host body, it almost always succeeds in eventually perverting and eroding it from within and underneath, to the point where the body (domestic and politic) bleeds/ejaculates/implodes to death. This is also the mythic corruption and fall of dynasties, and the female depraved powers to whom such a fall is attributed; or it is the abject death of Ximen Qing, and the women who sexually bled him dry.

The fascination with which such stories are always listened to, remembered, and retold should not be forgotten—just as Ximen will never tire of listening to Pan Jinlian's "stories," swayed each time into following her yin mou and putting them into effect. So, too, past readers have been enervated and strangely excited at the reading of these domestic combats, and in the process, become all the more persuaded of Pan Jinlian's (if not all women's) predilection, indeed innate tendency for evil and sexual murder.

Zhang Zhupo, for one, is convinced that the entire Song Huilian episode is to be read as a strategic writing of Jinlian's criminality in the guise of Song Huilian's liaison with Ximen Qing.

> There are ways of writing one person, without intending to write that person at all, thus such as Song Huilian. The original intent is to write of Pan Jinlian's evil, of Pan Jinlian's jealousy for Li Pinger. Yet in order to avoid a too hasty brushwork as well as the insufficiently broad structure and incomplete grammar of the text that would be its consequence, thus failing to produce the large book that this is, a Song Huilian must first be written in, to prepare for Jinlian's evil, serving as its testing ground

and as a model for Li Pinger's case. Only Huilian's death could sufficiently reveal Jinlian.[36]

(Textual work is envisaged as countering and operating the same techniques as those of Jinlian: she is deathly cunning and underhanded; so must the text be in order to sufficiently incriminate her.)

The "meaning" of the entire Huilian episode and especially that of her suicide-death is, according to Zhang Zhupo and countless readers following him (and his commentaries), then to be found in the figure of the arch-yinfu Jinlian, who is not only implicated in Huilian's suicide but whose absolute, ruthless immorality is therein revealed.

Pan Jinlian is so effectively framed, however, by both narrative and its biased readers that there is really no "saving" her in the sense of proffering another, slanted reading of the meaning or "motivation" of Huilian's death. Rather, the process and seemingly irrelevant details whereby this meaning is constructed may be reread, perversely, with interesting results.

Huilian commits suicide twice.[37] The first time is when she finally learns that Laiwang had not only been sentenced to return to his hometown and former status of commoner but had already left, without her being told, at the express orders of Ximen Qing (who had promised her that he would be released unscathed). She locks herself up in her room and attempts to hang herself with a long sash tied to the door frame, but is rescued by her next-door neighbor (the wife of another bond servant, Laizhao). She is consequently consoled and made much of, by Ximen especially, who has someone stay with her day and night, and even sends Jinlian to talk her into eating, without success. Huilian's refusal to eat is symptomatic of her refusal of Ximen's attempt to monopolize the use of her body—suicide constituting an active if suitably silent protest and resistance of a superior's, the master's, forcible and exclusive use of one's body and determination of one's actions. Her refusal to be persuaded by even Jinlian, who is sent by Ximen, signifies not only a continued resistance to a life subject to Ximen but also a refusal to give Jinlian "face," or to acknowledge her derived power, and in doing so, forming an "alliance" with Jinlian of the sort that exists between Jinlian and Chunmei (where the latter is made a favorite of Ximen at Jinlian's behest and consequently lives off of Jinlian's leavings, but both she and her mistress gain in the doubled attraction of their quarters for Ximen Qing).

The second time she attempts suicide with a pair of feet wraps, again tied to the door frame, from which she this time successfully hangs herself. What immediately precedes this suicide and would ostensibly be its "cause," both in terms of narrative syntax and according to what it declares outright, is a fight with Xue'e that had been instigated by Jinlian, who had gone to both Xue'e and Huilian telling each how the other had "told on" her, resulting in Laiwang's being got rid of. "Pan Jinlian, seeing the extent to which Ximen Qing was enamored of Song Huilian, devises a plan." The plan succeeds—if only in provoking the reader to outrage and the text to sentimental commiseration: "Poor woman, who had been unable to withstand the anger [of being slapped in the face by Xue'e]."[38]

But the detail of the instrument of suicide is singularly fixating: first a sash, probably used to tie a robe, and then a pair of feet wraps, those bandagelike things with which bound feet had to be wrapped and over which red shoes were worn. It is as if Huilian, in two attempts at hanging herself, had been disposing of her body sequentially: first, the body proper; then its extremities, or those body parts accorded excess and sumptuous commodity value. Or as if the narrative were simply, with two hangings, preparing (as in some necrophiliac bondage-suggesting foreplay) the reader for another hanging, the reverse of Song Huilian's in almost every sense but one: feet wraps are used again, this time for intercourse rather than death. For what strikes this reader at least is not how evil Pan Jinlian must be, to so feel driven to kill off potential, and even nonpotential, half-object foes and obstructors; for Pan Jinlian is driven in precisely the same way, to precisely the same degree, and just as (perhaps more) arbitrarily as the text itself is driven to implicate, incriminate, and finally execute her, with a relish that can only be a form of *moral sadism*, paradoxical as this may sound.

Thus the repetition of events and detail, with minute but inescapable differences that seem to mean nothing and yet too much—so that the reader seems in constant danger of either only reading and registering the same (with the differences subsumed to and enhancing the one "meaning" of the text), or continuously losing himself in the myriad proliferation of small details and minute differences. These are the two poles of one reading: one of which would condemn with growing conviction (succumbing to the moral imperative of repetitions), while the other would be dazed, seduced, and fascinated, examining every detail with the gaze of one lost in the "contemplation" of "obscenities and desire" (or obscene desires: yinyu).[39] The alternation between these two poles of one exemplary reading, encouraged by the text and prodded on by such as Zhang Zhupo, would pave the way for a Buddhist-Taoist closure—one that by voiding (vomiting) the entire narrative of obscene details and objects, would at once affirm and deny the latters' powers by precisely expelling these from a (the reader's) newly cleansed and remoralized body-self. This is a self-generation of sorts, by a curious cycle of excessive consumption followed by immediate and self-induced expulsion: a literary bulimia that would ideally induce sexual anorexia.

Only in this manner could the reader-subject seemingly "transcend" the pendulum movement of desire and punishment-condemnation that the text activates, and obtain a (false) exculpation. And the textual strategies that effect this moral "bowel movement" without aftereffect are precisely the same that in a reverse movement or series of narrative moves, entrap and sacrifice Pan Jinlian and her ilk, likewise guiltless and unrepenting. (This is not a world of sin and guilt after all but one of endless cycles of actions and retributions, within which the "offender" may be planted for eternity if need be, and from which some may fly in the throes of a transporting, abjecting morality.)

The narrative thus exposes Pan Jinlian's covert operations (which eventually lead to Laiwang's expulsion from the house and town, and Huilian's suicide)—revealing her mode of killing with a particular mode of feminine speech, which insinuates, persuades, and fascinates Ximen into partial though effective subjection, or into inhabiting the subject-position she constructs in her discourse. She is represented as that "something rotten" in the Ximen household, the killer behind the scenes of Huilian's drama with Ximen and Laiwang. Zhang Zhupo observes how "Jinlian's evil makes one's hair stand on its ends," and how her words to Ximen completely adhere to the logics of sentiment (qing) and principles (li), fully representative of the "machinations of treacherous power brokers [jian quan] throughout history."[40] Yet even these would not have succeeded so well had not Ximen (the deluded emperor) been already in a state of fascination (mi) (induced by his fantasy of sex, of the woman and her words) and therefore too easily emplotted.

To reiterate, the narrative's representation and exposure of treachery is itself duplicitous: interweaving seamlessly a double line of discourse, or one with an invisible lining that nevertheless shows through the texture of narrative weave. It is an ultimately moral exposition with obscene undertones and adumbrations; in its shadow, the reader may take (his) pleasure without having to pay for it (as Jinlian and the likes of her do, heavily). This is a free and exonerating joyride (echoing the "writer's" resounding laugh).

## Foot Bindings

> Although Pinger and Jinlian are of the same type, there is nevertheless between them a difference of depth and shallowness, thus the refinement of the "Kingfisher Hall" episode's subtle gorgeousness, and the absolute resentment of "the Grape Arbor's" bewitchingly obscene defilement. So very much does Pan Jinlian offend the author/writer.[41]

Juxtaposed to and immediately following the "tragic" death of Song Huilian is the grape arbor incident, infamous as one of JPM's most "juicy" and obscene parts. It is precisely for this reason that the scene has been the focus of moralists and "depraved" alike (but they'll say for the opposite reasons, of course)—the one censoring and erasing with as much verve as the other will read and reread. The bonding of death and sex, the moral and the obscene, are yet again repeated, with red sleep shoes, a pair of feet wraps, and a "swing" made not of rope and wood but this time of a woman's limbs hanging by her feet from a grape arbor.

For the Song Huilian affair had been taken care of, and her annoying troublemaking father taken to court on charges of blackmail. Unfortunately, he was unable to survive the beating they gave him—all because he tried to prevent the cremation of his daughter's body as a form of questioning the reasons behind her suicide. He, at least, had interpreted her self-inflicted death to have been the accusation (of slave–bond servant vis-à-vis owner, object vis-à-vis subject) it in fact was: one made often enough by women in such a position in those times and contexts, whose only way of speaking out was to use a body not legally theirs to dispose of as ultimate possession and voice, and kill it off in a last, silent cry. Ximen thus took care that her father was silenced for good as well, and turned to more pressing matters at hand, such as packing the sumptuous set of gifts that were to be finally taken to Dongjing for the coming birthday of Grand Preceptor Cai.

On one of those extremely hot early summer days, all the more so for being the first of the season (the first day of the sixth lunar month), Ximen had just two days ago sent the gifts off, and today decided to stay at home, "with his hair undone and his robe open, sitting in the bower by the Kingfisher Hall watching the boys watering the flowers in the garden."[42] Pan Jinlian and Li Pinger stroll into the garden, hand in hand and laughing, dressed in the most alluring of everyday clothing, described by the text in equally exquisite and fascinating detail down to the three tiny jade-colored flowers pasted on Jinlian's brow.

Depictions (of objects) in JPM never merely signify: they belong simultaneously to a narrative economy of excess and luxurious consumption. Here is evinced a collector's mania that has been studied in the adjacent discourses of object connoisseurship and garden keeping.[43] But in JPM, the collector's mania is not so much for material objects (as it is in handbooks on how to buy the correct furniture and vases). Rather, it is an *ultracultured* collector's mania whose object are *signs and language*, or that which designates specific attributes/aspects of these objects whose very multiplicity and variety daze the mind's eye. This is a mania for objects insofar as they always and already are the signs of what makes them objects; signs that can then be remade, put together in different modes, variously and *promiscuously* played with in an endless sequence, a continuous listing, strung together and recombined. It is as if these objects denote a process of becoming defamiliarized, fascinating things; a semio-philic description.

Thus the cup of tea especially prepared by Chunmei, who hands it to Jinlian for the latter to wipe off with her fingers what had spilled onto the saucer before handing it to Ximen. This is a cup of thick, rich, osmanthus, and rose-scented Liu An Sparrow-Tongue tea, with sesame seeds, salted bamboo shoots, chestnuts, melon seeds, walnuts, and preserved vegetables added. A cup of tea whose mere naming is a process conspicuously, extravagantly, and probably satirically (as in how vulgar) but nonetheless *promiscuously* encompassing all the possible or impossible elements and processes that went into its making.[44] (In the later XXJPM and ZZJPM editions, only the last four characters or the "name proper" of this cup of tea remain, which Clement Egerton translates as "Sparrow-Tongue tea").[45] It is as if the text would semiotically produce the totality of objects it could thereby fix for visual and mental consumption, as in some textual warehouse of curios. Women and certain parts of their bodies, their clothing and accessories, food and tea, flowers and plants, lanterns and tableware — all are to be "named" and "listed" in minutely desiring, extraordinary detail. It is this semio-philic portrait that later narratives will try to emulate, producing what Roland Barthes has termed a "reality effect" that is perhaps more of an accidental and mistaken aftereffect.[46]

In short, what has been mistaken for an early "realism" is actually an antiobject-motivated celebration of conspicuous object consumption. Not sufficiently cultured yet excessively object riveted, JPM's semio-philia registers the unease of the age (mid- and late Ming), its alternate fascination and repulsion with the extraordinary and conspicuous consumption of luxury items, both material objects and human part-objects (concubines and bond servants).[47]

Let us return to the hot spring day of the Grape Arbor scene. Ximen gives both women flowers with which to adorn their hair, and sends Jinlian off to fetch Meng Yulou and her *yueqin*, whereupon seeing her crimson silk underpants through the thin silk of her skirt in the sun's rays, the hint of flesh and limb beneath them, "his obscene heart was aroused [*yin xin ze qi*]."⁴⁸ Just as he is copulating with Li Pinger, taking her from behind in his favorite posture, Pan Jinlian, instead of fetching Meng Yulou, sends Chunmei to do so, and tiptoes back to eavesdrop on the two left alone in the hall. She hears the sounds of their lovemaking, and Ximen saying to Li Pinger, "My heart'n liver, your da loves nothing more than your so-white buttocks, and today they will give your da all the pleasure he wants."⁴⁹ Li Pinger does not respond immediately but after a while asks him not to take so long since she is still feeling unwell: "To tell you the truth, your slave/I am pregnant and hope you'll make do with [less time]."⁵⁰ Ximen is so overjoyed with the news of her pregnancy that he climaxes almost at once.

Again, Jinlian eavesdrops, this time not to hear herself directly denigrated in unfavorable comparison but even more dangerously, to hear of news that can cause Ximen to "climax" with joy. As the potential mother of a son, Li Pinger's pregnancy immediately places Li in a position of power that none except the official wife could equal, until of course the other concubines should also conceive and bear sons. Pan Jinlian's hypersensitivity to the nuances of intradomestic power plays (in the words of the text, "jealousy"), lead her to react (as she did with Song Huilian) by letting the two parties concerned know that she, too, is in on the secret. But perhaps she is less adroit than she was in the Song Huilian episode, or her greater disadvantage (lesser capital) works against her; for Li Pinger is not only "paler" (namely, her white buttocks) and "kinder" but wealthier and much better connected through previous marriages than Jinlian.⁵¹ Her pregnancy only adds to her substantial "capital," and Jinlian will be hard put in combating her. Finally, as usual, Ximen sways to the side of the stronger party, or sides with his favorite, which goads Jinlian further in her attempt to if not win, at least continue to matter.

Meng Yulou arrives to find Jinlian still outside Kingfisher Hall, and they go in together. Jinlian asks Ximen, "I've been gone all this time. What have you been doing? Why haven't you washed your face yet?" And when he replies that he's waiting for the maid to bring soap, she retorts, "I don't want to say this, but sending for soap . . . no wonder your face is even cleaner than others' buttocks." Later, when all four are seated around a small table with wine and fruit cooled in a bowl of water, Jinlian chooses to sit on a porcelain stool rather than a chair because, she says, "I for one am not afraid of freezing any fetus." Then, when Yulou comments on how Jinlian keeps eating uncooked fruits and cold water, Jinlian responds, "I don't have anything happening in my stomach, [so] why should I be afraid of cold food?" As Li Pinger's face flushes (with embarrassment) and pales (in anger) by turns, Ximen glares at Jinlian and exclaims, "You little whore; what bullshit are you saying!"[52]

Ximen is annoyed because Jinlian had been "hitting the bull's eye" too accurately for comfort, each of her remarks calculated for double effect, operating simultaneously on two semantic levels—the second silent yet singularly loud and clear as well as right on target. But Ximen will, of course, not allow the prospective mother of his child to be attacked without punishing the offender. And when Meng Yulou and Li Pinger decided to go back inside to help Yueniang string pearl flowers into a necklace, Ximen will not let Pan Jinlian follow them in and pulls her back outside, so hard that she almost falls to the ground, saying, "Little oily mouth, you're trying to slip off, but I just won't let you get away."[53]

Or not until you've been well and punished for letting your will to power get the better of Li Pinger, or in the language of the narrative, for being jealous of her conceiving the master's child, thereby becoming an even closer and more powerful "part" of the master than you can aspire to. For desiring to kill (her) with words, you shall in turn pay with having your vagina transformed into the gourd at which "I" will shoot plums for pleasure (a sexual variation on that favorite of domestic games: "aiming at the gourd"). Thus Ximen forces Pan Jinlian to stay behind, and proposes that they play a game of aiming at the gourd beneath the stone hill by the pond. He sends Chunmei for the wine that the loser of each round will have to drink, and Jinlian, plucking a pomegranate flower and placing it in her hair, jokes, "I'll wear a 'three-day-without-food, flowers-before-the-eyes.'"[54] Ximen, goaded, advances on her, "and seizing her *jinlian* and holding them high and apart, he laughingly exclaims, see if I don't fuck [*cao*] this little whore to death."[55]

All the editions of JPM (that I have seen) have the same version of this more-serious-than-joking threat of Ximen Qing's.[56] This is a warning of rape as it were, only "rape" as such being inconceivable and impossible in a society and at a time when the bodies of concubines and bondwomen were at the absolute disposition of their masters; and even more inconceivable in a narrative wherein this particular bondmaid-born concubine had been represented as—persistently and in the most diverse ways imaginable—

asking for it. Yet she would ask for it to the extent that, and insofar as, sex with the master was the only means available to (domestic and sociosymbolic) power, the only linkage to power for someone in her position (see chapter 7). Perhaps "woman's pleasure" in this narrative and such a context can only be read in terms of, as being founded on and informed by, opportunistic accession to and manipulative intercepting of the master's sexual power. It is a phantasmatic bondwoman's pleasure—unreadable, or readable only as madness.[57]

> The two play the game of aiming at the gourd until Jinlian, slightly drunk on the wine, decides to take a nap in the shade of the grape arbor. As Ximen goes off to pee, Jinlian places the bamboo mat and pillow on the ground beneath the arbor, takes off all [her] clothing, and lies down on the mat, with a pair of crimson-red sleep shoes on her feet, and fanning herself with a white silk fan. Ximen, approaching, saw her and was moved to licentious desire [yinxin], and taking advantage of his drunken state, also undressed, and sitting on a stool, used his toes to play with "the heart of her flower" until the obscene fluid flowed, like a saliva-spitting snail. At the same time he took off her red embroidered sleep shoes and played with them, then unraveled her feet wraps and tying them around both feet, hung them up from the two side frames of the arbor, like a dragon showing its claws.[58]

The scene is depicted (and here translated) in detail, precisely because of its difference from previous and following scenarios of copulation. If Jinlian seems to be "inviting" intercourse, Ximen is "resisting" the invitation, or playing with her parts as if with an object that must be at once assimilated and ejected, or "dealt with" punitively (naihe), suspended and taken apart in play to be later put together again, if only to show who's master and in which process the indiscriminate flow of anger/desire may be (s)played out.

Note the studied pictorial effect of the composition/writing: red embroidered shoes setting off silky white fan, marking the extremities of a naked vulnerable body ready for consumption; the contrast between the (feet's) red-textured stillness and (one hand's) white smooth movement, with the expanse of living flesh in between.

Note also the obsessive discursive focus on red shoes, feet, feet wraps, and their use.[59] Ximen uses his feet to play with the flower's heart, defiling the woman's clitoris; for in the hierarchical order of the body, feet occupy the lowest-end position in diametric opposition to the head, which touches the sky and dominates the entire body. Women's bound feet fascinate precisely to the degree that these are not only feet but feet highly processed and deformed, exuding the odor of their putrid state; in such fascination is surely crystallized a patriarchal order's deepest ambivalence and hatred/fear of "things" female.[60] Thus the fascination of the passage for the reader/rewriter, evoked with each mention of shoes (Zhang Zhupo keeps a close count of these in his commentaries, and in this sequence they number seventy-nine) and their close associates, feet and feet wraps.[61] The latter, so recently used to hang a woman's neck onto the rafter above the door, are now employed to hang a woman's feet from the rafters of a grape arbor. Feet wraps will hereafter be repeatedly put to just such use, Ximen perhaps finding "echoes" of this mode of "hanging" more exciting and the position easier for his body (recalling those Ming erotic prints that represent a threesome, with the "extra" body—of a bondmaid of course—utilized as a "prop"—precisely like the arbor in this case—to support the object/woman, while the man/subject takes it easy).[62]

But what after all is obscene, defiling, and misogynistic about the Grape Arbor scene?[63] It is not so much the language used and postures taken, both of which are after all pastiches of late Ming erotica (I would yet emphasize that these were rewritten to specific ends and effects in this particular narrative); nor even the details (that differentiate this from other similar texts), such as red shoes, feet wraps, and plums placed in and scooped out of vaginas, stringing the thread that links sex with death and copulation with sacrificial killing. Rather, and more sinisterly, it is how Ximen punishes Jinlian (for daring to step on the toes of his favorite, the mother of his child, in his presence) through precisely those techniques of "pleasure" whereby she had derived power from (servicing) him—by threatening to "fuck her to death."[64] This is a counterdisciplinary mode of punishment: one that "corrects" through measures that repeat the duplicitous and torturous tactics of the "offense," although the latter leaves no physical trace, while the "correction" seeks to mark, if not maim the body.

The Grape Arbor scene, in its unlikely yet prearranged sequencing, prefigures and inversely rehearses another climactic episode: Pan's sacrificial killing (I would deem it murder, too) by Wu Song, the hero.

> Wu Song grabbed a handful of burned-incense dust and stuffed her mouth with it so she would not cry out, then hitting her on the head, threw her to the ground; the woman struggled so, her headdress and combs fell all over the floor. Wu Song, afraid that she would struggle free,

used his oiled boots to kick her in the ribs, then with both legs on her shoulders, pinned her to the floor and said, "You whore, you think you're clever. I wonder what your heart looks like? I'll see for myself," and baring her breasts, faster than can be told, plunging his knife into the fragrant soft whiteness of her breast, he scooped a bloody hole, and the blood flowed; the woman's eyes fluttered half-closed, her limbs were still kicking; Wu Song put the knife in his mouth, and with both hands forced open her breast, "*pu chi*" [onomatopoeic sound-word], tearing her heart and guts out, and placed them dripping with blood on the altar of his brother.[65]

Ximen, however, in a more sublimated and eroticized mode, postpones finishing her off: he plays a round of aiming at the flesh gourd, throwing plums at her vagina/body, then placing one inside to much later scoop it out and force-feed it to her, reversing Wu Song's first stuffing her mouth with incense, followed by a bloody and violent extrication of organs from that same body. Pan Jinlian is a thing/body: to be punished and reformed by playing with its apertures and extremities, feeding it with its (symbolic) excrement, or stuffing it up and then disemboweling it, until one way or another it dies, or even better, as a sequence (of "deaths") increasingly violent and obscene. What is enacted, staged to the last detail, in this extended narrative of desire is a projection—onto the bodies of bondwomen-concubines—of the master-subject's fear of the sovereign self, its powers as subject, its borders, and the dissolution of this "self" in desire and its correlate affects. Projected onto the bodies of bondwomen-concubines, anxiety can then be fixated, played with, and perhaps postponed at length (as in the extended narrative)—thereby postponing the moment of reckoning, of ejaculation, of death as sacrifice.

CHAPTER 7

A Cat, a Dog, and the Killing of Livestock

Some will even taste of excrement, not to mention piss.
—XXJPM

This is the usual way of concubines, who will go to any length to seduce and ensnare [gu huo] their husbands, and remain unashamed despite body bending and humiliation, whereas the wife proper, upright and unafraid, would never assent to this [swallowing Ximen's piss].
—JPMC

Those who are not of the human(e) order, if one keeps them company, one will become not-human. Prostitutes take foster mothers, sons-in-law play with mothers-in-law, mistresses drink with servant boys, younger brothers commit adultery with wives of older brothers, all the world is become muddy chaos. As for adulterous men and licentious women, this is their innate nature, but to be a [human(e)] person contaminated by their habits, this is the extent to which one must not keep company with [nonpersons of the order of] birds-animals.
—Wen Long, commentary on ZZJPM

How are bondmaid-concubines represented as the epitome of "obscene things," thus figuring as powerfully illicit and dangerously intimate domestic and sexual appendages? This chapter reads several interwoven incidents in JPM and considers how "birds-animals" and excremental fluids (urine) are in too close proximity to as well as stand in for their "owners" who are themselves "owned" (as bondmaid-concubines) as luxury commodities, domestic and sexual appendages of the master of the household.

The accounts of economic and social historians on various modes of bond servitude both in the Ming and late Qing eras up through the colonial period (in Hong Kong) might be productively placed alongside the study of "idealized" representations of and by courtesans in the Ming-Qing.[1] The difficulties of "proving" and "finding" historical records for lowly and nearly invisible, yet all-too-present domestic bond servants and the trajectories of bondmaid to concubine/prostitution could then be seen as the shadowy counterpart of a discursive flowering of courtesans as subjects of/in writing in "idealized" or "romanticized" fictional and poetic representation. How might these two—one more of a silence or gap, or at most deadly negative representation; the other a breaking into writing and representation—be understood in relation to each other, or even as shading into one another, as reciprocally (de)constructive?

JPM can and has been read as a textual and even historical record of the obverse yet complementary side of Li Yu's aesthetic and celebratory "owner's manual" to the acquisition and apposite grooming of concubines (in the section titled "Voice and Facial Expression," in *Xianqing ouji*, or *Casual Expressions of Idle Feeling*).[2] In JPM, "bondmaids turned concubines" (*biqie*) are represented as the reverse of the properly groomed and domesticated. They would seem to be, in the words of Zhang Zhupo, "deeply hated" by the purported/projected author since the three main licentious women (*yinfu*) in the narrative—Pan Jinlian, her bondmaid Chunmei, and Li Ping'er, all of who die more or less fittingly gruesome deaths—come from this particular category of half-human, half-object persons.[3] (Their owner's almost equally animal-like death must be seen as implicating a "superior" gender-class of parvenu merchants.)[4]

In his work on caste and its meaning in Indian society, Louis Dumont has elucidated the concept of hierarchy as difficult to understand or even imagine from this side of the "modern" divide, and actively repressed by prevalent quasi-universal values of democratic and individual equality.[5] According to Dumont, the ideology of equality of "Western" modern societies makes it difficult to apprehend a hierarchical order fundamentally different, yet nonetheless relevant to reigning democracies. To the degree that the latter have disavowed unequal status between (all) groups and dissolved these into individuals, hierarchy has reappeared in the form of racial discrimination and somatic difference. Hierarchical (complex) societies, on the other hand, are visibly and avowedly distinguished among groups structured through a logic of encompassing and encompassed. Thus, differences are recognized and tolerated to the extent that they are differentiated by the hierarchical logic of encompassing and being encompassed. It would be interesting to think of the fluidity and tolerance of "Chinese" society in the context of Dumont's theory of hierarchy insofar as that fluidity could be seen to rest on precisely a self-adjusting order also comprehensible as encompassing and encompassed.[6] The lower the status, the smaller the significance and the more encompassed the situation. The higher the status, the greater the power (either symbolic-cultural or economic-political, or both), the larger the capacity for encompassing others. This is one way of thinking of the bondmaid-concubine/bondmaid-prostitute situation. These occupy the legal, familial, socioeconomic, and symbolic bottom of a hierarchy whose upper echelons it services daily in the most intimate proximity and manner. It is this very porous intimacy that produces both the greatest danger and greatest opportunity in terms of transformational personal-familial-social and even political (eunuchs, for example) trajectories. The "abuse" of such intimacy on the part of the bond servant can either mean immediate access to concubine (potential kinship and thus better social) status and power, and/or heightened danger of punishment and death (the punishment of bond servants being legally more severe than for commoners).[7]

In a recent sociohistorical and anthropological study tracing the life trajectories of women of bondmaid-concubine (rather than bondmaid-prostitute) status in Hong Kong from the late Qing period to the colonial 1950s, Maria Jaschok has raised crucial questions concerning the attitudes and practices of residual bond servitude in Chinese societies.[8] Jaschok finds these quasi-slavery practices to be relatively common among a parvenu class of compradors at a moment of socioeconomic and political change (in Hong Kong).[9] But more important, she also discovers how kinship terms (such as foster mother) will mask and retrospectively "naturalize" what had begun as master–bond servant relations.[10] The bond servant origin of concubines marked these women as permanent "outsiders" within the families to which they were bonded for life.[11] Such a

> marginal woman, detached from either paradigm, that of the male and the female worlds within orthodox kinship, could develop character-traits

that exploited the male-view, that women (for example, *mooi-jai* [bondmaids]) were no threat, by turning the physical proximity within a household into an invitation to greater intimacy—the intimacy of sex constituting her sole avenue to power.¹²

The bondmaid who turns concubine and thus is afforded the possibility of establishing kinship ties to a man (which is the only means to recognized social status for such base women) is better off than the bondmaid who remains a bondmaid in lifelong servitude to a family. In colonial Hong Kong, the latter's "slave [outsider] status positioned them within the twilight penumbra of social life."¹³ Their bodies, sexual and reproductive services, and labor could become mere extensions of the "master/mistress," completely instrumental. In such situations, "how does one measure regard, hostility, and contempt in a relationship"?¹⁴

A beginning step toward historically tracing the feelings of "regard, hostility, and contempt" toward bondmaid-concubines would include the study of eulogies of idealized courtesans, or the bondmaid-prostitute trajectory, as a discourse that might mark the distance between "poetics" and "praxis." It would also explore how such discourses influence or intervene in the lives and possibilities of the "vulgarized" prostitutes of the late Qing and early modern periods. (I am thinking here of the relation between institutional discourses and practicing prostitutes).¹⁵ The reading of such "negative representations" as JPM would afford a different angle—one ambivalently showing up both a historically earlier negative moral ideology against this entire category of female ("small" in the Confucian sense) persons in a form of narrative "dangerously" reproductive of the machinations and gyrations, the play and power of these persons who resemble nothing so much as not human(e) bird-animals, and/or marginal waste materials.

This, then, is how I read the following incidents/episodes in JPM: as simultaneously commentary on and exemplification/narrativization of the excess-obscene status of bondmaid-concubine in the intimate details and detailing of domestic and sexual servitude. Exceeding the boundaries of what may be written or recorded whether poetically or historically, the narration of such person-things and their behavior, feelings, and actions, their trajectories through life, could only be deemed obscene. Such a focus itself and the counterdominant perspective it might give rise to (as early readers of JPM worried) seemed sufficient to mark the tale as base as its purported subject, however limned with morality. (That is, until modern institutions of knowledge legitimated the study in anthropology, sociology, and history of erstwhile unworthy and debased person-things, sometimes instituting new dogmas that speak more to the state of research and ideology of the present.) I take the bondmaid-concubine as a life trajectory (which is to be distinguished from that of the bondmaid-prostitute) that is transformable and changeable (it may, for example, shift from concubine into wife) without eradicating the familial, social, and psychophysiological forces that go into the making of such a trajectory along with its varying positions and dispositions at different times and in different places.[16]

The excess that is integral to this trajectory and its disposition resonates with the notion of purity and danger that Mary Douglas has proposed, where purity and cleanliness express boundaries of self (and state or institution), and anxieties thereof. Douglas suggests that prohibitions and defilement reflect and express a society's structure in its divisions and contradictions, both internal and external. It is through such symbolic systems that social structures perpetuate themselves; dirt and filth are modes of classification and ordering where the social (or familial) body draws the purifying (internal and external) lines separating and distinguishing between the socially assimilable and beneficial, and the ejectable and dangerous. Douglas furthermore posits that the human body likewise might be seen to constitute such a symbolic system, whereupon the social maps itself, entrances, exits, margins, borders, and ejecta.[17]

Embedded within JPM is a document by an "upright" literati-official submitted to the emperor, in which the "evil" forces within and without the body politic are identified, and the appropriate cure advised:

> And since our own imperial Song dynasty was established, the great Liao has made incursions into the central plain for some time. But I have never heard of a state being threatened by barbarians from without when it did not already harbor barbarians within. As the proverb says: when frost descends the bell of Feng-shan sounds; when rain falls the plinth under the pillar sweats. That like breeds like is a necessary principle. The situation is analogous to that of a sick individual whose vital organs have long been ravaged by disease. When his natural vitality [*yuan qi*] is sapped from within he becomes susceptible to the penetration of malign influences from without. Once the entire body has become infected, not even Bian Que of Lu would be able to save him. How could he then long endure? The present situation of the empire is just like that of an invalid in the final stages of debilitation. The ruler resembles his head; the chief ministers resemble his vital organs; and the lesser officials resemble his four

> limbs. . . . These three officials have conspired to form a cabal that fosters corruption . . . and is like a noxious venom [gu] gnawing at Your Majesty's vitals. For years now their conduct has invited catastrophes and induced anomalies, destroying the health and vitality of the body politic.[18]

The body politic suffers from both internal poisoning and external dangers, but the internal poison must first be dealt with, identified, and expelled or exterminated before the body can successfully repel exterior evil influences. If three evil ministers are to blame for the disorder and enfeeblement of the state and empire, within the household narrated in JPM, three yinfu (Pan Jinlian, Li Ping'er, and Chunmei) and their keeper must die deaths befitting their debased status as no better than the cats and dogs that are their daily companion, their extension, objects to and instruments of their "abuse" of power.

Concubines and prostitutes are to bond servants what cats are to dogs, pigs, geese, and chickens. Like cats, the former belong to a category of (the master/subject's) "symbolic capital." They embody specific relations and modalities of pleasure; their use and consumption as "half-human, half-object" is often marked by a shade of excess, and sometimes associated with intemperance and immorality.[19] In their not-quite personhood and dubious "nature" as extra or surplus as well as "outsider" is constituted their (innate) negative value and moral ambiguity. They induce pleasure and impart symbolic power as much in being hoarded and accumulated as in being given away (as a gift or in punishment), or again, in being magnificently destroyed. Perhaps, too, concubines and prostitutes, more than the wife, are prone to keep cats: out of a feeling of affinity, but also as a substitute for the master('s penis-phallus), they can neither keep to themselves (being themselves kept rather than keepers) nor ever legitimately have access to.[20] Finally, both concubines and cats kill not disinterestedly, or concubines kill through cats, in the guise of cats, gloating or gleeful.[21]

## The Cat

Pan Jinlian keeps in her rooms a large, pure, white lion-cat (Persian?), with a black vertical mark on its forehead, named "sending charcoal in snowy weather."[22] It is also called "Snow Lion," and fondly nicknamed by Jinlian, "Snow Thief."[23] The cat was adept at retrieving handkerchiefs and fans, and when Ximen Qing failed to come at night (which was more often than not since the birth of his son by Li Ping'er), Pan Jinlian would sleep with the cat in her arms.[24] Perched on Jinlian's shoulders while she ate, Jinlian would feed Snow Lion; whenever she called, it would come, and when she wanted it to, it would leave. It was an incredibly pleasing and useful animal. Although whereas the cat refused to eat cow liver or dried fish, it would consume half a jin of raw meat, and had become so fat, strong, and well-fed that an egg could be hidden in its fur. Pan Jinlian was extremely fond of the cat, and holding it on her knees would fondle and play with it daily, "with dire intentions: for Li Ping'er and her son, Guange, liked cats, and when no one was around, [Jinlian] would wrap meat in a piece of red silk and have the cat pounce on it, snatching and eating it."

> It was bound to happen: Guange, having felt ill and taken Old Woman Liu's medicine for several days, was now slightly better; Li Ping'er dressed him in a red satin chemise and put him, with a small coverlet, on the bed in the outer room to play; Yingchun sat looking over him, while the nurse was eating beside the bed, without noticing that Jinlian's Snow Lion was on the bedrail; the latter, seeing Guange all in red, playing and moving on the bed, took him for the meat wrapped in red silk that was daily fed to him, suddenly jumped down, pounced on Guange, and clawed him all over; Guange shrieked then choked on his breath and was silent, hands and feet convulsing; the nurse threw down her bowl in alarm and taking him in her arms, spat continuously to contain his fright.[25]

Yingchun chased the cat outside, and Rui'er (the wet nurse), seeing that the baby's convulsions would not cease, sent the former to call for Li Ping'er. The birth mother (Ping'er) rushed back to her rooms with Yueniang (the wife mother) in a panic, only to see the child's eyes turned up so that the pupils could not be seen. Guange was foaming at the mouth, making the sounds of a small chicken, and his hands and limbs were convulsing. Li Ping'er, seeing him thus, felt as if her heart had been cut with a knife. She quickly took up the baby and, putting her face to his mouth, cried out, "My brother, you were all right when I went out. How come you've started convulsing?" Whereupon Yingchun and the nurse told her how Jinlian's cat had frightened him. Li Ping'er sobbed all the harder, saying, "My brother, you've been unable to please your 'parents-in-law,' and now unable to get away [stay alive], you've actually gone the way [of death]."[26]

Yueniang, who had arrived on hearing these words, remained silent for a moment. She then summoned Jinlian and asked her if "it was [her] cat that frightened the child." "Who said so?" queries Jinlian. "The nurse and Yingchun." Jinlian retorts:

*A Cat, a Dog, and the Killing of Livestock* 201

> How dare those old women speak with [their] eyes wide open; as if my cat hasn't been lying good and well in my room; say whatever you will, but don't try to put the blame on someone else for having frightened the child; claws only pinch where it's soft, [as if] we're that easy to pick on!

Yueniang turns to the nurse and Yingchun, asking, "How come her cat got into these rooms?" "It often comes here to play," says Yingchun. Jinlian immediately interjects, "You should have said so earlier. Why didn't it claw the baby before, [rather than] choosing to do so today, you bondmaid [*ya tou*]?" and again, with wide-open eyes, she remarks, "Let it be, don't stretch it [to the breaking point]. Just my bad luck."²⁷

It is at this point that the text breaks into narratorial aside-comments, headed "ye readers, listen well. . . .

> As the saying goes, even beneath flowers and leaves will there be hidden thorns, [so] how can man's heart not harbor poison? Pan Jinlian saw that since Li Ping'er had given birth to Guange, Ximen Qing complied absolutely with her wishes, so in the everyday competition for his favor, Pan Jinlian would often harbor the "influence" [*qi*] of jealousy and resentment.²⁸ Thus she resorted to "feminine tactics" [*yin mou*] and raised the cat expressly to frighten Li Ping'er's son to death, so that the latter's favor would wane, and Ximen would once more be [more] intimate with herself.²⁹

Whereupon Zhang Zhupo adds (with satisfaction) in between the lines: "Yet another clear proof."³⁰ Proof of what? Of Jinlian's culpability, of course; of her bad intentions and evil influence, which not only direct her cat to her/its object but eventually effect the death of the "precious" object's mother as well. The unknown commentator of XXJPM also notes in the margins of his text, above the narrator's words: "This is surely between the intentional and nonintentional, and may not be as bad as is here stated."³¹ There is a hint of uncertainty—or perhaps even a recognition of an impossible, debased, and nonperson disposition—leaking through the crack between Jinlian's psychological motivation (as represented in/by the text) and the text's equally motivated framing of Jinlian for murder.

Pan Jinlian's white, longhaired cat first appears in the ninth chapter preceding its final call onstage (chapter 51).³² Its appearance signals the convergence of a nexus of competitive and conflicting relations that knot together, eventually to explosively untie at the expense of its little cat life. Ximen Qing had only recently (chapter 49) obtained the yang-replenishing pills from a "barbarian monk" (see the following section) and was exuberantly trying its/his powers on various favorites, sequentially, with Wang Liuer first on the list and Li Ping'er a firm second (chapter 50). Ximen obtains the pills that can either preserve or kill, expressing thereby a will to imperial sexual power that he ought neither to have legitimately attained nor could have afforded, given his "originary" place in society.[33] So too Yueniang—in view of Li Ping'er's sudden "rise to power" with the birth of a son (chapter 30) and because of having miscarried (a male fetus) after falling down the stairs while visiting their newly bought house on Lion Street (chapter 33)—determines to ensure another, male birth, and asks Nun Wang for the appropriate "medicine."[34] Nun Wang promises to obtain at a high price the placenta and fetal membranes of a firstborn male; after having been washed in wine, these will be burned to ashes and mixed with the ashes of medicinal amulets (fu yao). This concoction must then be taken on a renzi (homophonic with man-child) day only, to be swallowed with yellow wine on an empty stomach; copulation that same night will ensure proper conception (of a male child).[35] "With great difficulty" Nun Wang finally gets these "ingredients" and brings Yueniang the "medicine" on the same night Ximen tries the pill/power he had obtained that very morning on a menstruating Li Ping'er, having already tried it with "extraordinary" results that afternoon at Wang Liu'er's (chapter 50).[36] Jinlian, noting the disappearance of the pouch of "obscene instruments" (yinqi) usually kept in her drawers and thinking that he must have taken them to use with Ping'er, gnashes her silvery teeth and goes to bed alone. She had been accumulating resentment of Li Ping'er's rising favor (chong) and influence (shi) over the past eight months, ever since the birth of the son.[37]

This night, she was so angry that she couldn't sleep, and the next morning before Li Ping'er had even risen, Jinlian went to Yueniang with an account of how Li Ping'er had "resented" Yueniang's imputations last night, which had cost her (Ping'er) to lose face before the women present. For the previous evening had been Li Jiaor's (the second wife) birthday, and Ximen, returning home drunk from Wang Liuer's, had not even bothered to come into the upper/inner quarters where the women were gathered to celebrate. Only the boy that had accompanied Ximen home came into the upper/inner quarters, and on being asked where the master was, said that he had gone into the "sixth mother's" rooms. Yueniang then exclaimed, "Will you look at the ill-behaved rogue! We're all waiting here for him, and now he won't come in." Li Ping'er anxiously hurried out front and said to Ximen, "Second mother is waiting for you in the back to offer you her birthday wine. Why in heaven have you come into my rooms?" Ximen laughing replied, "I'm drunk; let it wait till tomorrow." But Li Ping'er insisted, "Even if you're drunk, you should go and have a glass of wine. If you don't go, you'd offend second mother." And so Ximen goes in for a glass of wine.[38]

Of course, it is Pan Jinlian who is most offended and resentful, having been so for rather too long. For not only does Ximen refuse to notice such niceties of "polygamous" good behavior but even had he done so, he would still have in one way or another inevitably given face to one more than another. There is no such thing as an equitable distribution of favor and attention in a polygamous household. Everything depends on the microrelations of power between the master and his many women grouped in descending hierarchy according to complicatedly daily or even momentarily adjusting hierarchies of status, seniority, and intimacy, with the last least calculable and most manipulable. Add to this the relations among and between the women themselves as constitutive of domestic female kins (with their widely varied trajectories, positions, and dispositions making for intricate power negotiations and maneuverings).[39] Pan's telling the tale on Li Ping'er, or "repeating of her tongue, [xue she]," is of course immediately remarked on by the XXPJPM commentator as typical of Pan, as a putting of Jinlian's sentiment and style of speech in the mouth of Li Ping'er, and then ventriloquized by Jinlian.[40] Zhang Zhupo merely notes how again Jinlian has resorted to the old tactics that "killed" Huilian (that is, inducing animosity as well as potential rupture and combat between two parties whose interests clash, which could be any two women in a polygamous household). The Huilian episode, according to Zhang Zhupo, is preparation in miniature for the more gruesome and complex Ping'er death.[41]

Again different from Zhang, it is the XXPJPM commentator who finds it exquisitely entertaining (miao) that Jinlian should be made to sound, even when repeating another's tongue (xueshe), so like her own clever sharp self. This commentator further observes that Yueniang's immediate angry reaction is much more irritating (whereas Jinlian at least amuses and perhaps even beguiles?) since had she (Yueniang) not been angered, she would have noticed how Jinlian was in fact speaking for herself. Whereas Zhang Zhupo refuses to be either amused or irritated, but merely pronounces stern judgment, declaring Jinlian indubitably guilty in every word and act, attributing to her a consistency of motivation and action difficult to uphold in this polyphonic, multivoiced text.

Pan Jinlian's only "crime," in this case at least, is an irrepressible sense of having been sidelined for no good reason except the paramount one of not having given birth to a man-child, thereby becoming one of the three lesser-favored women in the household. The crime lies perhaps in how this sense of wrong is lodged *in the inappropriate category of personhood* for such self-righteous feelings of resentment (she is a bondmaid-concubine, and moreover not even pregnant), and could only then have come about from an *intimacy* that although in the "nature" of the relation to such a category of persons, had nonetheless *been taken in a manner* as inappropriate as the sentiment. Who does she think she is to "resent" and "feel wronged" of attention that is completely subject to the whims of the master?

Yet all the women cannot but keep a fine account of these daily changes of a whimsical "fate" and sentiment, and it is precisely such attentiveness to the distribution of attention that impels Li Ping'er in such anxious hurry back to her rooms that previous evening. She must use her (momentary) influence to ensure the redistribution of attention in such a way as to ward off retaliatory measures. Li Ping'er is thus more than aware of her (momentary) advantage over all the others to the extent where she is only second to Yueniang (who though wife, is neither as rich nor attractive, nor yet has a son). She also realizes the constant danger such an advantage entails in the resulting not unequal but rather inappropriate distribution of powers/privileges among her and her "sisters." Ping'er is acutely conscious of what that one reminder of Yueniang's ("we're all waiting here") implies. Ping'er's influence had overextended her (Ping'er's) position, and Ximen's actions merely express that surplus only he can "give"; "the rest of us" all know this, and "don't you think we don't." By these implications, Yueniang shows her privilege in not quite according Ping'er the "face" that goes with the latter's newly acquired surplus power; intentions do not count on this terrain since the outcome is the same.

By her ventriloquism of Ping'er, Jinlian reports what Ping'er—in the certainty of her (temporary) rise in favor as well as the security of her beauty, wealth, and motherhood—would never think or need to say. These are the bases of Ping'er's generosity and kindness, of her unfailing ability to swallow (tolerate) the anger and resentment that constitute the daily expenses of her parasitic power. This is why, when Big Sister Ximen (Ximen's married daughter) reports Jinlian's words back to Ping'er (the former had always been close to Ping'er since "when she [Big Sister Ximen] was short of needle and thread, Ping'er would give her whatever silks and cloth she had at hand, or handkerchiefs on the sly and of course silver as well"), Ping'er's arms become paralyzed and she remains speechless for a long while. She finally tearfully says, "I haven't ever said a word. When I heard the boys saying that dad had gone to my rooms, I came directly to hurry him on back. Whoever said a word? Your mother takes such care of me, how would I dare so ungratefully say such things? And even were I to have said it, to whom did I say it? There'd have to be proof."[42]

Li Ping'er is more upset by the accusation of having spoken out, than of what she was supposed to have actually said. In other words, she is worried that her reticence had been translated and ventriloquized perhaps aptly, but certainly not to her gain—quite the contrary. By acknowledging the "beneficence" of Yueniang, she is recognizing the only acceptable way of repayment: reticence in whatever feelings of resentment might nonetheless sometimes crop up. This, then, is Jinlian's crime throughout the narrative, and in the eyes of those who insist on her obscene "jealousy" and "evil."[43] Jinlian is of the bondmaid-concubine trajectory and position. She speaks in and for her "own" interest (instead of as a cohesive member of the domestic female kin grouping or encompassing family clan, although as concubine she does not have the place to speak for the latter) as if she could have any or could eventually accumulate enough to have a place. She not only speaks; she does so with a precision and knowledge of domestic intimate politics that disturb and upset the visible yet unspoken supposedly master-centered regulation of familial movements and resource (re)distributions.

This might partially explain the sympathy and goodwill accorded to the figure of Li Ping'er in some recent criticism: she is interpreted as a fittingly passive, silent "victim" of the polygamous system as well as the politics of domestic and sexual intimacy that go with it. As such, she is a "safer" figure to rescue from traditional ignominy.

And yet does not this tendency to approve of only the silent, passive, self-immolating victims of a "past" patriarchy precisely repeat and reinforce the gender configurations of a gentry-literate class femininity in the process of reconstruction? It is as different from, say, a bondmaid-concubine trajectory "femininity," although the latter would always already have congealed into "essence" only in a negative sense as a "minor" and wrong sort of femininity altogether, especially in the retrospective light of a present-day modernity without shadows.[44]

Jinlian, in her "repeating the tongue" of Li Ping'er significantly "identifies" with the latter in the sense of wanting to inhabit her position of influence (with/over the master). Rather than as the XXPJPM commentator would have it—that is, imputing to Ping'er her own sentiment and language—it is a projecting onto Ping'er a situation that she, Jinlian, had been fantasizing for many months. "Why does the man not stay in the inner/upper rooms [after I, Ping'er, had told him to go] but instead return to 'my' rooms? The two of them said intimate words to each other all night; only his heart and innards did he fail to pour out to 'me.'"[45] That one slip into the third person is where Jinlian's long-frustrated desires and its envious jealousy burst forth.

The white cat first appears that same evening while Ximen is (finally) in bed with Jinlian, having "challenged" her to perform fellatio on his magically transformed penis, saying that if she could bring it to ejaculation, he would give her one tael of silver. For Jinlian, wager or no, the "bet" cannot be refused, just as she had had to put up with his "play" under the grape arbor, and not only put up with it but even play back. For only thus, by playing his game each time and appropriating whatever "pleasure" she could from it, could she ensure a modicum of power from this master-to-bondmaid-concubine relation. Her only resource besides intelligence was precisely her catlike "disposition for intimacy," a propensity for pleasure parasitic to a will to please/take pleasure at whatever cost (since there was nothing to lose).

> Ximen looked down at the fragrant flesh of the woman by the light that shone through the gauze mosquito net, gazing at her fine hands holding that hairy thing, putting it in and out of her mouth, its to-and-fro movement in the light, not noticing that a white lion-cat sat right beside them, and seeing the movement, taking it for who-knows-what, pounced forward to snatch it with its claws. Ximen used the gold-speckled fan he held in his hands to tease the cat, when suddenly the woman seized the fan and hit the cat hard, and it ran off from under the net. She looked up at Ximen and said, "You shameful enemy of mine, you're always making things difficult for me. There you are now teasing it so that it'll get more and more daring. What if it should claw one's face? What's to be done then? See if I'll continue doing this job for you." Ximen said, "You funny little whore; you're really difficult, aren't you?" The woman replied, "Why don't you have Li Ping'er suck this for you. It's always in my rooms that you'll play these punishing tricks. I don't know what stuff you've eaten, sucked, and sucked, and nothing's happened."[46]

In a moment of displaced anger at the cat who cannot tell the difference between the penis and the face, a cat that somehow condenses both Ximen and Li Ping'er, or becomes the relation between those two—a relation that threatens to disrupt/disturb Jinlian's hold on the penis, preventing her from servicing the master's power/pleasure in exchange for whatever of the phallus may leak her way—Jinlian again speaks what should have remained silent yet understood among the various players. The rules of the game are any which way against her, for Ximen, with his little rituals of "punishment," knows to pick on one who can least refuse to play (whereas Yueniang and Li Ping'er can and do: the one as wife; the other as mother). Paradoxically, this abject position of the picked on will allow her a little space for retaliation. In her low-faced speech, in the effrontery of calling his card (blackmail), albeit in the guise of anger at the cat, she is enabled (again) to "blackmail" in turn, thus gaining some points, a slight advantage.

*Dog Pee*

Guange is a "fragile" baby, as perhaps all firstborn sons in these polygamous households are bound to be: destined from the moment of birth to carry too great a symbolic value for the body of a not-yet-human but assuredly phallic "thing."[47] The road, in this polygamous household, to the particular positionality of secure masculine manhood (nanzihan) and eventually familial patriarch that is by rights the firstborn son's is one fraught with dangers. Or so his mother must feel, and Li Ping'er does feel, almost without respite. For his immanent power constitutes at once the greatest protection—a nurse, bondmaids in constant attendance, the fond attention of the father, and those "mothers" who wish not to usurp his power but rather share in its leftovers—and greatest danger in the eyes of those who would resent this purely chance access to so much power. The latter would then presumably plot either to undermine it (with rumors of illegitimate origins—the "wrong" father, for example) or destroy its present incarnation (through the agency of cats, a dog, and an ill-favored maid). On the other side, Guange is a baby especially prone to fear: as if he'd been born with the prescient knowledge of all the complicated "evil influences" surrounding and against him. Hence, his father will say to the Taoist priest at whose temple he has asked for the boy to be nominally registered that "the boy is too easily frightened; even with three or four maids and a nurse who take turns looking after him, he is still afraid, so much so that we do not even dare allow cats or dogs to approach him."[48] And much later, after Guange had been frightened by a black cat under the palm trees, Old Woman Liu is summoned to "contain his fright" (*shou jing*). As she mutters a string of formulaic phrases above the sleeping child's head, his mother discerns "that cat" among her words: "Heaven fright earth fright human fright demon fright cat fright dog fright. . . ." Ping'er immediately says, "That's it, Guange's fright *was* caused by a cat."[49]

But dogs are dangerous, too. Dogs, and dog excrement, can become agents of a baby boy's fearful disease in a most roundabout manner, once more featuring Jinlian plus that "obscene" thing: her red shoe. The previous day had been Ximen's birthday, and today, Yueniang had prepared a feast of crabs for the women who had stayed on from the celebration (chapter 58). Jinlian had gotten quite drunk, and tottering back to her rooms that evening,

> because she'd seen Ximen stay with Li Ping'er the previous night, and call in Doctor Ren for her this morning, [Jinlian] felt very angry, and knowing that the child was unwell, just as she entered the gate [to her rooms in the garden], suddenly, with the convenience of heaven's help, in the dark [she] stepped [in] a shoeful of dog pee.[50]

These few lines will initiate an incident that must be seen as a prologue to "The Event" of the child's death. It is an incident that would again ascertain, as if she were insufficiently "guilty" of the intention of murder, the arch-yinfu's interest and "influence" in the diseases and deaths of both birth mother and son. It is precisely at such a crucial initiatory moment that one finds another "textual slip," whose significance lies not so much in its "inconsistency" with a detail mentioned on just the previous page but rather in how it discovers a certain textual urgency and investment in the full psycho-textual motivating of Pan Jinlian as murderess. This urgency and vested interest betray a certain pleasure of the text and its recorded/ projected writer/readers.

For Jinlian *and* the text misremember that Ximen had not retired to the rooms of Li Ping'er the night before, nor even the night before the last. This particular chapter begins with how because of all the women (kin and prostitutes who have become foster daughters) visiting at the house, Ximen is forced to go to Xue'e's rooms for the night. On the night of his birthday the next day, he goes into Yueniang the wife's rooms (in accordance, for once, with propriety). The text misremembers this detail, perhaps in its desire to appropriately motivate Jinlian's anger and subsequent tirade. Thus the "thievish" (duplicitous, to borrow the text's own terms for Jinlian and her cat) remark introduced between "knowing that the child was unwell" and "in the dark stepped a shoeful of dog pee." For "entering the door—who would have thought—heaven knows—so conveniently" could be read as either Jinlian's thoughts word for word, or the narrator interpolating these thoughts, "reading" and rewriting them for the reader sarcastically (how convenient for her, this would-be murderess!). This reader suddenly realizes that this is how Jinlian repeats another's tongue or recounts "stories" with a "lining," either to her own interests and/or to implicate some person/animal/object onto which blame/ill may then be transferred. In the latter case, she will usually "slide" free from under her "rereading" (not without witnesses—the reader for one). Repeating her tactics, the text recounts Pan Jinlian's story, reading/writing her feelings, thoughts, and actions in a specific arrangement of narrative syntax that will at once camouflage its (the text's) interests and transfer its desire/dis-ease onto the woman.[51]

Pan Jinlian conveniently (for the text and indeed for all concerned) steps on dog pee. She immediately calls for Chunmei and a lantern to examine the filth that had dirtied her new red satin shoes. Her eyebrows arch and her eyes open wide in rage, and closing the gate, she takes up a huge stick to beat the dog, who sets up a queer howling. Li Ping'er then sends her maid over with the request that the fifth mother cease beating the dog since Guange has only just fallen asleep after taking the cinnabar pills given him by Old Woman Liu. Jinlian lets the dog out of the garden, and gazing at the dog-piss-sullied shoe, gets more and more angry. She calls for Qiuju (the least favored of her two maids)—who she upbraids in a "typically" fascinating double-edged discourse—slaps her with the defiled shoe until Qiuju bleeds at the mouth, and then has her kneel down so she can whip her into screaming like a "knifed pig," whereupon Guange wakes up in shocked fear. Li Ping'er again sends her maid over to plead for Qiuju (not for Guange). Jinlian's mother, who was visiting with Jinlian, had meanwhile been trying to stop her daughter to no avail, and seeing that Li Ping'er had sent her maid over a second time, snatched the whip from Jinlian's hand and told her to cease the beating "for it's making the sister over there talk, and will frighten the big brother; to take up a stick for a mule is fine, only take care not to hurt the redbud tree." Jinlian is roused into a purple-faced fury. She pushes her mother away and says, "You don't know anything, besides which you're on their side against me. Take your old cunt off tomorrow. See if they dare do a thing to me."[52] The old woman retires to bed in tears, and Jinlian continues to beat Qiuju until the latter's skin is torn and flesh aflower, whereupon she pinches with her pointed nails Qiuju's face to shreds.[53] Li Ping'er next door covers up Guange's ears with her hands and cries in silent anger.

The scene is bloody and overtly sadistic. Nothing need be disguised; everything must be told down to the last detail of the pointed nails and shredded cheeks (in sharp contrast to the moving touch of a tearful, reticently angry mother with hands covering her baby son's ears). Only thus will Jinlian's sadism be confirmed enough to go with Wu Sung's equally sadistic, bloody, and detailed killing of her. More than that, Wu Sung's punitive, revengeful, and ritual killing will be seen to complete and complement this and other scenes like it of abuse, where Jinlian acts out murderous anger at the triad (Ximen/Ping'er/Guange) onto bodies-persons just as, if not more marginal and valueless than her own.

Shortly after the dog scene, Guange, the sole son and heir, is attacked by Jinlian's white lion-cat and has another fit of "infantile convulsion" (*jing feng*), ostensibly the culmination of a cumulative series of frights (chapter 59). Old Woman Liu is summoned and administers a last desperate remedy in the form of a decoction of "rush pith" (*deng xin*), peppermint, gold, and silver, pounded to powder and wrapped in gold foil into a pill, and moxa burned directly on Guange's wrists and chest. Neither have much effect, and the man-child sleeps in a heavy coma, not waking even after Ximen's return home. On learning from Yueniang of what had caused the boy's falling into a coma, Ximen rushes in a furious rage to Jinlian's rooms, picks up her cat by its feet, and dashes the animal against the stone steps of the corridor outside the room, against which the cat's brains explode with a sharp sound into a thousand peach blossoms, its teeth shattering into fragments of jade.[54]

The moxa burned in five places on the baby's body had, instead of curing the infant, "driven the wind influences back into the body." The convulsions had become chronic (*man feng*) and finally affected the viscera, with the body ultimately expelling its wastes uncontrollably, the excrement five-colored, while the eyes opened and closed fitfully. Guange could no longer take in anything and died that same night.

What a frightful, abject death, wherein the body seems to entirely lose control, refuse all intake, and expel everything that had been inside, liquid and matter flowing out of apertures that had been in the case of "others" forcibly opened (Snow Lion the cat, and Pan Jinlian her mistress). Guange's death renders him suddenly disintegrated, as he becomes the incarnation of a murdered husband (Li Ping'er's Hua Zixu come for revenge in the form of a too-loved, short-lived son). What is it about these violent dramas of death that so repel and transfix at the same time? How can one understand (though he may not have meant to be thus "reread") Zhang Zhupo's affirmation that the second half of JPM—filled with blood, semen, and deaths—is meant for the "real" reader, one who can truly appreciate a deeply moral obscenity?

For the record, it must be noted that Guange—from the details of his medication and symptoms—most probably died much less sensationally than the narrative would have it of mercuric sulfide poisoning. After all, Old Woman Liu prescribes it for him the day he returns from a trip to the family cemetery, where he had been frightened by the loud music (chapter 48), and thereafter he is often given the cinnabar pill (chapters 53 and 59). Children in modern-day Taiwan are still given this medicine: the China Times of 18 July 1991 records the case of a baby boy with convulsions because of a high amount of mercury in his blood: he had been fed an "infantile convulsion powder" every day since four days after his birth. The report further states that in 1983, a five-month-old girl baby with the same symptoms had died of mercury poisoning after having been fed the same kind of powdered medicine since birth.

Guange lives one year and two months. The meaning with which his body, life, and death were overinvested may be judged by the degree to which the narrative and discourses that fed into it or were sustained by it sought to tie that death around the body of a particularly catty bondmaid-concubine, and to sink the latter once and forever, in some grand ceremony like the ones all the men of the village used to attend when a licentious adulteress had been found and was to be publicly drowned naked or paraded in the streets sitting astride a spiked halter on a mule, with blood running down the sides, in a terrible caricature of one mode of her crime—illicit sexual intimacy. Again, such punishment evokes and intertwines with pleasure, the obscene shades of a punitive morality. Only thus, perhaps, could pleasure and desire be liquidated along with its prohibited and dangerous object—in this case, the bondmaid-concubine yinfu.

### The Obscene Mother

JPM represents in detail the deaths of impure, debased (jian) bondmaid-concubines—impure women who die in ways fitting to their state, with their bodies transfigured into emblems of impurity, excess, and obscenity. Li Ping'er, both bondmaid-concubine adulteress *and* mother, for embodying such a paradox, must slowly bleed to death in an inversion of pregnancy. The punishment reverses the crime of an infidel conception; the baby becomes the reincarnation of a wronged husband returned to extract the blood that was due him, that should have enwrapped and produced his seed/son. And finally, an abortionlike hemorrhage is induced by the semen of the adulterer in a moment of transgressive intercourse with a menstruating woman.

For Li Ping'er is that impossible, unthinkable thing, an "obscene" (erotic) mother, with all the undertones of incest that the text would mute and displace onto the less transgressive relations between Pan Jinlian and the son-in-law, Chen Jingji. Incest appears in the inverted guise of retribution and reincarnation, the husband becoming/displacing the son through excessive resentment and an implacable will to revenge. Li Ping'er's death is integrally linked to those of both Guange her son, whose death precedes and induces her own in the form of a prolonged melancholy and the accompanying psychophysiological reactions, and that of Ximen Qing her lover, whose demise is then construed as the result of a double, complementary contamination: contact with the unclean blood of a mother/yinfu, and to top it off, an overdose of aphrodisiac fed him by an insatiable and barren arch-adulteress.

After acquiring the one hundred pills and pink ointment from a foreign monk (hu seng) who Ximen meets at the Temple of Eternal Fortune (chapter 49), Ximen, as I have already noted, proceeds to try their effects first with Wang Liuer, that same night with Li Ping'er, and the following two nights with Pan Jinlian. He finds Li Ping'er already in bed with her son in her arms. On seeing him, she asks, "Why don't you go and sleep in back? Why come here? The baby's just gone to sleep, and is sleeping so well. I feel rather anxious and am menstruating; it isn't convenient."[55] Ximen insists, and tells her to get the maid to bring some water and wash herself, and Li Ping'er replies, "Now this is funny. Where have you been drinking? . . . Even were I to wash, it would still be unclean; a woman's menstruation dirtying a man's body, how filthy and unlucky. Were I to die tomorrow, you'd still hold me responsible." But Ximen remains adamant, and Li Ping'er washes herself to then copulate with him on the bed.[56] Guange, who had been asleep on the same bed, suddenly wakes up. Ping'er coaxes him back to sleep, only to have him again wake up, and this occurs three times. The mother has the maid take the baby into the outer room to sleep with his nurse. Ximen then copulates with Li Ping'er from behind, liking to "gaze at her snow-white bottom" and the movement of his penis alternately disappearing and appearing therefrom. Ping'er, afraid that the movement would bring blood with it, unceasingly wipes it and herself with a handkerchief. Finally, Ping'er asks Ximen to go slower since she feels pain, and he replies,

"Since you feel pain, I'll let it go" and ejaculates, as the monk had directed, by swallowing a cup of cold tea.[57]

Li Ping'er's words of warning disregarded by Ximen are nevertheless prophetic. Not only does she eventually die of a hemorrhage brought on by "semen clashing with blood vessel."[58] Ximen, too, will die of having come into contact with "unclean" menstrual blood, but also from the very pills that he is so eager to try with/on her. Yet strangely, despite the mention of menstrual blood and Ping'er's attempts to wipe off its traces during copulation, it is not until the evening after the next, when Ximen copulates with a Jinlian who is not menstruating, that a "bloody penis" appears, resonantly in the "wrong" place with the "right" person. For with Jinlian, Ximen seems (again) less accommodating. With the mother he had insisted, but was at least willing to hasten discharge. With Jinlian he must have anal intercourse; she protests to no avail of course and finally submits, though soon after asks him to go slower (in the same words as Ping'er) because of the pain. Ximen tells Jinlian not to mind the pain and that he'll buy her a new set of multicolored, flower-embroidered clothes. Soon after, she again begs him to ejaculate since she feels extreme pain. Ximen ignores her, "holding her buttocks and gazing/playing with its in-out movement"; he tells her to call him "dada" and thereby induce ejaculation. After ejaculating, Ximen withdraws a penis "of a bloody red" that the woman then wipes clean.[59]

Witness the polluting menstrual blood, even more so perhaps for the mother than the master, but from which encounter both will (in part) die abject deaths in the profusion of blood that will flow, as if triggered by that single moment of defiling contact. In contrast is the base though strongly erotized anal blood of Jinlian, yet another trace in a bloody text of the waste that flows from base bodies in the thrashings, beatings, and killings of bondmaid-concubines, bond servants, bondmaids, and a cat. Blood is as significant or insignificant, as powerful or powerless, as the bodies from which it flows or spills. Note the silence of both the XXPJPM commentator and Zhang Zhupo, neither of whom comment on the anal blood that covers the penis. Whereas in the case of the menstrual blood of the mother, both observe how it signifies "the source of disease" (bing gen) for both Ping'er and Ximen.

The obscene mother Ping'er's death is extended.[60] From the onset of her disease at the death of her son and the angry "influences" (qi) she receives from Jinlian, to her final lingering and withering away in a pool of blood, there are eight chapters of escalating fear and horror on the part of both the text and reader in anticipation of the inevitable outcome. Ping'er's death, like Jinlian's, was "meant" from the very beginning, with the former's seduction of Ximen and subsequent murder by inattention of her husband Hua Zixu. Yet since her "marriage" to Ximen (which like her death is roundabout and delayed), and with her residing in the same front rooms in the garden with Jinlian outside the women's quarters proper signaling the two's (even more than the others') appended and uncertain status, Ping'er has come to function both as Jinlian's complement and contrast. Although her death is that of an impure bereaved mother narrated in a rhythm slow and heavy, with each mention of her symptoms (a sudden vertigo, a sudden warm flow between the legs, then nausea, and an inability to swallow any food) aiming for maximum affect that is certain to arouse pity and horror in the reader, who is expected to recall his own mother in her perpetual sorrow (the sorrow of birth, separation, and death). In juxtaposition to this death of the mother, one reads of the death of the mostly barren and obscene-excessive woman (Jinlian), explosive and inducing the shock of a sudden release, a complete exorcism of a complex tension, as in sexual discharge. As such, the verse following Jinlian's sacrificial death claims to mourn her: "Poor Jinlian, truly pitiful, clothes torn off [and] on her knees before the altar, who would have thought Wu the second would knife her thus. We thought Ximen was tying up her legs to play with."[61] The collapsing of Ximen's play with/on her body along with Wu Sung's splitting it open and disemboweling it in revenge, makes of both an acting out and discharging on the body of a *base* woman, an obscene yet supremely moral force.

It is this same force that is undone, almost disintegrated, in the duration and aftermath of Ping'er's death; in a purifying renunciation of aggressive powers, as the latter is dissolved in tears. The tears of Ximen are those of an incestuous eros. He cries, again and again, with Zhang Zhupo keeping count of how many times as well as with what strength and function. His is a childlike outpouring of grief. A sense of emptiness seems evoked at the death of this beautiful, wealthy, favored bondmaid-concubine adulteress birth mother that presages the tone with which the narrative will end: separation from the mother (Yueniang) and renunciation of worldly sensual desire as the only means whereby the son may survive whole and complete—thereby saving as it were the familial-social body politic through leaving it, separating from it, yet paradoxically preserving it whole and unharmed for the future. The highest filiality and morality would then consist of not a denial or negation but rather a transubstantiation (*huan hua*) of the son and desire into emptiness and out-of-the-worldliness (renunciation), thus transcending the maternal figure and her familial (uterine) powers. The perversions of the maternal in this case (the birth mother as adulteress, the son Guange as reincarnating the dead ex-husband, and the present master Ximen as mourning the most favored concubine brokenhearted like a "son") would likewise cease to seduce not just because exorcised and expelled (as with the arch-yinfu) but rather and much more effectively because emptied of affect.

The slow bleeding to death of Ping'er is one stage preceding a final sacrificial rite (Wu Song's ritual slaying of Jinlian) of the emptying of maternal-umbilical-uterine waste from the (becoming-masculine) body of the text. This is a process in which the reader is projected to have participated either siding with the already-dead Guange and the tearful Ximen or perhaps from a safer, more distant position such as Zhang Zhupo's.[62] With the latter the reader would be able to weigh the death, ponder the (meaning of so much) blood, and pass judgment on the drama and its players. On the other hand, Jinlian's anal blood on Ximen's bloodied penis would, like that of her lion-cat's blood splattered all over the stairs, contrastively mark the borders outside of which all such base ejecta must and will eventually have to be dumped—not as in when Jinlian has an aborted fetus of a male child dumped in the latrine, only to be discovered by the latrine cleaner and told in a story around town, of how a Ximen concubine conceives then kills a fetus *after* the death of the master (the disloyal, licentious thing!). For that would be making too much (excess meaning, desire, and pleasure) out of refuse as Ximen the improper master cannot seem to resist doing. He is seduced and fascinated by excremental things along with the borders and apertures of the bodies whenceforth these enter and exit, losing not only his body/self therein but his will as well, as in the doxa "playing with things [makes one] lose one's will" (*wanwu sangzhi*). All of this will ensure his end at a time and in a manner between that of the obscene mother who bleeds to death and the obscene adulteress who is disemboweled. Ximen will lose control of his penis, and (through) it will discharge all the semen/essence stored in his body until finally only blood flows forth.[63] This is a death excessively metaphoric. Truly, the vaginal doors that gave him birth are now the instrument of his death, as if all women were as dangerous, as prone to becoming yinfu—the embodiments of seduction and death. And yet this is not completely so, for at the moment of his death, Yueniang his widow finally gives birth to the man-child so carefully and calculatingly conceived.

Lo and behold, Ximen is reborn as her son, or so the text's cyclical retributive logic would have it.

### The Killing of Livestock

Following the death of Li Ping'er, a "surrogate" figure too quickly seems to replace her in the affections and attentions of Ximen Qing. This is the wet nurse Rui'er, who had stayed on after the death of Guange as one of the retinue in Ping'er's rooms to await the birth of Yueniang's child. During the mourning period, Ximen would often spend the night in the deceased Ping'er's rooms, refusing to allow any change to be made, and one night while being served tea by the nurse is seduced by her maternal breast and copulates with her. Thereafter, she receives (in exchange for maternal coupling) much that had belonged to her mistress, from their master. Jinlian detects the liaison with her usual flair, and one day when Rui'er dares to refuse Chunmei the use of the baton for clothes washing, Jinlian rushes to where Rui'er is washing her master's intimate clothing and screams at her for wanting to keep the baton to herself.[64] But first, she tells her off for daring to explain and talk back: "Thievish, crooked-spined, man-fucking, obscene woman, you dare speak with a hard mouth. Who's the one who serves dad his tea and covers him up in the middle of the night? Who's asked him for a robe? What have you been doing behind our backs? You think I don't know? Even if you should steal a stomachful [bear him a child], I'm not afraid of you." Rui'er replies, "Even those who really did bear a child are dead; we'd never get that far." Jinlian furiously grabs her hair and beats her in the stomach, exclaiming, "Shameful, man-hooking hussy, the rest of us have little enough to do here, and you actually come in here to fuck [the] man. [You better take a good look at] who's in here with you. Even if you were Laiwang's wife reborn, I wouldn't be afraid of you."[65]

Jinlian's vehemence and tornado tongue, in both her tirade against Rui'er and later vertiginous retelling of the Rui'er episode to Yulou, with all its implications for the relations of power in the domestic women's circle, precisely reveal the fear she harbors and wards off with an excess of words. The fear of "motherhood" in yet another, this time a bondmaid already fertile (she is after all a wet nurse) who might then again exchange with the value that a child constitutes the share of power that could otherwise have been more securely Jinlian's in proportion to her position, talents, tactics, and vigilance.[66]

Soon after, Ximen arrives home from a second trip to the capital—where he had been promoted—tired and frightened by the windstorm in which he had been caught on the way back.[67] The second night of his arrival he retires to Pan Jinlian's rooms. They copulate and he ejaculates, then,

> the woman wanted to hold on to Ximen's heart; moreover having been apart for more than half a month, she had been lonely and was afire with obscene sentiments [yin qing]. Now she had him. She wished she could bore into his stomach, and played with the thing in her mouth all night. ... When Ximen wanted to get out of bed to urinate, the woman wouldn't let him, and said, "My dear, however much urine you have, let it pass in my mouth, I'll swallow it for you. A warm body, you'll catch cold getting out of bed. It isn't worth it [would cost too much]."[68]

Jinlian wants both to bore into Ximen and become his child, an inseparable part of his body, thus ensuring the most intimate linkage-association to him. She simultaneously expresses this desire by incorporating his penis and what flows out of it, as if this would ensure her becoming a part of him through the intake and assimilation of his waste. Abjection is the half-human, half-object's becoming waste, in relation to the master's precious, infinitely more valuable body. This is then from a base (jian) waste-like bondmaid-concubine place, to accede to becoming (even as little as) the superior albeit waste matter of the master, to be played with by the master, reincorporated and ejected at the master's whim and will. This is a fantasy of base personhood who by assimilating to superior waste matter, manage to live (better) off of the residues of an obscenely overvalued masterly power and wealth of resources. The XXPJPM commentator sarcastically notes, "Some will even taste of [other's] excrement, not to mention urine."[69] But the text offers its own reading: "This is the usual way of concubines, who will go to any length to seduce/ensnare [gu huo] their husbands, and remain unashamed despite body bending and humiliation, whereas the wife proper, upright and unafraid, would never assent to do this."[70] The wife would not need to become or assimilate to waste insofar as she has already acceded to the position of person—a position that guarantees a share that concubines have to secure via scrupulously calculated and managed intimacies, which moreover the death of the master would immediately forfeit since it would place them at the mercy of the mother (or wife) of the inheriting son, or the head of the family clan.

Ximen subsequently demands Rui'er to do the same: "Your fifth mother, afraid that I'd catch cold, will not even let me get down off the bed but will swallow my urine for me."[71] This is the danger for masters in the face of assiduously assimilating waste-bodies and services: the seduction and fascination of a completely centripetal (fascist) world and life. This is no doubt a perversion of true filiality, yet nonetheless distantly linked, since in the domestic hierarchy Ximen is Rui'er's and indeed everyone's symbolic father. She too calls him "dad," and in his illness nurtures him with her milk. The difference between urine and breast milk is signified in this text by the superior value of breast milk disregardful of the "carrier's" status, so long as she is healthy, whereas urine, although perhaps considered beneficial after having been carefully processed, is in these two urine-drinking instances in the text read by commentators as waste matter.[72] Thus Zhang Zhupo on how both instances are designed to caricature "those who lick carbuncles and suck hemorrhoids."[73] That parasites, middlemen, go-betweens, kiss asses, and their kind are so figured at least suggests the ambivalent powers/pleasures obtained through introjecting base fluids. This is a reterritorializing of sites and matter soiled and debased, at the borders of the "superior" (rather than simply clean and proper) body and that body's concomitant symbolic order.

Ximen's death, long prepared for and augured, is immediately preceded by a series of sexual couplings with women who will then be held responsible for his eventual demise—the last one most of all, and with the least grounds for vindication. At least two of these sexual couplings are marked by a pronounced sadism, as pain seems to more and more supersede pleasure in the complex of affect Ximen desires to produce in the reactions and on the bodies of his (part) objects. This is perhaps the better to signify Ximen's proximity to and approximation of the base status of the obscene things, the half-human, half-objects he has become enthralled to. Ximen decides to burn incense on the bodies of the women he copulates with, wanting to see (and perhaps smell?) female-body-surface-turned-burned-flesh. Between the breasts, below the stomach, on the vulva—finding direct gaze insufficient, he finally places a mirror so he can better see the "intensified" mirrored scene.[74] Perhaps this is a final preparatory textual incrimination of the master's subjection to his objects of putrid fascination: his enthrallment to the very smell of burned flesh, waste-bodies.

But it is his last "round" with Pan Jinlian that will, for the text and readers ever since, too easily "kill" him off as if he were livestock (*chu sheng*). Ximen had spent that wintry afternoon with Wang Liuer, and played again at hanging her feet up by her feet wraps. He returns home late. It is cold and dark in the streets, and just as his horse comes to a stone bridge, a black shadow appears from beneath the bridge and reaches as if for Ximen. The horse veers away in fright and Ximen has a shaking fit. He then drunkenly whips the horse, who gallops off until he reaches the house. Ximen can hardly stand as he gets off the horse, and helped by the boys, he enters the house and goes straight into Jinlian's front rooms.

> All would have been well had he not come, but having come, he would be like "the lost souls who meet with Wu Dao, the hungry ghost who bumps into Zhung Kuei." For Jinlian had not yet slept and was waiting for Ximen. . . . The moment Ximen's head touched the pillow, he was snoringly asleep and could not be awoken. The woman . . . turned this way and that; how could she resist the fires that burned her body, the obscene heart a-swing with desire? She kept playing with the thing in her hand and, bending over, sucked at it to no avail. She became extremely anxious and asked Ximen, pushing him awake, "Where is the monk's medicine?" Ximen drunkenly scolded her, "You funny little hussy, why do you keep asking? You want dada to 'manhandle' [*baibu*] you, but your dada is too lazy to move today. The pills are in a box in my sleeves; you eat it, and if you're able, play it until it rises. It'll be your luck." The woman found the box in the sleeves, opened it; there were only three or four pills left. She took the gourd of warm wine, poured a cup, swallowed one pill herself, and the three remaining pills—afraid one wouldn't be powerful enough—she should never, never have fed into Ximen's mouth along with some warm wine. A drunken man, what can he know? With eyes closed he swallowed the whole. . . . The woman seeing that he was still asleep, sat astride his body, placed some pink ointment in the "horse's eye," and put the penis into the vagina. . . . The woman changed handkerchiefs five times, discharged twice. Ximen would not ejaculate; the "turtle's head" seemed increasingly swollen and purplish, its tendons clearly visible, hot as fire. Ximen, feeling as if about to burst, had the woman remove the ring at its root, then, still feeling it swelling, had the woman use her mouth . . . , after a meal's period of time, the semen in the pipe surged forth, flowing out like mercury from a tube, the woman barely able to swallow it in her mouth, as it continued to pour forth. At first it was still semen, but then became blood, and could not be stopped. Ximen had fainted, four limbs spread loose. The woman panicked, and taking a red jujube, fed it to him. The semen, having all flowed out, was followed by blood, and after all the blood had flowed, only cold "qi" was left to be expelled, and this continued for a long time before stopping.[75]

The text must then further drive its moral home, as if the above were insufficiently incriminating:

> Ye readers, a person's spirit [jing shen or semen-essence-soul] is finite, this world's sexual desire is infinite, and again, those who are deeply addicted to desire/pleasure, their heavenly fate is shallow. Ximen Qing knows only the greed and pleasure of obscene/excessive sex and does not know that the lamp will extinguish when the oil dries up, and man dies when his marrow is used up. Just so do women('s)-sex [nüse] entrap men into certain failure following success.[76]

The upshot and answer to the mythic riddle of Ximen's illness and the text's dis-ease is obvious and simple: woman-sex (my translation of the term nüse, which combines and collapses the two characters, woman and sex/desire, to form one semantic and deadly compound). Woman-sex: the sensualities particular to female (yin) dispositions. Sensual entanglement with (certain) women: the baser the latter, the more sexually, hygienically, and sociopolitically harmful, eventually even destructive. Woman as sensualities/sex and vice versa: the figure of woman merging into desire, pain/pleasure, and copulation, as if sexual desire were a "femininity" within, a tendency toward dissolution and death within an insufficiently cultivated and undisciplined, thereby false master-subject. Thus the imperatives of such a narrative; narration becomes a slow, rhythmic, and incantatory exorcism of both the myriad things that seduce from without and the equally illusory figures that ensnare from within—by destroying and dissolving the boundaries that ensure the moral well-being and physiological amplitude of the man.

For both the XXPJPM commentator and Zhang Zhupo, the death of Ximen repeats the poisoning of Wu Da: both are fed drugs (aphrodisiac and arsenic) by Jinlian, and Jinlian will sit astride both—in the one case for pleasure; in the other for murder by suffocation and poisoning. "What is the difference between this medicine and Wu Da's? Where is the difference in the way each is made to swallow it? And the reader suddenly realizes, here is the eternal cycle of cause and effect [karmic retribution]."[77] In the margins above the description of Ximen's bloody and continuous discharge, the unnamed commentator writes, "Gazing at such a scene, how is it different from the killing of livestock?" "pitiful [Ximen]," and "How does this compare with Wu Da? Having gazed at the various dispositions in the Kingfisher Hall and the Grape Arbor, one must also gaze on this."[78] Note here the peculiar incriminating logic of the correspondences established that emphasize the sameness of woman-sex (nüse) in whatever situation. Jinlian murders Wu Da to now symmetrically murder Ximen; the one is cause to the latter's effect; the playing with base women (who are prone to kill) will lead to one's body/self being killed in turn; and the arrangement of female bodies in the Kingfisher Hall and Grape Arbour chapters must be juxtaposed to the particular disposing of the male body by woman-sex in this final chapter of Ximen's spectacular death. Evidently the pleasure of both text and readers inscribed in that purportedly particularly obscene episode (JPMC 27 hui, see also previous chapter) has been grossly and bloodily turned inside out, reversed and perverted into a much more equivocal and painful orgiastic death.

> Sixteen year-old beauty curd-like body
> Beneath the waist a sword kills men who're fools
> Although tumbling heads are never seen
> Unknowing [she'll] suck dry your bone marrow.[79]

*Intimate Politics*

"Of the animals kept in one's domicile on an everyday basis, besides chickens and dogs, are cats. . . . The cat is considered by its master to be very close and intimate to him, he therefore eats all his meals with the cat, and there are some masters who will even allow it to sleep in their rooms and beds with them. . . . There is a saying that goes, those who prefer cats to chickens and dogs, are like those [kings] who have an obsession for accommodating officials and coquette young men who are good at pandering and seducing and being generally agreeable (*pi xiechen meizi*). This is because they will come without the master's having called for them, and will not leave even upon being scolded. It is because of their *intimate disposition* [*qin*] that the master is close to them, and not because of any reason to being intimate with them."[80]

When and where half-human, half-object, catlike base persons such as bondmaid-concubines (and eunuchs and young male favorites) exceed their "originary," purely centripetal use and instrumental function by and for their master-subject, is when and where an "equalizing" liberatory moment (always excessive and escapist from the centripetal hierarchical point of view) surfaces. Such a moment is elusive and ephemeral, penumbra-like, when cats have the temporary and superficial power to transvalue the master as livestock, then kill the master made over into livestock. This is that nonreadable moment of base-inferior bondmaid-concubine revenge on not parvenu Ximen Qing or the superior reader but all of their fated place in the obscene hierarchical order that places cat-dogs on the borders of a human(e) order that encompasses all—human(e) and animal.

CHAPTER 8

Very Close to Yinfu and Ënu; or,
How Prefaces Matter for *Jin Ping Mei*
(1695) and *Ënu Shu* (Taipei, 1995)

This final chapter attempts to think through the politics and erotics of prefacing problematic, in this case erotic/pornographic texts. It also tangentially raises the question of excavating enabling readings of past texts in juxtaposition to present-day discourses, so that each might speak to the other and cross-fertilize meanings otherwise not legible under the cumulative weight of dominant institutions of writing and reading; meanings that might begin to indicate a flight away from centripetal, docile, hierarchical tendencies (see chapter 7). I have chosen to place together two nonequivalent but homologous prefatorial texts for comparison. They are nonequivalent in the sense that I deal with only one small detail and section of a definitive "how-to-read" essay printed around 1695 Qing China (Zhang Zhupo on JPM), and the entirety of the preface to a collection of lesbian erotic short stories published in 1995 in Taipei, Taiwan (Yang Zhao on Ënu Shu). Then, too, they are nonequivalent in the sense that the regimes of printing in the first case and publishing in the second are not the same, and therefore cannot be thought of as identical or even continuous formations. Neither can the printing and circulation of commentaried fiction in early Qing China and its cultural effects in terms of its practices of reading be equated to the publishing technologies and strategies of a modern market in books. Yet I suggest that a *homology,* a structural similarity in function, does obtain if one thinks of prefaces as a discourse that works to actively *place* its text in a projected or specified field of writing (the field in question can usually be deduced from the preface itself, and thus, it may be the field of popular vernacular fiction authored or authorized by eminent literati figures as writer or reader-commentator; or as in the case of Yang Zhao's preface to *Ënu Shu,* a literary field wherein the prefacer may hold an interested position as arbiter and judge of new entrants into that field).[1]

My reading assumes this homology insofar as the *literary* effects of the two prefaces in question can be assumed. Thus, Zhang Zhupo's prefaces plus commentaries constitute a singular JPM, an "authorized" (in an ethical-aesthetic sense at least) version that simultaneously proved to be the most circulated and long-lived one. In a way, it could be seen as securing JPM's continued reading and circulation through time within a circumscribed space of letters (it had undergone adequate literati mediation and authorization, whatever the profit or price to the individual literatus concerned).[2] Yang Zhao's preface, on the other hand, has already since its publication been variously quoted in approval, critically refuted, and analyzed.[3] One might almost worry that it had superseded the text it was meant to introduce if there were not (as I will later clarify) a clear disjuncture, in this case, between different classes or groups (perhaps even personhoods) of consumers. That is, those who have been interested in noting the preface have positioned their responding discourse within the field of academia—more specifically, literary criticism. This does not mean that these same persons might not consume the stories in other ways but rather that they have chosen to focus on the preface in the guise and service of articulating as well as furthering particular positions in an academic literary field (this chapter included).[4]

Given that both these prefaces have successfully put their object-texts in their seemingly rightful cultural-literary place, I shall proceed to question the erotics of such a placement, to suggest that placement and reading entail complicated and complicating relations of desire not only to the object-text but also the text as object. JPM is, for Zhang, an object of desire that accords with the rules of aesthetic and ethical writing. The only problem, and an onerous one at that, is the *form* this object takes. Yet its beauty is its ugliness—an ugliness of manner, but even more of its subject of representation, especially in its too many licentious women and illicit sexual acts.[5] Zhang resorts to a figure of Buddhist rhetoric, *xianshen shuofa,* to account for the provenance of ethical aesthetics in a muddy world. For Zhang, that source is the projected writer of JPM, a male literatus filled with filial ressentiment whose genius is proved in virtually *becoming* the bad objects—becoming licentious women⁶—who are the fictional embodiments of his exemplary literary and ethical teachings. In seeing double, the two in one, licentious women and the talented writer doubled (the latter in virtual drag is my way of putting it), Zhang "saves" the text from its own misogynist erotic. But what of the (the strange or queer) desire that leaks through such a figuration, that enables it and drives it? What of that desire that must remain unreadable and yet might be recuperable anachronistically as virtually queer?

Yang Zhao, by contrast, prefaces a self-proclaimed lesbian writer's first collection of short stories, all female homoerotic narratives.⁷ But Ënu Shu clearly does not "fit" with Yang Zhao's model of what he defines to be *literary* lesbian and gay writing; nor does it fit with his imaginary of either a lesbian-enunciating or representational subject. It is the sexual and literary politics of this mismatch that I am interested in reading. Too clearly perhaps, Yang's preface does not evoke a desiring relation to its object-text. How is it nondesiring, and what are the literary and erotic effects of a nondesiring relation to an explicit female homoerotics?

## Is There a Heterosexual Male Subject in This Text?

I have previously tried to claim, in an essay on Zhang Zhupo and his JPM, a "heterosexual male desire" in the strategies of reading whereby both textual object (yinfu) and reading subject (a virtual, virtuous male reader) are constructed, simultaneously and reciprocally.⁸ After presenting that essay (an earlier version of chapter 4) some years ago, I remember a friend saying to me afterward that she couldn't agree with the use of "heterosexual" in the context of a late Ming–early Qing JPM (or something to that effect). I was too busy worrying about how to prove the blatant "narrative misogyny" with which Zhang Zhupo's commentaries so clearly colluded, and that certainly (it seemed to me) his commentaried edition had helped to crystallize as part of the JPM mythology. It was only in thinking through this chapter, and attempting to rethink one line in Zhang Zhupo's *Dufa*, that I began to understand anew my friend's reservation about the notion of a "heterosexual" male desire in a late Ming–early Qing context.

JPM is undoubtedly "about" a polygamous household, and crucially "about" the sexual relations between the head of that household (Ximen Qing) and mostly the women, but also some boys in that household. Significantly, the latter—whether women or boys—are all ritually, symbolically, and in ways familial-social and politico-economic inferior to Ximen Qing. Such an "inferiority" no longer resounds with the weight and meanings it would have had in the time-space wherein the narrative was produced and mostly read, until about a century ago. To nonproblematically "name" the modality of desire as represented in the narrative as well as between the "virtual" reader that is the commentator and the text filled with his interjections, a "heterosexual" male desire, is to assume a seamless continuity between representations of male-female desire and sexual relations in the late Ming–early Qing period and the present. This is not even to bring up the complexities of translation and transposition of ideas and practices concerning and surrounding gender and sexuality in the present moment between, say, English and different regions/gradations of "Chineseness." If "heterosexual" has been in at least some fields (I am thinking of gay and lesbian studies, feminist and queer theories) deeply problematized and deconstructed, returned as it were to history and the social, then I must rethink the relations of desire and sex on at least two levels in my project on JPM: at the level of the representation of sexual relations within the narrative; and in the space between the narrative and at least two of its "virtual" reader(s), who may be said to engage in relations of desire with the text and its representations.

I am interested in this chapter in reformulating the Zhang Zhupo commentaries' relation of desire to its host text. I shall try to show how one line in his 108 Dufa items might be read as a stray thread that could well undo any attempt (even or especially my own) to stabilize and cohere any one sexualized proclivity on the part of its virtual reader, be it desire and fear or nondesire. I continue to hold that JPM, especially in its Zhang Zhupo version, is a deeply misogynist narrative, but I can no longer think it so in a total way without any leaks or letups (which perhaps will take time and changes in our conditions to misapprehend and apprehend in turn).

I would like to use this reformulation of Zhang Zhupo's (and my own) shifting relation to a desired object-text to reflect for the moment on another problematic text that appeared in Taiwan in 1995. This is a short story collection titled Ënu Shu (The Book of Bad Women; "bad" as in evil, malignant, degenerate, licentious, immoral, and so forth), written by Chen Xue and published by Huang Guan, a popular press in Taiwan. The work appeared as one of three books in a new series called xin ganguan xiaoshuo—that is, "new sensual narratives" or "new erotica." All three writers were, at the time of publication, first-time, young, self-proclaimed queer authors. The book appeared with the first wave of lesbian and gay groups in several universities in Taiwan, and followed on the international success of Li An's film, *The Wedding Banquet*. (*The Wedding Banquet* was so successful abroad that the then-president of Taiwan decided to see it with his entire family. A "Taiwanese" father's acceptance of his son's gay marriage in New York had become an international then local hit, a film for family viewing.) Of the three "new erotica" books, however, Chen Xue's was the only one sold in a plastic cover, usually reserved for "pornographic" materials such as *Penthouse* and *Playboy*, with an additional stamp forbidding all those under eighteen from purchasing the book. The material inside was deemed unsafe for the consumption of the young and innocent. All three books came with prefaces by well-known Taiwan cultural critics and/or writers. Yet only Chen Xue's preface came with a caveat: a warning to the author and an explanation to all potential readers. The warning defined "how to write" properly literary rather than merely escapist works, while the explanation belabored "how to read" insufficiently self-affirming narratives of unclassifiable though highly suspect female homoerotic desires.

*Becoming Licentious Women*

> The author of JPM must have experienced danger, difficulty, poverty, and sorrow and must have been thoroughly acquainted with the ways of the world in order to be able to depict the inner spirit of his characters with such verisimilitude [*moshen*].[9]

In his *Dufa* item number fifty-nine, Zhang Zhupo explains the writer's (*zuo Jin Ping Mei zhe*) success in authentically representing the various characters in his narrative in terms of the writer's surmised autobiographical experiences.[10] Only one who has gone through *huannan qiungchou* and *renqing shigu*, the vicissitudes of life and relations to (other) men and the social world, and experienced this world and its relations in its depth, could have the understanding necessary to accurately cast (*mo*) each character's internal structure of feeling.[11] In thus understanding the experiential conditions for the writer's talent, Zhang Zhupo immediately comes up against a difficulty, one that arises from Zhang's reading of what seems to take up a major part of the book: the varied passages detailing *yinfu touhan*, licentious women stealing men, engaging in illicit sex. What kind of experience can the writer have had of such situations, not to mention the positions/perspectives entailed in the depiction of such situations, to produce the verisimilar, sometimes inflammatory, always finally punitive effects of such episodes in the narrative?

> However, if the author had felt it necessary to have personally experienced everything he describes in order to produce this book, the Chin P'ing Mei could never have been written. Why is this? The various licentious women in the book engage in illicit relations with men in a variety of different ways. If the author had to have personally experienced all of these things in order to understand them, how could he have done it? Thus, it is apparent that there is nothing a genius [caizi] cannot apprehend if he concentrates his mind on it.[12]

There are two points worth noting here. One is how in the sequence of thought from item fifty-nine to sixty, Zhang Zhupo changes his mind. Experience of the world is all-important for a talented writer to realize that talent in fictional writing. Yet in the case of this fiction, experience cannot explain all—in fact, experience cannot explain portions of the narrative that are immensely memorable to this virtual reader (Zhang Zhupo). The second point has to do precisely with what Zhang remembers most in regard to (and what would later in the history of its dissemination become most associated with) JPM. Another way of putting this would be: When and where in the narrative is Zhang Zhupo the virtual reader very interested? How might one, reading his text today, ascertain and understand some of these moments and placements of interest? I suggest that one of these blocks of readerly interest is reached in this item of Zhang's *Dufa*. For Zhang Zhupo, who is more often than not identified with the purported writer of JPM (see chapter 4), the question raised here is an urgent one: What in the writer's practical experiences can possibly explain the verisimilar narrative effect in the casting of all these licentious women and their variegated illicit sexual engagements? What is simultaneously affirmed in this question is the "truth-effect" of these representations as well as the genius of their identifiably virtuous male literati writer. Zhang Zhupo's answer, however, seems a bit ad hoc, the repeating of a quasi-Buddhist cliché: anything can be apprehended to the concentrated force of the heart-mind that is one (not scattered, not dispersed).

As if he too felt this insufficient, Zhang goes on to elaborate in item sixty-one that

> once his concentration has enabled him to apprehend what he needs to know about a character, the author [writer] must be able to become that

character himself [*xianshen*] before he can speak for him. Thus, he has actually become the various licentious women whom he describes, and he is able to expound his lesson through them.¹³

Apprehension, presented as the ability of the one to partake of all and any, is not enough to speak for each of these diverse characters. In order to successfully ventriloquize such varied figures, the writer must phantasmically become each, so as to speak for/as if (in the virtual corporeality of) each (*shi you zhenge xianshen ifan fang shuode ifan*). Hence, it is in the writing process (*xie zhu yinfu*) that the writer actualizes the becoming of each licentious woman in the representation of her personhood (*zhen nai ge xian yinfu ren shen*) so as to speak his (the writer's) lessons (*fa*) to all. Through the process of writing, it is as if the writer becomes one licentious woman after another, the better to speak in their (immoral feminine) voice *his* (moral and masculine) lessons for his readers. Yet in using this quasi-Buddhist rhetoric as trope for how the writer could have written in such detail of what was surely not beyond but rather *beneath* his (gender, sexual, and class/caste) experiential knowledge, Zhang Zhupo inadvertently skews certain axes of the writable and readable for one in his (and the writer's putative) position. A quasi-Buddhist rhetoric (*i xin; xian shen shuo fa*) facilitates and masks this skewing and its potentially queer consequences. The latter is, of course, only anachronistically excavatable. Let me now try to detail how in proposing the becoming various yinfu on the part of the genius writer in order the better to present his lessons to the reader, this particular process and trope may be seen to skewer narrative "truth" (the register of the verisimilar), aesthetic pleasure (the register of affect), and moral-lesson (the register of an ethics of learning). I use skewer here, as in rendering askew, but also as in forcibly stringing and weaving the three together.

How, then, can we understand Zhang Zhupo's particular and, on second and third readings, increasingly defamiliarizing use of xianshen shuofa, a by-now-cliché Buddhist trope? What does this Buddhist trope do to Zhang Zhupo's elucidation of, first, the writer's intentions; second, the seemingly improper objects of that intention—the many yinfu of JPM; and finally, the virtual reader's reading of those objects, and through the latter, his apprehension of the writer's lessons (as actualized intentions)?

For one thing, the trope metaphorically renders the writer as a Buddha-like teacher who in order to convincingly speak his teachings, speaks in the guise of the (partial and encompassed) object of these teachings. Thus, yinfu as representation is an illusion (fiction) whose sole verity ("truth" effect) lies in the writer's intentions or moral-lessons, and in the reader's retrieval of the latter by reading through illusion to lesson. To some extent, the reader must invert the process of writing, and go from each particular yinfu and her illicit sexual engagement to the lesson that speaks in yinfu form, to the writer ventriloquist whose voice and lesson must be carefully discerned despite, or even because of its being—in drag?

If not in drag, the lesson is as it were embodied and elucidated in the form of a problematic, indeed a devalued and profane object, a clearly "bad" object, if only in terms of this object's distance from the projected writer's and virtual reader's positions—whether morally, or in terms of gender, status (shenfen), and sexual practices. Such an object plainly ne-cessitates the presence and explanations of a virtual reader who knows the trick to a correct and purgative reading. At the same time, the explanation given—that the writer has had to *ge xian yinfu renshen*, that is, to become each and every one of these awful debased women so as to speak their particular evil truths in the dual tonal register that will resonate with his more "general" voice and lesson—is at the very least, a strange (qi) explanation. This is strange in the imagery of a writer (and virtual reader) whose ultimately women-fearing and desire-devaluing voice and teachings are embodied in precisely the negative bodily forms (apparitions, of course) that are their objects of opprobrium. Where does the one start and the other begin? How is one to discern the two levels of voices—the one dissolute; the other stern and lecturing? It would have been discursively so much more consistent and less paradoxical to align one's virtuous languages and selves to virtuous widows and filial *guixiou* feminine practices.[14] The purported writer of JPM and virtual reader that is Zhang Zhupo in this instance face a much more arduous task. To dress up as bad objects and enact virtuous teachings is dangerous—unless one is Buddhalike, devoid of desires. Otherwise, at what point and in what guise might some stray desiring thoughts (of identificatory pleasures even if relayed and twice removed, as in the case of Zhang Zhupo) *not* seep into, leak out of, this long process of writing and reading that constitutes ge xian yinfu renshen. This is why I have anachronistically chosen to overread this particular usage of Zhang Zhupo as a moment of a possibly relayed identificatory pleasure taken with yinfu (he—the writer has become yinfu; I, Zhupo, become him, and through him, yinfu). For if sexual desire for licentious women is evil and to be eradicated, then perhaps one (leaky) way out for an unspeakable, not-writable desire on the part of a virtuous male (and female) reading position is through sexual desire *as bad objects*.

But to recapitulate on the signifying process involved in Zhang Zhupo's use of xianshen shuofa, a residual Buddhist ideology in Zhang's considered use (specifically to explain the inexplainable: how without experiential knowledge, a genius male writer could write yinfu into such verisimilar forms and contortions) would seem to establish the differential value and ontological status of each. The writer and virtual reader are in the position of the subject as either enunciator/writer of (eternal) truths, or reader-retriever of gems (truth, meaning, and so on) amid dross (flotsam, illusory waste material); this is the order of the upright, superior, weightier. Whereas the many licentious women and their illicit sexual engagements are of another, lesser, encompassed order of things, bad and ephemeral objects whose negative value and illusory (fictive) status serve to *embody* another subject, a higher other's teaching.

To push this line of thinking a bit further, one could then say yinfu are by definition fake insofar as they are illusory fiction, written and read as such in the service of human(e) mankind's realization of the equally illusory nature of his desires (for bad objects). Paradoxically, this realization and its attendant purge or attenuation of sexual desire relies on the *degree* of verisimilitude achieved by the representation in question. Bad objects notwithstanding, these have to be bad *enough* to call forth and transfix the (male) desire that will then wither at its root when it encounters the lesson that inheres within these seductive forms. The greater the verisimilitude, the more invested the reader, and the more effective the lesson and process of a purgative cure.[15]

At the same time, the greater the verisimilitude, the more totalizing the momentary strategic transposition whereby writer becomes yinfu—albeit working toward the purgation of the virtual reader. Yes, Zhang Zhupo seems to be conceding, having cornered himself by referring to the experiential knowledge necessary for a narrative aesthetic and ethical verisimilitude, that the writer had to virtually become yinfu, and that is why one can take pleasure in reading (even in reading yinfu) that is not ultimately *immoral*. For it is in the process of reading, as an inversion of the process of writing, that one may realize or penetrate to the moral bone–teachings of these ephemeral seductive body-figures.

But what if this moral pleasure is leavened, slightly bloated (or gloating or ecstatic-hysteric), and more ambivalent than it needs to be by the fantasized merge, the becoming two in one, of writer-subject and yinfu-object? What if this fantasized transformation of gender and ontological status were one aspect of the imaginative and desiring effects of a Buddhist trope?[16] Imagine becoming base bondmaid-concubine for even just a second!

I think one might consider the possibility of Zhang Zhupo as having strategically deployed an available Buddhist figure of speech in order to resolve a knot in his ethico-aesthetics of JPM. It would be precisely such a strategy that would then allow Zhang Zhupo to construct between two ethically polarized but aesthetically parallel effects of writing (the projected writer-virtual reader; the object of writing-reading), a linkage forged in Buddhist transformational thinking yet limned in a gender-skewing, status-inverting desire.[17]

### Queer Subjects, Straitened Readings

> The lesbian sentiment [nutongxinglian ganqing] that we read in Ënu Shu are almost all intentionally extracted from [a] social context, and yet the more it [lesbian sentiment?] wishes to escape society's interventions the more it will express that part of it which is society's slave.
>
> In Chen Xue's writing, every passage of lesbian erotics is filled with guilt [zuïe gan]. But what guilt need the lesbian have? What guilt need women's erotics have? Why is it necessary to place lesbian erotics at a great distance from everyday situations? Does not Chen Xue's persistent "escape by way of exoticism" [yizhi taobi] precisely reflect the overarching shadow of society's restrictions?[18]

This is the blurb on the back cover of Chen Xue's Ënu Shu. It is taken from the preface to this short story collection—a preface written by one of Taiwan's foremost fiction writers and critics Yang Zhao for the generation now under forty.[19] The blurb differs from that on the back of the other two books released simultaneously as part of the same "new erotic writing" series by one of Taiwan's largest commercial presses, primarily known as the publisher of romances for women; it is also markedly different from most blurbs advertising the books that this press aims to place and sell. It differs in how the set of rhetorical questions posed by Yang Zhao serves as both interpretation and rebuke. Yang interprets Chen's title and the collection's various evil women (ënu) as suffering from guilt—a guilt that he deems both source and proof of (continued) enslavement to social repression and restrictions. The proof of guilt, according to Yang, lies in the author's *intentional* extraction of lesbian sentiment and thematics from any recognizable social context that nevertheless succeeds in extending its shadowy influence through the very forms used to escape it. These forms must then be seen as enslaved to the same social mechanisms they would seem to deny.

For Yang Zhao, the three forms that indict Chen Xue's lesbian subjects as "guilty" of continued enslavement to a sexually repressive social regime are: a first-person narrator evincing what Yang considers to be "false consciousness" (in English in parentheses in the original); the projection of lesbian sentiment onto mother-daughter (incestuous) relations, or onto the transfigurations of a narcissistic narrator; and the situating of her stories in an "alien" space (*yizhi kongjian*), an "exotic place" (*yi jie*). On the latter, Yang writes that Chen Xue has "borrowed from the magic realism of South America," and what with "a teeny bit of Mo Yan and Han Shaogong [modernist writers in the People's Republic of China] added in, has created an exotic place" (15). What Yang is of course implying (and the patronizing tone is not an addition in my translation) is that there is nothing new here—nothing, that is, apart from the "lesbian subject" that in any case is dealt with altogether problematically. As such, he concludes, "Why must lesbian erotics be situated at such a great distance from the everyday? Chen Xue's persistent 'escape by exoticism' precisely serves to reflect the immense shadow cast by society's restrictions" (15). Chen Xue escapes through a reactive extraction of the narrative self from the recognizably "everyday" (the latter is rendered exotic and alien)—an everydayness that constitutes the specific restrictions of this particular society toward female homoerotics and homosexuality. In short, Chen Xue's fictional topography is insufficiently "everyday Taiwan" just as her fictional erotics are not "Lesbianism per se."

But an even greater problem, besides the shadows cast on a situatedness that cannot therefore somehow sufficiently be concretized (in Yang's reading), is a homoerotics that is likewise insufficiently *sure of itself*, and therefore projected onto and dependent on modalities of desire that are *not* lesbian but defective (how is not made clear), perhaps even heterosexist.

> Although Chen Xue focuses her writing on lesbians, yet the homoerotics of women in her stories are lacking in the legitimacy of an assertive existential mode [*lizhi qizhuang cunzai de hefaxing*]. She will habitually write homosexuality as a fictive projection of a [daughter's] mother-complex (as in [the short story] "Searching for the Lost Wings of the Angel"), or as the myriad transformations of a narcissistic desiring formation (as in "Labyrinth of the Night" [another short story]). Having written a whole

book of/about/filled with lesbians [*yi zhengben de nutongxinglian*], paradoxically, Chen Xue is actually denying "Lesbianism per se" [*nutongxinglian qingyu de shizhi zishen*, or the actual substance of a female homoerotics].[20]

"Habitually" (*xiguan xingde*) again registers a devaluation. It is as if, for Yang, the author had slipped up here, had fallen back into modes of thinking, writing, and desiring that *cannot be lesbian* since they are so patently something else, something recognizable and categorizable to this particular reader (Yang Zhao) as a "mother-complex," or an extreme case of "narcissism" and autoerotic transformations. This leads Yang to state categorically that the central paradox of Chen Xue's book is its *denial* (*foren*) of what he terms "Lesbianism per se," which in a book "filled with/about lesbians" can only be seen as a denial of its own "subject."

This denial, according to Yang, is exemplified at the level of narration and in the voice-person of the narrator.

> Moreover, in terms of form, these four short stories uniformly use the first-person confessional mode, without other experimentation in narrative form. Chen Xue's confessional mode is a superficial one, with the narrator detailing her thoughts and actions as if these were actual, with the effect of a seeming sincerity, as if she were telling the truth. Yet reading on to the end, we clearly feel a huge tension in the text, and this tension arises from the conflict and struggle between the narrator's consciousness and subconsciousness. What the narrator self-consciously presents as a sincere confession is actually none other than a "false consciousness" [*huanjia yishi*], and [her] true feelings and thoughts are repressed, distorted, and hidden between the lines. The source of this repression is of course not personal but social.[21]

The crux of the problem with Chen Xue's collection, for Yang Zhao, is simply this: the author and all the first-person narrators of her stories are afflicted with a "false consciousness" of which they are insufficiently aware, and this then would explain not just the "surface" or "superficial" quality of the first-person narrations but also the thematic representation of pseudo-lesbian relations (mother-daughter erotism; narcissistic autoerotism) as well as the formal recourse to "alien" or "exotic" places and situations. Further, this so-called false consciousness is diagnosed as one shared by both the author (Chen Xue) and her narrators, as evidenced in Yang Zhao's noting Chen Xue's "intentionality" in thematic and formal choices. But it is her use of a "sincere" first-person narrator that is finally most damning.

It is important to restate that Yang Zhao's preface is both typical and atypical in its relation to the text it is prefacing. On the one hand, it is typical in its "assessment" of the new author on first publication, and therefore, constitutes a sort of "stamp of approval" pending a newcomer's entrance into the field of fiction and literature. It is atypical in the relative sternness or even harshness of its judgment, and in the fact that the commercial press in question did not ask the author to agree to this particular writer-critic for her preface.[22] Yang Zhao's preface pronounced the book in *literary* terms adequate but barely so. Literature is, declares Yang Zhao, "simultaneously deeply embedded in the network that is society, yet at the same time transcends and even leads society."[23] Insofar as Chen Xue's stories inadvertently, despite their author's intentions, "reflect the overarching shadow of society's restrictions" (15), they must be seen as lacking in literary inventiveness and of positive value only to the extent to which they (passively) reflect social embeddedness. In short, they cannot help being flawed, and that is exactly how they may still be read as socially illuminating (of the alleged false consciousness with which they are ridden). And yet, without this preface, or what in effect amounts to a "how to read Chen Xue's first novel," the "unknowing" reader might never have quite defined literature in this way, nor read Chen Xue in this particular light (as failed contender for lesbian literariness) and context. (Incidentally, Yang Zhao's judgment eerily recapitulates certain Chinese critics on JPM in the first half of the twentieth century. JPM is considered too "naturalist" or insufficiently "realist" in failing to provide textual point d'appui for critique. See chapter 1.)

But what precisely is the context provided by this prefacer who can so offhandedly define literature, judge what counts and what doesn't, and finally as an aside, decide who, what, and how is Lesbianism per se?

The context or continuum in which Chen Xue's collection is placed, measured, and found lacking is an interesting one. Yang Zhao begins his preface by outlining two works: one written in 1891 by Harry Campbell on biological differences between the sexes, and the other a recent analysis by Bram Dijkstra of Western phallocentrism's feminine idols of perversity. For Yang Zhao, the preceding century in the West is marked by male anxiety over the "discovery" of female sexuality. "What if women have desires? What would be the difference between the desires of women and that of men? More important, what would be the influence, the effects, of women's desires on men?"[24] The discovery of women and women's sexual desires along with their attendant male anxiety produced a flurry of works that "superficially idolized the newly discovered female sexual desire, but actually deeply and in the harshest way condemned it, equating female sexual desire to the evil power that seduces people to criminality, and this is what those European males did, at the end of the last century" (8).

A hundred years later, a new question arises. It is now the age of "men discovering men, and women discovering women," says Yang Zhao. If the heterosexual romance has been overwritten, then it is now possible to enter into a new field, "a barren field awaiting tilling"—that is, the erotic adventures of women with women, and the erotic seductions of men and men.[25] And it is at this point that Yang Zhao proceeds to define literature, turning to two examples of laudable literary work in this new field. The two are Zhu Tienwen's novella *Huangren Shouji* and Qiu Miaojin's novel *Ë U Shouji*, or *Journal of a Crocodile*. It is after having read and admired the literary accomplishments of these two that Yang Zhao finally explores *Ënu Shu*.

But if

> at the end of the nineteenth century, men were horrified by the newly discovered potentials of female sexual desires, and thereupon created a whole spectrum of evil figures representing desiring women, then, in the same way, at the end of the twentieth century, when women find out about other women's internal desires, they will also panic and fear and feel unused to such desires, and therefore take measures in writing that hedge with, escape and justify these ambivalent feelings.[26]

This, then, is how Yang Zhao understands and situates Chen Xue's work. Chen Xue is *analogous* to the men who hated and idolized women's sexuality at the turn of the nineteenth century. Her work both escapes from and seeks to justify a perverted lesbian erotics in ways parallel to what European men tried to do with European women's sexuality one hundred years ago. The implicit accusation is that Chen Xue and her narrators are too guilt ridden to adequately represent (in writing, as representative voice and "identity") a sufficiently contextualized Taiwanese Lesbianism per se.

Chen Xue is twice boxed in. The larger encasement is the context of a discourse of (European) male discovery and fear of women's sexuality; the second box is a 1990s' Taiwanese literary field.[27] The first establishes the reactive modality of her representations of female homoeroticism; the second shows up the degree to which her first error (fear of women who desire women; lack of an in-your-face *lizhi qizhuang* attitude) extends to become a second, more serious failure—that is, the ability to "represent" a local, locatable in a readable everyday Lesbianism per se. Chen Xue is therefore twice inauthentic. Her fear approximates that of *European* men who fear and fantasize about women's sexuality. Her writing reproduces a homoerotics that mimics what it ought not to mimic, and ensconces that mimicry in a mystifying alien surrounding—as if that could save its inauthenticity from being detected.

But is not inauthenticity an effect, rather than cause, of the boxes envisaged in this preface?

The central contradiction in Yang Zhao's preface is his devaluing of Chen Xue's literary value, while basing that devaluation on the collection's failure to correctly and positively (that is, in the mode and voice Yang deems necessary) represent ënu, or homoerotic relations and sentiments of lesbians in particular in Taiwan. But how, one might ask, is such a "correctness" or "positivity" to be read and measured? What pretexts and contexts might have provided the necessary trajectories, even if only of reading—a reading that must activate, if not challenge both one's history as well as conditions of knowledge and desires? Such a reading would not be "individualist" but would take into account one's multifaceted linkages with and formations through various "modernizing" institutions in Taiwan, including family, school, and state?

What is this lizhi qizhuang, this rationally self-affirming, in-your-face lesbian representation embedded in an everyday (Taiwanese) sociohistoric that would measure up to Yang Zhao's expectations? How would it be configured and marked to ensure its "immediate" legibility to "anyone"? Where and how would such an "authentic" and "authenticating" discourse and its enunciating positions exist? Might there not be specifically Taiwanese sociohistoric but also economic and cultural conditions for its apparent nonexistence, its invisibility and nonlegible practices, excepting in forms and places hardly recognizable as such—that is, ascertainably "Lesbian" and certifiably "Taiwanese"?[28] Might not one of Yang Zhao's preface's paradoxical discursive effects be to precisely erase, or at least devalue, emergent though as yet indefinable female homoerotic writings and readings in the face of their sprouting and spreading?

Embodiments of Ënu?

Let me now juxtapose to Yang Zhao's reading two anecdotes and one hypothesis that will serve to encircle my question: What are some of the situations and contradictions that might reciprocally constitute a taiwanese lesbian representation and discourse as diffuse, one among many, easily unnoticed and unrecognized, but never completely unlinked?

The first story is of one Taiwanese lesbian telling a queer female friend of the difficulty among the former's circle of friends in getting their hands on Chen Xue's book. This book has sold like wildfire. It has sold out in many of the larger bookstores. It's become the bedside book—yes, of course. Silence and knowing smiles.

The second story is of a large family gathering at one of those typical festivities in Taiwan where the patriline must be emotionally and sociopolitically reaffirmed, and when all manner of sexual rebels and emotional escapees sometimes find themselves stranded in rather straitened circumstances. One nunnish aunt finds, not so surprisingly, a copy of Chen Xue's book in her tomboyish high-school dropout niece's bedroom. The niece's "best friend"/lover is unexpectedly present at the familial gathering, and though not a stray word passes between the three, the year will be a better one for them all, the aunt decides, when burning incense and kowtowing to the now amiable ancestors.

Such stories abound among lesbian and queer persons in Taiwan and are passed around with relish. They attest to "other" readings of and around Chen Xue's book as well as female homoerotic uses of Chen Xue's stories that displace and make somewhat irrelevant "serious" critical judgment, especially when these come in the guise of such as Yang Zhao's preface. But I also wish to seriously address this very "irrelevance." How has this irrelevance come about if not through just the kind of "invisibility effect" that Yang Zhao ironically attributes to Chen Xue, thus producing it as an effect of her textual "denial" and "false consciousness"? In fact, Yang Zhao writes "guilt" onto evil (queer) women and other persons whose lives and practices are shameless, and between who transpire queer desires oftentimes encoded as "incestuous."[29] Perhaps this is an active perversion, a perverted appropriation of the residual overvaluation of filiality and familial ties by precisely those persons most condemned in that "old" moral hierarchical order. But does not the active unknowing of homoerotic contexts and queer modalities of reading constitute its own particular denial and false consciousness—if only of its (straitened) relations of desire to its object text?[30]

To frame Chen Xue's stories and narrators as analogous to that of panicked European males of a previous turn of a century in the face of their discovery of female sexuality (no less imaginary and phastasmic than their previous unknowing of female sexuality) would have been disingenuous had it not been so revelatory of the preface's particular labor of unknowing and the erotics of that ignorance. Chen Xue's denial and false consciousness must be aligned to that of *European* male fantasies at the turn of the nineteenth century, just as the erotics of her stories are seen to slavishly reproduce certain hegemonic (hetero-)social sexual taboos and clichés. The missing mediating subject here is, of course, the geopolitically situated and gendered reader who couples these together. One is almost tempted to read, in the place of European, an authoritative voice of the Taiwan literary establishment, and in the instance of taboos and clichés, the "straight mind" retracing its own laws. Denial and false consciousness revert back to their mediating subject, and a slavish (hetero-)erotics stalls and sputters in the closed circuit that makes up a "straight" (correct, *lizhi qizhuang*) literary and mental field of reading.

Now for the hypothesis. Yang Zhao has glossed the semantics of ënu as guilt ridden. I have said that in thus reading ënu and its varied embodiments in Chen Xue's stories, he is inscribing guilt as a cover-up for a reticent shamelessness (*wuchi*) in representation and practice.[31] In reading ënu as shameless homoerotic female figures in Chen Xue's fiction, I would like to suggest their emotional and erotic affiliations with the various types of *feinu*, or "nonfemales" produced in a medico-hygienic discourse of the late Ming period. These were women who were deemed deficient solely due to their being incapable of sexual reproduction.[32] On the other hand, ënu etymologically recalls the undesirables of sexual-hygienic manuals of that same (and earlier) periods, women whose physical attributes and aggressive sexual practices signaled their malignant qualities for men. If ënu used to circulate as "objects to avoid" in sex manuals for male readers, then Chen Xue's ënu now circulate as objects of desire among lesbians, female readers of homoerotic tendencies, and queers.

*Reading "Very Close to" Yinfu and Ënu*

Prefaces matter. Their matter is the stuff of literary capital (its accumulation, depletion, or exchange from the currency of nearby fields, such as the political or academic), just as it is the stuff of market salespersonship. Since the book markets of the late Ming Jiangnan region, prefaces have helped to ensure the place, price, and circulation of their books. But great differences obtain since the time when nonentities could make a lasting literary (*wenren* at large) name for themselves by putting out their own editions of popular, infamous, or reknowned fictional works or poetry anthologies (I am thinking of Jin Shengtan, for one example). Whereas in today's literary market in Taiwan, nobodies must find famous names to preface their first publication and/or win a major literary prize as a mark of literary worth. Yet narratives of female sexuality, then considered dangerously licentious and now seen as problematically homoerotic, continue to demand prefacing, commentaries, and interpretation. It is as if the labor of a preliminary and preparatory knowing and telling would divert whatever damage was believed would follow on an uninitiated reading. How else to explain the urgency and seriousness of a Zhang Zhupo's and Yang Zhao's "how to read"?

But here, too, there are telling differences. A "Zhang Zhupo" had no doubt that these were "verisimilar yinfu" he was reading, nor was he worried that other readers would fail to recognize such finely brushed up lascivious and seductive yinfu and their sexual acts. (He could thus, of course, be "accused" of producing the very "yinfu" he was reading/writing—as I have done in chapter 4.) The only thing Zhang was worried about was that the particular products of this talent for fictional verisimilitude would be held against their genius writer. Thus, Zhang devises two strategies for reading. First, read in the place of the writer, as if you were the writer, or at least as if in the place of the virtual reader (that is, the place of Zhang's pre-hui and interlinear commentaries): "You must read it as though it were your own work in order not to be deceived by it. . . . Only if you start out with the assumption that you will have to work out every detail for yourself in order to avoid being deceived will you avoid being deceived."[33] And second, read all these yinfu and their sexual escapades recitatively, out loud (dui ren du), as if the writer (and you the complicit reader) were reciting (performing?) yinfu for their exposure and his/your purgative cure. "Nowadays, if a scholar [du shu zhe] reads JPM his parents and teachers are sure to forbid it, and they themselves do not dare to read it openly [dui ren du]. People do not understand that only a true scholar is able to read JPM properly. Anyone who reads it on the sly is really reading an obscene book."[34] The answer (and secret) to not falling for illusory licentious base women is simply to "become" licentious yinfu for the duration of an acting out, a purge, and a reading (out loud).

As for Ënu Shu, one could well repeat Zhang Zhupo only changing the value and accent on "obscene": "Anyone who reads it on the sly is really reading an obscene book." Even those who read it to each other, out loud, may well be reading obscenely, an obscene book. Hence the need for a plastic cover, an age limit, and a censorious preface—censorious not as in "how to read pleasurably yet not fall prey to the pleasures of this text" but rather as in "how to read and police whatever desires, however unknowable, misrecognizable, in this text and reading." The 1990s in Taiwan were not, at least not in a totalizing way, a place where multifarious sexual pleasures and desires could be written and read only in the name of an eventual (Confucian-Buddhist?) enlightenment and/or (Buddhist-Taoist?) purgation. Yet other techniques of management and control set in and began their work, quietly and effectively. This, together with state policy's accelerated bringing of all informal and illegal economies (sexual and otherwise) to legal light and regulation (for instance, the police harassment of gays on Chang De Road just outside of what is now no longer called the New Park; the "abolishing" of licensed prostitution in Taipei as part of an antiobscenity and antipornography campaign and policy). Yang Zhao's reading of Chen Xue's ënu figures and female homoerotics accomplishes the policing of several boundaries at once. One line is the "1990s' Taiwan literature" that Chen Xue remains just this side of, not firmly inside but not quite outside for good either (a borderline case).[35] Then there is the line of fictional representation of and the book's implied representativeness as a particular Lesbianism per se, which again Chen Xue falls short of due to the "escapism" in her representation of situatedness (is this anywhere in Taiwan? not really, says the preface) and the "incest" topoi of her narratives (how can this be a "proper" lesbianism?).

Against and in response to the increasingly imperious demand for readings that either police or incarcerate in "representative" positionalities, I should like to recite a passage—stealing from Gayatri Spivak's quotation of it[36]—written to enjoin readings and writings that neither occupy the place of nor seek to speak authoritatively on but rather hover very close to yinfu and ënu.

> Don't claim to "speak for" or, worse, to "speak on," barely speaking next to, and if possible *very close to*: these are the first of the solidarities to be taken on by the few Arabic women who obtain or acquire freedom of movement, of body and of mind.[37]

For those who continue to find (some part of) themselves for one unspeakable/illegible reason or another residing in the space and time of base (jian, considered inferior and immoral, incorrect, perverted, queer, homosexual, bisexual, transsexual or all of the above) modes of sexual practices and familial-social personhood. It is imperative that those parts/persons that/who have acquired "freedom" in this encompassed order stay centrifugally, counterintuitively, not falling in with the weightier side of the watermelon, very close to so as to struggle alongside of penumbra (non)subjects, social movements, and aggregations for sustenance and survival.

NOTES

## Preface

1 Ming-Shui Hung, *The Romantic Vision of Yuan Hung-tao, Late Ming Poet and Critic* (Taipei, Taiwan: Bookman Books, 1997), 77.
2 Reprinted in Yijia Wang, *Gudian Jinkan* (Taipei, Taiwan: Yee, 1989), 185–98.
3 Li Yu [Qing], *Xianqing ouji* (Shanghai: Wenyi chubanshe, 1992), 115–63. Photocopy of the 1936 Beiyeshanfang edition.
4 This would seem to concur with Mathew Sommer's argument for the shift in late Ming through Qing legal discourse from what he terms "status performance" to "gender performance," and the concomitant "peasantization" of both civil law and sexual morality via criminal liability. See Mathew Sommer, *Law, Society, and Culture in China* (Stanford, Calif.: Stanford University Press, 2000), 5–14, 308–11.
5 On the changing concept of *liang* as legal term, see Sommer, *Law*, 312–20: "From the Tang through the eighteenth century, the term's emphasis shifted from free commoner legal status to moral goodness, especially in a sexual sense" (312). On the gender and sexual politics of recent "state feminist" reforms in Taiwan law, see Naifei Ding and Jen-peng Liu, "New Taiwanese are (Good) Women Unused to Fornication" (Xin Taiwanren shi bu xi yu yinxing de nuren), unpublished manuscript.
6 C. T. Hsia, *The Classic Chinese Novel: A Critical Introduction* (New York: Columbia University Press, 1968), 170.

7 Kai-wing Chow suggests that the growth of literati (some as "professional writers") interest in novels and plays may even have "contributed to the increasingly positive reception and tolerance of 'heterodox ideas' and vernacular expressions in the examinations" ("Writing for Success: Printing, Examinations, and Intellectual Change in Late Ming China," *Late Imperial China* 17, no. 1 [June 1996]: 144). Thus, the reading and editing of "popular" fictional forms would have influenced institutionalized orthodoxy, just as the latter "contributed" its forms of exegeses to the beginnings of a fictional "criticism" in the form of prefaces, commentaries, and so forth.

8 For a recent account of the authorship debates, see Bu Jian, "Jin Ping Mei zuozhe zhi mi" ("The Riddle of JPM's Author," in *Jin Ping Mei zhi mi* (*The Riddles of Jin Ping Mei*), ed. Liu Hui and Yang Yang (Beijing: Shumu wenxian chuban she, 1989), 33–64.

9 On a rereading of Zhuangzi's penumbra and how it speaks to contemporary reticent homophobic formations in Taiwan, see Jen-peng Liu and Naifei Ding, "Reticent Poetics, Queer Politics," *Working Papers in Gender/Sexuality Studies*, nos. 3 and 4 (September 1998): 109–55.

10 As Sommer writes: "The best recent work on women in late imperial China has focused on the Yangzi Delta elite, because only in that privileged stratum did some women enjoy the resources to write and publish. . . . In contrast, Qing legal cases tell us precious little about the elite. . . . Instead, the legal archives provide an unprecedented opportunity to glimpse the lower strata of society, to look beyond the state and elite to learn something firsthand (or close to it) of the lives of peasants and marginalized people" (*Law*, 15–16). Sommer further notes how the evidence provided in these legal cases "sheds new light on the role sex played in survival strategies of poor and marginalized people" (*Law*, 16).

11 On how Qing marginal subjects connived with and against increasingly severe legal regulations of gender and sexuality, see Sommers, *Law*, 316–20.

12 Louis Dumont, *Homo Hierarchicus: The Caste System and Its Implications*, trans. Mark Sainsbury, Louis Dumont, and Basia Gulati (Chicago: University of Chicago Press, 1980). See also chapter 7.

13 Maria Jaschok, *Concubines and Bondservants: The Social History of a Chinese Custom* (London: Zed Books, 1988), 108–9.

14 Ibid., 108. See also chapter 7.

15 Li, *Xianqing Ouji*, 115–63.

16 On unorthodox household patterns in Qing court cases as survival strategies of the marginal peasantry, see Sommer, 320.

17 See David Rolston, *Traditional Chinese Fiction and Fiction Commentary* (Stanford, Calif.: Stanford University Press, 1997). See also chapter 3.

18 Elizabeth Long, "Textual Interpretation as Collective Action," in *The Ethnography of Reading*, ed. Jonathan Boyarin (Berkeley: University of California Press, 1993), 180–211.

19 Gayatri Chakravorty Spivak, "Literature," in *Critique of Postcolonial Reason* (Cambridge, Mass.: Harvard University Press, 1999), 112–97.

20 These are identified as editions A, B, and C in Patrick Hanan, "The Text of the Chin

P'ing Mei," *Asia Major* 9, no. 1 (1962): 1–57. For a succinct account of the different editions and current state of scholarship concerning them, see also Andrew H. Plaks, *The Four Masterworks of the Ming Novel* (Princeton, N.J.: Princeton University Press, 1987), 56–72; and Liu Hui, "Jin Ping Mei banben zhi mi" (The riddle of JPM's different editions), in *Jin Ping Mei zhi mi* (The riddles of Jin Ping Mei), ed. Liu Hui and Yang Yang (Beijing: Shumu wenxian chuban she, 1989), 65–89.

21 In his book on Yuan Hongdao, Ming-Shui Hung (*Romantic Vision*) defends the late Ming "liberals" as no less concerned with affairs of the state than their counterparts in the bureaucracy. That this point should constitute a defense (they are not to be faulted morally or scapegoated politically for their lack or failure in service to the state) may serve as evidence of the endurance of such a value and structure of feeling.

22 See Josephine Ho, "Self-Empowerment and Professionalism: Conversations with Taiwanese Sex Workers," *Inter-Asia Cultural Studies* 1, no. 2 (August 2000): 283–99; and Naifei Ding, "Prostitutes, Parasites, and the House of State Feminism," *Inter-Asia Cultural Studies* 1, no. 2 (August 2000): 305–18.

23 See Kristofer Schipper, *The Taoist Body* (Berkeley: University of California Press, 1993), 55.

CHAPTER 1  Jin-ology

1 Zhang Yuanfen, "Zuo buyuan de meng," in *Wo yu Jin Ping Mei* (Chengdu: Chongdu chubanshe, 1991), 41. Jin-ology is the name coined for the study of JPM in the 1980s in China, following the hallowed usage of Red-ology (the study of the *Hung Lou Meng* or *Dream of the Red Chamber*).

2 Tonglin Lu, *Rose and Lotus: Narrative of Desire in France and China* (Albany: State University of New York Press, 1991).

3 The effect here is interestingly the reverse of what Roland Barthes has noted in his *S/Z* (trans. Richard Miller [New York: Hill and Wang, 1974]) as the "innocence" of the denotative in classic realist novels; this innocence of the denotative in novelistic language serves as alibi for the force of connotative meanings (126–28). The literal naturalizes and camouflages the metaphoric and metonymic networks of meaning. With JPM, it is the literal that incriminates, and generations of commentaries have sought refuge in its metaphoric and metonymic meanings. To avow in this instance to the literal is to condemn the text (its writer and reader-critic) to the base level of the literally obscene.

4 See Chi-p'ing Chou, *Yuan Hung-tao and the Kung-an School* (Cambridge, U.K.: Cambridge University Press, 1988), esp. 113–22.

5 Raymond Williams, *Marxism and Literature* (Oxford: Oxford University Press, 1977). See also *Problems in Materialism and Culture* (London: Verso, 1980), 22–27.

6 I am thinking of the Columbia school of neo-Confucian thought, and its several volumes on variations of "self and society" in the late Ming era.

7 The conditions for such a convergence are not coincidental either. Late Ming writers continue to be recognized and made into a sort of "native" origin for a so-called Chinese modernity in written language and potentially populist lit-

erary aesthetics — via the beginnings of a vernacular literature in print, plus the advocacy of a transcendental authentic aesthetic cultivation, paradoxically both compromised yet made possible through the medium of print. See Ming-Shui Hung, *The Romantic Vision of Yuan Hung-tao, Late Ming Poet and Critic* (Taipei, Taiwan: Bookman Books, 1997), 196.

8 Lin Yutang, *The Importance of Living* (New York: John Day, 1937). "Literary beauty is only expressiveness. The dangers of this school [of self-expression] are that a writer's style may degenerate into plainness (Yuan Chunglang) [Yuan Hongdao], or he may develop eccentricity of ideas (Chin Shengtan) [Jin Shengtan], or his ideas may differ violently from those of established authorities (Li Chowu) [Li Zhi]. That is why the school of self-expression was so hated by the Confucian critics. But as a matter of fact, it is these original writers who saved Chinese thought and literature from absolute uniformity and death. They are bound to come into their own in the next few decades. Chinese orthodox literature expressly aimed at expressing the minds of sages and not the minds of authors, and was therefore dead; the *hsingling* school of literature aims at expressing the minds of authors and not the minds of the sages, and is therefore alive" (391).

9 See C. T. Hsia, *The Classic Chinese Novel: A Critical Introduction* (New York: Columbia University Press, 1968), 2.

10 Kai-wing Chow, "Writing for Success: Printing, Examinations, and Intellectual Change in Late Ming China," *Late Imperial China* 17, no. 1 (June 1996): 144.

11 Williams, *Marxism*, 122.

12 Hsia, *Classic Chinese Novel*, Bloomington: Indiana University 1980, 1, 6.

13 Ibid., 4.

14 Ibid., 5.

15 Ibid., 6.

16 Ibid., 1, 6.

17 See Michael M. Ames, *Cannibal Tours and Glass Boxes: The Anthropology of Museums* (Vancouver: University of British Columbia, 1992), 73.

18 Hsia, *Classic Chinese Novel*, 168.

19 Andrew H. Plaks, *The Four Masterworks of the Ming Novel* (Princeton, N.J.: Princeton University Press, 1987), x–xi.

20 Ibid., xi.

21 Ibid., 17.

22 Ibid., 23.

23 Ibid., 51–52.

24 "First, my readings of these 'amazing books' are based on the conviction that they yield the most meaningful interpretations when viewed not simply as compendia of popular narrative materials, but as reflections of the cultural values and intellectual concerns of the sophisticated literary circles of the late Ming period" (Plaks, *Masterworks*, ix).

25 For a detailed comparison of Hu Shi and Lu Xun, though rather more favorable to Hu Shi, see Chou, *Yuan Hung-tao*. Chou emphasizes the paradigmatic importance of these two figures in terms of their writings on literature.

26 Yi, Zhuxian, ed., *Hu Shi Lun Zhongguo Gudian Xiaoshuo* (Hubei: Changjing Wenyi Chu-

ban She, 1987), 2. To a certain extent, the editor's careful noting of how Lu Xun defers to Hu Shi on questions of dating for the Honglou Meng exemplifies how Lu Xun continues to function as guarantor of an ideologically correct attitude toward fiction.

27 Qian Xuantong had written: "To extend your argument, JPM certainly cannot be spoken of alongside all these books that specialize in obscenities. [JPM] is a reflection of a decadent society marked by profligate excess, licentiousness, and ignorance of manners, honor, propriety, and shame. If one looks at the people narrated in this book, they may be officials or literati-genry, men or women, on the face of it 'masters' and 'mistresses' and 'little misses,' yet the moment they open their mouth or lift a finger, not one of their words or movement is not of the most extreme indecency and shamelessness; theirs is the reality of those who today accumulate immoral capital, play poker all day, frequent bordellos, and collect concubines. The point of JPM is the same as that of Honglou Meng [HLM]. (If one were to say that HLM is an incarnation of JPM, I would agree). It is only that [JPM] describes too many obscenities and thus finally cannot but be seen as an 'obscene book'" (Yi, Hu Shi Lun Zhongguo Gudian Xiaoshuo, 579).

28 Hu Shi, "Da Qian Xuantong shu" (Letter to Qian Xuantong), in Wenxue Gailiang Zouyi, Hu Shi Zuopin ji, vol. 3 (Taipei, Taiwan: Yuanliu, 1986), 43.

29 Ibid., 53.

30 For an account of the political work of the nineteenth century's novelistic cult of domesticity in producing domestic (middle-class) women and domesticated (family) men, see Nancy Armstrong, Desire and Domestic Fiction (New York: Oxford University Press, 1987).

31 Lu Xun, Zhongguo xiaoshuo shilue (Hong Kong: Wenxue yanjiu she, 1973), 149. In translating this passage, I have referred to Hsien-yi Yang, and Gladys Yang's translation in A Brief History of Chinese Fiction (Peking: Foreign Language Press, 1976), 225–26.

32 But what does it mean to suggest that Hu Shi at a moment of translating modernity into Chinese should disavow a vernacular xiaoshuo's representation of sex? Could this be read as an allegory of the founding of a colonial subjectivity and sexuality?

33 "Actually, many researchers might very well have the same feelings while reading as the common reader, yet when they write articles, these are always full of high-sounding phrases. And even though we may clearly detect the 'faking' quality of some critical pieces, where even the title will leak the make-believe of its righteous and severe words, yet, this very posturing signals the reality and strength of that kind of thinking. And it is that kind of thinking that force people to do this [posturing]. And once one has done it for long enough, there is a kind of self-deceptive effect, where it becomes hard to say whether it is real or fake. For example, in dealing with the representation of sex in JPM, I must admit that in my essays there is a degree of camouflaging" (Zongyi Ning, "Entering Uncertainty," in Jin Ping Mei and I (Wo yu Jin Ping Mei) (Chengdu: Chubanshe, 1991), 180, 91, 305.

34 Wu Han, "Jin Ping Mei de zhuzuo shidai ji qi shehui beijing" (1934), in Lun Jin

Ping Mei, ed. Hu Wenbin and Zhang Qinshan (Beijing: Xinhua shudian, 1984), 29; and Zheng Zhenduo, "Tan Jin Ping Mei Cihua" (1933), in Lun Jin Ping Mei, ed. Hu Wenbin and Zhang Qinshan (Beijing: Xinhua shudian, 1984), 57.

35  Wu, "Jin Ping Mei," 41.
36  Zheng, "Tan Jin Ping Mei Cihua," 50, 57–58. Especially notable is the metaphor of suffering the existence of JPM, and its reading, as one would the presence of a needle in one's eye. On how such a painful reading may actually yield a transcendent aesthetic experience, see chapter 4.
37  Ibid., 51–52. Note the incipient violence of moral cleansing.
38  Li Xifan, "Shuihu he Jin Ping Mei zai woguo xianshizhuyi wenxue fazhan zhong de diwei" (1959), in Lun Jin Ping Mei, ed. Hu Wenbin and Zhang Qinshan (Beijing: Xinhua shudian, 1984), 285.
39  Ibid.
40  "Although Jin Ping Mei's aesthetic contributions cannot be negated, in its basic literary penchant, it has veered away from realism toward objectivism, and has therefore forfeited the chance of robbing Shuihu Zhuan's certain and honorable title as pioneer [of realism]" (ibid., 287–88).
41  This is what one recent venture into risky waters suggests, as will be discussed later in this chapter. See Chen Dongyou, Jin Ping Mei Wen Hua Yanjiu (Taipei, Taiwan: Guanya wenhua, 1992), 134.
42  See Song Mouyang, "Luelun JPM pinglun zhong de yimei qinxiang," in Jin Ping Mei lunji, ed. Xu Shuofang and Lin Hui, 182. According to Sung, from 1930 to 1949, twenty-two articles on JPM were published. From 1949 to 1965, ten articles appeared. None were published from 1965 to 1978. From 1978 to 1984, sixty-three were written and published. "From 1919 to 1949 . . . only forty articles were published. And from 1949 to 1978, only about ten or so articles appeared. The study of JPM is a virgin land that is just being developed" (Zhou Juntao, "Wei yi xiao de ren qiao cui," in Jin Ping Mei and I, ed. Zhou Juntao [Chengdu: Chubanshe, 1991], 112).
43  Zongyi Ning, "Zoujin kunhuo," in Jin Ping Mei and I, ed. Zhou Juntao (Chengdu: Chubanshe, 1991), 175. Ning and others also talk about how the teaching, talking, and writing about JPM brought them political trouble both in 1958 and later during the Cultural Revolution.
44  See Wu Gan, Zhang Zhupo yu Jin Ping Mei (Tianjin: Baihua wenyi chubanshe, 1987), 117.
45  Zhang Yuanfen, Jin Ping Mei xinzheng (Jinan: Qiru shushen, 1984), 6.
46  Huang Lin, "Wogguo pulu wenxue de jiegou JPM," in Jin Ping Mei Lunji, ed. Xu Shuofang and Lin Hui. (Beijing: Renmin Wenxue Chubanshe, 1986), 111.
47  Ibid., 112, 125. The former may be a reference to Li Xifan's 1959 article wherein he claims that in no way can JPM be seen as superior to SHZ.
48  Ibid., 125.
49  Quoted in David Rolston, How to Read the Chinese Novel (Princeton, N.J.: Princeton University Press, 1990), 241.
50  Dongyou Chen, Jin Ping Mei Wenhua Yanjiu (Taipei, Taiwan: Guanya wen hua, 1992), 17.

51 Ibid., 31.
52 Ibid., 33.
53 This had already been done by Zhang Zhupo—made all the more easy by censorship so that the exact number of obscene characters could be counted. Since the arithmetic accuracy of this method provides for certain objectifying and scientific satisfaction along with peace of mind, Plaks (*Masterworks*) too does this.
54 Chen, *Jin Ping Mei Wenhua Yanjiu*, 135.
55 Ibid., 149.
56 Ibid.
57 Li Jianzhong and others all compare JPM to *Lady Chatterley's Lover* in this respect only. Perhaps this has to do with the political-economic opening up and the vogue in sexual matters, as if *Lady Chatterley's Lover* constituted an exemplary literary pornography?
58 Thus, the aesthetic value of JPM is, according to Chen, a "true representation of life in accordance with the rules inherent within life itself, which then reveals the essential qualities of life and the trajectories of human struggles therein." More important, "the representation of sex in this work is an inextricable part of it, and we cannot deny these descriptions being an organic part of the human life force, therefore JPM is able to break through the limitations of time and space, and after three hundred years, continue to be transmitted into the future" (*Jin Ping Mei Wenhua Yanjiu*, 321).
59 Shuyu Sun, *Jin Ping Mei de Yishu* (Taipei, Taiwan: Shibao Wenhua, 1978).
60 On its unsuitability for youths, see ibid., 121. On its flaws, see ibid., 1–5. On the author-writer's sincerity of intent, and thus the guarantor of the hidden meaning of the work, see ibid., 2.
61 Ibid., 117.
62 Ibid., 118.
63 See Joseph A. Dane's excellent study of the history and institutionalization of irony as a literary-critical term in *The Critical Mythology of Irony* (Athens: University of Georgia Press, 1991). Sun Shuyu's use of irony is consonant with "the destroying of illusion" that is one among many definitions of romantic irony in modern scholarship (see Dane, *Critical Mythology*, 73), but has the added "historical" dimension of Cleanth Brooks's notion of irony as a "late form," thus indicative of literary and aesthetic maturity (ibid., 154).
64 Again, it seems no accident that the shift in authority from text to author to reader-critic that develops over two centuries in Europe may be seen condensed in the span of two generations of readers in a Chinese context. See Dane, *Critical Mythology*, 11. I would suggest that this is attributable to colonialism's "compressed development" yet also must be explained as a repetition of the increasingly sophisticated and self-justificatory reception of JPM from its appearance in manuscript form to its rewriting by Zhang Zhupo. See chapters 2 and 3 herein. See also Rolston, *Traditional Chinese Fiction*, where the point is made concerning Ming-Qing commentaries of fiction and their publication.
65 The trajectory of Chinese readings of JPM in the twentieth century fantasmatically repeats one line in the thematics of reading rehearsed by readers from Ming

Wanli through Qing Kangxi. Precisely, that one line has to do with a gradual awareness of JPM as a (potentially) widely disseminated text, rather than one that is only available to the elite few. Thus in Sun Shuyu and Huang Lin, shades of Zhang Zhupo abound, attributable to their common concern for ensuring in an age of possibly wide dissemination at least a "correct" reading, as well as their own place as the most qualified and authoritative readers.

66 Sun, *Jin Ping Mei de yishu* 97 n. 16.
67 Ibid., 121–24.
68 The publisher of Sun's book is one of the largest commercial publishing houses in Taiwan, and the book is clearly aimed at both academic and nonacademic audiences.
69 Hsia, *Classic Chinese Novel*, 185.
70 Ibid., 169.
71 Ibid., 186.
72 Ibid., 186.
73 Ibid., 181.
74 Ibid., 178.
75 Plaks, *Masterworks*, 87.
76 Ibid., 138–39.
77 Ibid., 139.
78 A strategy of reading very much recommended by Zhang Zhupo.
79 Plaks, *Masterworks*, 142–45.
80 Shades of Zhang Zhupo can again be noted, as Plaks virtually becomes the neo-Confucian reader-writer by whom and for whom, as he claims, these narratives were written. Plaks's reading might then be seen as instituting the very kind of reader he argues the text as having been written by and for—Just as, to some extent, this book must try and instantiate a base-feminist reading that is as much forgotten or misremembered as it is not yet realized in the text and the readings that make it up.
81 David T. Roy, trans., *The Plum in the Golden Vase or Chin P'ing Mei* (Princeton, N.J.: Princeton University Press, 1993), xxiv–xxv.
82 Ibid., xxxvii.
83 Ibid., xlvii.
84 Ibid., xlviii.
85 Victoria Cass, "Celebrations at the Gate of Death: Symbol and Structure in Chin P'ing Mei" (Ph.D. diss., University of California at Berkeley, 1979), 101.
86 Ibid., 113.
87 Ibid., 101.
88 Katherine Carlitz, *The Rhetoric of Chin P'ing Mei* (Bloomington: Indiana University Press, 1986).
89 Ibid., 50–51.
90 Ibid., 45.
91 Ibid.
92 Chen Dongyou makes this point.
93 For the foundational use of women as both instrument and other of self-cultiva-

tion, see Maram Epstein, "The Beauty is the Beast: The Dual Face of Woman in Four Ch'ing Novels" (Ph.D. diss., Princeton University, 1992), esp. conclusion.
94 Zongyi Ning and Derong Luo, eds., Jin Ping Mei dui xiaoshuo meixue de gongxian (Tianjin: n.p., 1992).
95 See Bu Jian, "Jin Ping Mei zhong de meichou qingyi," in Jin Ping Mei dui xiaoshuo meixue de gongxian, ed. Zongyi Ning and Derong Luo (Tianjin: , 1992), 264–79.
96 See Zhang Guofu, "Renwu, xing, yu shenmei," in Jin Ping Mei dui xiaoshuo meixue de gongxian, ed. Zongyi Ning and Derong Luo (Tianjin: n.p., 1992), 279–95.
97 Roy, Plum, xlv.
98 Ning and Luo, Jin Ping Mei dui xiaoshuo meixue de gongxian, 285.
99 Ibid., 285.
100 Ibid., 291–92.
101 Plaks, Masterworks, 144.

CHAPTER 2   *The Manic Preface: Jin Shengtan's (1608–1661) Shuihu Zhuan*

Pierre Bourdieu's work on the sociology and phenomenology of knowledge, its institutions and historical conditions, are everywhere in this chapter, and the entire part 1 of this book. My aim has been to ask how might details of readings (of SHZ, of JPM) be considered as social and literary practices, accomplishing particular forms of literary, social, and psychic work. Such questions concerning the practices of reading, concerning reading as practice, entail the establishment of dynamic interrelations between writing, reading, and their material cultural conditions. My debt to Bourdieu's work and ideas is minimally recognized in the epigraph (at this chapter's opening) that serves as commentary on both the object of this chapter and the chapter itself. I do not deal with Bourdieu at length in the body of the chapter because the extent and success of the cross-fertilization of his work in a context entirely removed from that which produced it must rest finally on the appropriation and extension itself.

1 Henri-Jean Martin, *The History and Power of Writing*, Lydia G. Cochrane, trans. (University of Chicago, 1994), 225–26.
2 For a comprehensive account of how reading and writing between the lines of published fiction affected the reading and writing of fiction in pre-twentieth-century China, as well as a detailed examination of the major commentator-editors, see David Rolston, *Traditional Chinese Fiction and Fiction Commentary* (Stanford, Calif.: Stanford University Press, 1997).
3 Ibid., 2–4.
4 Ibid., 3.
5 For biographical references to Jin Shengtan's "arrogance," see Robert Hegel, *The Novel in Seventeenth-Century China* (New York: Columbia University Press, 1981), 68–70. See also John C. Y. Wang, *Chin Sheng-t'an* (New York: Twayne, 1972). On Jin Shengtan's "larger-than-life" presence in his commentaries, see David Rolston, ed., *How to Read the Chinese Novel* (Princeton, N.J.: Princeton University Press, 1990), 124 ff. On the ego of third-stage commentators, see Rolston, *Traditional Chinese Fiction*, 8.

6 See Kai-wing Chow, "Writing for Success: Printing, Examinations, and Intellectual Change in Late Ming China," *Late Imperial China* 17, no. 1 (June 1996): 136–44.
7 See Laura Hua Wu, "Jin Shengtan (1608–1661): Founder of a Chinese Theory of the Novel" (Ph.D. diss., University of Toronto, 1993).
8 See Chun-shu Chang and Shelley Hsueh-lun Chang, *Crisis and Transformation in Seventeenth-Century China: Society, Culture, and Modernity in Li Yu's World* (Ann Arbor: University of Michigan Press, 1992), 272–73. ("The national literacy rate for males rose to 40–50 percent in Li Yu's [1611–1680] day, over 65 percent of the male urbanites in these great metropolises could read and over 40 percent of them were financially able to purchase popular reading materials in fiction and drama," 272–73).
9 For a succinct account of the origins of wenren as a category of "professional" writers in the late Yuan, see Chen Wanyi, "Wan Ming xiaopin yu Mingji wenren shenghuo," in *Wan Ming Xiaopin yu Mingji wenren sheng huo* (Taipei, Taiwan: Daan Chubanshe, 1988), 54–57. Chen also elucidates the different names (*shanren, buyi, chushi, mingshi*) whereby late Ming literati "without a position" could and did maintain a certain social distinction and status, not without much discoursing on who was what and how authentically. Many of the ideas in this chapter find verification in the inspiring first two essays of Chen's book. Our conclusions differ in my emphasis on the social and symbolic profit of editorial work in the late Ming literary field, whereas Chen generously refrains from such demystification.
10 On changing attitudes in the sixteenth century toward success in the examination in this region, see John Meskill, *Gentlemanly Interest and Wealth on the Yangtze Delta* (Ann Arbor, Mich.: Association for Asian Studies, 1994), esp. 10, 163.
11 See Chen, "Wan Ming," 85–115; and Jr-lien Tsao, "Remembering Suzhou: Urbanism in Late Imperial China" (Ph.D. diss., University of California at Berkeley, 1992).
12 See Chen, "Wan Ming," 98.
13 See Hegel, *Novel*.
14 Susan Cherniack, "Book Culture and Textual Transmission in Sung China," *Harvard Journal of Asiatic Studies* 54, no. 1 (1994): 5–125.
15 *Jin Shengtan Quanji* (vol. 1), Guan Huatang diwu Caizi Shu Shuihu Zhuan (Yangzhou: Jiangsu Guji Chubanshe, 1985), 6.
16 Recent studies have begun to explore what Elizabeth Eisenstein has called in the European context "the unacknowledged revolution" that accompanied the advent of print culture (*The Printing Press as an Agent of Change: Communications and Cultural Transformation in Early-Modern Europe* [Cambridge, U.K.: Cambridge University Press, 1979], 3). Anne E. McLaren analyzes how Ming vernacular publishing produced different editions of the "same" text to accommodate different levels and classes of readers (*The Chinese Femme Fatale: Stories from the Ming Period* [Honolulu: University of Hawaii Press, 1994], 51–80). Chen Wanyi has shown how a generation of Wanli wenren reconfigured the literary field and its reigning poetics through the editing and printing of new anthologies of the Song poet Su Shi. He notes how in so doing, these editors (including such luminaries of the day as Li Zhi and Yuan Hongdao) succeeded in redefining for their own times

and purposes, for their literary battles and symbolic profit, the meaning of Su [Shih's] body of works (Chen, "Wan Ming"). Finally, Dorothy Ko has expounded the "other" side of this story of late Ming print culture along with its social and cultural coordinates; she examines the new gendered culture of learning and the communities of women readers/writers that evolve alongside a "revolution in the economics of publishing" (*Teachers of the Inner Chambers: Women and Culture in Seventeenth-Century China* [Stanford, Calif.: Stanford University Press, 1994], 34–67).

17 See Cherniack, "Book Culture," 53–55, 65. Cherniack notes how silent reading (*moshi*) was a rare phenomenon in early medieval China, just as it was in the medieval West and Western antiquity. While Cherniack does not explicitly link the stress that Zhu Xi puts on an internalized consciousness (in his formulation, "the ancients did not have written texts") with the print culture of which Zhu Xi was an integral part, she does point to Zhu Xi's ambivalence toward the new medium of print. "The combination of skepticism about authority in print and the nostalgia for preprint culture are symptomatic of the reaction to print-culture in twelfth-century China" (53–55). Furthermore, "the complexity of Zhu Xi's position may be imagined, when we recall that he supported himself by running a printing business, which he also used to promote his ideas"(65).

Cherniack also explains how print culture produced a public medium and space in print wherein individual writers and editors became responsible for their writings in an intellectual, social, and political manner not possible in a manuscript age. "Thus Zhu Xi thought it a worthwhile investment, despite his chronically troubled finances, to attempt to squelch an unauthorized imprint of some of his works by an academy official in Wuzhou, by offering to buy up the entire stock of copies from the printer" (65).

18 A recent special issue of *Late Imperial China* focuses on "Publishing and the Print Culture in Late Imperial China." In this issue, Timothy Brook examines the building of school libraries in county seats, and suggests that the relation between these buildings is a form of symbolic capital ("the authority of textual knowledge") and "the inner history of elite life in the Ming dynasty" ("Publishing and the Print Culture in Late Imperial China," *Late Imperial China* 17, no. 1 [June 1996]: 103, 114). Brook notes how the cultural and symbolic meanings of library buildings in the mid- and late Ming in their subjective and intellectual aspects await further elucidation of the "inner history" of elite intellectuals of that time. Kai-wing Chow further shows how "the combined effects of commercialization and printing in the sixteenth and early seventeenth centuries had transformed a significant segment of the Chinese literati from custodians of Classical truths to professional writers who attempted to help their readers succeed in examinations" ("Writing for Success," 144). Chow's study, in effect, delineates the outer contours and material conditions of the inner history that Brook has called for. Moreover, Chow points out the contemporaneous "growth of interest in novels and plays," as well as how the new breed of professional writers were "actively involved in the development of theories for different genres" (144). The readings in the first part of this book seek to extend this particular line of inquiry

from a microtextual perspective. That is, the inquiry into the relation between what Brook has noted as an increasingly bookish culture ("Publishing," 116)—of the mid-Ming—and the custodians-turned-professional writers (Chow, "Writing for Success," 144) in the midst of this culture—in terms of the readings of quasi-professional writers of one particular new textual object of consumption that first appears in Ming Wanli, the JPM. These readings are then analyzed for a taste of their mood and tendencies; their discursive strategies and the latter's social and psychic uses; and their place in a history of the sexual politics of reading JPM.

19 Ko, *Teachers of the Inner Chambers*, 39.
20 On the peasant rebels and Manchu forces, see James Bunyon Parsons, *Peasant Rebellions in the Late Ming Dynasty* (Ann Arbor, Mich.: Association for Asian Studies, 1970), 257–58. On the economic depression, see Cynthia Brokaw, *The Ledgers of Merit and Demerit: Social Change and Amoral Order in Late Imperial China* (Princeton, N.J.: Princeton University Press, 1991), 11–13.
21 Quoted in Chen, "Wan Ming," 38.
22 The reading of Jin Shengtan's preface in this chapter is in danger of "taking seriously" precisely what David Rolston warns might have been penned facetiously, contradicting as it does commentaries later in Jin's SHZ text (*Traditional Chinese Fiction*, 35, 42). I seek, however, to place these prefaces in another context: not that of Jin Shengtan's oeuvres as a whole, thus indicative of editor-commentorial integrity but rather a certain prefatorial mode and style is juxtaposed to an earlier one to which it seems to respond, in order to gauge the engagements of both to a print market culture wherein they participated, to their profit. I was early warned that the renown of Li Zhi and Jin Shengtan would obstruct the very point I am trying to make, as to how figurative flourish successfully camouflages material context and commercial-professional concerns.
23 Parsons, *Peasant Rebellions*, 258.
24 Brokaw, *Ledgers of Merit*, 13. On absentee landlordism and the demographic move to urban centers, see Mi Chu Wiens, "Socioeconomic Change during the Ming Dynasty in the Kiangnan Area" (Ph.D. diss., Harvard University, 1973).
25 Ko, *Teachers of the Inner Chambers*, 39.
26 For a discussion of how the "public" aspect of "private practices" has been misread in the essentializing tendency of previous sinological practices, see Craig Clunas, *Fruitful Sites: Garden Culture in Ming Dynasty China* (Durham, N.C.: Duke University Press, 1996). The excess of quotations in this paragraph indicates the tentativeness of the usage of "public" and "private" where such usage has not been sufficiently understood in its historical and theoretical dimensions.
27 Ji Shaofu, ed., *Zhongguo Chuban Jianshi* (Shanghai: Xuelin, 1991), 157–58.
28 Goodrich, L. Carrington, and Fang Chao-Ying, eds., *Dictionary of Ming Biography* (New York: Columbia University Press, 1976), 791.
29 Lang Ying, *Qixiou Leigao*, juan 45.
30 Ji Shaofu, *Zhongguo Chuban Jianshi*, 158.
31 Zhang Xioumin, "Mingdou Nanjing de yinshu," in *Lidai Keshu Gaikuang* (Shanghai: Yinshua Gongye Chubanshe, 1991), 283; Cao Zhi, "Shilun Mingdai banke

de Chengjua," in *Lidai Keshu*, 285; Shen Xieyuan, "Ming dai Jiangsu keshu shiye gaishu," in *Lidai Keshu*, 311.
32 Yang Shengxin, "Lida Kegong Gongjia Chutan," in *Lidai Keshu*, 559–60; and Ko, *Teachers of the Inner Chamber*, 35.
33 Yao Boyue, "Mingdai Wuxing Min Ling Zrshide Taoban Yinshu," in *Lidai Keshu*, 301–5.
34 Interestingly, whereas the imperial examination is largely regarded as both the source of and justification for this technical innovation (the first book printed in red and black ink in 1616 in Wuxing is the *Chunqiu Zuozhuan*), it seems more than coincidental that this technique should be "rediscovered" at a moment and in a region when urbanites—both literati and nonliterati—are, as one older contemporary unapprovingly puts it, "in thrall to the new and the strange." The famous, indeed trendsetting poet of the day, Zhong Xing (1574–1625), anthologized a best-selling volume, *Shi Gui*, that ran through at least six editions before 1644, with "at least one printed in three colors (black for the prefatory material and poetry, red for Zhong Xing's commentary, and blue for Tan Yuanchun's commentary)" (Nancy Norton Tomasko, "Chung Hsing (1574–1629): A Literary Name in the Wan-Li Era (1573–1620) of Ming China" (Ph.D. diss., Princeton University, 1995), 307.
35 In the Jiangsu (the eastern part of Ming southern Zhili) area alone, there were 496 private publishers or sike and 92 print shops or fangke for the entire Ming period. Of these private publishers, 417 engraved and printed books from the Jiajing through the Chongzhen (1522–1645) (Jiang Chenpo, Du Xinfu, Du Yongkang, eds. *Jiangsu Keshu* [Jiangsu: Jiangsu renmin chubanshe Jiangsu 1993], 72–226). The predominance of sike in number was made up for by the continuity and sheer volume of the fangke's printed output.
36 See *Jiangsu Keshu*, Jiang Chengpo, Du Xinfu, and Du Yongkang, eds. (Jiangsu: Jiangsu renmin chubanshe, 1993), 116–43; and Cao and Zhi, "Shilun," 283.
37 Ji Shaofu, *Zhongguo Chuban Jianshi*, 151–52.
38 See *Jiangsu Keshu*, Chengpo, Xinfu, and Yongkang, eds.
39 See Lin Qixian, *Li Zhuowu shiji Xinian* (Taipei, Taiwan: Wenjin, 1988).
40 Zhu Guozhen (1557–1632) writes in his *Yongchuang xiaopin* under the heading "Li Zhuowu" of having once met Li Zhi on a boat and recollecting how he had read his books—"The madness of today's literati originate in such readings; they no longer read the Four Books, [but] instead each has under his arms a copy of Li's *Cangshu* and *Fenshu*, which they consider marvelous possessions [qi huo], [which actually] demoralize one's heart-mind and harm social mores; one wonders where such catastrophes will end" (*Ming Qing Biji Congkan* [Shanghai: Zhonghua Shuju, 1959], 365–38).
41 See Chen, *Wan Ming*, 85–98.
42 On how the market was "flooded with bogus Li Zhi commentaries" in Rolston's second stage of fiction commentary, see *Traditional Chinese Fiction*, 3, 31.
43 Li Zhi, *Fenshu/Xu Fenshu* (Taipei, Taiwan: Janjing Wenhua, 1984), 76.
44 Chih-P'ing Chou, *Yuan Hung-tao and the Kung-an School* (Cambridge: Cambridge University Press, 1989).

45 Ibid., 25.
46 Ibid., 26.
47 Elizabeth Eisenstein has claimed as one of the effects of early European print culture how "veneration for the wisdom of the ages was probably modified as ancient sages were retrospectively cast in the role of individual authors—prone to human error and possibly plagiarists as well. Treatment of battles of books between 'ancients and moderns' might profit from more discussion of such issues" (Printing Press, 122). A reconsideration of the material aspects of Li Zhi's well-known iconoclasm and their relation to the book culture of his day would be extremely interesting.
48 For an analysis of how the discourse on gardens shifts in the sixteenth century toward an ever clearer separation between the economic and aesthetic, see Clunas, Fruitful Sites. The separation of these two fields of garden discourse produces two distinct classes of consumers: one comprised of ruling-class garden owners, urban aesthete literati at large, and the other including commoners and aspirers to a social and cultural capital that they did not "naturally" possess. "With the commodification of absolutely everything in the late Ming, and no barriers other than wealth to the possession of attributes formally limited to a relatively small elite, that elite began to fear a collapse of the social and wealth hierarchies into each other" (90).
49 I have referred to Martin W. Huang's translation (Literati and Self-Re/Presentation: Autobiographical Sensibility in the Eighteenth-Century Chinese Novel [Stanford, Calif.: Stanford University Press, 1995], 18) for this section of Li Zhi's text, but have retained my own translation.
50 Shuihu Ziliao Huibian, ed. Ma Tiji (Beijing: Zhonghua Shuju, 1980), 4; and Li, Fenshu/Xu Fenshu, 3, 109.
51 Shuihu Ziliao Huibian, 2.
52 Ibid., 9–10.
53 See Rolston, How to Read the Chinese Novel, 124; Andrew H. Plaks, The Four Masterworks of the Ming Novel (Princeton, N.J.: Princeton University Press, 1987), 292; and Wu, "Jin Shengtan," 23–24, 268. I chanced on Wu's "Jin Shengtan" after having finished this chapter. I have not modified the chapter since my aim has been to contextualize Li Zhi's and Jin Shengtan's prefaces to different editions of SHZ in terms of their slightly yet significantly different market concerns. Wu's excellent study of Jin Shengtan as "founder" of an "indigenous" narrative theory to a certain extent presupposes the very print market effects that are of concern in this chapter. The material presence and cultural-symbolic possibilities of a print market in fiction would, from a different angle, partly account for Wu's ("Jin Shengtan," 277) question as to why Jin Shengtan succeeded in incorporating vernacular fiction within the field/space of elite cultural work, whereas Li Zhi did not.
54 Jin Shengtan Quanji, vol. 1, 7; Guanhuantang diun caizi shu Shuihu Zhuan, 2 vols. (Jiangsu: Jiangsu Guiji Chubanshe, 1985).
55 In his translation of the Jin Ping Mei cihua, David T. Roy has rendered these two modes of reading (in the Pearl-Juggler of Eastern Wu preface, 1617–1618) as "ad-

monitory" (jie) and "hortatory" (quan) (*The Plum in the Golden Vase or Chin P'ing Mei* [Princeton, N.J.: Princeton University Press, 1993], 6). I have used "prohibitive" and "exhortational" to stress the effects of reading implicated in these distinct yet linked lines of reading strategies.

56 Translated in Rolston, *How to Read the Chinese Novel*, 131–32.
57 See Clunas, *Fruitful Sites*; and Chen, "Wan Ming."
58 Patricia Sieber, "Rhetoric, Romance, and Intertextuality: The Making and Remaking of Guan Hanqing in Yuan and Ming China" (Ph.D. diss., University of California at Berkeley, 1994), 7.
59 Quoted in Chen, "Wan Ming," 38.
60 *Jin Shengtan Quanji*, 1.
61 Ibid., 2.
62 Ibid., 3–6.
63 See Rolston, *How to Read the Chinese Novel*, 129.
64 See Ji Shaofu, ed., *Zhongguo chuban jianshi* (Shanghai: Xuelin Chubanshe, 1991), 147.
65 Lang Ying, *Qixiou Leigao*, 2 vols. (Taipei, Taiwan: Shijie Shuju, 1984), 45.
66 See Hegel, *Novel*, 68–70.
67 As in adjusting one's pose in front of a mirror (the market) so as to see oneself reflected from an appropriate angle and size. After a while, one begins to assume the most flattering pose without thinking; the mirror-market is now in one's bones—a disposition of the body-mind.
68 Translated in Rolston, *How to Read the Chinese Novel*, 145.
69 *Jin Shengtan Quanji*, 6.
70 Li Zhi, *Fenshu/Xu Fenshu*, 76.
71 See Meskill, *Gentlemanly Interest*; and Clunas, *Fruitful Sites*.
72 Or an expression of that expansiveness, in Walter Benjamin's terms: "Marx describes the causal connection between economic system and culture. The expressive relationship is what matters here. The expression of an economic system in its culture will be described, not the economic origins of culture" ("N [Re the Theory of Knowledge, Theory of Progress]," trans. Leigh Hafrey and Richard Sieburth, in *Benjamin: Philosophy, Aesthetics, History*, ed. Gary Smith [Chicago: University of Chicago Press, 1983], 46).

CHAPTER 3  *A Cure for Melancholy: Yuan Hongdao (1568–1610) and Qifa (Seven Stimuli)*

1 For an excellent study of the Yuan brothers and Gongan school, see Chou, *Yuan Hung-tao*. This section—indeed this chapter—is deeply indebted to Chou's study, and may be seen as an extension of a dialogue with a small part of that book, mediated through the works of Pierre Bourdieu, wherein literary schools and arguments are analyzed in terms of the reproduction of institutional practices. For an in-depth literary and biographical study, see Ming-Shui Hung, *The Romantic Vision of Yuan Hung-tao, Late Ming Poet and Critic* (Taipei, Taiwan: Bookman Books, 1997).
2 Hung, *Romantic Vision*, 5.

3 These men were not, or were not primarily—and this is important—politically and bureaucratically powerful, although each had served as an official at some point. Rather, they were more powerful and influential culturally and socially—not just regionally but transregionally as well, thanks in part to the printing trade and book market. This latter power was already at this age relatively autonomous from, although not unallied with, political power in strictly bureaucratic forms. On the increasing professionalization of the literati in an urban setting, see Jr-lien Tsao, "Remembering Suzhou: Urbanism in Late Imperial China" (Ph.D. diss., University of California at Berkeley, 1992). In the first century of the Ming, the world of literature was led by highly ranked scholar-officials, yet by the Wanli, an inversion of this state of literary affairs took place; see Chou, Yuan Hung-tao, 9.
4 See W. T. de Bary, ed., Self and Society in Ming Thought (New York: Columbia University Press, 1970).
5 Craig Clunas, Fruitful Sites: Garden Culture in Ming Dynasty China (Durham, N.C.: Duke University Press, 1996), 69–70. See also Nelson Wu, "Tung Ch'i-ch'ang: Apathy in Government and Fervor in Art," in Confucian Personalities, ed. Arthur F. Wright (Stanford, Calif.: Stanford University Press, 1962).
6 See Chou, Yüan Hung-tao, 35–60.
7 Quoted in ibid., 38.
8 Ibid., 31.
9 Ibid., 39.
10 Ibid., 44.
11 See ibid., 3–4.
12 See Wei Ziyun, Mingdai Jin Ping Mei Shiliao Quanshi (Taipei, Taiwan: Guanya Wenhua, 1992), 13 n. 6.
13 Yuan Hongdao, "Wenchao," in Yuan Zhonglang Quanji, ed. Yang Jialuo (Taipei, Taiwan: Shijie Shuju, 1990), 14 (my translation). A part of this passage is quoted in Chou, Yuan Hung-tao, 49.
14 Ibid., "Wen chao," 14.
15 On "a nationalist 'modern individualism'" reading, see Zhou in Chou, Yuan Hung-tao, 4. On "a quintessentially Chinese aesthetics of the everyday, see Yutang Lin, The Importance of Living (New York: John Day, 1937). Modern scholarship (this one included) has extended—albeit modifying and refining—the positive pole of reception, reproducing its affirmation and teleology, even as it has sought to become more self-reflexive of the dual articulation of geo-historical and institutional (academic) forces in and of its own project. An example of the latter tendency may be found in the works of Craig Clunas—most recently, in his analysis of the discourses that constitute the Ming garden, wherein he traces an evolving separation of the economic from the aesthetic, with the latter serving social and cultural functions of distinction within an increasingly wealthy and competitive urban class of consumers. See Clunas, Fruitful Sites.
16 See Shih-shan Henry Tsai, The Eunuchs in the Ming Dynasty (Albany, N.Y.: State University of New York Press, 1996).
17 "Preparatory students used the squared wrapper cap, but when Chen Jiru appeared on the scene, they began using two fluttering ribbons at the top. . . . At the

beginning of spring, they always put on crimson shoes. The young men among the scholars always put on light red informal dress." So notes Fan Lian, in a tone that is somewhat disapproving and at least a little bemused. This passage and others are quoted in John Meskill, *Gentlemanly Interests and Wealth on the Yangtze Delta* (Ann Arbor, Mich.: Association for Asian Studies, 1994). Meskill's work details, through the *biji* of four writers from different generations of the Sungchiang prefecture in the sixteenth century, the increasingly wealthy and consumption-oriented state of urban society as represented in the eyes of local nonofficial elites. See also Tsao, "Remembering Suzhou."

18 On the changes in urban centers, see Mi Chu Wiens, "Socioeconomic Change during the Ming Dynasty in the Kiangnan Area" (Ph.D. diss., Harvard University, 1973); Dorothy Ko, *Teachers of the Inner Chambers: Women and Culture in Seventeenth-Century China* (Stanford, Calif.: Stanford University Press, 1994); and Clunas, *Fruitful Sites*.

19 Meskill, *Gentlemanly Interests*.

20 Clunas, *Fruitful Sites*, 21.

21 "Although the rise of wealth among commoners cannot be fully traced . . . it has been noted that from the time of the raids Huizhou merchants became prominent in several coastal cities, active in a variety of businesses including the salt monopoly, publishing, engraving, and the selling of brushes, ink, tea, and lumber. . . . Obviously, changes [in the late sixteenth century] affected many more people than scholar-officials alone. Others whose lower status had once been marked by the utter inferiority of their living now were not always so clearly set apart. . . . Among 'the people,' some, presumably the richer, were beginning to emulate the cultivation of higher classes" (Meskill, *Gentlemanly Interests*, 108, 147). This prompted one contemporary to complain, "How is it that excellence that was extraordinary and rare among the ancients now occurs in one and all in Sungchiang?" (Fan Lian, quoted in Meskill, *Gentlemanly Interests*, 148). Finally, "class distinction, which had once been made clear by, among other things, possessions, became in that aspect blurred, as the measure of one's standing became one's pocketbook" (Meskill, *Gentlemanly Interests*, 155). In the words of Fan Lian again, "The use of sectioned boxes for parties began in the Longqing period and became universal in the Wanli. At first only gentlemen and officials used them. In recent years, servants, pimps, all have used sectioned boxes, whether drinking wine or strolling in the hills, inside the city or out" (Fan Lian, qtd. in Meskill, *Gentlemanly Interests*, 146). And finally, Ho Liangjun said, "Yet just now, in a degenerate age, who does not think well of being superior? That each seeks to outdo the other has gradually become the custom" (quoted in Meskill, *Gentlemanly Interests*, 146, 154). For a structural, historical analysis of changes in gentry-class formation, see Atsushi Shigeta, "The Origins and Structure of Gentry Rule," in *State and Society in China: Japanese Perspectives on Ming-Qing Social and Economic History*, ed. Linda Grove and Christian Daniels (Tokyo: University of Tokyo Press, 1984). "It is a mistake however to hierarchically divide the two groups of literati — that is, those who were on the official rolls and who had held official posts, and those who had never held official posts. Rather we should think of the two groups as standing side by side. One group, the gentry and gentry officials, regardless of

their examination degree or official success, consisted of those who had dominant power in rural matters and who advised the local officials. The other group included urban recluses [shiyin] who were at best active champions of righteousness through criticisms of current situations and at worst, peevish critics considered 'eccentric' by their fellow townsmen. They constituted a source of public opinion formed in the seclusion in a town or village, and thus aloof from the pursuit of fame and profit" (Tanaka, "Popular Uprisings," 177). With the print culture of the late Ming, such localized "public opinion" could easily through the medium of print—reach a translocal audience, and thereby conduce to fame and symbolic profit. This, at least, is what I argue in the case of a melancholic Yuan Hongdao in early retirement.

22 "Many people have died unnoticed / But I shall die with fame / I only worry about these superfluous people / Who might prevent me from achieving a name" Li Zhi to Yuan Hongdao, quoted in Hung, *Romantic Vision*, 47).

23 Judith Zeitlin, in *Historian of the Strange: Pu Songling and the Chinese Classical Tale* (Stanford, Calif.: Stanford University Press, 1993), quotes Yuan as epitomizing what she terms "the late Ming craze for obsession" (70). In a short history of the literary discourse of "obsessions," Zeitlin traces the late Ming "craze" to, on the one hand, a radical reformulation of a self-expressive poetic—thus obsession as "a self-reflexive act . . . the self loving the *self*" (70)—and on the other hand, a parallel discourse of qing, or love/sentiment—whereby obsession becomes an exteriorization of qing, or genuine and therefore moral sentiment, capable in the form of poetry and fiction of moving. Both lines of filiation, it seems to me, show up a relation between the subjects of obsession, their modes or field of writing, and a newly problematized *authority* in writing/reading.

24 *Yuan Zhonglang Quanji*, 21.

25 Chou, *Yuan Hung-tao*, 99. See also Lin, *Importance of Living*, 314.

26 *Yuan Zhonglang Quanji*, 21.

27 Tsao, "Remembering Suzhou."

28 As Li Yu, in his *Casual Expressions of Idle Feeling* (Xianqing ouji [Shanghai: Wenyi chubanshe, 1992]), writes in a section on illness and its medicines, that which one's nature (benxing) loves obsessively *is* an antidote to illness because "where there is an obsession, there is life itself [*pi zhi suo zai, xingming yu tong*]" (362).

29 *Yuan Zhonglang Quanji*, 21. See also Wei, *Mingdai Jin Ping Mei*, 1–4; and Chou, *Yuan Hung-tao*, 55.

30 Chou, *Yuan Hung-tao*, 55. See Chou's reading (54–60) of this letter; my indebtedness to his book and this particular section cannot be overestimated. Given the context of my own reading (see introduction), my differences with Chou's reading are very much a function of that context.

31 Wei, *Mingdai Jin Ping Mei*, 34, 42, 30.

32 Chou, *Yuan Hung-tao*, 54–60.

33 Ibid., 55–56.

34 On the poet's name as ultimate fetish, see Zhong Xing (1574–1627), Yin Xiou Xuan ji (Shanghai: Guji chubanshe, 1992), 267. See also Nancy Norton Tomasko, "Chung

Hsing (1574–1625): A Literary Name in the Wan-Li Era (1573–1620) of Ming China" (Ph.D. diss., Princeton University, 1995).

35 This would not contradict readings of Yuan Hongdao as the exceptional literary talent. It would, however, point to the conditions for—at least partially sustaining if not directing—that talent. See, for example, Hung, *Romantic Vision*: "Yuan Hung-tao's appraisal of *Water Margin* and *The Golden Lotus* is significant not only because he was ahead of his contemporaries in recognizing the value of these two novels, but also because it was probably the first time an erotic novel was so openly praised by a Chinese literary man" (72). "Openly" indexes the print market whereby influential appraisals could be disseminated.

36 In terms of the "didactic" model of reading, let me press the point by suggesting that it seems to be Chou who sounds "justificatory" when he writes that "the tone of this letter is very casual. After having read the first part of the JPM, Yuan Hongdao found the novel very enjoyable, and as his curiosity was aroused by the incomplete story he very much wanted to obtain the latter half of the novel. There is nothing unusual about this reaction" (*Yuan Hung-tao*, 55). Chou is perhaps denying, like other Ming Wanli respondents to Yuan's remarks, the possibility of a concupiscent interest in Yuan's wanting to read the whole manuscript, having glimpsed a portion.

37 I use "reading" here and not "criticism" because such records of reading as Yuan's, or the prefaces of printed fiction in Ming Wanli, did not yet constitute criticism in the sense, for example, that Roland Barthes uses it in "Truth and Literature." Readings, random jottings, and records of reading on fiction were in the Ming Wanli not quite a part of the literary institution, though they indeed contribute to the inclusion of certain fiction into the literary line. Yuan Hongdao's mention of JPM on two occasions certainly helped this new text to establish its more or less serious readability. The problem with theorizing everyday practices of reading, such as in Michel de Certeau's work, is a tendency to valorize and privilege reading, to idealize it in relation to a repressive regime of production and writing, and so on. De Certeau thinks primarily of contemporary "modern" nameless readers (in front of television sets, consuming dime novels and romances, and so forth). Without other "histories" and situations of everyday readings, however, reading becomes homogenized and ahistorical, undifferentiated. For Barthes, on the other hand, reading is to be distinguished from criticism precisely to maintain a distinction between scientific and nonreflexive practices. But what of nonscientific, reflexive, and authoritative "readings," notes on reading, commentaries to texts, not-quite-professional, half-casual, certainly exerting "influence," and incrementally so, through print market circulation circa 1600 in Ming Jiangnan?

38 In compiling late Ming written and printed items that have to do with JPM, Wei Ziyun appends his own comments and interpretation/translation to each item. Yuan's letter is, of course, the first item in this volume, and Wei reads Yuan's passing comparison as "proof" that the manuscript in Yuan's hands is one that must have been *significantly rewritten* to become the earliest JPM *cihua* printed edi-

tion "rediscovered" in the early 1930s (Wei, *Mingdai Jin Ping Mei*, 5). This is because for Wei, *Qifa* is obviously "about" political remonstrance (*zhengzhi jianzheng*), whereas JPM *cihua* seems obviously not (primarily) about political remonstrance, although Wei is then led to surmise that some earlier version could and must have been. Wei's reading takes Yuan's comparison as historico-philological evidence for a manuscript version of JPM markedly different from either the Wanli or Chonzhen editions that are still in circulation today. In order to do so, however, he has had to forcibly link an erotic haze not to the line that precedes it, and that syntactically furnishes the perused erotics with a material site and subjective state of reading, but rather the line that follows from it, that functions more in the manner of an afterthought (albeit an important one) or a supplement. "Glancing through it while leaning against a pillow, its pages emit an erotic haze; it is greatly superior to Mei Sheng's *Qifa*." Thus, Wei takes the "pages [that] emit an erotic haze" as referring less to JPM and more to *Qifa* (ibid., 2). Interestingly, a history of the readings of both *Qifa* and JPM would at least demonstrate that as regards the practices of readings that constitute these "two" texts, erotics was always and already political, and vice versa. But my point is that Wei's thematic assumptions about, and supposed opposition between a "political" text (*Qifa*) and a "nonpolitical" one (the Wanli or Chongzhen JPM), prevent him from positing a continuity not in subject matter but in a distinct structure of reading both evoked and reconstituted in Yuan's "quoting" *Qifa*, through the literary and social negotiations that transpire in thus articulating two generically different, historically discontinuous, and linguistically/literarily distant texts.

39 Chou, *Yuan Hung-tao*, 54.
40 With minor changes, I have used Hans H. Frankel's translation of Mei Sheng's *Qifa* here. See Hans H. Frankel, *The Flowering Plum and the Palace Lady: Interpretations of Chinese Poetry* (New Haven, Conn.: Yale University Press, 1976), 186–89.
41 Liu Xie, *The Literary Mind and the Carving of Dragons* trans. Vincent Yu-chung Shih (Hong Kong: Chinese University Press, 1983), 147 n. 2.
42 Sources for this section include Chen Hongtian, ed. *Zhaoming wenxuan yizhu* (Changchun: Jilin wenshi chubanshe, 1994), 5: 1–30; Frankel, *Flowering Plum*, 186–211; Dore Levy, *Chinese Narrative Poetry: The Late Han through T'ang Dynasties* (Durham, N.C.: Duke University Press, 1988), 20–53; Li Wai-yee, *Enchantment and Disenchantment: Love and Illusion in Chinese Literature* (Princeton, N.J.: Princeton University Press, 1993), 3–46; and David R. Knechtges, trans., *Rhapsodies on Metropolises and Capitals*, vol. 1 of *Selections of Refined Literature (Wen Xuan)* (Princeton, N.J.: Princeton University Press, 1982), 1–35. This interpretation of Yuan Hongdao's allusion to *Qifa* "found" itself, so to speak, in Frankel's essay on this particular fu. Apropos of the sequential arrangement (order) of the seven stimuli, Frankel holds that this "makes sense artistically and 'medically.'" In my use, in the context in which Yuan "rereads" it alongside JPM, the *Seven Stimuli* forges "sense" out of JPM aesthetically and hygienically (Frankel, *Flowering Plum*, 206).
43 Rather than "psychosomatic." "In classical medical thought, emotional and bodily pathology were not bifurcated around a body-spirit split; rather, madness was a symptom with roots in the whole organism. Nor did doctors think

in terms of the psychosomatic, that is, a somatic displacement of fundamentally psychic problems. . . . In the Chinese medical imagination consciousness (shen = psyche) was an aspect of the functioning of the Heart system, and emotion could destabilize Blood and cloud the psyche. But the path of influence also ran the other way: erratic motions of Blood might manifest themselves in the derangement of madness, the flare of Liver Fire in the surge of anger, the dispersal of qi in the withdrawal of melancholy" (Charlotte Furth, A Flourishing Yin: Gender in China's Medical History, 960–1665 [Berkeley: University of California Press, 1999], 88).

44 See Levy, Chinese Narrative Poetry, 48; and Frankel, Flowering Plum, 202.
45 Levy, Chinese Narrative Poetry, 37–38.
46 Frankel, Flowering Plum, 201–2.
47 Ibid., 188–89.
48 Frankel, Flowering Plum, 204.
49 Ibid., 197–201, with my own few alterations. Emphasis in original.
50 Frankel, Flowering Plum, 197.
51 Li, Enchantment, 9.
52 Frankel, Flowering Plum, 188.
53 For a "genealogy of disenchantment" in fu rhetoric, see Li, Enchantment, 3–46.
54 For an account of a contemporary Taoist regime of a "Chinese" everyday body, see Kristofer Schipper, The Taoist Body (Berkeley: University of California Press, 1993). His book suggests that this regime of the body coexists and has become synthesized with a "Confucian" body and a "Buddhist" body at the very least, and perhaps with a "Westernized" colonial body (itself hybrid) in present-day Taiwan. The Taoist Body further contends that the structure of reading I will claim inheres in Yuan Hongdao's reading of JPM (via his allusion to Qifa) is primarily Taoist, aligned with and structured through Taoist languages, practices, and knowledges. The military language and violence in Qifa recall what Schipper describes as "punitive expeditions" conducted with the help of "mediums or puppets against the demons that have invaded a faithful's dwellings and body" (53).
55 I have consulted the following in translating this passage: Liu Xie, The Literary Mind and the Carving of Dragons, trans. Vincent Yu-chung Shih (Hong Kong: Chinese University Press, 1983), 146–49; and Lu Kanru and Mo Shijin, eds., Wenxin Diaolong (Jinan: Qiru shushe, 1988), 165–78.
56 Frankel, Flowering Plums, 146–47.
57 James Legge, trans. Confucius: Confucian Analects, the Great Learning, and the Doctrine of the Mean (New York: Dover, 1971). Legge's translation for gui is "spirtual beings," but in his exegesis, he notes Zhu Xi's gloss as "the mysterious, or spiritual operations apparent in the course of nature" (201).
58 Frankel, Flowering Plum, 198.
59 Liu, Literary Mind, 147.
60 Vincent Chih, 147.
61 For details of princely conditions aspired to by social and cultural parvenu types —merchants, urban absentee landlords, clerks and yamen runners, arrogant bond servants, and even "tradeswomen" who had been bond servants in power-

ful urban households—see Tsao, "Remembering Suzhou"; and Meskill, *Gentlemanly Interests*.

62 The JPMC includes two prefaces—one by the "Master of Delight" and another shorter one by the "Pearl-Juggler" of Eastern Wu—and a colophon by a certain "Nien-gong." To sum up these prefaces' crucial difference from Zhang Zhupo's early Qing rewriting: The Master of Delight is, as his name tells it, a connoisseur of pleasures, in particular the efficacy of the pleasures of reading in curing melancholy [*you*]. Thus the JPMC is recommended primarily for its ability to beguile the reader into "forgetting his melancholy with a smile" (3). As for these readers, they are specifically those many who "have been unable to achieve enlightenment in their hearts, and who do not have access to the riches of the classic tradition to alleviate their melancholy." The Master of Delight seems, in alignment with the historical moment in which he wrote the preface, to be one of the heterodoxically inclined or merely professionalized literati who envisions for this text a reader that is, by any definition, a cultural parvenu. His is a populist reading of JPM—one that subsumes morality to pleasure. More significant, his allusion to such parvenu readers signals a Ming Wanli subject's vision of vernacular fiction *in print* as reaching a much wider urbanized reading public, who may not have classical resources but will experience comparable human sentiments as the classically educated literati. New venues of vicarious experience, such as the reading of fiction in print, would provide for and produce new structures of sentiment. The second preface by the Pearl-Juggler, however, already forebodes the stern notes of Zhang Zhupo's reading. Likewise, the last colophon by Nien-gong reads JPMC as a contemporary version of Zheng's and Wei's deleterious airs, which were not entirely deleted only because they served as a negative example. Thus, two of the three Wanli prefaces already tend toward the reading that Zhang Zhupo would fully elucidate at the end of the seventeenth century.

63 David T. Roy, trans., *The Plum in the Golden Vase or Chin P'ing Mei* (Princeton, N.J.: Princeton University Press, 1993), 6. I have used Roy's translation in the main, but have rendered *jie* as "prohibitive" rather than "admonitory," and *quan* as "exhortational" rather than "hortative," wishing to retain a focus on the text-object and its effects as realized through reading processes rather than stressing authorial motivation.

64 "Our bodies . . . are formed through the coagulation of energies, and this coagulation obeys a transformational dynamic inscribed in time. . . . When the individual grows up, seminal essence, whose generative power transcends the individual, is distilled from the Original Breath. Chinese physiology often insists on the limited quantity of seminal essence our bodies are able to produce" (Schipper, *Taoist Body*, 156).

65 Roy, *Plum in the Golden Vase*, 3–5.

66 Wei, *Mingdai Jin Ping Mei*, 30.

67 Ibid., 34.

68 This last point is implied in Xie's offhand reference to Cai Yong insofar as this reference is glossed by Xu Bo (1570–1642). Xie Zhaozhe's friend, the commoner-

bibliophile Xu Bo, wrote a preface for Xie's *Collected Works* (Tienqi 7). Xu Bo also authored his own collected notes, *Essential Words from the Brush of Master Xu* (*Xushi Bijing*, 856–551). In this collection, he includes among contemporary notable book collections that of his friend Xie Zhaozhe. Xie is, according to Xu, truly obsessed with books (*you shu shi*) and known for his acute finds, which he does not mark with jottings or comments (*ruiyi souluo bushi pidian*). In a subsequent entry headed "Secret Books" ("Mi Shu"), Xu Bo records how Cai Yong had secreted Lun Heng into his rooms while sending off the tens of thousands of books in his collection to Wang Can. Why did Cai do this? Because whoever might have found Lun Heng might not have been a man after Cai Yong's heart (*wei Yong yizhongren*), while Wan Can was a man of such exceptional talent (*yi cai*) as would be able to withstand the (inordinate) gift of tens of thousands of books (*bu wei shang hui*). What is important is that what is appropriate be done. Yet today, books have become mere gifts and are given to the rich (*guiren*) in great numbers and volumes (*lianpian leidu*). Those who receive the gift do not at all know to appreciate it, and it is cake for the ants and food for mice. The gift giver is not a Cai Yong, and the recipient not a Wang Can. Books are thus endangered. Rather than becoming the waste matter of the rich, how much better to hide them in one's rooms. See Xu Bo, "Mi Shu" (Secret books), in *Xu Shi Bijing* (Siku Biji Xiaoshuo Congshu), (Shanghai: Guji Chubanshe, 1992), 854–56. Xu Bo laments a time and situation where books have become ordinary objects of consumption and exchange. Books are now as everyday as gifts that are exchanged on first meeting or visiting someone, with no discrimination as to the recipient or to the fate of the book in question. The fate of the book—its potentially falling into hands that would sully it, to eyes and heart that would fail to share the knowledge of its value—becomes implicit in Xie Zhaozhe's oblique reference to Cai Yong's keeping a book (the Lun Heng) secretly in his rooms. JPM is then just such a book, according to Xie Zhaozhe. It is a book that is a must for the select few who know enough to use it in the appropriate manner—without doing harm to the book itself, with maximal pleasures and benefit to the self. Interestingly, this is how JPM is largely read and kept today by many male scholars and wenren in Taiwan—as a secret, in one's bedroom or closet, not to be read or mentioned in public but to be "appreciated" in leisure and with one's friends; a collectible item whose new editions are to be bought and put away.

69 Li, *Xiangqing ouji*, 364–65.
70 See Patrick Hanan, *The Invention of Li Yu* (Cambridge, Mass.: Harvard University Press, 1988), esp. chapter 1.
71 Shen Defu, *Wanli Yehuo Bian*, vol. 25 (Taipei, Taiwan: Xinxing, Shuju, 1983), 652.

CHAPTER 4  *Tears of Ressentiment: Zhang Zhupo's (1670–1698) Jin Ping Mei*

1 The three main seventeenth-century versions are: *Jin Ping Mei Cihua* (with preface dated 1618, referred to as the Cihua edition, hereafter JPMC), ed. Wei Ziyun (Taipei, Taiwan: Zengnizhi Wenhua Shiye, 1982); *Xinke xiouxiang piping Jin Ping Mei* (or the Chongzhen edition, hereafter XXPJPM), ed. Qi Yan and Ru Mei (Hong Kong,

Shandong: San Lian, Qiru Shushe, 1990); and *Zhang Zhupo Piping Diyi Qishu Jin Ping Mei* (or the Zhang Zhupo commentary edition; hereafter ZZJPM), ed. Wang Rumei, Li Zhaoxun, and Yu Fengshu (Jinan: Qiru Shushe, 1991). Zhang Zhupo read and commented on a Chungzhen edition of JPM, whose "anonymous" commentaries clearly "influenced" Zhang's reading. For interpretations of Zhang Zhupo's reading, see Andrew H. Plaks, "Chin P'ing Mei: Inversion of Self-Cultivation," in *The Four Masterworks of the Ming Novel* (Princeton, N.J.: Princeton University Press, 1987), 55–66; Peter Rushton, "The Daoist's Mirror: Reflections on the Neo-Confucian Reader and the Rhetoric of Jin Ping Mei," *Chinese Literature* 8, nos. 1–2 (July 1986): 63–82; and David T. Roy, "Chang Chu-p'o's Commentary on the *Chin P'ing Mei*," in *Chinese Narrative: Critical and Theoretical Essays*, ed. Andrew H. Plaks (Princeton, N.J.: Princeton University Press, 1977). The three editions of JPM differ in how each evinces greater textual and ideological coherence as well as consistency in representing the effects of a transgressive (female) sexuality. An earlier version of this chapter was presented at the forty-seventh Asian Studies Association conference, Washington, D.C., 6 April 1995; and at the Workshop on Woman, Culture, and Difference, University of Washington at Seattle, May 1995, subsequently published in *positions: east asia cultural critique* 3, no. 3 (1995): 663–94. I am deeply indebted to Patricia Sieber, Colleen Lye, Kuan-hsing Chen, Kim Besio, Hsu Pi-ching, Tani Barlow, Motoo Kobayashi, and two anonymous readers for their support, critique, suggestions, and comments.

2  The homology between a piece of writing and the human heart-mind that produces it is analogistically worked out in Liu Xie's sixth-century founding text of literary criticism. "Literary expressions are conditioned by the bone in much the same way as the standing posture of a body is conditioned by its skeleton; feeling gives form to the wind very much as a physical form envelops the vitality which animates it" (Liu Xie, "The Wind and the Bone," in *The Literary Mind and the Carving of Dragons*, trans. Vincent Yu-chung Shih [Hong Kong: Chinese University Press, 1983, 313). See also Lu Kanru and Mou Shijin, eds., *Wen Xin Diao Lung* (Jinan: Qiru Shushe, 1988), 2: 108.

3  For details concerning the different editions of JPM, see Liu Hui, "Jin Ping Mei Banben Kao," in *Jin Ping Mei Lunji* (Taipei, Taiwan: Guanya Wenhua, 1992), 138–68.

4  "Zhang's edition was not only the most widely disseminated, but also the most influential [of all the extant editions]" (Wang Rumei, ZZJPM, 1).

5  On how all the "third-stage" commentators do this, see David Rolston, *Traditional Chinese Fiction and Fiction Commentary* (Stanford, Calif.: Stanford University Press, 1997), 3.

6  As mentioned earlier, the story of JPM is an extensive reworking of one episode from SHZ: the story of the hero Wu Song, who after killing a tiger, must combat an even more dangerous "animal"—his lascivious sister-in-law, Pan Jinlian. JPM is more "her" story than "his," and therefore as sexually transgressive as SHZ was seen to be politically transgressive.

7  On how late Ming editorial and anthologizing practices "constructed" a Yuan zaju informed by late Ming institutional and ideological concerns, see Patricia Sieber, "Rhetoric, Romance, and Intertextuality: The Making and Remaking of

Guan Hanqing in Yuan and Ming China" (Ph.D. diss., University of California at Berkeley, 1994).

8  I find useful Pierre Bourdieu's concept of cultural or symbolic capital in understanding the social yet not necessarily economic, or even material, benefits of attaining the status and identity (*shenfen*) of wenren—literati in the larger sense of acknowledged competence and practice in the various activities that might define and constitute scholarly status. Such competence and practices were never fixed; rather, they were terrains of contestations and negotiations of power. See Pierre Bourdieu, *Language and Symbolic Power*, trans. Gino Raymond and Mathew Adamson (Cambridge, Mass.: Harvard University Press, 1991).

9  See T'ien Ju-K'ang, *Male Anxiety and Female Chastity: A Comparative Study of Chinese Ethical Values in Ming-Ch'ing Times* (Leiden, Netherlands: E. J. Brill, 1988).

10  Katherine Carlitz, "Desire, Danger, and the Body: Stories of Women's Virtue in Late Ming China," in *Engendering China: Women, Culture, and the State* (Cambridge, Mass.: Harvard University Press, 1994), 34–67.

11  Hsu Pi-ching, "Celebrating the Emotional Self: Feng Meng-Lung and Late Ming Ethics and Aesthetics" (Ph.D. diss., University of Minnesota, 1994).

12  See Chow Kai-wing, *The Rise of Confucian Ritualism in Late Imperial China* (Stanford, Calif.: Stanford University Press, 1994). In the introduction and first chapter, Chow notes how the received "empiricist" thesis in intellectual historians' studies of the Qing tend to "treat the moral and social commitments of Qing Confucians as a given or as something eroded by the critical edge of evidential scholarship" (2). In fact, as Chow shows, the opposite is the case. He further traces how even for the Taizhou school of populist and syncretic Confucianism, their "zeal in popularizing basic Confucian morals among villagers was nothing less than religious. If their zeal was religious and their approach populist or perhaps radical, the moral message of their lectures remained traditional" (28).

13  Zhang Zhupo, "The Number One Marvelous Book is Not an Obscene Book," in ZZJPM, 20. For David T. Roy's English translation of Zhang Zhupo's "How to Read [JPM]," see "Chang Chu-p'o on How to Read the *Chin P'ing Mei*," in *How to Read the Chinese Novel*, ed. David Rolston (Princeton, N.J.: Princeton University Press, 1990), 196–243. Subsequent quotations from Zhang Zhupo's "Dufa" (How to read) will be in Roy's translation unless otherwise noted.

14  Zhang, "Dufa," 53, 17, 108 (page numbers indicate both the Chinese and the Roy, *How to Read the Chinese Novel* translation). For the Chinese text, see ZZJPM, 25–50. Subsequent references to the "Dufa" will be from this edition.

15  Zhang Zhupo would fail five times in all. For a detailed account of Zhang Zhupo's life and writings, his early talent and continual straitened circumstances, as well as how the publication of his version of JPM brought him regional fame and familial opprobrium, see Wu Gan, *Zhang Zhupo yu Jin Ping Mei* (Tianjin: Baihua wenyi chubanshe, 1987).

16  Again, one finds in Liu Xie's *Wen Xin Diao Lung* the figuration of text as body, and of the writer's (in Liu Xie's thesis; whereas in Zhang Zhupo's I am arguing for the reader transplanting the writer, stepping into his shoes, writing in his shadow) work as needlework, crafting the clothing that constitutes a second, aesthetic-

ethical skin, as it were, to the textual body. "[Organization] may be compared to the role of the foundation in the building of a house and the tailor's pattern in the making of a dress, both necessary in their respective fields.... [I]t consists of feelings and ideas as the soul, of facts and meaning as the bone and marrow, of linguistic patterns as the musculature and integument, and of *kung* and *shang*, that is, the resonance of the language, as its voice and breadth" (Liu Xie, "Organization," in *The Literary Mind and the Carving of Dragons*, trans. Vincent Yu-chung Shih [Hong Kong: Chinese University Press, 1983], 437). See also Lu and Moü, *Wen Xin Diao Lung*, 2: 288.

17 Richard Sugarman, in his study of ressentiment in Friedrich Schlegel and Friedrich Nietzsche, notes how "resentment" fails to convey the "sense of time-lag between offenses suffered and displeasure or indignation expressed" (*Rancor against Time: The Phenomenology of "Ressentiment"* (Hamburg: Meiner, 1980), x.

18 Zhang Zhupo, "Zhupo's Idle Musings," in ZZJPM, 8. The "sour Confucian" (*suanru*) is a figure of derision and contempt by the mid- and late Qing. A genealogy of this figure, its uses and shifts in meaning, would be an interesting topic for further study. Zhang Zhupo, in 1695, wrote more in terms of yuan, noting how yuan turns sour with time and feelings prevented from expression.

19 Sugarman, *Rancor against Time*, x, 41.

20 On how the excess quantities of *shengyuan*, or first-level degree holders, had as it were rotted the foundations of good government in the last decades of the Ming, see Gu Yenwu, Ri Zhi Lu (Taipei, Taiwan: Shangwu, 1978), 3: 56–62. See also T'ien, *Male Anxiety*; Carlitz, "Desire, Danger, and the Body."

21 Not just any women but the two who, in comparison with all the obscene women in the narrative, Zhang Zhupo considered to be sufficiently marginal in a contaminating text—marginal therefore embodying some virtue. For comments on Aijie, see ZZJPM, 26; for comments on Yulou, see ZZJPM, 34.

22 See Wai-yee Li, *Enchantment and Disenchantment: Love and Illusion in Chinese Literature* (Princeton, N.J.: Princeton University Press, 1993), esp. 17–23.

23 Thanks to Patricia Sieber for this line of thought.

24 In his postface to Shi Ji, Sima Qian writes of his castration and imprisonment, and of how he was inspired to continue writing by the illustrious examples of Confucius and Qu Yuan, Han Fei and Sun Zi, all of whom produced writing in moments of great personal difficulties; "When the will of men is obstructed, and prevented from flow and expression, then they will narrate the past, thinking of the future" (3300). For Sima Qian, the writings of the sages of the past are motivated by *fen*, righteous indignation, not yuan (Shi Ji, 130 juan, *Tai shi gong zixu*, Zhong Hua Shuju, 1959, 3300). But Confucius in the *Analects* does refer to yuan as one of the sentiments that the *Book of Songs* produces (Legge, *Confucius: Confucian Analects*, book 17, section 9). The Confucian yuan is one of four exemplary affects of the *Book of Songs*: the first being *xing*, or exhortation; the second, *guan*, or observation; the third, *qun*, or fraternal community; and finally yuan, or critique (in Legge's translation, "how to regulate feelings of resentment"). Confucian yuan is an oblique sentiment, a veiled remonstrance (of imperial misconduct), marked

by its position of lesser power vis-à-vis the subject of speech and song. It is this aspect that is resuscitated, with a twist, in Zhang Zhupo's evocation of yuan.
25 Zhang, "Idle Musings," 8.
26 Ibid., 9.
27 A biographical anecdote illustrates the efficacy of Zhang Zhupo's grafting of his voice and emotions onto the work he was commentating: in the family records, all mention of JPM are excised, and the reason given is, "Relying on his talent, Zhang Zhupo looked down on others. He wrote a commentary on JPM that is full of hidden allusions and satiric remarks and violates the clan code of behavior. This is surely an improper use of his talents! That he died early and that his descendants have not prospered is surely not without cause" (quoted in Rolston, *How to Read the Chinese Novel*, 199). Clearly, one of his clansmen (Zhang Xiangxien, 1796–1857) at least read his commentaries as expressing more of his own views and feelings than elucidating the moral literariness of JPM.
28 Zhang, "Idle Musings," 10.
29 For a genealogy of the concepts, imagery, and functions of "wind" in Chinese thinking on the "body," see Shigehisa Kuriyama, "The Imagination of Winds and the Development of the Chinese Conception of the Body," in *Body, Subject, and Power in China*, ed. Angela Zito and Tani E. Barlow (Chicago: University of Chicago Press, 23–41). To say that a text is filled with a certain quality of air is to claim this quality as both definitive of and powerfully affective on the (discriminating) reader.
30 Zhang, "Idle Musings," 9.
31 Zhang Zhupo elsewhere notes, "I shall ignore the theory that Ximen Qing was intended to represent Yen Shifan [1513–1565]. . . . As for the person who wrote this book, I shall simply refer to him as the author. Since he did not choose to attach his name to the book, why should I try to second-guess him?" ("Dufa," item 36).
32 Zhang, "Dufa," 16, 23 (page numbers indicate both the Chinese and the Roy, *How to Read the Chinese Novel* translation). I have retranslated this passage since Roy's translation reduces (slightly) Zhang Zhupo's stress on the aggressive will/desire of the author to kill not just Pan Jinlian but all those who have had anything to do with the production of such a monster: "[The author] wanted to put them all to death, and then [he could obtain] relief [*jie yu zhi zhi sidi er fang chang ye*]," in ZZJPM, 31. Roy's translation: "As for Lady Lin, she serves as a vehicle for expressing the incalculable resentment the author feels in his heart for P'an Chin-lien. Not only does he have her [P'an Chin-lien] murdered and mutilated, but he is not satisfied until he has damned even the household in which she got her start in life and the persons who taught her to be what she is" (23).
33 Zhang, "Dufa," item 36.
34 Patricia Sieber has used "moral voyeurism" in the context of her study of the Ming fabrication of Yuan zaju. I have claimed, in my dissertation, that JPM evinces a moral sadism—that is, the taking of an ethical (yes, but) pleasure (nonetheless) in the narrative embodiments of sexual women and their horrify-

ing deaths. This is very much in line with what Katherine Carlitz has noted as the sensual overtones of morally edifying tales of virtuous women.
35  Zhang, "Idle Musings," 9.
36  Zhang, "Dufa," item 47.
37  ZZJPM, 1564; and JPMC, 496.
38  Interestingly, this telling phrase does not occur in the earlier JPMC, where there is only mention of the passing of a night (dang ye guo le yi su).
39  ZZJPM, 1564, item 100.
40  Zhang, "Dufa," item 51.
41  "The body of a man is given him by his parents. Thus my body will follow the life and death of my parents' bodies" (Zhang Zhupo, "Embittered Filiality," ZZJPM, 19).
42  One is reminded here of the Buddhist chants that read the female body in such a way as to produce an affect of objectification and revulsion. Thus, as it is retold in a late Ming (?) compilation titled "The Words of Gentlemen on Food and Sex" (Lung Zunxu)

> i. There was once a lascivious king, who the teacher advised with this Buddhist verse,
> ii. [Her] eyes are cavities of tears and mucus, [her] nose a dirt- and snot-filled bag, [her] mouth a container for saliva, [her] stomach a warehouse for shit and urine. Alas, the king lacks the eyes of wisdom with which to see, and continues to indulge in sexual pleasures.

43  Zhang, "Dufa," item 106.
44  Ibid., items 40, 71, 82.
45  Ibid., item 48.
46  Ibid.
47  See Lung Zunxu, ed., Shise shenyan, in Congshu jicheng xinbian (Taipei, Taiwan: Shangwu, 1965), 47: 234.
48  See Kangxi zidian, Zhang Yushu, ed., Shanghai: Shanghai shudian chubanshe, 1985, 893.
49  In fact, in the first hui of both JPMC and the Zhang Zhupo edition, there is the following list of the five ills that attend Mr. Zhang's "having his way" with a young Jinlian:

> No. 1: his loins began to ache.
> No. 2: his eyes began to tear.
> No. 3: his ears began to grow deaf.
> No. 4: his nose began to run.
> No. 5: his urine began to drip. I quote this list from David T. Roy's trans., The Plum in the Golden Vase or Chin P'ing Mei (Princeton, N.J.: Princeton University Press, 1993), 27.

50  Zhang, "Dufa," item 42.
51  The term buliang fu appears in a story collected in a late Ming work of anecdotal

fiction, *Furong jing yuyan*, edited and written by Jiang Dongwei, a juren of 1606 (reprint, Zejiang: Zejiang Guji chubanshe, 1986), 257.

52  See Susan Mann, "Learned Women in the Eighteenth Century," in *Engendering China: Women, Culture, and the State*, ed. Christina Gilmartin et al. (Cambridge, Mass.: Harvard University Press, 1994); and Dorothy Ko, *Teachers of the Inner Chambers: Women and Culture in Seventeenth-Century China* (Stanford, Calif.: Stanford University Press, 1994).

53  Translated in Rolston, "How to Read the Fifth Book of Genius," in *How to Read the Chinese Novel*, item 69, 145.

54  Zhang, "Dufa," item 82.

55  By the mid–fifteenth century, book merchants were already publishing novels for an "improperly" literate audience. For an illuminating account of the print commercialization of the book market and its relation to the increasing professionalization of literati subjects, see Jr-lien Tsao, "Remembering Suzhou: Urbanism in Late Imperial China" (Ph.D. diss., University of California at Berkeley, 1992), esp. chapters 1 and 4. Ye Sheng (1420–1474) writes that "peasants, artisans, [and] merchants hand copied the words and illustrations [of novels]; and imbecilic women are especially obsessed with [these stories], which some busybodies have termed "Female Chronicles" [Nü Tongjian]," (*Shuidong riji*, 21: 213–14, quoted in Tsao, "Remembering Suzhou," 211–12). By the Wanli era, Shen Defu notes the laughable quality of Guangling prostitutes' vaunted abilities to read and write: "If you buy them home, and then have them read for you, [you will find that] excepting for a few characters [such as *jie yuan, hui yuan*] they are unable to decipher any other word" (*Wanli Yehuo Pian* [Taipei, Taiwan: Xinxing Shuju, 1983], 23: 597). On the publishing boom and birth of a reading public in Ming Jiajing (1522–1566), see also Ko, *Teachers of the Inner Chambers*, 34–67.

56  Echoing of (others') tongues (*xueshe*) is Pan Jinlian the arch yinfu's primary mode of speech. She is represented as surviving the cutthroat polygamous familial compound through the deployment of gossip as mimicry, as the nuanced echoing of an other's speech in such a way as to incriminate the mimicked subject, while seeming to transport words interest free. The treachery of this yinfu lies in her agile use of mimicry. Yet the text that represents her deadly use of repetition likewise repeats, mimicks yinfu, to produce an equally treacherous feminized fictional form. Thus Zhang Zhupo's comment that in order to so "realistically" represent such a variety of yinfu, the author must have metamorphosized (*huanhua*) into all of these yinfu. There is a successive ventriloquism of different voices: Zhang Zhupo for the author, the author for yinfu, and Pan Jinlian for those yinfu who stood in her way.

57  Zhang, "Dufa," item 90.

58  Ibid.

59  See Zhang, "Dufa," item 106.

60  Kai-Wing Chow notes that "this professionalization of the literati [in the late Ming] diluted gentry culture. The classical education the literati acquired was put to uses not directly related to the examination system or government service.

... As professional writers they had to cater to the diverse needs and interests of the reading public" (*Rise of Confucian Ritualism*, 23).

61 Bernard Faure notes in the "tradition" of Chan Buddhism how a rhetoric of equality serves to mask a practical misogyny, or misogyny as practice. It also served the purpose, in the context of Buddhism's "rivalry—and complementarity—with Confucianism" to attract women who wanted "to run away from their gender-determined roles" (243). More revealing are the three types of women Faure finds in Chan Buddhist discourse and imaginary: the non-feminine "old woman"/mother, the virgin, and the whore. Faure also notes the important role of "repulsion" in Chan Buddhism, particularly how "repulsion" is a sentiment used to counter the rising of feelings of desire. See Bernard Faure, *Rhetoric of Immediacy: A Cultural Critique of Chan/Zen Buddhism*, Stanford, Calif.: Stanford University Press, 1994. Zhang Zhupo's reading of Pan Jinlian partakes especially of this aspect of Buddhist misogyny, in his interpretation of key passages wherein the emplotting of Jinlian in JPM serves to induce revulsion, in a contrapuntal movement to stirrings of desire.

CHAPTER 5   Seduction: Tiger and Yinfu

1 I also refer to Jin Shengtan's commentated and shortened edition, the *Guanhua tang diwu caizi shu Shuihu Zhuan*, in vols. 3 and 4 of *Jin Shengtan Quanji* (Yangzhou: Jiangsu Guji Chubanshe, 1985), as the Jin Shengtan SHZ. For a comprehensive account of and the state of scholarship on SHZ's textual history, see Andrew H. Plaks, *The Four Masterworks of the Ming Novel* (Princeton, N.J.: Princeton University Press, 1987), 280–303.

2 The warrior ethos of SHZ is both obvious yet masked by what C. T. Hsia terms its comic effects, the sadism of its violence (to the "modern" reader), and the incomprehensibility of its indulgence in wine and food simultaneous with a pronounced sexual puritanism. See C. T. Hsia, *The Classic Chinese Novel: A Critical Introduction* (New York: Columbia University Press, 1968), 88–92.

3 See Wang Jing, *The Story of the Stone: Intertextuality, Ancient Chinese Stone Lore, and the Stone Symbolism of Dream of the Red Chamber, Water Margin, and the Journey to the West* (Durham, N.C.: Duke University Press, 1992), 261–67.

4 The late Ming might have been such a moment; the cultural revolution or 1975 in China seems to have been another such moment, as was the late 1990s in Taiwan, when the television series based on the one-hundred-chapter SHZ made in China became all the rage. The periodic political usefulness of a narrative of the heroic code at large (with the people) rather than at court (state aligned) signals the possibility of reactivating sentiments embedded in an otherwise seemingly outdated paternalist imperial system.

5 See Hsia, *Classic Chinese Novel*, 41.

6 See Pierre Clastres, *Archeology of Violence* (New York: Semiotexte, 1994). Clastres juxtaposes in such war-driven, stateless societies masculinity to death and femininity to life (biological reproduction): "Slaves of death, men envy and fear women, mistresses of life.... The myths, by reversing the real order, attempt

to think of society's destiny as masculine destiny; the rituals, a theatrical setting in which men play out their victory, are used to ward off, to compensate for the too obvious truth of this destiny. Weakness, dereliction, inferiority of men in the face of women? This is indeed what myths almost everywhere in the world that imagine the lost golden age or paradise to conquer as an asexual world, as *a world without women*, recognize" (194–95).

7 This chapter will primarily focus on JPMC in two editions: one, a modern typeset edition (Taipei, Taiwan: Zengnizhi wenhua shiye youxian gongsi, 1982) to which page numbers will refer; and two, a photocopy edition of the original, *Quanben Jin Ping Mei Cihua*, reprinted by Taiping Shuju (Hong Kong, 1982)—the chapter or hui numbers following the page numbers in parentheses will refer to this photocopy edition. XXPJPM, reprinted by San Lian and Qiru Joint Publishing (Hong Kong, 1990), will also be referred to. Finally, ZZJPM will be extensively cited and reread as well. For more detailed information concerning editions used, see introduction and bibliography.

All translations are my own unless otherwise noted. I have consulted David T. Roy's meticulous translations in *The Plum in the Golden Vase or Chin P'ing Mei* (Princeton, N.J.: Princeton University Press, 1993). In this chapter, I have for the most part retained my own translations to acknowledge how the interpretations in this and the following two chapters "remake" the text as much as any translation.

8 Incidentally, the journals of Mathew Ricci provide an interesting "outsider's" view of the military in the late Ming period; see Louis J. Gallagher, trans., *China in the Sixteenth Century: The Journals of Mathew Ricci, 1583–1610* (New York: Random House, 1953), 55–56, 89–90. "Policies of war are formulated and military questions are decided by the Philosophers [namely, literati] only, and their advice and counsel has more weight with the King than that of military leaders" (55–56). Furthermore, "The whole military is under the jurisdiction of the Philosophic Senate, which issues their pay as well as their military supplies and rations. . . . There probably is no class of people in the country as degraded and as lazy as the soldiers. . . . The greater part of the army are bondsmen to the crown, and serve in slavery either for their own crimes or for those of their ancestors" (89–90).

9 See Jean Baudrillard, *Seduction*, trans. Brian Singer (London: Macmillan, 1990).

10 Thus, for example, Jin Shengtan's obsessive attacks on Song Jiang, whose perfidy is put in terms of a hypersensitivity to money and (self-)profit.

11 For instance, the several infamous women in SHZ, and their continuing fascination for readers of fiction and audiences of drama, are Pan Jinlian (Wu Song) and Pan Qiaoyun (Song Jiang), to name just two.

12 In a recent literary-political scandal in Taiwan, Li Ang's new novel, *Beigang Xianglu Renren Cha* [Everyone puts their incense sticks in the Pei-kang incense burner], features a female protagonist who fucks her way up the political ladder to the very top echelon of the major opposition party. The heroine of the novel, Lin Lizi, is characterized throughout as "that Lin Lizi," a debasing strategy analogous to SHZ's treatment of its licentious female walk-on parts.

13 SHZ, 357. See also Jin Shengtan SHZ, 348. When Wu Song reads the public notice posted on the gate of a temple at the foot of the ridge he was going to cross,

more than half drunk, he realized "that there really was a tiger, and was about to turn back and return to the wineshop," but he decided that he could not go back without being laughed at. This moment and phrase of hesitation is erased in the JPMC version.

14 Jin Shengtan SHZ, 347.
15 Ibid., 356.
16 SHZ, 365; and Jin Shengtan SHZ, 356.
17 Jin Shengtan SHZ, 357.
18 Jin Shengtan's reading—and his abridged edition of SHZ—has become almost better known than its "original." This makes of him both the ultimate "ideal" reader, the record of his reading having become nearly inseparable from the text itself, and the ultimate "rewriter," since his, and in fact any, reading constitutes at the same time a (figural) rewriting, though there is always the chance (ruse) of literally rewriting while pretending to only comment. Zhang Zhupo, in commentating on JPM, followed closely in Jin Shengtan's footsteps. See chapters 2 and 4. See also David Rolston, *Traditional Chinese Fiction and Fiction Commentary* (Stanford, Calif.: Stanford University Press, 1997).
19 In terms of the tiger-killing episode, Jin Shengtan's recurring comment was: "*hai ren*" (terrifying); fear would seem to have been the primary affect. George Bataille has most suggestively noted the underground linkage between fear and laughter as two poles of erotic affect; see his *The Tears of Eros*, trans. Peter Connor (San Francisco: City Lights, 1989), 66.
20 Bataille, *Tears of Eros*, 33. Incidentally, the pseudonym of the "writer" of JPM is *xiaoxiao sheng*, literally "the one who laughs."
21 The decapitation of Pan Jinlian could be seen as a historical remainder, a textual trace of dismemberment and decapitation especially as befitting slaves and (non)persons of inferior position/status and denoting sacrificial objects. For a careful account of the archaeological findings of burial sites of the Shang era (1600–1100 B.C.E.) in which slaves were buried as/along with sacrificial animals, decapitated and prostrate, see Sha Wenhan, *Zhongguo nuli zhidu de tantao* [An inquiry into the Chinese slave system] (Shanghai: shehuik exueyuan chubanshe 1984), 5–9.
22 I have found Bataille's theory of the homogeneous society and duality of heterogeneous elements immensely fertile in thinking through the *zhanghui* form and its correlations as well as interconnections with Ming monarchical society. See especially George Bataille, "The Psychological Structure of Fascism," in *Visions of Excess: Selected Writings, 1927–1939* (Minneapolis: University of Minnesota Press, 1985). It is Bataille's anthropological and cultural semiotic aspect that has most influenced the reading in this chapter.
23 Readings that stress the progressiveness of SHZ in its subversion of traditional hierarchies and power tend to "miss" this transfiguration and transvaluation, or ignore it.
24 Jin Shengtan SHZ, 355.
25 Here again is a further example of how the heterogeneous ruling elements will, in order to consolidate its ties to the homogeneous masses, oppose and seek to

exterminate those heterogeneous elements at the base of society—for instance, licentious women. This pits the likes of Wu Song (bums and rebels) against those who compete with them for the same space and resources at the bottom of society—adulteresses who also live more by consumption and pleasure than production. Wu Song must exterminate and expel that which mirrors and parodies his state, for in so doing he will simultaneously represent and reproduce the morality that will ultimately legitimate and valorize his difference.

26  Yi translates to righteousness/honor between men, and zhong as loyalty to one's state/ruler. The fact that SHZ stressed the former—that is, homosocial bonding between men—has been taken as an implicit critique of the latter, or at least as pointing up a potential contradiction between these two highest of all values in the "Chinese" polity. For a systematic critique of these ethical values and how they sustain a particular micropolitics of hierarchy in everyday life in the context of a family-state continuum, see Zhu Hanmin, *Zhongxiao daode yu chenmin jingshen* (Lushan, Henan: Henan Renmin Chubanshe, 1994).

27  Although SHZ and JPM have come to be seen as inaugurating two distinct lines and genres of zhanghui (wuxia or martial art/brotherhood versus domestic drama/worldly sentiment), and despite the great differences between Wu Song in these two groupings of texts (the Wu Song of SHZ as the martial hero, and in JPM therefore difficult to assimilate into a muddy world of inferior and nonhumane persons). Nonetheless, it is useful to see how JPM could be read as a rewriting of SHZ, turning inside out and expanding indefinitely one small episode in the latter. Thanks to an anonymous reader for this line of thought.

28  Jin Shengtan SHZ, 360–61.

29  JPMC, 55–56 (1).

30  Yuan Hongdao on drinking aestheticizes a refined ritual of wine drinking that would replace this more everyday and base version of the game. Instead of the hierarchy of those who physically outdo all others, Yuan installs another hierarchy—one more cultural and literary or poetic. Drinking is thus redefined for the literary elite (who is not necessarily a drinker but has more "know-how"). See Yuan Hongdao, "The Treatise for Drinkers," in *Yuan Zhonglang Quanji*, ed. Yang Jialuo (Taipei, Taiwan: Shijie Shuju, 1990), 23–26; translated in Ming-Shui Hung, *The Romantic Vision of Yuan Hung-tao, Late Ming Poet and Critic* (Taipei, Taiwan: Bookman Books, 1997), 152–59. This is where Yuan lists JPM as among the drinker's "Extraordinary Canon": "Anyone not familiar with these books cannot be regarded as a real drinker but simply as a man with jar-like intestines who can drink like a butler" (Hung, *Romantic Vision*, 158). For a "modern" version of the aesthetic rather than vulgar drinker—that is, "people who had the 'sentiment for wine' without having an actual capacity for it" (240), see Yutang Lin, *The Importance of Living* (New York: John Day, 1937).

31  Quoted in Roy, *Plum in the Golden Vase*, 34. See also JPMC, 53 (1).

32  This is precisely what SHZ is all about: the thirst and hunger for wine, meat, and sacrificial blood, to be consecrated at the altar of a renewed community of virile men.

33  I must note here in passing the peculiar form of seduction known as *sa jiao*, lit-

erally meaning to perform the baby coquette—a form of cultural flirtation in the northeast Asian world in the figure of the girlish woman-child who never quite matures, much to the delight of all the "fathers" who adopt and spoil her. "Femininity" in this sense is an enhanced and eroticized "childlikeness" honed into an art, including a certain nasal quality to the voice, artlessness in facial expression, and a distinct prepubescent disposition of the body. Perhaps again, this includes residual elements of the eroticization of a gendered familial and social position that must be marked as inferior and submissive, as the child's is to the parent.

34 Note the dissymmetry of names: she calls him Shushu, the appellation for the younger brother of one's father, whereas he calls her Saosao, the appellation for the wife of one's elder brother (or the wife of a senior friend). For the woman, the difference in gender will already have given the man a generational advantage and privilege. Shushu is both intimate and respectful; and when Pan Jinlian for the first time shifts to a too-intimate "ni" (one only addresses intimates directly in the second person), closing as it were that generational (incestuous) gap, Wu Song immediately reacts violently to reinstate the proper distance between them—countering with a threat of closing the same gap in his way: "My fists shall not recognize the Saosao that I see with my eyes." In a skewed sense, he will finally be impelled to give her what she had asked for.

35 JPMC, 64 (2).

36 Quoted in David T. Roy, "Chang Chu-po's Commentary on the Chin P'ing Mei," in *Chinese Narrative: Critical and Theoretical Essays*, ed. Andrew H. Plaks (Princeton, N.J.: Princeton University Press, 1977), 236.

37 See Laura Mulvey, "Visual Pleasure and Narrative Cinema," in *Visual and Other Pleasures* (Bloomington: Indiana University Press, 1989), 19.

38 Fan Lien, translated and quoted in John Meskill, *Gentlemanly Interests and Wealth on the Yangtze Delta* (Ann Arbor, Mich.: Association for Asian Studies, 1994), 146.

39 Lady Lin is the "widow of Imperial Commissioner Wang I-hsuan, mother of Wang Ts'ai, former mistress of Pan Jinlian who learns to play musical instruments and to sing as a [bond] servant in her household. [Lady Lin] carries on an adulterous affair with His-men Ch'ing under the transparent pretext of asking him to superintend the morals of her profligate son" (Roy, *Plum in the Golden Vase*, lxxv).

40 Fan Lien, translated and quoted in Meskill, *Gentlemanly Interests*, 149. From another source (Li Shaowen's *Yunjian Zashi*), Meskill writes how Saleswoman Wu "was a servant in the establishment of Fan Wei-yi, the distinguished official.... A beautiful woman, Saleswoman Wu was admitted to the great houses to sell jewelry and came to be on familiar terms with all the gentlemen living in them. Soon she was manufacturing aphrodisiac toys and medicines and urging them on women who enjoyed erotic pleasures. Her business prospered so much that she rode everywhere in a sedan chair. She dressed and ate like someone from a rich house. In 1592, Kan Shijie, an investigating censor on tour in Songjiang took note of the group and had them all seized and beaten. Saleswoman Wu came off very

badly. She was turned over to the Huating magistrate, who punished her with great zeal, having her stripped and beaten and her wealth taken away. The commerce stopped for a year and then began again, often carried on by servants of the great houses" (148). The career of Saleswoman Wu, her sexual and commercial opportunism, recall the rise and fall of Pan Jinlian, down to the details of her punishment as well as the zeal with which that punishment is carried out, witnessed, and recorded in writing. Both occupy positions that in Ming Jiajing and Wanli, in the Yangze delta region, offered new possibilities for lines of flight from bond servitude and concubinage, for amassing wealth and living the (temporary) good life.

CHAPTER 6   Red Shoes, Foot Bindings, and the Swing

1  JPMC, 420 (28). As mentioned earlier, the chapter or hui number following the page number in parentheses refers to the photocopy edition of the original, Quanben Jin Ping Mei Cihua, reprinted by Taiping Shuju (Hong Kong, 1982).
2  Ibid., 75 (3).
3  Ibid., 88 (4).
4  Ibid., 356 (24).
5  Ibid., 331–32 (22).
6  Ibid., 373 (25), in the venomous words of Jinlian to Yulou.
7  Ibid., 332 (22).
8  Ibid.
9  JPMC, 332 (22).
10 Ibid. All the wives, maids, and servants of the house address Ximen Qing with the intimate form of father, die, which I have translated as "dad" because of the phonetic resemblances. This records the master as father of all in the "family," including "nonbiological" bond servant–retainers (thus the usage of jia ren for bond servants in general). Acquaintances of equal or inferior social position to Ximen would call him "venerable old one" (lao ye). The household was thus basically conceived of as an extended family, structured along generational, gender, and class/status lines. "Prior to the Zhengde period [1506–1521] one in every ten commoners was an official, and nine out of ten were working the land. . . . During the last forty to fifty years the land tax has been increasing daily and service labor getting heavier. The people cannot bear it and they all change their occupations. In former days resident officials [xiangguan] did not have too many family servants [jia ren]. At present the number of people that give up agriculture to become family servants of resident officials is already ten times what it was previously" (He Liangjun, quoted in Atsushi Shigeta, "The Origins and Structure of Gentry Rule," in *State and Society in China: Japanese Perspectives on Ming-Qing Social and Economic History*, ed. Linda Grove and Christian Daniels [Tokyo: University of Tokyo Press, 1984], 369). "Many of the literati [shidafu] in Jiangnan today practice this custom [of keeping bond servants]. As soon as they pass the examinations, these people compete to be admitted to their families, large followings number-

11  JPMC, 333 (22).
12  "Men are swayed by two simultaneous emotions: they are driven away by terror and drawn by an awed fascination. Taboo and transgression reflect these two contradictory urges. The taboo would forbid the transgression but the fascination compels it" (George Bataille, *Erotism: Death and Sensuality*, trans. Mary Dalwood [San Francisco: City Lights, 1986], 68; see also 63–64).
13  JPMC, 199 (13).
14  This is an oblique challenge to Jean Baudrillard's absolute "seduction" (Jean Baudrillard, *De la Seduction* [Paris: Editions Galilée, 1979], 120–21). Is Baudrillard not seducing us into believing that women always used to win at this game between the sexes?
15  For a study of prostitution in the Ming period and JPM, see Tao Muning, *Jin Pingmei zhong de qinglou yu jinu* (Beijing: Wenhua yishu chubanshe, 1993).
16  Such as Wang Liu'er's case in chapters 37–79 of JPM. As Zhang Zhupo notes, she is Pan Jinlian's second "double" and successor to Huilian's place in terms of relations with Ximen Qing. Her less "tragic" end is directly linked to the position she occupies: the wife of one of Ximen's hired shopkeepers, she lives outside the compound with her husband, who also acts as passive pimp to his employer's visits with his wife. She does not therefore encroach spatially on the territory of the wives in the domestic compound.
17  JPMC, 334 (22).
18  Ibid., 347 (23).
19  Ibid.
20  ZZJPM, 348. According to Zhang's prechapter commentary, Pan Jinlian had only to use a little bit of quan shu to cause the slightest rift between Ximen and Huilian—just enough for her to slowly fit a wedge in and complete the rupture, sacrificing in the process both Huilian and Lai Wang. "And the evil of Jinlian already overflows even the silence (about it)" ZZJPM, 348.
21  See Zhang Zhenjun, *Chuantong xiaoshuo yu zhongguo wenhua* (Gulin, Guangxi: Guangxi Shifan daxue chubanshe, 1996), 269, where Zhang contrasts Jinlian's "selfishness" and Huilian's "child-like innocence."
22  For the continued importance of smell in the appraisal of bondmaids and concubines into the modern era, see Maria Jaschok, *Concubines and Bondservants: A Social History of a Chinese Custom* (London: Zed Books, 1988), 16.
23  That is, the two items given Ximen Qing by Wang Liu'er shortly before his death: a tress of glossy black hair braided with five-colored silk ribbons onto a lover's knotted ring (*tung xin jie tuor*), with two cotton strings, and an embroidered, purple, two-mouthed bag filled with melon seeds. Both are signifiers of desire: the one phallic, the other oral. See JPMC (79). Other occasions where "the assimilating gaze" appears include chaps. 27, 29, 50, 78, and 79.
24  The phrase consistently used throughout is: "*man xin huan xi*."
25  JPMC (25).

26 Ibid. (15).
27 In JPM, the story of adultery is suspended (6–7) and the woman kept waiting, the better to whet the reader's appetite, while the adulterer enjoys a change of fare and marries another for money. Adultery will be resumed only to be further suspended and, this time, endlessly repeated (22, 37, 78, 80)—suspension becoming repetition, or a mirror reflecting another mirror in a mirage of infinite reflections. It is the reader's desire that is played with finally. Caught in the reflection of itself that is the narrative, the reader's desire is continuously enthralled and at stake in these strategies of writing.
28 "And Yueniang will actually have him send off the swing [for the wives]. At such a time, even someone who had the willpower and could exert self-control would be hard put to learn from Liu Xiahui and Lu Nanzi [men who could withstand seduction in any form], not to mention such a flighty rake as Jingji" (ZZJPM, 375).
29 JPMC, 372 (25).
30 Ibid., 373 (25).
31 Ibid., 376 (25).
32 Ibid., 377 (25).
33 Ibid., 386 (26).
34 Ibid.
35 Ibid., 387 (26).
36 ZZJPM, 388.
37 JPMC, 390–95 (26).
38 Ibid., 394 (26).
39 ZZJPM, 376.
40 Ibid., 389 (26).
41 Ibid., 407 (prechapter commentary to chapter 27).
42 JPMC, 401 (27).
43 See Craig Clunas, *Fruitful Sites: Garden Culture in Ming Dynasty China* (Durham, N.C.: Duke University Press, 1996).
44 "Dian le yi jian nongnong yanyan zhima yanxun lixi guaren hetaoren jia chunbulao haiqing na tiane muxi meigui polu Liuan queshe yacha" (JPMC, 38 [72]).
45 JPMC, 39 (72, vol. 3); XXPJPM, 1001 (72); and Clement Egerton, *The Golden Lotus: A Translation, from the Chinese Original, of the Novel Chin P'ing Mei* (London: Routledge, 1974), 3: 72.
46 As in the case of *Hong Lou Meng*, with so much more encrusted and domesticating narrative meaning for each name and thing named, so that the text will no longer seem too obesely/obscenely (to use yet an association of Jean Baudrillard's, though mostly differently, from his "Figures du Transpolitique," in *Les Strategies Fatales* [Paris: Grasset, 1983]) replete with objects (as in JPM), but more seriously and hygienically meaningful and properly acculturated.
47 Residues of an outrightly negative attitude toward material things that is recorded as the correctly moderate nonconsumer of the mid-Ming: "[Gu Qing, 1460–1528,] was content though poor. When a rich family wanted to exchange betrothal gifts with him, he wrote a motto that said, 'Do not covet things and

be weakened by them. Do not get used to things and be controlled by them'" (Sun Chengen, quoted in John Meskill, *Gentlemanly Interests and Wealth on the Yangtze Delta* [Ann Arbor, Mich.: Association for Asian Studies, 1994], 59 n. 85).

48  JPMC, 402 (27). A yueqin is a four-stringed plucked instrument with a full-moon-shaped sound box.

49  JPMC, 403 (27).

50  Ibid.

51  After her death, Ximen will be inconsolable and repeatedly mourn his "sister who is good and virtuous," forgetting that she was the only one of the concubines who could afford even a semblance of goodness and virtue.

52  JPMC, 404 (27).

53  Ibid., 405 (27).

54  This is one of the innumerable word games at which Jinlian and Ying Bojue (the arch-mediator-parasite) are experts: playing with words being the most deadly and effective of strategies, for these never leave a trace (of blood) and kill or please at will. In this case, putting on "flowers-before-the-eyes" that are the result of three days without food, translates into "I'll pretend not to see what's happening before me." This further implies, "But I do see and know; don't think you've deceived me."

55  Egerton's translation is, in this case, what Pan Jinlian would call a "powdered and made up" presentable version of the Chinese. Cao was, and today still means, "fuck," with connotations of aggressive penetration; both are commonly used as cusswords, or expletives, expressing forcefully sensations of anger and aggression. The ideogram designates the act: "enter" perched on top of the character "flesh." Egerton's translation reproduces a gendered perspective: "Hsi-men Ching seized her tiny feet. 'You little villain,' he cried, 'if I weren't afraid of somebody seeing us, I'd make you die of delight'" (*Golden Lotus*, 1: 382).

56  Even the unknown commentator of the XXPJPM edition notes in the margins following this phrase that this "inscribes [how he is] both loving and angry." It is a love-hate relation. JPM is at least exemplary in refusing to sentimentalize/romanticize, though its negation (of late Ming discourse of sentiment or qing, usually seen as a rebellion against orthodox neo-Confucian strictures, which makes it no less neo-Confucian) is unfortunately or predictably likewise made at the expense of women.

57  On the youngest sister of a twentieth-century bondmaid-concubine whose "mental retardation" consisted of a "single-minded pursuit of her obsession with sex, luxuries and instant gratification—regardless of loss of face and the social repercussions of her actions on the family," see Jaschok, *Concubines and Bondservants*, 31.

58  JPMC, 407 (27).

59  Incidentally, the *Ciyuan* dictionary records under "red" (*hong*) the phrase "red embroidered shoe" (*hong xiou xie*), denoting an instrument of torture used during the Ming: a shoe made of iron and burned until red for the criminal's express wear. The outcome must inevitably have been the peeling off of at least a part of one's feet with the shoe; the reverse, as it were, of having them bound. This was

undoubtedly inspired by (the fascination with) women's bound feet and the red embroidered shoes that figure so often in erotic and romantic fiction. Red shoes go with desire and pleasure, torture and punishment.

60  For the theory that would delineate such ambivalence concerning borders and extremities along with their secretions and excretions, and how the latter constitute in certain orders and contexts a threat to the reigning body (individual/politic), see Mary Douglas, *Purity and Danger: An Analysis of the Concepts of Pollution and Taboo* (London: Routledge, 1966); and Julia Kristeva, *Powers of Horror: An Essay in Abjection*, trans. Leon Roudiez (New York: Columbia University Press, 1982).

61  ZZJPM (27–29), with the "last" shoe/word (for this sequence) mention appearing on page 435 (29).

62  Bataille would uphold this view: the association between death and sex is precisely what gives the latter its powers to fascinate. Also, feet wraps are used in just such a manner again, in chapters 61 and 79, with Wang Liu'er, Jinlian's second shadow-double. On women as props, see Robert H. van Gulik, *Erotic Colour Prints of the Ming Period* (Tokyo: n.p., 1951), which refuses to find anything "unusual" in such uses of bodies. Thus, one is used in the mode of a chair or back support, while another is a cushion placed horizontally beneath the waist of a woman (looking vaguely bored).

63  A retelling of the scene would read as follows: Ximen begins to copulate with Jinlian until Chunmei suddenly appears with the wine they had asked for, and seeing her "mother" hanging by the feet, runs away to the top of the stone hill— whereupon Ximen leaves Jinlian to run after Chunmei and carries her back to the arbor, holds her on his knee, and drinks wine with her. Ximen then proposes a game of "aiming at the flesh gourd," and using golden plums, aims at Jinlian's vagina, striking the target three times. He orders Chunmei to feed Jinlian a glass of wine (having drunk three himself, one for each "hit") and places another plum inside Jinlian, leaving it there. Jinlian calls out in protest, to no avail; Ximen continues to drink, ignoring her, and finally falls asleep. He wakes up after about an hour and, seeing Jinlian still suspended from the arbor, "a pair of white fleshy thighs hanging to both sides, says: "Whore, I'll give [diou] it to you." But before doing so, he does not forget to scoop the plum out and feed it to her. He takes out a small bag filled with various sexual aids, placing a silver ring, then changing it for a sulphur one, around his penis. Pan Jinlian is, according to the text, in a frenzy by this time and calls out to him, "Dada, get in quickly, this whore's really anxious. I know you're angry at me because of Li Pinger and have purposely done all this to 'get at me.' After today's lesson, I'll never dare provoke you anymore." Finally, the sulphur ring breaks inside of her and she faints in a coma, barely breathing, the tip of her tongue icy cold, hands and limbs spread limp (JPMC [27]).

64  Bataille, too, writes of climax as *la petite mort*.

65  JPMC, 318 (87). There is an illustration of Aztec human sacrifice around 1500 in George Bataille, *The Tears of Eros* (trans. Peter Connor [San Francisco: City Lights, 1989], 207) with a strangely familiar scooping out of the heart sacrificial scene.

CHAPTER 7   *A Cat, a Dog, and the Killing of Livestock*

1  I am especially thinking of the studies of bond servitude and bond servants in relation to late Ming landownership, urban gentry, and urban popular uprising by Masaaki Oyama ("Large Landownership in the Jiangnan Delta Region during the Late Ming–Early Qing Period," in *State and Society in China: Japanese Perspectives on Ming-Qing Social and Economic History*, ed. Linda Grove and Christian Daniels, eds. [Tokyo: University of Tokyo Press, 1989], 101–164); and Masatoshi Tanaka ("Popular Uprisings, Rent Resistance, and Bondservant Rebellions in the Late Ming," in *State and Society in China*, 165–214. On fictive family relationships that mask bond servitude, see Oyama, "Large Landownership," 133–35. On the legal status of bond servants in the Ming through Qing periods, see Tanaka, "Popular Uprisings," 192–93. "Because bondservants were given the right to have their own possessions and families, a great gap in wealth and economic position arose between the bondservants who owned nothing and could be used without restraint by their master and 'brazen' servants, such as the bondservant managers, who were often able to acquire considerable wealth. In short, not all bondservants shared identical class interests" (ibid., 193). On the other hand, I am thinking of what Paul S. Ropp has termed the "ambivalent position of courtesan culture" and "courtesanship in Ming and Qing society" ("Ambiguous Images of Courtesan Culture in Late Imperial China," in *Writing Women in Late Imperial China*, ed. Ellen Widmer and Kang-I Sun Chang [Stanford, Calif.: Stanford University Press, 1997], 18, 43). What are the relations between familial bondmaid-concubine yinfu and famous prostitutes? Might they not share a similar socioeconomic trajectory? What are the relations between the representations of such diverse, perhaps even polarized figures?

2  See Tao Muning, *Jin Pingmei zhong de qinglou yu jinu* (Beijing: Wenhua yishu chubanshe, 1993); and Zhang Zhenjun, "Ruoxiao shengling de Kangzheng: Lun Jin Ping Mei nubi xingxiang de suzao," in *Chuantong xiaoshuo yu Zhongguo wenhua*. Tao Muning provides an overview of *qinglou wenxue* or "blue-building [brothel] literature" (Dorothy Ko's translation in "The Written Word and the Bound Foot: A History of the Courtesan's Aura," in *Writing Women in Late Imperial China*, ed. Ellen Widmer and Kang-I Sun Chang (Stanford, Calif.: Stanford University Press, 1997, 75) in relation to the representation of prostitutes in JPM, 82–110. Zhang Zhenjun reads JPM as representing the world of domestic bond servitude, yet faults the narrative for its insufficiently inspiring (positive) portrayal. For Li Yu on concubines, see Patrick Hanan, *The Invention of Li Yu* (Cambridge, Mass.: Harvard University Press, 1988), 200–202. As Hanan observes of Li Yu's tastes in concubines: "It is not true passion in a girl that is being celebrated—the emotions implied lack the reciprocity of love—but a naive, unsophisticated charm that induces in her husband moods ranging from aesthetic admiration through piquant enjoyment to the onset of erotic feeling. It is certainly not mere sensuality; Li Yu detests girls who make up for their lack of accomplishment by fawning on their husbands" (201). The likes of Pan Jinlian, then, would only be attractive to boors

(as is Ximen Qing), or are only good for reading (consumption) and not for acquiring—jaded, sensual, and without real accomplishment as she is.

3 See ZZJPM, post-hui commentary for chapter 1; and *Huiping Haijiao Jin Ping Mei* (hereafter HHJPM), ed. Liu Hui and Wu Gan (Hong Kong: Tiandi Tushu, 1994).

4 On how "even wealthy merchants managed, by chicanery or bribery, to get military commissions and [take] part in grabbing state lands," to the extent that "military service became a sort of commodity market where businessmen could buy military commissions and the soldiers could purchase free time to pursue what they pleased," see Shih-shan Henry Tsai, *The Eunuchs in the Ming Dynasty* (Albany, N.Y.: State University of New York Press, 1996), 77–78. The trajectory of Ximen Qing precisely.

5 See Louis Dumont, *Homo Hierarchicus: The Caste System and Its Implications*, trans. Mark Sainsbury, Louis Dumont, and Basia Gulati (Chicago: University of Chicago Press, 1980), esp. introduction, chaps. 5 and 6, and "Postface: Toward a Theory of Hierarchy."

6 On how ledgers of merit and demerit encouraged social fluidity and upward mobility, without "challenging in any significant way the terms of the Chinese social hierarchy," see Cynthia Brokaw, *The Ledgers of Merit and Demerit: Social Change and Moral Order in Late Imperial China* (Princeton, N.J.: Princeton University Press, 1991); "It simply made a virtue, even a moral necessity, of what was already a principle of Chinese social organization, the possibility of movement between different social stations. . . . Indeed it is hard to imagine a more optimistic moral affirmation of both the validity of the social hierarchy and the benefits of upward mobility" (232–34). For the economic, political, and social conditions of a "fluidity" that does not significantly challenge social hierarchy in the late Ming, see Tsai, *Eunuchs*, 26–27. Tsai discusses the "growing social malaise" of the late Ming amid population growth, worsening poverty for the lowest peasant strata, and capital shifts from land to commerce and craft (26–27).

7 There are residual traces of hierarchical master–bond servant affect and relations in the "new" labor relations between Taiwanese middle-class housewives and Philippino, Thai, and Indonesian domestic labor. An anthropologist conducting research has told me of housewives who consider foreign domestic "help" as a kind of "property" that can and must be "fully" used, thus "lending" her to friends and relatives. Newspaper articles have also reported of arbitrary and random physical abuse. At the same time, the media has extensively discussed the sexual "threat" foreign domestic help pose to the "integrity" of the nuclear family in terms that might signify the transposition of class distinction onto ethnic-national or racial discrimination.

8 Maria Jaschok, *Concubines and Bondservants: A Social History of a Chinese Custom* (London: Zed Books, 1988). "The *mooi-jai* (bondmaid) institution was abolished in 1923 . . . but its underlying social evaluations and attitudes have survived, to be reckoned with today as much as yesterday" (39).

9 For slavery in the Shang and Chou periods, see Sha, *Zhongguo nuli zhidu de tantao*. For a recent general historical account of the traffic in persons, see Ma Yushan,

*Zhongguo gudai renkou maimai* (Taipei, Taiwan: Taipei shangwu yinshuguan, 1999). For the Han era, see C. Martin Wilbur, *Slavery in China during the Former Han Dynasty 206 B.C.–A.D. 25* (New York: Russell and Russell, 1967). For a history of concubinage, see Wang Shaoxi, *Xiaoqieshi: Qiezhilousu de lishiyange* (Shanghai: Wenyi chubanshe, 1995). For bond servitude in the Ming period, see Brokaw, *Ledgers of Merit and Demerit*: "At worst these bondservants, who, as "base people" (*jianmin*), occupied a very low status in Ming law, might be more or less at the mercy of their masters, with no recourse to justice in the face of brutal exploitation. . . . But there was a type of bondservant who managed to thrive in the status, despite its low social and legal standing, and who may indeed have seen bondservitude as an opportunity for economic advance on the coattails of wealthy and powerful masters" (6–10). See also Tsai, *Eunuchs*: "Even though the Ming Code did not sanction slavery, it allowed people to employ servants. By collusion with officials and falsifying the records, daring people openly made a travesty of legal integrity. When wealthy families purchased slaves, they put in the bond such words of euphemism as *adopted sons* and *adopted daughters* or simply called them *employed servants*. . . . One writer reported that in a single county the number of slaves amounted to 20 to 30 percent of the whole population. It was indeed a buyer's market. . . . Military commanders, public officials, wealthy merchants, and affluent landlords universally practiced concubinage and kept large numbers of slaves. Of course, the biggest slave owner of the Ming period was the emperor himself, and although ordinary slaves could be bought and sold, castrated eunuchs were an imperial monopoly" (26–28). See also the journals of Mathew Ricci, recorded precisely at about the time JPMC was first read: "Many of [these people], not being able to forgo the company of women, sell themselves to wealthy patrons, so as to find a wife among his female servants, and in so doing, subject their children to perpetual slavery. Others buy a wife when they can save money enough to do so, and when their family becomes too numerous to be supported, they sell their children into slavery for about the same price that one would pay for a pig or a cheap little donkey—about one crown or maybe one and a half. Sometimes this is done when there is really no necessity, and children are separated from their parents forever, becoming slaves to the purchaser, to be used for whatever purpose he pleases. The result of this practice is that the whole country is virtually filled with slaves; not such as are captured in war or brought in from abroad, but slaves born in the country and even in the same city or village in which they live. . . . The only ameliorating feature in this traffic of children is the fact that it lessens the great multitude of the extremely poor who have to labor incessantly in the sweat of their brow to eke out a miserable living" (Louis J. Gallagher, trans., *China in the Sixteenth Century: The Journals of Mathew Ricci, 1583–1610* [New York: Random House, 1953], 86).

10 See Oyama, "Large Landownership," 112–13. Oyama quotes Xiao Yong on how although "the law does not allow commoners to keep bondservants (nu). Those that provide services are called *adopted sons and adopted wives*" (113).

11 "The termination of the [bondmaid] status, when it occurred, was not automati-

cally succeeded by a full integration of the former [bondmaid] into the rank of free women. The more far-reaching her upward-mobility, the heavier the legacy of her past was encumbered with prejudices and reservations. The fear of her was the fear of her former ambiguous status; the fear of the corruptive influences associated with the polluting 'baseness' of her [bondmaid] existence. She could never be trusted to have internalized the proper models of behaviour and, like the notorious Imperial concubines of the past, she was prone to abuse power, to violate the boundaries that existed to protect society from chaos. . . . The threat was to male-dominated values, but no less to woman-centered uterine units whose existence and survival were dependent on the former" (Jaschok, *Concubines and Bondservants*, 67). This "tendency" to "abuse" power both marks her inferior status and agential will as one who has a catlike "intimate disposition."

12 Ibid., 68. See the previous chapter on Pan Jinlian's avenue to (temporary) power, her need to secure it, and Ximen Qing's punishment of her, via the sex that had been her means of survival.

13 Ibid., 76. On the penumbralike status of queers, homosexuals, and other sexual marginals and dissidents in Taiwan under the invisible regime of reticent familial and social disciplinary powers, see Jen-peng Liu and Naifei Ding, "Reticent Poetics, Queer Politics," *Working Papers in Gender/Sexuality Studies*, nos. 3 and 4 (Sept. 1998): 109–55.

14 Jaschok, *Concubines and Bondservants*, 32. In the words of granddaughters of differently positioned bondmaid-concubine grandmothers, the bondmaid-concubine is remembered and reviled as the "most successful sex-object" (25), or at the opposite extreme, as a "political person in the sense that [my grandmother] could help herself and make her fortune despite her poor background. So she sold herself as a *mooi-jai* and became strong, she was clever and made positive decisions in her life." (60). Both "readings" are mediated through and by "modern" ideologies of abject "objecthood" (the selling of the self) and willed free choice (self-determination), neither of which was quite in the situation of the grandmothers. Herein, too, is the dilemma of present-day feminism—not only in historical studies of past female personhoods but also in coming face to face with residual practices and attitudes of bond servitude (in both the master/mistress and neo-slave form).

15 Dorothy Ko, "The Written Word and the Bound Foot: A History of the Courtesan's Aura," in *Writing Women in Late Imperial China*, ed. Ellen Widmer and Kan-I Sun Chang (Stanford, Calif.: Stanford University Press, 1997), 100.

16 As such a trajectory, it is less an identity with the latter's connotation of "modern" egalitarian individualism as it is a position, habitus, and psychophysiological assemblage.

17 "The body is a model which can stand for any bounded system. Its boundaries can represent any boundaries which are threatened and precarious. The body is a complex structure. The functions of its different parts and their relation afford a source of symbols for complex structures. We cannot possibly interpret rituals concerning excreta, breast milk, saliva and the rest unless we are prepared to see in the body a symbol of society, and to see the powers and dangers credited to

social structure reproduced in small on the human body" (Mary Douglas, Purity and Danger: An Analysis of the Concepts of Pollution and Taboo [London: Routledge, 1966], 115).
18 JPMC, 258 (17); the translation of this quotation is by David T. Roy, in The Plum in the Golden Vase or Chin P'ing Mei (Princeton, N.J.: Princeton University Press, 1993), 343–44.
19 See Tanaka, "Popular Uprisings," 193.
20 On the preference for cats among imperial concubines, see Shen Defu, Wanli Yehuo Pian (Taipei, Taiwan: Xinxing shufu, 1983), 812.
21 On the interestedness of cat's killing, see Li Yu's little story "Expelling the Cat" in Xianqing ouji, translated and quoted in Hanan, Invention of Li Yu, 193. The problem with cats is that they don't just kill mice but *enjoy* eating them. This is very instructive as to the problem with bondmaid-concubines like Pan Jinlian or Chunmei. Hanan notes how officials have been represented as cats ("appointed to catch mice and keep order" [195]), which could be seen as bringing forth another aspect to the identification of the literatus-official with courtesan-concubine.
22 A phrase that signifies "helping those in need," or "timely help"—obviously ironic and timely indeed, for the text and its readers even more than for Jinlian.
23 JPMC, 388 (59).
24 On the birth of Ximen Qing's son, see ibid., 448 (30).
25 Ibid., 388–89 (59).
26 Li Ping'er is alluding to Pan Jinlian, of course, referring to her son as being like a daughter-in-law unable to please her parents-in-law, and with no other means of escape, having finally resorted to death. This comparison reverses the positions of the two concerned: for Jinlian as barren concubine has no legitimate power at all over the firstborn son of the family, even though he is the son of another, junior concubine. But as a baby (precious object and not yet grown) he is vulnerable—all the more so in a household where his very birth would influence (in the strongest material sense of the word) the balance of power between the wife, concubines, and master, the center of power. Thus invisible, illegitimate, feminine/feline power and its tactics will be used, both to liquidate the heir, and on another, textual level, to ensure the punishment and death of the "murderer," or so we are told to believe.
27 "Let it be, why pull the arch so full, as if we had neither time nor luck were with us" (thanks to an anonymous reviewer for this revised translation). To have neither time nor luck: it is as if those with power were simply fated to having it, and those without must abide time and luck. As if power itself were somehow magical/demonic, as with the (good) influence that is thought to emanate from those who live a correct life (adhering to the place assigned him/her), or the evil that exudes from those who err and go astray, leading/seducing others with them. This is precisely the kind of doxa that would keep everyone in their proper place, except that Jinlian twice questions this formula, ending both her speeches with this point: we're unlucky, this is not our time, therefore you'll pick on us, just as claws will pinch where it's soft. Of course, the text may have intended the "claws" to be ironic, but more than irony, claws at this juncture (dis)articulate

an entire chain of meanings and questions: whose claws, how used, and to what effect?

28 In translating qi as "influence," meaning it to be taken in the strongest and most material of senses, I have followed Paul U. Unschuld, *Medicine in China: A History of Ideas* (Berkeley: University of California Press, 1985). Given the etymology of the character and the history of its use, it designates not just the sentiment of anger, resentment, joy, and so forth but that "finest-matter influence" that underlies these sentiments and links them to their psychophysiological expressions.

29 JPMC, 390 (59).
30 ZZJPM, 388.
31 XXPJPM, 781.
32 JPMC, 251 (51).

33 We witness here what, in Mary Douglas's terms, would be a resorting to non-institutional means and powers (the pills provided by a foreign monk, or *hu sen*) to enhance one's own limited powers in a situation of transgressive ascendancy in a stratified (hierarchical) society.

34 Nun Wang is one of two nuns who often frequent, along with numerous old women go-betweens, the Ximen household. Yueniang especially favors the nuns because of her Buddhist fervor; Zhang Zhupo, the narrative, and most literati deem the nuns an unfortunate and misleading tendency on the part of women and unlettered commoners. Thus, the homophobic ferocity with which the narrative represents these nuns' deceptions, struggle for money, promiscuity, and homoerotic relations (chapter 50). Zhang Zhupo faults/hates Yueniang perhaps even more than Jinlian, for the latter is after all merely a whorish concubine, while the former, as pious wife and daughter of a low-level bureaucrat/literatus —hence not a *base* woman—has pretensions to "good breeding" and can therefore be held responsible for much that goes "wrong" in the women's quarters. But the final "responsibility," of course, is still the husband's since he must lead, and she can only follow.

35 The logic is obviously a mixture of the correspondence between the demonic and magical that Paul Unschuld (*Medicine in China*) traces back to the Shang and Chou dynasties, two millennia prior to the Ming Period. Thus, renzi is phonetically identical to renzi, the son of man; thereby the "influences" at work on that specific day. The consumption of the excremental elements of childbirth must likewise influence and reproduce similar processes within the body of the "receiver." Just so is the eating of animal brains still considered today as "nourishing" to one's own brain, and the eating of congealed pig's blood, good for one's blood. The killing of inhuman "livestock" by promiscuous "cats" could be considered an ethical "like" to "like" situation.

36 If Ximen's precious essence/semen should come into contact with the foul blood —the unborn fetuses—of women, this will cause him to die of "contagion," or so the narrative, Zhang Zhupo, and the XXPJPM commentator repeatedly ascertain, while Ping'er will significantly bleed to death (punishment?)—a symptom, among other things, of the clash between "essence/semen" and "blood" (chapter 54).

37  See esp. JPMC, chaps. 38, 39, 41, 43.
38  JPMC, 236 (50).
39  "The boundaries of the women's territory were set not so much by men as individual actors, but by the rules of patriarchal society that both men and women had to respect as a thing apart from the strength or weakness of the individual male. Within these boundaries, on the 'inside,' women faced women as rivals: for emotional hold over 'key' males; for financial control; for power over others" (Jaschok, Concubines and Bondservants, 24).
40  XXPJPM, 653 (51).
41  ZZJPM, 747 (51).
42  JPMC, 242 (51). The relationship between Ping'er and Big Sister Ximen and the latter's position mirrors in the Huilian-Laiwang episode the position of Laipao, who had an interest in siding with Jinlian against Laiwang. Let us not forget that Jinlian was at the time very much among Ximen's favorites, and that Ping'er's pregnancy had not yet been announced.
43  ZZJPM, 745 (51). The first phrase of this chapter's prechapter commentary reads: "This chapter sums up the jealousy [du], the [obscene] promiscuity [yin], the evil [xie] of Jinlian, and with the affair between Guijie and Wang Sanguan, and the affair of the Nun Wang and Nun Xue, makes an entirely evil and obscene world quite complete/replete [manzu]."
44  Thus the listing in court cases of female bond servants in Hong Kong of their "characteristics," which read, according to Maria Jaschok, "like an inversion of what were considered the attributes of respectable females excelling in the virtues of filial piety and obedience, reticence, loyalty, literal adherence to prescribed conventions. Mooi-jai were commonly described as stupid and ungrateful, they were thieves, they were licentious . . . they were wayward . . . , were untrustworthy, troublesome, willful, and always hungry and ate too much" (Concubines and Bondservants, 108–109). JPM would strangely enough corroborate these court testimonials of the early twentieth century in Hong Kong. Or perhaps the court case testimonials attest to the narrative's "realist effect" as even more powerful than imagined.
45  JPMC, 241 (51); and Quanben JPMC, vol. 3, 1330 (51). See ZZJPM, vol. 2, 747 (51), where this third-person is "corrected" to first-person.
46  JPMC, 251 (51).
47  On the fragility and perpetual childlikeness of male children in thrall to strong women and maidservants, whose part-subject, part-object lives are ensured by their power/influence over the "precious object" that is the son-master, see Jaschok, Concubines and Bondservants, 23–25. "All of [Meng's sons] were weak and dependent, totally submissive to the father, smothered emotionally by mothers and numerous servants. The authority of these men was precarious, yet they continued to be propped up—publicly—by structural paradigms of male dominance and superiority. Raised and indoctrinated with belief in their own infallibility, they were 'towers of male authority' only insofar as their female nurturers continued to provide the props" (23). Jaschok's study can be read in conjunction with JPM, with JPM a late Ming narrative of structures of commodity and com-

modified intimacy that recur in the marginal colonial society of late-nineteenth-century Hong Kong among a new parvenu class: the compradors.
48 JPMC, 75 (39).
49 Fright and the resulting convulsions have traditionally been one of the primary "ills" of babies, identified as such in Chinese medicotheory and still, today, treated with the same kind of medicine as Liu Pozi (Old Woman Liu) gives to Ping'er for Guange: cinnabar (red mercuric sulfide) pills (zhusha wanyaor). See Dictionary of Traditional Chinese Medicine (Taipei, Taiwan: Southern Materials Centre, 1985), 200, 247, 332.
50 JPMC, 370 (58). All three editions that I have seen have exactly the same version, with only one character different: in the XXPJPM and Zhang Zhupo versions, dog shit, rather than the urine of dog, which it is twice in the Cihua edition. Perhaps this is a miswriting again on the part of some semiliterate copier. Certainly dog shit seems more "logical" a reading, according to everyday experience, which would make the liquid form of dog waste perceptible and offensive more in touch and smell than in sight.
51 For the Chinese vernacular as it was written and read in late Ming extended narratives was not punctuated but merely marked with pause indicators; add to which JPM not only represents characters' direct speech but also their feelings and thoughts. The effect sometimes approximates that of a "free indirect style," where the distance between narratorial and character viewpoint and language decreases to almost nil, and the two can barely be differentiated (the narrator's voice is, of course, most distinct in the "ye, readers" passages). Jinlian is an expert in this particular art of double speech, and she puts it to killing uses (for instance, chaps. 23, 51); but the text is perhaps even more adroit, even more of a "feminine tactician."
52 JPMC, 371 (58). This is an abridged translation.
53 This kind of (base) person mistreatment of and cruelty to baser persons is also noted by Maria Jaschok in her social history of bondmaid-concubines: "Women rather than men seemed to excel in cruelty to their mooi-jai. . . . A considerable number of concubines in the middle-class stratum of Chinese society stood before magistrates accused of maltreating their slave-girls. The explanation given to me was that concubines were raised by amahs, had little education (meaning 'moral' education) and therefore were more likely to abuse their power over their vulnerable 'toy'" (Concubines and Bondservants, 103).
54 JPMC, 391 (59). The bit of verse that follows is prophetic: "No longer among the living [will it] catch mice, but [it will have] returned among the dead to become a fox spirit." Yueniang twice mentions the incarnation of a nine-tailed fox spirit in the household—the first time implying and the second time directly referring to Pan Jinlian (JPMC, 384 (26), 112 (75)).
55 JPMC, 236 (50).
56 Ibid., 237 (50).
57 Ibid.
58 Ibid., 433 (61).
59 Ibid., 264 (52).

60 Ping'er tells Ximen after he forces her to copulate with him while she is menstruating that ever since she has had the child, her body has remained "unclean," her face has become sallow, and food has seemed unappetizing (XXPJPM, 710 [54]). After the death of Guange, and the "heavy influences of anger" that she has kept to herself, Ping'er develops an incessant dripping of blood (JPMC, 403 [60]). A month later, during celebrations for the Double Yang festival, Ping'er is forced to leave the banquet because of a sudden sense of heat flowing; she returns to her rooms and sits astride the toilet pail, while the blood flows like urine, her eyes black out, and standing up in a fit of vertigo, she falls forward in a faint (ibid., 429 [61]). She is diagnosed as having chronic uterine bleeding, whose source is "semen clashing with blood vessels" (ibid., 433 [61]). She is thereafter bedridden, with grass paper placed underneath her, to be changed every once in a while. She finally dies in a pool of blood, which Ximen disregards in his grief as he holds and kisses her corpse (ibid., 457 [62]).

61 Ibid., 319 (87).

62 Zhang Zhupo nevertheless cannot refrain, at times, from a hysterical fit of sobbing laughter, for "literati write with such finesse and effort, and a heart constant over thousands of years, and yet who will ever understand? I cannot but sob [*da ku*] tens, hundreds, thousands of days, without ceasing, and yet also roar with laughter [*da xiao*] incessantly" (ZZJPM, 1123 [73]).

63 According to the narrative logic, Ximen will have exchanged his life (insofar as it was ensured only in the case of control even to the point of eradication of desire and its manifestations) for a penile power from which he derives the most elusive and illusory of pleasures. He exchanges it via a monk who is the embodiment of a penis. What eventually kills him, however, is the embodiment of a vagina in the figure of Jinlian. See JPMC (49).

64 JPMC, 25–28 (72).

65 Ibid., 27 (72).

66 I must note in passing the XXPJPM commentator's admiration of and fascination with Jinlian's language: as deeply ensnaring and persuasive, as yet another "talent" with which to ensure her "fair" share of power. In Yulou's slightly barbed words: "Sixth little slave, you really are a strategist, aren't you?" (JPMC, 27–28 [72]).

67 Strong winds will sweep clean, but also destroy. In this text, the strong wind on Ximen's return trip will have given him a fright, from which he will never fully recover, until his last bloody discharge on another cold, windy night (chapter 79).

68 JPMC, 34 (72).

69 XXPJPM, 997 (71).

70 Ibid.

71 JPMC, 95 (75).

72 See Joseph Needham, *Chemistry and Chemical Technology, Part V: Physiological Alchemy*, in vol. 5, part 5 of *Science and Civilization in China* (Cambridge, U.K.: Cambridge University Press, 1983), 304–14. Incidentally, in Japan and Taiwan, the drinking of

one's own urine first thing in the morning is considered by some to be beneficial to one's health.

73 ZZJPM, 1109 (72).
74 See JPMC, 175 (78), with Madame Lin; and ibid., 180 (78), with Juier.
75 JPMC, 201–2 (79).
76 Ibid., 202–3 (79).
77 XXPJPM, 1143–44 (79).
78 Ibid., 1143 (79); and ZZJPM, 1277 (79).
79 XXPJPM, 1143 (79); and as the commentator writes above the verse, "To end with the inaugurating verse, this is where the author's great meaning lies"—no doubt referring to the sword between her waist. Could the sword be the same one as Li Yu's comment on how the brush of the literati is in some cases even more dangerous to his enemies than a sword? Wouldn't it then be something like a fantasized prosthetic implantation? In the XXPJPM edition, this verse is placed at the beginning of the first chapter, and resurfaces following Ximen's bloody discharge. But it does not inaugurate the less "polished" and perhaps more "confused/seduced" JPMC edition. I note here an anonymous reviewer's thought: that vagina could also be "read" as the "feminine way," where "way" is homophonic with "knife-sword," thus semantically secreting the ultimately killing powers of female se(x).
80 Li Yu, Xianqing ouji (Shanghai: Wenyi chubanshe, 1992), 344.

CHAPTER 8  *Very Close to Yinfu and Ënu; or, How Prefaces Matter for Jin Ping Mei (1695) and Ënu Shu (Taipei 1995)*

1 For a sociology of the literary field and the epistemological politics of tracing its historical formation, see Pierre Bourdieu, *Rules of Art: Genesis and Structure of the Literary Field* (Stanford, Calif.: Stanford University Press, 1995). For a comprehensive study of textual thresholds, or paratextual matters and their convergent effects (in the European contexts primarily), see Gérard Genette, *Seuils* (Paris: Editions du Seuil, 1987), esp. 182–218, 219–70. I thank Yu Chi-chong for lending me a copy of the latter book.
2 "Zhang's edition was not only the most widely disseminated but also the most influential [of all the extant editions]" (Wang Rumei, in ZZJPM, 1. For details of the familial repercussions for commentating an "obscene" book, see also Wu Gan, *Zhang Zhupo yu Jin Ping Mei* [Tianjin: Baihua wenyi chubanshe, 1987]).
3 For a detailed rebuttal to Yang Zhao, and a queer "how to read Chen Xue," see Ji Dawei's preface to Chen Xue, *Mengyou 1994* (Taipei, Taiwan: Yuanliu, 1996). In *Chung-Wai Literature* (1995), Ma Sen reviews the three "new erotica" books together and basically agrees with Yang Zhao's assessment. Thanks to Joy Tu for bringing this last to my attention and for an unpublished chapter analyzing Ma Sen's article.
4 This chapter first appeared in Chinese as an invited essay to a special queer issue of *Chung-Wai Literature* guest edited by Liu Liangya. I thank Wo Ching-ling for

the translation, and Liu Liangya for the invitation to write as well as insightful suggestions that helped improve the paper.
5 I have tried to show this elsewhere. See Naifei Ding, "Tears of Ressentiment; or Zhang Zhupo's Jin Ping Mei," positions: east asia cultures critique 3, no. 3 (1995): 663–94. For a contrasting position, see Ping Zhong Shen Chou.
6 I have followed David T. Roy's translation (in "How to Read the Chin P'ing Mei," in How to Read the Chinese Novel, ed. David Rolston [Princeton, N.J.: Princeton University Press, 1990]) of xianshen as "becoming." The use of this translation here might also retrieve two instances in English (also translated) of literary transpositions and theoretical transversality: Gustave Flaubert, "I am Madame Bovary," in and Felix Guattari, "Becoming a Woman," in Molecular Revolution: Psychiatry and Politics, trans. Rosemary Sheed (New York: Penguin, 1984).
7 "That woman can thus deeply love another woman, it took me incredibly six years to realize" (Chen Xue, "Written to Qing," in Enu Shu (Taipei, Taiwan: Huangguan, 1995], 248).
8 See Ding, "Tears," 666.
9 Zhang Zhupo, Dufa, item 59. Item numbers from this and subsequent quotations from Zhang's "Dufa" also correspond with the item number in Roy, "How to Read the Chin P'ing Mei."
10 I have used "writer" for Zhang's zuo Jin Ping Mei zhe since the "modern" notion of an "author" was perhaps still in the stages of sociohistorical formation in the early Qing.
11 My reading of this section differs from Ye Lang's in his Zhongguo Xiaoshuo Meixue (Aesthetics of the Chinese Xiaoshuo) in that Ye is primarily interested in tracing the historicity of aesthetic categories established by five major critic-commentators of the extended narrative form. Thus, this passage in Zhang Zhupo is noted for its emphasis on the writer's need to have actively engaged with the social (ru shi), garnering therein the experiential basis for the accurate representation of each characters' ren qing (relational sentiment). According to Ye Lang, Zhang Zhupo's notion of renqing is more complex in denoting how each character's internal substance is determined by his/her social relations, constituting for each a distinct "structure of sentiment." I use "structure of sentiment" here in accordance with Raymond Williams's notion of "structure of feeling," likewise social, but more important for Williams, historical in its specificities. See Ye Lang, Zhongguo Xiaoshuo Meixue (Taipei, Taiwan: Liren shuju, 1987), 220–22; and Raymond Williams, Marxism and Literature (Oxford: Oxford University Press, 1977).
12 Zhang, "Dufa," item 60.
13 Ibid., item 61.
14 See Katherine Carlitz, "Desire, Danger, and the Body: Stories of Women's Virtue in Late Ming China," in Engendering China: Women, Culture, and the State, ed. Christina Gilmartin et al. (Cambridge, Mass.: Harvard University Press, 1994), 34–67. See also Patricia Sieber, "Corporeality and Canonicity: A Study of Technologies of Reading in Early Modern Zaju Drama," Graven Images 2 (1995): 171–85 and Kimberly Besio, "On the Borders of the Han: Gender, Cultural Identity, and Canon Formation in Early Modern Drama," manuscript.

15 On JPM's purgative effect, though his conclusion differs from mine in this and previous chapters, see Peter Rushton, "The Daoist's Mirror: Reflections on the Neo-Confucian Reader and the Rhetoric of *Jin Ping Mei*," *Chinese Literature* 8, nos. 1–2 (July 1986): 63–82. I have also used "virtual reader" in this essay in a way consonant with his use of "virtual" for Zhang Zhupo's position in the text.

16 I have used the following texts in reading this Buddhist trope: Kenneth K. S. Ch'en, *Buddhism in China* (Princeton, N.J.: Princeton University Press, 1964); W. T. de Bary, ed., *The Buddhist Tradition in India, China, and Japan* (New York: Vintage Books, 1972); Diana Y. Paul, *Women in Buddhism* (Berkeley: University of California Press, 1979); and a facsimile copy of the *Foxue Dacidian* (Taipei, Taiwan, 1985). See especially Paul's introduction to and translation of sutras in the chapter titled "The Bodhisattvas with Sexual Transformation."

17 "More generally, then, every 'dissident' organization of the libido necessarily makes common cause with the feminine body in its becoming, as an escape route from the repressive social structure, as a possible route to a 'minimum' of sexual becoming, and as the last life-buoy to cling to for safety from the established order. I stress this point particularly, because the becoming of the female body must not be confused with the category of woman as considered in marriage, the family and so on. This kind of category can only exist within the particular social field that defines it, in any case. Women as such does not exist at all. . . . Conversely, anything that infringes the norms, that breaks with the established order, is in some way related to animal becoming, feminine becoming and the rest. Wherever there is a semiotic system being broken down, there is also a sexualization being broken down. We should not, it seems to me, discuss the problem of homosexual writers, but rather try to discover the homosexual element in every great writer, even one who is heterosexual in other respects" (Guattari, "Becoming a Woman," 234–35). Zhang Zhupo was perhaps "intending" the reverse of Guattari's proposal: that is, to gloss and read a dissipated, overfeminized text in such a way as to enable its reinsertion into the literary patriline. The market achieved what he tried to do, without however mitigating the paradox of his attempt. In Zhang's moral overreadings lie the flickerings of a dissident libidinal charge.

18 Chen, Ënu Shu, 14–15. All subsequent quotations of Yang Zhao's preface to Ënu Shu will refer to this edition.

19 This is from the blurb for Yang Zhao's new collection of essays.

20 Yang Zhao, preface to Ënu Shu, 14–15.

21 Ibid., 14.

22 Chen Xue, personal communication with author, Taipei, Taiwan.

23 Yang, preface to Ënu Shu, 11.

24 Ibid., 7.

25 Ibid., 9.

26 Ibid., 13.

27 Ibid., 11–15.

28 Both "Lesbian" and "Taiwanese" may be considered hotly contested discursive terrains in 1990s Taiwan. Of course, there is a huge discrepancy in the stakes,

size, and location of these terrains. Whereas the former is debated primarily within one sector of the cultural field, plus a segment of the Internet, the other is in ascending and cumulative construction nationwide, at all levels and in all domains. I will use the lowercase "lesbian" and "taiwanese" for alternative and nondominant (nonstatist) senses of these two nouns.

29 This is a point that has also been made in Chao Yen-ning, "Chugui huo bu chuguei—Zheshi yige youguan heian de wenti" [To come out of the closet or not to come out of the closet—This is a question that has to do with darkness), *Sao Dong* (Stir) 3 (January 1997): 61: "In the works of Chen Xue, incest is the primary trope of multiple states of desiring (or 'queerness')."

30 "If *ignorance* is not—as it evidently is not—a single Manichean, aboriginal maw of darkness from which the heroics of human cognition can occasionally wrestle facts, insights, freedoms, progress, perhaps there exists instead a plethora of *ignorances*, and we may begin to ask questions about the labor, erotics, and economics of their human production and distribution" (Eve Kosofsky Sedgwick, "Privilege of Unknowing: Diderot's *The Nun*," in *Tendencies* (Durham, N.C.: Duke University Press), 25).

31 For the reticent shamelessness of Chen Xue's writing, see Amie Parry, "A Search for the Lost Dialectics of the Invisible Po: Chen Xue's anti-realism and anti-reticence." Paper presented at the Third International Super-Slim Conference on Politics of Gender/Sexuality. November 1999: National Central University, Chungli, Taiwan.

32 See Charlotte Furth, "Androgynous Males and Deficient Females: Biology and Gender Boundaries in Sixteenth- and Seventeenth-Century China," *Late Imperial China* 9, no. 2 (December 1988): 1–31.

33 Roy, "How to Read the Chin P'ing Mei," 224.

34 Ibid., 232.

35 Yang, preface to *Ënu Shu*, 15.

36 From a panel discussion at which Spivak and Assia Djebar spoke at the University of California at Berkeley in the summer of 1995.

37 Assia Djebar, *Women of Algiers in Their Apartment* (Charlottesville: University Press of Virginia, 1992), 2.

# GLOSSARY

| | | | |
|---|---|---|---|
| *ayia* | 呵呀 | Cai taishi | 蔡太師 |
| *baibu* | 擺佈 | *caise* | 財色 |
| *baixing* | 百姓 | *caizi* | 才子 |
| Baohan lou keben | 寶翰樓刻本 | Cang Di | 蒼帝 |
| *baoru* | 褒儒 | Cang Jie | 倉頡 |
| *bi shang Liangshan* | 逼上梁山 | Cang Shu | 藏書 |
| *bi* | 筆 | *cao* | 肏 |
| Bian Juan | 便娟 | Chang De Road | 常德街 |
| Bian Que | 扁鵲 | Chen Dongyou | 陳東有 |
| *biandu yiyi* | 變度易意 | Chen Duxiu | 陳獨秀 |
| *biaoli bui* | 表裡不一 | Chen Jingji | 陳經濟 |
| *bing gen* | 病根 | Chen Jiru | 陳繼儒 |
| *bing* | 病 | Chen Longzheng | 陳龍正 |
| *bingqing weizhi shaoque* | 病魔為之稍卻 | Chen Wanyi | 陳萬益 |
| *biqie* | 婢妾 | Chen Xue | 陳雪 |
| Bu Jian | 卜建 | *cheng* | 誠 |
| *bu liang* | 不良 | *chong* | 寵 |
| *bu mingyu* | 不名譽 | Chongzhen | 崇禎 |
| *buliang fu* | 不良婦 | Chou Chih-p'ing | 周質平 |
| C.T. Hsia | 夏志清 | Chu Xiaoxiu | 褚孝秀 |
| Cai Guoliang | 蔡國梁 | Chunmei | 春梅 |
| Cai Yong | 蔡雍 | *chusheng* | 畜生 |

| | | | |
|---|---|---|---|
| chusheng | 儲生 | Fenshu | 焚書 |
| ci tianxia guaiyi guei guan ye | 此天下怪異詭觀也 | foren | 否認 |
| | | fu yao | 符藥 |
| cier | 雌兒 | fu | 賦 |
| da | 達 | Fujian | 福建 |
| dang fu | 蕩婦 | ganyi yao gusui | 甘意搖骨髓 |
| dang ye chou chu bu jue | 當夜躊躇不決 | ge xian yinfu renshen | 各現淫婦人身 |
| dang (qiu qian) | 盪（鞦韆） | Gongan | 公安 |
| dao yin xuan yu zhi you | 導淫宣欲之尤 | gongsheng | 貢生 |
| dao | 刀 | gouda | 勾搭 |
| de | 德 | gouzhi | 狗彘 |
| deng xin | 燈心 | gu huo | 蠱惑 |
| Dong Jieyuan | 董解元 | Gu Yenwu | 顧炎武 |
| Dong Qichang | 董其昌 | gu | 蠱 |
| Dongjing | 東京 | guai | 怪 |
| dong nian | 動念 | guan huei xiao yier | 慣會小意兒 |
| dong qing | 動情 | guan wan | 觀玩 |
| doulan | 兜攬 | guanbi minfan | 官逼民反 |
| Du Fu | 杜甫 | Guange | 官哥 |
| du shu xingling bu ju getao | 獨抒性靈不拘格套 | guanke | 官刻 |
| | | guanren | 官人 |
| du shu zhe | 讀書者 | Gufen | 孤憤 |
| dufa | 讀法 | gui | 鬼 |
| dui ren du | 對人讀 | guixiou | 閨秀 |
| dui | 懟 | guiyuan shi | 閨怨詩 |
| Dutou | 都頭 | gujin jingshu xingfei | 古今經書興廢 |
| du yao | 毒藥 | guojia | 國家 |
| Ë u Shouji | 鱷魚手記 | guoyu | 國語 |
| ë wu | 惡物 | Han Aijie | 韓愛姐 |
| Ënu Shu | 惡女書 | Han Shaogong | 韓少功 |
| ënu | 惡女 | Han | 漢 |
| ermu zhi yu | 耳目之欲 | Hangzhou | 杭州 |
| fa han | 發汗 | hanliu mozhui | 汗流沬墜 |
| fa | 法 | hansuan baoyuan | 含酸抱（阮）怨 |
| fa | 發 | | |
| fafen zhushu | 發憤著書 | Hanyu dacidian | 漢語大辭典 |
| fan wei xiu shen zhi lei | 反為修身之累 | nüse | 女色 |
| fangke | 坊刻 | hao nüse | 好女色 |
| Fangla | 方臘 | hao shi zhi | 好事者 |
| feinu | 非女 | haohan | 好漢 |
| fen shu | 焚書 | haoyong dohen | 好勇鬥狠 |
| Feng Menglong | 馮夢龍 | hengbao zhi ji | 橫暴之極 |
| fengguan zhi wanni | 封關之丸泥 | hengyi | 橫議 |
| fengliu | 風流 | Honglou Meng | 紅樓夢 |
| fenmen | 憤懣 | Hsu Wei | 徐渭 |

| | | | |
|---|---|---|---|
| hu seng | 胡僧 | jie zao qi tudu | 皆遭其荼毒 |
| Hu Shi | 胡適 | jie | 戒 |
| Hua Zixu | 花子虛 | Jin Ping Mei cihua | 金瓶梅詞話 |
| huagong | 化工 | Jin Ping Mei | 金瓶梅 |
| huai ren xinshu | 壞人心術 | Jin Shengtan | 金聖嘆 |
| huan hu | 幻化 | jin xue | 金學 |
| Huang Guan | 皇冠 | jin | 斤 |
| Huang Lin | 黃霖 | jin | 禁 |
| Huangren Shouji | 荒人手記 | jing feng | 驚風 |
| huanhu ruo yi ting shengren bianshi zhi yan | 渙乎若一聽聖人辯士之言 | jing shen | 精神 |
| | | jing ying | 經營 |
| | | Jinlian | 金蓮 |
| huanhu | 渙乎 | jinshi | 進士 |
| huanjia yishi | 幻假意識 | jinxin xioukou | 錦心繡口 |
| huannan qiungchou | 患難窮愁 | jinzhen | 金針 |
| Huguang | 湖廣 | jiujiu | 揪揪 |
| hui shu | 穢書 | jiuping zhuang xinjiu | 舊瓶裝新酒 |
| hui | 回 | ju shijin zhi huo | 居市井之貨 |
| Huilian | 蕙蓮 | juan | 卷 |
| huo | 貨 | juedao | 絕倒 |
| i xin | 一心 | junzi | 君子 |
| ji gumei zhi shengse | 極蠱媚之聲色 | juren | 舉人 |
| jia ren | 家人 | kanben | 刊本 |
| Jia Sanjin | 賈三近 | Kangxi Zidian | 康熙字典 |
| jia | 假 | Kangxi | 康熙 |
| jiadi | 假弟 | ke yi yaoyian miaodao shuei er qu ye | 可以要言妙道說而去也 |
| jiafu | 假父 | | |
| Jiajing | 嘉靖 | keben | 刻本 |
| jiake | 家刻 | Wen | 文王 |
| jian quan | 奸權 | Zhou | 周王 |
| jian | 賤 | kuai | 快 |
| Jiang Cong | 蔣聰 | kuali fenghai | 夸麗風駭 |
| jiang wei jie zhe er fan jiang wei quan ye | 將為戒者而反將為勸耶 | Laiwang | 來旺 |
| | | Laixing | 來興 |
| Jiangnan | 江南 | Lang Ying | 郎英 |
| jiangti | 匠體 | laopo shetou | 老婆舌頭 |
| jianu | 駕駑 | laoren sifu | 勞人思婦 |
| Jiao hong | 焦竑 | Laozi | 老子 |
| jiao tung | 交通 | late Ming Jiangnan | 晚明江南 |
| jiao yi | 交易 | lengre | 冷熱 |
| jiao | 交 | Li An | 李安 |
| jiaozao | 焦躁 | Li Guijie | 李貴姐 |
| jiashi | 假飾 | Li Jaoer | 李嬌兒 |
| jiaxiung | 假兄 | Li Kaixian | 李開先 |
| jiazi | 假子 | Li Pinger | 李瓶兒 |

| | | | |
|---|---|---|---|
| Li Rihua | 李日華 | mingren keshu er shuwang | 明人刻書而書亡 |
| Li Xifan | 李希凡 | | |
| Li Yu | 李漁 | Mingshi | 明史 |
| Li Zhi | 李贄 | minke | 閩刻 |
| Li Zhowu piping Zhongyi Shuihu zhuan | 李卓吾批評忠義水滸傳 | Mo Han Zhai | 墨憨齋 |
| | | Mo Yan | 莫言 |
| | | mo | 摹 |
| li | 利 | molisan er fashu | 莫離散而發曙兮 |
| li | 理 | | |
| liang fu | 良婦 | mooi-jai | 妹仔 |
| Liang Shan | 梁山 | moshen | 摹神 |
| Liang Zhongshu | 梁中樞 | Mozi | 墨子 |
| liang | 兩 | Mudan Ting | 牡丹亭 |
| Liangshan | 梁山 | naihe | 奈何 |
| liao bing | 療病 | nanzihan | 男子漢 |
| Liao | 遼 | nei shu | 內書 |
| liaodou | 撩鬥 | Niang | 娘 |
| Lin Yutang | 林語堂 | Nian Gong | 念公 |
| Ling Mengchu | 凌濛初 | nianran hanchu | 涊然汗出 |
| ling ren luo lei | 令人落淚 | Ning Zongyi | 寧宗一 |
| Liu Hui | 劉輝 | nü bang xian | 女幫閒 |
| Liu Xie | 劉勰 | Nun Wang | 王姑子 |
| lizhi qizhuang cunzai de hefaxing | 理直氣壯存在的合法性 | nuo | 諾 |
| | | nüse | 女色 |
| lizhi qizhuang | 理直氣壯 | nütongxinglian ganqing | 女同性戀感情 |
| Longqing | 隆慶 | nütongxinglian qingyu de shizhi zishen | 女同性戀情慾的實質自身 |
| Loyang | 洛陽 | | |
| Lu Xun | 魯迅 | Pan An | 潘安 |
| lueguan | 略觀 | Pan Jinlian zhi Qianshi Jinsheng | 潘金蓮之前世今生 |
| lunchang | 倫常 | | |
| man feng | 慢風 | Pan Jinlian (P'an Chin-lien) | 潘金蓮 |
| man pian laopo shetou eryi | 滿篇老婆舌頭而已 | | |
| | | pi xiechen meizi | 癖諧臣媚子 |
| Manchu | 滿州 | pi | 癖 |
| Mei Sheng | 枚乘 | pian xizhi | 偏喜之 |
| Mencius | 孟子 | pingdian | 評點 |
| Meng Yulou | 孟玉樓 | po er hu zhe bu ze sheng | 迫而呼者不擇聲 |
| mi mu | 瞇目 | | |
| mi | 迷 | pu chi | 樸忔 |
| miao | 妙 | pulu | 暴露 |
| miaoshi | 妙事 | qi | 奇 |
| miaowen | 妙文 | qi | 氣 |
| ming | 名 | Qian Xuantong | 錢玄同 |
| Ming | 明 | qiangren | 強人 |
| Ming-Qing | 明清 | Qiao | 喬 |

| | | | |
|---|---|---|---|
| Qifa | 七發 | shi you zhenge xianshen ifan fang shuode ifan | 實又真個現身一番方說得一番 |
| qin yan | 擒艷 | | |
| Qin | 秦 | | |
| qin | 親 | shi | 勢 |
| Qing Kangxi | 清康熙 | shidao zhi jiao | 市道之交 |
| qing | 情 | Shiji | 史記 |
| Qing | 清 | Shijing | 詩經 |
| Qingho | 清河 | shishi | 事實 |
| qingse | 情色 | shishou zhe yi | 失守者易 |
| qingyu | 情慾 | shiwen | 時文 |
| qingzhen | 情真 | shiwen | 詩文 |
| Qiu Miaojin | 邱妙津 | shixie mozheng | 始邪末正 |
| Qiuju | 秋菊 | shiye | 事業 |
| Qu Ping | 屈平 | shiyu | 嗜欲 |
| quan shu | 權術 | shou jing | 收驚 |
| quan | 勸 | shouxing de rouyu | 獸性的肉慾 |
| quanyou | 勸誘 | shu ji fei shu du yi fei du | 書既非書讀亦非讀 |
| ququ zhezhe | 曲曲折折 | | |
| ran fengyi quan bai shi bu zifan | 然諷一勸百勢不自反 | shu | 書 |
| | | shuei er chu | 說而出 |
| ranze tao he qi zai | 然則濤何氣哉 | shuei er qu | 說而去 |
| renqing shigu | 人情事故 | Shuihu Zhuan | 水滸傳 |
| renren zhishi | 仁人志士 | Shuinan | 說難 |
| renzi | 壬子（人子） | shuren | 庶人 |
| Rui'er | 如意兒 | Shushu | 叔叔 |
| San Guo | 三國 | Shutung | 書童 |
| san niangzi | 三娘子 | si shen er fei zhe san | 似神而非者三 |
| Sanguo Yanyi | 三國演義 | si shu | 私書 |
| Saosao | 嫂嫂 | Sichuan | 四川 |
| se | 色 | si ke | 私刻 |
| shen zao qi nan | 身遭其難 | Sima Qian | 司馬遷 |
| shen | 神 | sishen er fei | 似神而非 |
| shen | 身 | siwen zhi gongchen | 斯文之功臣 |
| shendu | 慎獨 | siwen | 斯文 |
| shenfen | 身分 | Song Jiang | 宋江 |
| sheng jing | 聖經 | Song Ren | 宋仁 |
| shengong guifu zhi bi | 神工鬼斧之筆 | Su Shi | 蘇軾 |
| shengren xuewen | 聖人學問 | Sui | 隨 |
| shenjing | 聖經 | Sun Shuyu | 孫述宇 |
| shenwu guaiyi bu ke shengyan zhi shi ren bo yan | 神物怪疑不可勝言直使人跂焉 | Sung | 宋 |
| | | Sungjiang | 松江 |
| | | suoyi jie gaoliang zhi zi ye | 所以戒膏粱之子也 |
| shenwu guaiyi | 神物怪疑 | sushi | 俗士 |
| shenzui | 深罪 | Suzhou | 蘇州 |
| Shi Naian | 施耐庵 | | |

Glossary 301

| | | | |
|---|---|---|---|
| Taibei Pinglun | 台北評論 | Wu Sung | 武松 |
| Tang Xianzu | 湯顯祖 | Wu Xian | 巫咸 |
| Tang | 唐 | wuchi | 無恥 |
| Tao Xiaoruo | 陶孝若 | Xi You Ji | 西遊記 |
| taoban | 套版 | Xi | 檄 |
| T'ien Ju-K'ang | 田汝康 | Xianqing ouji | 閒情偶寄 |
| timu | 題目 | xianshen shuofa | 現身說法 |
| tongren guibing | 通人貴病 | xianshen | 現身 |
| tongzhi | 同志 | xianxian | 鮮鮮 |
| touhan | 偷漢 | Xiao Tong | 蕭統 |
| Tsao Jr-lien | 曹志漣 | Xiao Xiao Sheng | 笑笑生 |
| Tu Fu | 杜甫 | xiaoren | 小人 |
| Tu Long | 屠龍 | xiaoshun | 孝順 |
| tudu | 荼毒 | xiaoshuo | 小說 |
| Wang Daokun | 汪道昆 | xiaozi tidi | 孝子悌弟 |
| Wang Fuzhi | 王夫之 | Xie Zhaozhe | 謝肇淛 |
| Wang Liuer | 王六兒 | xie zhu yinfu | 寫諸淫婦 |
| Wang Mang | 王莽 | xieqi | 邪氣 |
| Wang Po | 王婆 | xiguan xingde | 習慣性的 |
| Wang Shizhen | 王世貞 | Ximen Qing | 西門慶 |
| Wang Yangming | 王陽明 | (Hsi-men Ch'ing) | |
| Wang Yijia | 王溢嘉 | xin ganguan xiaoshuo | 新感官小說 |
| Wang Zhideng | 王稚登 | xing ë lun | 性惡論 |
| Wanli | 萬曆 | xingling pai | 性靈派 |
| wannong | 玩弄 | xinjue qijin | 心絕氣盡 |
| wanwu sangzhi | 玩物喪志 | xiong wu | 凶物 |
| wei feng zhe | 為風者 | Xixiang Ji | 西廂記 |
| Wei Xiao | 隗囂 | xixiao numa | 嘻笑怒罵 |
| Han Gu Guan | 函谷關 | xixin qizhong | 悉心其中 |
| wen sheng | 文勝 | Xiyou Ji | 西遊記 |
| Wen Xuan | 文選 | Xu Cangshu | 續藏書 |
| wen | 文 | Xu Fenshu | 續焚書 |
| wenfa | 文法 | Xu Shuofang | 徐朔方 |
| wenjia zhi bifa | 文家之筆法 | Xue Gang | 薛岡 |
| wenren | 文人 | xue she | 學舌 |
| wenshi | 文士 | Xue'e | 雪娥 |
| wenzhang zhi zhipai xiayu zhi mozao | 文章之支派暇豫之末造 | xueshi taifu | 學士大夫 |
| | | xuexing | 血性 |
| wenzhang | 文章 | Xunzi | 荀子 |
| wo xin le ci pu wei pi ye | 我心樂此不為疲也 | Xuzhou | 徐州 |
| | | ya tou | 丫頭 |
| Wu Da | 武大 | yamen | 衙門 |
| Wu Han | 吳唅 | Yan Song | 嚴嵩 |
| Wuhu Laoren | 五湖老人 | yanchen zhi le | 淹沈之樂 |
| Wu maipo | 吳賣婆 | yanci dong hunshi | 艷詞動魂識 |

| | | | |
|---|---|---|---|
| Yang Zhao | 楊照 | yuanru | 怨儒 |
| Yang Zhu | 楊朱 | yuci yungou | 腴詞雲搆 |
| Yanggu | 陽穀 | yue se | 悅色 |
| yaoyen miaodao | 要言妙道 | Yueniang | 月娘 |
| yaoyin zhi wu | 妖淫之物 | yueqin | 月琴 |
| Ye Zhou | 葉晝 | Yulou | 玉樓 |
| yi jie | 異界 | yunxia manzhi | 雲霞滿紙 |
| yi shu | 異書 | Yuxiao | 玉簫 |
| yi zhengben de nutongxinglian | 一整本的女同性戀 | Yuxiao | 玉簫 |
| | | yuzhe si dangzhe huai | 遇者死當者壞 |
| yi | 義 | yuzhi | 語直 |
| yin mou | 陰謀 | za wen | 雜文 |
| yin qing | 淫情 | zaju | 雜劇 |
| yin shu | 淫書 | zao | 藻 |
| yinfu touhan | 淫婦偷漢 | Zhan He | 詹何 |
| yinfu | 淫婦 | Zhang Dahu | 張大戶 |
| Ying Bojue (Ying Po-chueh) | 應伯爵 | Zhang Guofu | 張國富 |
| | | Zhang Shen | 張勝 |
| Yingchun | 迎春 | Zhang Yuanfen | 張遠芬 |
| Yinger | 迎兒 | Zhang Zhupo ben | 張竹坡本 |
| yinhua | 淫話 | Zhang Zhupo | 張竹坡 |
| yinmou | 陰謀 | Zhanguo Ce | 戰國策 |
| yinqi | 淫器 | zhen jing | 真境 |
| yinshu | 淫書 | zhen nai ge xian yinfu ren shen | 真乃各現淫婦人身 |
| yinxin | 淫心 | | |
| yinyin | 裀裀 | zhen | 真 |
| yinyu | 淫欲 | zhen/jia | 真／假 |
| yishi zhi junzi | 宜世之君子 | Zheng Aiyue | 鄭愛月 |
| yishu | 異書 | zheng jing xie | 正經寫 |
| yiwei yuyi | 以為羽翼 | Zheng Zhenduo | 鄭振鐸 |
| yizhi kongjian | 異質空間 | zhengjing zhengshi | 正經正史 |
| yizhi taobi | 異質逃避 | zhenjia | 真假 |
| yizuo zhi shu yi dan jin fei | 已作之書一旦盡廢 | Zhenzhong Yi | 枕中囈 |
| | | zhiji | 知己 |
| you chengdu de duzhe | 有程度的讀者 | Zhili | 直隸 |
| Youju Feilu | 游居柿錄 | zhiti zhi an | 支體之安 |
| youyu | 憂鬱 | Zhong Xing | 鍾惺 |
| yu | 鬱 | Zhong yi Shuihu zhuan | 忠義水滸傳 |
| Yuan Hongdao | 袁宏道 | | |
| yuan qi | 元氣 | zhong | 忠 |
| Yuan Zongdao | 袁宗道 | Zhongni | 仲尼 |
| Yuan Zhongdao | 袁中道 | Zhu Tienwen | 朱天文 |
| Yuan | 元 | Zhu Xi | 朱熹 |
| yuan | 怨 | Zhuang Zhou | 莊周 |
| yuanhen | 怨恨 | Zhuangzi | 莊子 |

Glossary 303

| | | | |
|---|---|---|---|
| zhuhou | 諸侯 | zouzou | 嫊嫊 |
| Zhung Kuei | 鍾馗 | zui | 罪 |
| zi bu yu guai li luan shen | 子不語怪力亂神 | zuiě gan | 罪惡感 |
| | | zuo Jin Ping Mei zhe | 作金瓶梅者 |
| zixie | 自泄 | zuo shu | 作書 |
| zong yu | 縱慾 | Zuozhuan | 左傳 |
| zong | 縱 | | |

WORKS CITED

*Works in Chinese*

PRIMARY SOURCES

Jin Ping Mei Cihua 金瓶梅詞話. Photocopy of the Taipei National Palace Museum Wanli edition 明萬歷丁巳刻本. Taipei 台北, Taiwan 台灣: Lianjing 聯經, n.d.

Jin Ping Mei Cihua (3 vols.) 金瓶梅詞話（三冊）. Edited by Wei Ziyun 魏子雲. Modern typeset Wanli edition. Taipei 台北, Taiwan 台灣: Zengnizhi Wenhua Shiye Youxian Gongsi 增你智文化事業有限公司, 1982.

Quanben Jin Ping Mei Cihua (6 vols.) 全本金瓶梅詞話（六冊），蘭陵笑笑生撰. Photocopy edition of Beijing Library Ming Wanli (now in the United States). 明萬歷年間刊本，舊藏北京圖書館，現藏美國，以 1933 年『古佚小說刊行會』名義影印本為底本重印. Hong Kong 香港: Taiping Shuju 太平書局, 1982.

Xinke xiouxiang piping Jin Ping Mei (2 vols.) 新刻繡像批評金瓶梅（上、下冊）. Edited by Qi Yan and Ru Mei 齊煙、汝梅校點. Chungzhen edition. Hong Kong 香港, Shandong 山東: San Lian 三聯書店, Qiru Shushe 齊魯書社, 1990.

Zhang Zhupo piping diyi qishu Jin Ping Mei (2 vols.) 張竹波批評第一奇書金瓶梅（上、下冊）. Zhang Zhupo commentary edition. Edited by Wang Rumei 王汝梅, Li Zhaoxun 李昭恂, and Yu Fengshu 于鳳樹. Jinan 濟南: Qiru Shushe 齊魯書社, 1991.

Huiping Huijiao Jin Ping Mei (5 vols.) 會評會校金瓶梅（五冊）. Combined commentary edition. Edited by Liu Hui 劉輝, and Wu Gan 吳趕. Hong Kong 香港: Tiandi Tushu 天地圖書, 1994.

*Yibai ershi hui de Shuihu* (3 vols.) 一百二十回的水滸（三冊）. Modern typeset of the "Li Cho-wu" commentary edition with 120 hui. Hong Kong 香港: Shangwu Yinshu Guan 商務印書館, 1969.

*Guanhua tang diwu caize shu Shuihu Zhuan* 貫華堂第五才子書水滸傳. In vols. 3 and 4 of *Jin Shengtan Quanji* 《金聖嘆全集》第三、四冊. Jin Shengtan commentary edition. Yangzhou 揚州: Jiangsu Guji chubanshe 江蘇古籍出版社, 1985.

SECONDARY SOURCES

Cai Guoliang 蔡國梁. *Jin Ping Mei kaozheng yu yanjiu* 金瓶梅考證與研究. Xian 西安: Sanxi Renmin Chubanshe, 1984.

———. *Jin Ping Mei pingzhu* 金瓶梅評註. Guilin 桂林, 1986.

———. *Ming Qing xiaoshuo tanyou* 明清小說探幽. Hangzhou 杭州: Zhejiang wenyi chubanshe 浙江文藝出版社, 1985.

Cao Zhi 曹之. "Shilun Mingdai Banke de Chengjiu" 試論明代板刻的成就. In *Lidai Keshu Gaikuang* 歷代科書概況. Shanghai 上海: Yinshua gongye chubanshe 印刷工業出版社.

Cao Zhi 曹之. *Zhongguo yinshu shu de qiyuan* 中國印刷術的起源. Wuhan daxue chuban 武漢大學出版, 1994.

Chen Delai 陳德來, ed. *Pan Jinlian biezhuan* 潘金蓮別傳. Zhejiang: Wenyi chubanshe 浙江文藝出版, 1990.

Chen Dongyou 陳東有. *Jin Ping Mei wenhua yanjiu* 金瓶梅文化研究. Taipei 台北, Taiwan 台灣: Guanya wenhua 貫雅文化, 1992.

Chen Hongtian 陳宏天. *Zhaoming wenxuan yizhu* 昭明文選譯注, vol. 5. Changchun 長春, Jilin 吉林: Jilin wenshi chubanshe 吉林文史出版社, 1994.

Chen Jiru [Ming] 陳繼儒〔明〕. *Yangsheng fuyu* 養生膚語, 1 juan 卷. *Congshu jicheng xinbian* 叢書集成新編, 24 juan 卷. Taipei 台北, Taiwan 台灣: Xinwenfeng chubanshe 新文風出版社, n.d.

Chen Wanyi 陳萬益. *Wan Ming xiaopin yu Mingji wenren sheng huo* 晚明小品與明季文人生活. Taipei 台北, Taiwan 台灣: Daan chubanshe 大安出版社, 1988.

Chen Xue 陳雪. *Ënu Shu* 惡女書. Taipei 台北, Taiwan 台灣: Huangguan 皇冠 1995.

Chen Xue 陳雪. *Mengyou 1994* 夢遊 1994. Taipei 台北, Taiwan 台灣: Yuanliu 遠流, 1996.

Cheng Zhongying 成中英. "Lun Rujia xiao de lunli ji qi xiandai hua" 論儒家孝的倫理及其現代化. *Hanxue Yanjiu* 《漢學研究》 4, 1 (June 1986): 83–106.

Du Weimo 杜維沫, and Liu Hui 劉輝, eds. *Jin Ping Mei yanjiu ji* 金瓶梅研究集. Jinan 濟南: Qiru shushe 齊魯書社, 1988.

Gao Mingcheng 高明誠. *Jin Ping Mei yu Jin Shengtan* 金瓶梅與金聖嘆. Taipei 台北, Taiwan 台灣: Shuiniu chubanshe 台北水牛出版社, 1988.

Gao Yuefeng 高越峰. *Jin Ping Mei renwu yishu lun* 金瓶梅人物藝術論。 Jinan 濟南: Qiru shushe 齊魯書社, 1988.

Gong Pengcheng 龔鵬程, and Zhang Huoqing 張火慶. *Zhongguo xiaoshuo shi luncong* 中國小說史論叢. Taipei 台北, Taiwan 台灣: Xuesheng shuju 學生書局, 1984.

Gu Yenwu [Qing] 顧炎武〔清〕. *Ri Zhi Lu* (6 vols.) 日知錄（六冊）. Taipei 台北, Taiwan 台灣: Shangwu 商務, 1978.

Gu Yenwu [Qing] 顧炎武〔清〕. *Tinglin shiwenji* 亭林詩文集. Taipei 台北, Taiwan 台灣: Zhonghua shuju 中華書局, 1970.

Hou Zhongyi 侯忠義, and Wang Rumei 王汝梅, eds. *Jin Ping Mei Ziliao Huibian* 金瓶梅資料匯編. 北京 Beijing: Beijing daxue chubanshe 北京大學出版社, 1985.

Hu Shi 胡適. "Da Qian Xuantong shu" (Letter to Qian Xuantong). *Wenxue Gailiang Zouyi* 文學改良芻議, Hu Shi Zuopin ji, vol. 3 胡適作品集 3. Taipei, Taiwan: Yuanliu 遠流, 1986.

Hu Wenbin 胡文彬. *Jin Ping Mei shulu* 金梅梅書錄. Liaoning 遼寧: Liaoning renmin chubanshe 遼寧人民出版社, 1986.

Hu Wenbin 胡文彬, and Zhang Qingshan 張慶善, eds. *Lun Jin Ping Mei* 論金瓶梅. Beijing 北京: Xinhua shudian 新華書店, 1984.

Huang Lin 黃霖. "Wugguo pulu wenxue de jiegou Jin Ping Mei" 我國暴露文學的傑構. In *Jin Ping Mei lunji* 金瓶梅論集. Beijing 北京: Beijing renmin wenxue chubanshe 北京人民文學出版社, 1986.

Huang Lin 黃霖. *Jin Ping Mei kaolun* 金瓶梅考論. Shenyang 瀋陽: Liaoning renmen chubanshe 遼寧人民出版社, 1986.

Huang Lin 黃霖, and Wang Guoan 王國安, eds. *Riben yanjiu Jin Ping Mei lunwenji* 日本研究金瓶梅論文集. Jinan 濟南: Qiru shushe 齊魯書社, 1989.

Huang Zongxi [Qing] 黃宗羲〔清〕. *Mingru xuan* 明儒學案. Taipei 台北, Taiwan 台灣: Zhengzhong shuju 正中書局, 1979.

Huang Zongxi [Qing] 黃宗羲〔清〕. *Mingyi daifanglu* 明夷待訪錄. Taipei 台北, Taiwan 台灣: Jinfeng chuban 今風出版有限公司, 1979.

Ji Shaofu, ed. *Zhongguo chuban jianshi*. Shanghai: Xuelin chubanshe, 1991.

Jiang Chengpo 江澄波, Du Xinfu 杜信孚, and Du Yongkang 杜永康, eds. *Jiangsu Keshu* 江蘇刻書. Jiangsu 江蘇: Jiangsu renmin chubanshe 江蘇人民出版社, 1993.

Jiang Dongwei. *Furong jing yuyan*, Zejiang: Zejiang Guji Chubanshe, 1986.

Kang Zhengguo 康正果. *Chongshen fengyue jian: Xing yu zhongguo gudian wenxue* 重審風月鑑：性與中國古典文學. Taipei 台北, Taiwan 台灣: Ryefield 麥田, 1996.

Lang Ying 郎英. *Qixiou Leigao* 七修類稿, 2 volss. Taipei 台北, Taiwan 台灣: Shijie shuju 世界書局, 1984.

Li Ang 李昂. *Beigang xianglu renren cha* (Everyone puts their incense sticks in the Peikang incense burner) 北港香爐人人插. Taipei 台北, Taiwan 台灣: Ryefield Publishing 麥田, 1997.

Li Bihua 李碧華. *Pan Jinlian zhi qianshi jinsheng* 潘金蓮之前世今生. Taipei 台北, Taiwan 台灣: Crown 皇冠, 1989.

Li Jianzhang 李健章. *Yuan Hongdao jijianjiao zhiyi, Yuan Zhonglang xingzhuang jianzheng, Bingzhuo ji*《袁宏道集箋校》志疑・袁中郎行狀箋證・炳燭集. Hubei 湖北: Renmin chubanshe 人民出版社, 1994.

*Li Xianfang yu Jin Ping Mei* 李先芳與《金瓶梅》. Edited by Liaocheng Shuihu Jin Ping Mei yanjiu xuehui 聊城《水滸》《金瓶梅》研究學會. Ningxia 寧下: Ningxia Renmin chubanshe 寧夏人民出版社, 1988.

Li Yu [Qing] 李漁〔清〕. *Xianqing ouji* 閒情偶寄. Beiye shanfang 貝葉山房 1936 photocopy edition. Shanghai 上海: Shanghai wenyi chubanshe 上海文藝出版社, 1992.

Li Zhi [Ming] 李贄〔明〕. *Fenshu/Xu fenshu* 焚書／續焚書. Taipei 台北, Taiwan 台灣: Hanjing wenhuashiye 漢京文化事業, 1984.

*Lidai keshu gaikuang* 歷代刻書概況: *Zhongguo yinshua shiliao xuanji*. Vol. 3 中國印刷史料選集（之三）. Beijing 北京: Yinshua gongye chubanshe 印刷工業出版社, 1991.

Lin Qixian 林其賢. *Li Zhuowu de fuxue yu shixue* 李卓吾的佛學與世學. Taipei 台北, Taiwan 台灣: Wenjin chubanshe, 1992.

Lin Qixian 林其賢. *Li Zhuowu shiji xinian* 李卓吾事蹟繫年. Taipei 台北, Taiwan 台灣: Wenjin chubanshe 文津出版社, 1988.

Liu Hui 劉輝, and Yang Yang 楊楊, eds. *Jin Ping Mei zhi mi* 金瓶梅之迷. Beijing 北京: Beijing shumu wenxian chubanshe 北京書目文獻出版社, 1989.

Liu Hui 劉輝. *Jin Ping Mei lunji* 金瓶梅論集. Taipei 台北, Taiwan 台灣: Taipei Guanya wenhua 台北貫雅文化, 1992.

Liu Jen-peng 劉人鵬, and Ding Naifei 丁乃非. "Wangliang wenying: hanxu meixue yu kuer zhenglue" 罔兩問景：含蓄美學與酷兒政略. *Xingbie Yanjiu* 性別研究 3/4, (October 1998).

Liu Lie 劉烈. *Ximen Qing yu Pan Jin Lian: Jin Ping Mei Cihua zhurengong ji qita* 西門慶與潘金蓮—金瓶梅詞話主人公及其他. Harbin 哈爾濱: Heilongjiang jiaoyu chubanshe 黑龍江教育出版社, 1989.

Liu Xie 劉勰. *Wenxin diaolong yizhu* (2 vols.) 文心雕龍譯注（上下冊）. Lu Kanru 陸侃如 and Mo Shijin 牟世金, eds. Jinan 濟南: Qiru shushe 齊魯書社, 1988.

Lu Kanru, and Mo Shijin, eds. *Wexin Diaolong*. Jinan: Qiru shushe, 1988.

Lu Kun [Ming] 呂坤〔明〕. *Wanli ben shenyin yu* 萬曆本呻吟語. Taipei 台北, Taiwan 台灣: Hanjing wenhua chubanshiye 漢京文化出版事業, 1981.

Lu Xun [Zhou Shuren] 魯迅〔周樹人〕. *Zhongguo xiaoshuo shilue* 中國小說史略. *Lu Xun Quanji* 魯迅全集 (8). Hong Kong: Wenxue yanjiu she 文學研究社, 1973.

Lung Zuxu [Ming] 龍遵敘〔明〕. *Shise shenyan* 食色紳言. In *Congshu jicheng xinbian* 叢書集成新編, 82 juan 卷. Taipei 台北, Taiwan 台灣: Shangwu 商務, 1965.

Ma Yushan 馬玉山. *Zhongguo gudai renkou maimai* 中國古代人口買賣. Taipei, Taiwan 台灣: Taiwan shangwu yinshuguan 台灣商務印書館, 1999.

Mang Zheng 馬征. *Jin Ping Mei zhong de xuanan* 《金瓶梅》中的懸案. Sichuan: Renmin chubanshe 四川人民出版社, 1994.

Mou Zongsan 牟宗三. *Zhongguo zhexue de tezhi* 中國哲學的特質. Taipei 台北, Taiwan: Xuesheng shuju 學生書局, 1975.

Ning Zongyi 寧宗一. "Zou jin kun huo" 走進困惑. In *Wuo yu Jin Ping Mei: Haixia liangan xueren zishu* [*Jin Ping Mei and I*]. Chengdu: Chengdu chubanshe, 1991.

Pu Jian 卜鍵. *Jin Ping Mei zuozhe Li Kaixian kao* 金瓶梅作者李開先考. Lanzhou 蘭州: Gansu renmin chubanshe 甘肅人民出版社, 1988.

Qiu Chuji [Yuan] 丘處機〔元〕. *Shesheng xiaoxi lun* 攝生消息論. In *Congshu jicheng jianbian*, 82 juan 《叢書集成簡編》82 卷. Taipei 台北, Taiwan 台灣: Shangwu 商務, 1965.

Ren Jiyu 任繼愈. *Zhongguo Daojiao shi* 中國道教史. Shanghai 上海: Renmin chubanshe 人民出版社, 1990.

Sha Wenhan 沙文漢. *Zhongguo nuli zhidu de tantao* [An inquiry into the Chinese slave system] 中國奴隸制度的探討. Shanghai 上海: Shanghai shehuikexueyuan chubanshe 上海社會科學院出版社, 1984.

Shen Defu [Ming] 沈德符〔明〕. *Wanli Yehuo Pian* 萬歷野獲編. Taipei 台北, Taiwan 台灣: Xinxing shuju 新興書局, 1983.

Shi Fang 石方. *Zhongguo xing wenhua shi* 中國性文化史. Heilongjiang 黑龍江: Renmin chubanshe 人民出版社, 1993.

Song Mouyang 宋牟. "Luelun Jin Ping Mei pinglun zhong de yimei qingxiang" 略論金瓶梅中的溢美傾向. In *Jin Ping Mei lunji* 金瓶梅論集. Beijing 北京: Beijing renmin wenxue chubanshe 北京人民文學出版社, 1986.

Sun Shuyu 孫述宇. *Jin Ping Mei de yishu* 金瓶梅的藝術. Taipei 台北, Taiwan 台灣: Shibao 時報, 1978.

Sun Xun 孫迅, and Chen Zhao 陳詔, eds. *Hong Lou Meng yu Jin Ping Mei* 紅樓夢與金瓶梅. Ningxia: Renmin chubanshe 寧夏人民出版社, 1982.

Sung Yuanfang 宋原放, Li Baijian 李白堅, and Chen Shengzheng 陳生錚. *Zhongwai chubanshi* 中外出版史. Beijing 北京: Shifan daxue chubanshe 師範大學出版社, 1993.

Tao Muning 陶慕寧. *Jin Pingmei zhong de qinglou yu jinu* 金瓶梅中的青樓與妓女. Beijing 北京: Beijing wenhua yishu chubanshe 北京文化藝術出版社, 1993.

Tian Binge 田秉鍔. *Jin Ping Mei renwu lun*《金瓶梅》人物論. Shanghai 上海: Xuelin chubanshe 學林出版社, 1996.

Wang Chao 王超. *Zhongguo lidai guanzhi yu wenhua* 中國歷代官制與文化. Shanghai 上海: Renmin chubanshe 人民出版社, 1989.

Wang Rumei 王汝梅. *Jin Ping Mei tansuo* 金瓶梅探索. Changchun 長春: Jinling daxue chubanshe 金陵大學出版社, 1990.

Wang Shaoxi 王紹璽. *Xiaoqieshi: Qiezhilousu de lishiyange* 小妾史：妾制陋俗的歷史沿革. Shanghai 上海: Wenyi chubanshe 文藝出版社, 1995.

Wang Shouren [Ming] 王守仁〔明〕. *Wang Wencheng Gong wenji* 王文成公文集. Taipei 台北: Shangwu 商務.

Wang Yijia 王溢嘉. *Gudian Jinkan—Cong Kong Ming dao Pan Jinlian* 古典今看—從孔明到潘金蓮. Taipei 台北, Taiwan 台灣: Yehe 野鶴, 1989.

Wang Yupo 王玉波. *Zhongguo jiazhangzhi jiatingzhidushi* 中國家長制家庭制度史. Tianjin 天津: Shehui kexue yuan chubanshe 社會科學院出版社, 1989.

Wei Ziyun 魏子雲, ed. *Jin Ping Mei Cihua zhushi* 金瓶梅詞話注釋. Taipei 台北, Taiwan 台灣: Zengnizhi 台北增你智, 1981.

Wei Ziyun 魏子雲. *Jin Ping Mei de biannian jishi* 金瓶梅的編年紀事. Taipei 台北, Taiwan 台灣: Juliou 巨流, 1981.

Wei Ziyun 魏子雲. *Jin Ping Mei de wenshi yu yanbian* 金瓶梅的問世與演變. Taipei 台北, Taiwan 台灣: Shibao 時報, 1981.

Wei Ziyun 魏子雲. *Jin Ping Mei tanyuan* 金瓶梅探源. Taipei 台北, Taiwan 台灣: Juliou 巨流, 1979.

Wei Ziyun 魏子雲. *Mingdai Jin Ping Mei shiliao quanshi* 明代金瓶梅史料詮釋. Taipei 台北, Taiwan 台灣: Guanya wenhua 貫雅文化, 1992.

Wei Ziyun 魏子雲. *Xiaoshuo Jin Ping Mei* 小說金瓶梅. Taipei 台北, Taiwan 台灣: xuesheng shuju 學生書局, 1987.

Wu Gan 吳敢. *Zhang Zhupo yu Jin Ping Mei* 張竹坡與金瓶梅. Tianjin 天津: Baihua wenyi chubanshe 百花文藝出版社, 1987.

*Wuo yu Jin Ping Mei—Haixia liangan xueren zishu* 我與金瓶梅—海峽兩岸學人自述. Chengdu 成都: Chengdu chubanshe 成都出版社, 1991.

Xu Bo [Ming] 徐勃〔明〕. *Xushi bijing* 徐氏筆精. Shanghai 上海: Shanghai guji chubanshe 上海古籍出版社, 1992.

Xu Shuofang 徐朔方 and Liu Hui 劉輝, eds. *Jin Ping Mei xifang lunwen ji* 金瓶梅西方論文集. Shanghai 上海: Shanghai guji chubanshe 上海古籍出版社, 1987.

Xu Shuofang 徐朔方, and Liu Hui 劉輝, eds. *Jin Ping Mei lunji* 金瓶梅論集. Beijing 北京: Beijing renmin wenxue chubanshe 北京人民文學出版社, 1986.

Yan Yiping 嚴一萍, ed. *Yi Xin Fang* 醫心方. Photocopy edition of Tamba Yasuyori's 丹波康賴 1857 edition. Taipei 台北, Taiwan 台灣: Yiwen shuguan 藝文印書館.

Yang Shengxin 楊繩信. "Lidai Kegong gongjia chutan" 歷代刻工工價初探. In *Lidai Keshu Gaikuang* 歷代科書概況, Shanghai 上海: Yinshua gongye chubanshe 印刷工業出版社, 1991.

Yang Weijie 楊維傑. *Huangdi neijing suwen jieshi* 黃帝內經素問解釋. Taipei 台北, Taiwan 台灣: Lequn wenhua 樂群文化, 1976.

Yao Boyue 姚伯岳. "Mingdai Wuxing Min Ling ershi de taoban yinshua" 明代吳興閔凌二氏的套版印刷. In *Lidai Keshu Gaikuang* 歷代科書概況, Shanghai 上海: Yinshua gongye chubanshe 印刷工業出版社.

Ye Dehui 葉德輝. *Shuangmei jingan congshu* 雙梅景闇叢書. Photocopy edition of 1903 and 1914 Changsha 長沙 edition. Kyoto, Japan 京都: Zhongwen chubanshe 中文出版社, 1986.

Ye Guitong 葉桂桐, Liu Zhongguang 劉中光, and Yan Zengshan 閻增山. *Jin Ping Mei zuozhe zhi mi* 《金瓶梅》作者之迷. Liaocheng Shuihu Jin Ping Mei yanjiu xuehui bian 聊城《水滸》《金瓶梅》研究學會. Liaocheng 聊城: Ningxia Renmin chubanshe 寧夏人民出版社, 1988.

Ye Lang 葉朗. *Zhongguo xiaoshuo meixue* 中國小說美學. Taipei 台北, Taiwan 台灣: Liren shuju 立人書局, 1987.

Yi Zhuxian, ed. *Hu Shi lun Zhongguo gudian xiaoshuo*. Hubei: Changjing wenyi chubanshe, 1987.

Yuan Hongdao [Ming] 袁宏道〔明〕. *Yuan Zhonglang quanji* 袁中郎全集. Yang Jialuo 楊家駱, ed. Taipei 台北, Taiwan 台灣: Shijie shuju 世界書局, 1990.

Yuan Hongdao [Ming] 袁宏道〔明〕. *Pinghua zhai zalu* 瓶花齋雜錄. In *Congshu jicheng xinbian* 叢書集成新編, 88 juan 卷. Taipei 台北, Taiwan: n.p., n.d.

Yuan Huang [Ming] 袁黃〔明〕. *Shesheng Sanyao* 攝生三要. In *Congshu jicheng xinbian* 叢書集成新編, 24 juan 卷. Taipei 台北.

Zhang Fenghung 張風洪. *Pan Jinlian* 潘金蓮. Sichuan: Wenyi chubanshe 四川文藝出版社, 1986.

Zhang Guofeng 張國風. *Jin Ping Mei miaohui de shisu renjian* 《金瓶梅》描繪的世俗人間. Beijing 北京: Beijing shumu wenxian chubanshe 北京書目文獻出版社, 1992.

Zhang Shudong 張樹棟 and Li Xiouling 李秀領. *Zhongguo hunyin jiating de shanbian* 中國婚姻家庭的嬗變. Hangzhou 杭州: Zhejiang renmin chubanshe 浙江人民出版社, 1990.

Zhang Xioumin 張秀民. "Mingdai Nanjing de yinshu" 明代南京的印書. In *Lidai Keshu Gaikuang* 歷代科書概況.

Zhang Yuanfen 張遠芬. "Zuo bu yuan de meng" 做不圓的夢, in *Wuo yu Jin Ping Mei: Haixia liangan xueren zishu* (Jin Ping Mei and I). Chengdu: Chengdu chubanshe, 1991.

Zhang Yuanfen 張遠芬. *Jin Ping Mei xinzheng* 金瓶梅新證. Jinan 濟南: Qiru shushe 齊魯書社, 1984.

Zhang Yushu [Qing] 張玉書 [清], ed. *Kangxi zidian* 康熙字典. Shanghai 上海: Shanghai shudian chubanshe 上海書店出版社, 1985.

Zhang Zhenjun 張振軍. *Chuantong xiaoshuo yu Zhongguo wenhua* 傳統小說與中國文化. Guilin 桂林, Guangxi 廣西: Guangxi Shifan daxue chubanshe 廣西師範大學出版社, 1996.

Zhao Yenning 趙彥寧. "Chugui huo bu chuguei—Zhe shi yige youguan heian de wenti" 出櫃或不出櫃—這是一個有關黑暗的問題. *Saodong* (Stir) 3, (January 1997).

Zheng Run 鄭潤. *Jin Ping Mei han Tu Lung* 金瓶梅和屠隆. Shanghai: Xuelin chubanshe 上海學林出版社, 1994.

Zhong Xing [Ming] 鐘惺 [明]. *Yin Xiou Xuan ji* 隱秀軒集. Shanghai 上海: Guji chubanshe 古籍出版社, 1992.

Zhou Juntao 周鈞韜. "Wei yi xiao de ren qiaocui" 為伊消得人憔悴. In *Wuo yu Jin Ping Mei: Haixia liangan xueren zishu* (Jin Ping Mei and I), ed. Zhou Juntao. Chengdu: Chengdu chubanshe, 1991.

Zhou Zhiping [Chou Chi-p'ing] 周質平. *Hu Shi luncong* 胡適論叢. Taipei 台北, Taiwan 台灣: Sanmin shuju 三民書局, 1992.

Zhu Guozhen [Ming] 朱國禎 [明]. *Yongchuang xiaopin* 湧幢小品. In *Ming Qing biji congkan* 明清筆記叢刊. Shanghai 上海: Zhonghua shuju 中華書局, 1959.

Zhu Hanmin 朱漢民. *Zhongxiao daode yu chenmin jingshen* 忠孝道德與臣民精神. Lushan 魯山, Henan 河南: Henan renmin chubanshe 河南人民出版社, 1994.

Zhu Yixuan 朱一玄, and Liu Yuchen 劉毓忱, eds. *Shuihu ziliao huibian* 水滸傳資料彙編. Tianjin 天津: Baihua wenyi chubanshe 百花文藝出版社, 1981.

Zhu Yixuan 朱一玄, ed. *Jin Ping Mei ziliao huibian* 金瓶梅資料彙編. Tianjin 天津: Nankai daxue chubanshe 南開大學出版社, 1985.

## Works in English

Ames, Michael M. *Cannibal Tours and Glass Boxes: The Anthropology of Museums*. Vancouver: University of British Columbia, 1992.

Armstrong, Nancy. *Desire and Domestic Fiction*. New York: Oxford University Press, 1987.

Armstrong, Nancy, and Leonard Tennenhouse, eds. *The Violence of Representation: Literature and the History of Violence*. New York: Routledge, 1989.

Barthes, Roland. *S/Z*. Translated by Richard Miller. New York: Hill and Wang, 1974.

———. *The Pleasure of the Text*. Translated by Richard Miller. New York: Hill and Wang, 1975.

Bataille, George. *Literature and Evil*. Translated by Alastair Hamilton. New York: Urizen Books, 1981.

———. *Visions of Excess: Selected Writings, 1927–1939.* Edited by Allan Stoekl. Minneapolis: University of Minnesota Press, 1985.

———. *Erotism: Death and Sensuality.* Translated by Mary Dalwood. San Francisco: City Lights, 1986.

———. *The Tears of Eros.* Translated by Peter Connor. San Francisco: City Lights, 1989.

Baudrillard, Jean. "Figures du Transpolitique." In *Les Strategies Fatales.* Paris: Grasset, 1983.

———. *Seduction.* Translated by Brian Singer. London: Macmillan, 1990.

Benjamin, Walter. "N [Re the Theory of Knowledge, Theory of Progress]," translated by Leigh Hafrey and Richard Sieburth. In *Benjamin: Philosophy, Aesthetics, History,* edited by Gary Smith. Chicago: University of Chicago Press, 1983.

Besio, Kimberly. "Gender, Loyalty, and the Reproduction of the Wang Zhaojun Legend: Some Social Ramifications of Drama in the Late Ming." *Journal of the Economic and Social History of the Orient* 40 (1997): 251–82.

Besio, Kimberly. "On the Borders of the Han-Gender, Cultural Identity, and Canon Formation in Early Modern Drama," unpublished manuscript.

———. "Zhang Fei in Vernacular Literature: Legend, Heroism, and History in the Reproduction of the Three Kingdoms Story Cycle." *Journal of Yuan Studies* 27 (1997): 63–98.

Birch, Cyril, ed. *Studies in Chinese Literary Genres.* Berkeley: University of California Press, 1974.

———, trans. *The Peony Pavilion (Mudan Ting).* Bloomington: Indiana University Press, 1980.

Bourdieu, Pierre. *Language and Symbolic Power.* Translated by Gino Raymond and Mathew Adamson. Cambridge, Mass.: Harvard University Press, 1991.

———. *Rules of Art: Genesis and Structure of the Literary Field.* Stanford, Calif.: Stanford University Press, 1995.

Boyarin, Jonathan, ed. *The Ethnography of Reading.* Berkeley: University of California Press, 1993.

Brokaw, Cynthia. *The Ledgers of Merit and Demerit: Social Change and Amoral Order in Late Imperial China.* Princeton, N.J.: Princeton University Press, 1991.

———. "Commercial Publishing in Late Imperial China: The Zou and Ma Family Businesses." *Late Imperial China* 17, no. 1 (June 1996): 49–92.

Brook, Timothy. *The Confusions of Pleasure: Commerce and Culture in Ming China.* Berkeley: University of California Press, 1988.

———. "Edifying Knowledge: The Building of School Libraries in Ming China." *Late Imperial China* 17, no. 1 (June 1996): 93–119.

Carlitz, Katherine. "Codes and Correspondences in Jin Ping Mei." *Chinese Literature: Essays, Articles, Reviews* 8 (1986): 7–18.

———. *The Rhetoric of Chin P'ing Mei.* Bloomington: Indiana University Press, 1986.

———. "Desire, Danger, and the Body: Stories of Women's Virtue in Late Ming China." In *Engendering China: Women, Culture, and the State.* Cambridge, Mass.: Harvard University Press, 1994.

———. "Desire and Writing in the Late Ming Play Parrot Island." In *Writing Women in Late*

*Imperial China*, edited by Ellen Widmer and Kang-I Sun Chang. Stanford, Calif.: Stanford University Press, 1997.

Cass, Victoria. "Celebrations at the Gate of Death: Symbol and Structure in Chin P'ing Mei." Ph.D. diss., University of California at Berkeley, 1979.

Chan, Wing-tsit. *A Source Book in Chinese Philosophy*. Princeton, N.J.: Princeton University Press, 1963.

———. "The Ch'eng-Chu School of Early Ming." In *Self and Society in Ming Thought*, edited by W. T. de Bary. New York: Columbia University Press, 1970.

Chang, Chun-shu, and Shelley Hsueh-lun Chang. *Crisis and Transformation in Seventeenth-Century China: Society, Culture, and Modernity in Li Yu's World*. Ann Arbor: University of Michigan Press, 1992.

Chartier, Roger, ed. *The Culture of Print: Power and Uses of Print in Early Modern Europe*. Translated by Lydia G. Cochrane. Oxford, U.K.: Polity Press, 1989.

Cheang, Eng Chew. "Li Chih as a Critic: A Chapter of the Ming Intellectual History." Ph.D. diss., University of Washington, 1973.

Ch'en, Kenneth K. S. *Buddhism in China*. Princeton, N.J.: Princeton University Press, 1964.

Cherniack, Susan. "Book Culture and Textual Transmission in Sung China." *Harvard Journal of Asiatic Studies* 54, no. 1 (1994): 5–102.

Ch'ien, Edward. "Chiao Hung and the Revolt against Ch'eng-Chu Orthodoxy." *The Unfolding of Neo-Confucianism*, edited by W. T. de Bary. New York: Columbia University Press.

Chou, Chi-P'ing. *Yuan Hung-tao and the Kung-an School*. Cambridge, U.K.: Cambridge University Press, 1988.

Chow, Kai-wing. *The Rise of Confucian Ritualism in Late Imperial China*. Stanford, Calif.: Stanford University Press, 1994.

———. "Writing for Success: Printing, Examinations, and Intellectual Change in Late Ming China." *Late Imperial China* 17, no. 1 (June 1996): 120–57, ed. William T. Rowe.

Chu, T'ung-tsu. "Chinese Class Structure and Its Ideology." In *Chinese Thoughts and Institutions*, edited by John K. Fairbank. Chicago: University of Chicago Press, 1957.

Clastres, Pierre. *Archaeology of Violence*. New York: Semiotexte, 1994.

Clunas, Craig. *Fruitful Sites: Garden Culture in Ming Dynasty China*. Durham, N.C.: Duke University Press, 1996.

Crawford, Robert B. "Chang Chu-Cheng's Confucian Legalism." In *Self and Society in Ming Thought*, edited by W. T. de Bary. New York: Columbia University Press, 1970.

Dane, Joseph A. *The Critical Mythology of Irony*. Athens: University of Georgia Press, 1991.

Dardess, John W. *Confucianism and Autocracy: Professional Elites in the Founding of the Ming Dynasty*. Berkeley: University of California Press, 1983.

Davis, Lennard J. *Resisting Novels: Ideology and Fiction*. New York: Methuen, 1987.

de Bary, Wm. Theodore. "Chinese Despotism and Confucian Ideals." In *Chinese Thought and Institutions*, edited by John K. Fairbank. Chicago: University of Chicago Press, 1957.

———. *Principle and Practicality*. New York: Columbia University Press, 1979.

----. *Neo-Confucian Orthodoxy and the Learning of the Mind-and-Heart.* New York: Columbia University Press, 1981.
----, ed. *Self and Society in Ming Thought.* New York: Columbia University Press, 1970.
----, ed. *The Buddhist Tradition in India, China, and Japan.* New York: Vintage Books, 1972.
----, ed. *The Unfolding of Neo-Confucianism.* New York: Columbia University Press, 1975.
Deleuze, Gille. *Masochism: Coldness and Cruelty.* New York: Zone Books, 1989.
*Dictionary of Traditional Chinese Medicine.* Taipei, Taiwan: Southern Materials Centre, 1985.
Ding, Naifei. "Tears of Ressentiment; or, Zhang Zhupo's Jin Ping Mei." *positions: east asia cultures critique* 3, no. 3 (1995): 663–94.
----. "Prostitutes, Parasites and the House of State Feminism," *Inter-Asia Cultural Studies* vol. 1 no. 2, August 2000, 305–318.
Djebar, Assia. *Women of Algiers in Their Apartment.* Charlottesville: University Press of Virginia, 1992.
Douglas, Mary. *Purity and Danger: An Analysis of the Concepts of Pollution and Taboo.* London: Routledge, 1966.
----. *Natural Symbols: Explorations in Cosmology.* New York: Pantheon, 1970.
----. *Implicit Meanings: Essays in Anthropology.* London: Routledge and Kegan Paul, 1975.
Dumont, Louis. *Homo Hierarchicus: The Caste System and Its Implications.* Translated by Mark Sainsbury, Louis Dumont, and Basia Gulati. Chicago: University of Chicago Press, 1980.
----. *Essays on Individualism: Modern Ideology in Anthropological Perspective.* Chicago: University of Chicago Press, 1986.
Eberhard, Wolfram. "What is Beautiful in a Chinese Woman?" In *Moral and Social Values of the Chinese: Collected Essays.* Taipei, Taiwan: Chinese Materials and Research Aids, 1971.
----. *Social Mobility in Traditional China.* Taipei, Taiwan: Southern Materials Center, 1984.
Ebrey, Patricia, and James L. Watson, eds. *Kinship Organization in Late Imperial China, 1000–1940.* Berkeley: University of California Press, 1986.
Edwards, Louise. "Women in Honglou Meng: Prescriptions of Purity in the Femininity of Qing Dynasty China." *Modern China* 16, no. 4 (October 1990): 407–29.
----. "Representations of Women and Social Power in Eighteenth-Century China: The Case of Wang Xifeng." *Late Imperial China* 14, no. 1 (June 1993): 34–59.
Egerton, Clement. *The Golden Lotus: A Translation, from the Chinese Original, of the Novel Chin P'ing Mei.* 4 vols. London: Routledge, 1974.
Eisenstein, Elizabeth. *The Printing Press as an Agent of Change: Communications and Cultural Transformation in Early-Modern Europe.* 2 vols. Cambridge, U.K.: Cambridge University Press, 1979.
Elvin, Mark. "Tales of Shen and Xin: Body-Person and Heart-Mind in China during the Last One Hundred and Fifty Years." In *Fragments for a History of the Human Body, Part Two,* edited by Michel Feher. New York: Zone Books, 1989.
Epstein, Maram. "The Beauty is the Beast: The Dual Face of Woman in Four Ch'ing Novels." Ph.D. diss., Princeton University, 1992.

Fairbank, John K., ed. *Chinese Thought and Institutions*. Chicago: University of Chicago Press, 1957.
Faure, Bernard. *Rhetoric of Immediacy: A Cultural Critique of Chan/Zen Buddhism*. Stanford, Calif.: Stanford University Press, 1994.
Foucault, Michel. *The History of Sexuality, Volume I: An Introduction*. Translated by Robert Hurley. New York: Vintage, 1980.
———. *The Use of Pleasure: The History of Sexuality, Volume II*. Translated by Robert Hurley. New York: Pantheon, 1985.
———. *The Care of the Self. The History of Sexuality*. Vol. 3. Translated by Robert Hurley. New York: Pantheon, 1986.
Frankel, Hans H. *The Flowering Plum and the Palace Lady: Interpretations of Chinese Poetry*. New Haven, Conn.: Yale University Press, 1976.
Furth, Charlotte. "Androgynous Males and Deficient Females: Biology and Gender Boundaries in Sixteenth- and Seventeenth-Century China." *Late Imperial China* 9, no. 2 (December 1988): 1–31.
———. *A Flourishing Yin: Gender in China's Medical History, 960–1665*. Berkeley: University of California Press, 1999.
Gallagher, Louis J., trans. *China in the Sixteenth Century: The Journals of Mathew Ricci, 1583–1610*. New York: Random House, 1953.
Gardner, Daniel K. "Transmitting the Way: Chu Hsi and His Program of Learning." *Harvard Journal of Asiatic Studies* 49, no. 1 (June 1989): 141–72.
Gates, Hill. "The Commoditization of Chinese Women." *Signs: Journal of Women in Culture and Society* 14, no. 41 (1989): 799–832.
Genette, Gérard. *Seuils*. Paris: Editions du Seuil, 1987.
Goodrich, L. Carrington, and Chaoying Fang, eds. *Dictionary of Ming Biography, 1368–1644*. 2 vols. New York: Columbia University Press, 1976.
Granet, Marcel. *Chinese Civilization*. Cleveland, Ohio: Meridian Books, 1958.
Grimm, Tilemnann. "Ming Educational Intendants." In *Chinese Government in Ming Times*, edited by Charles O. Hucker. New York: Columbia University Press, 1968.
Grosz, Elizabeth. "Animal Sex: Libido as desire and death," in *Sexy Bodies: The Strange Carnalities of Feminism*, E. Grosz and E. Probyn, ed. (Routledge 1995), pp. 278–300.
Guattari, Felix. *Molecular Revolution: Psychiatry and Politics*. Translated by Rosemary Sheed. New York: Penguin, 1984.
Gulik, Robert Hans van. *Erotic Colour Prints of the Ming Period*. Tokyo, 1951.
———. *Sexual Life in Ancient China: A History of Ideas*. Leiden, Netherlands: Brill, 1974.
Hanan, Patrick. "The Text of the Chin P'ing Mei." *Asia Major* 9, no. 1 (1962): 1–57.
———. "Sources of the Chin P'ing Mei." *Asia Major* 10, no. 2 (1963): 23–27.
———. *The Chinese Short Story*. Cambridge, Mass.: Harvard University Press, 1973.
———. *The Chinese Vernacular Story*. Cambridge, Mass.: Harvard University Press, 1981.
———. *The Invention of Li Yu*. Cambridge, Mass.: Harvard University Press, 1988.
Handlin, Joanna. *Action in Late Ming Thought: The Reorientation of Lu K'un and Other Ming-Dynasty Scholar-Officials*. Berkeley: University of California Press, 1983.
Haun, Saussy. *The Problem of a Chinese Aesthetic*. Stanford, Calif.: Stanford University Press, 1993.

Hegel, Robert. *The Novel in Seventeenth-Century China.* New York: Columbia University Press, 1981.

Higonnet, Margaret. "Speaking Silences: Women's Suicide." In *The Female Body in Western Culture*, edited by Susan Rubin Suleiman. Cambridge, Mass.: Harvard University Press, 1985.

Ho, Josephine. "Self-Empowerment and Professionalism: Conversations with Taiwanese Sex Workers." In *Inter-Asia Cultural Studies* 1:2 (August 2000): 283–99.

Ho Ping-ti. *Studies on the Population of China, 1368–1953.* Cambridge, Mass.: Harvard University Press, 1959.

———. *The Ladder of Success in Imperial China, 1368–1953.* New York: Columbia University Press, 1962.

Hsia, C. T. *The Classic Chinese Novel: A Critical Introduction.* Bloomington: Indiana University Press, 1980.

———. "Time and the Human Condition in the Plays of T'ang Hsien-tsu." In *Self and Society in Ming Thought*, edited by W. T. de Bary. New York: Columbia University Press, 1970.

———. "Classical Chinese Literature: Its Reception Today as a Product of Traditional Culture." In *Chinese Literature: Essays, Articles, Reviews* 10 (1988).

Hsiung Ping-chen. "Constructed Emotions: The Bond between Mothers and Sons in Late Imperial China." *Late Imperial China* 15, no. 1 (1994): 87–117.

Hsu Pi-ching. "Celebrating the Emotional Self: Feng Meng-Lung and Late Ming Ethics and Aesthetics." Ph.D. diss., University of Minnesota, 1994.

Huang, Martin W. *Literati and Self-Re/Presentation: Autobiographical Sensibility in the Eighteenth-Century Chinese Novel.* Stanford, Calif.: Stanford University Press, 1995.

———. *Taxation and Government Finance in Sixteenth-Century Ming China.* Cambridge, U.K.: Cambridge University Press, 1974.

———. *1587: A Year of No Significance.* New Haven, Conn.: Yale University Press, 1981.

Hucker, Charles. *The Traditional Chinese State in Ming Times.* Tucson: University of Arizona Press, 1961.

———. *The Censorial System in Ming China.* Stanford, Calif.: Stanford University Press, 1966.

———. *The Ming Dynasty: Its Origins and Evolving Institutions.* Ann Arbor: Center for Chinese Studies, University of Michigan, 1978.

———. *A Dictionary of Official Titles in Imperial China.* Taipei, Taiwan: Southern Materials Center, 1988.

———, ed. *Chinese Government in Ming Times.* New York: Columbia University Press, 1968.

Hung, Ming-Shui. *The Romantic Vision of Yuan Hung-tao, Late Ming Poet and Critic.* Taipei, Taiwan: Bookman Books, 1997.

Idema, Wilt. *Chinese Vernacular Fiction: The Formative Period.* Leiden, Netherlands: Brill, 1974.

Irwin, Richard. *The Evolution of a Chinese Novel.* Cambridge, Mass.: Harvard University Press, 1966.

Jahshan, Shaun Kelley. "Reader-Oriented Polyphony? Zhang Zhupo's Commentary on the Jin Ping Mei." *Modern Language Quarterly* 56, no. 1 (March 1995): 1–29.

Jameson, Fredric. "Pleasure: A Political Issue." In *Formations of Pleasure*. London: Routledge, 1983.
Jaschok, Maria. *Concubines and Bondservants: A Social History of a Chinese Custom*. London: Zed Books, 1988.
Jing, Wang. *The Story of the Stone: Intertextuality, Ancient Chinese Stone Lore, and the Stone Symbolism of Dream of the Red Chamber, Water Margin, and the Journey to the West*. Durham, N.C.: Duke University Press, 1992.
Judd, Ellen R. "Niangjia: Chinese Women and Their Natal Families." *Journal of Asian Studies* 48, no. 3 (August 1989): 525–44.
Knechtges, David R., trans. *Rhapsodies on Metropolises and Capitals*. Vol. 1 of *Selections of Refined Literature (Wen Xuan)*. Princeton, N.J.: Princeton University Press, 1982.
Ko, Dorothy. *Teachers of the Inner Chambers: Women and Culture in Seventeenth-Century China*. Stanford, Calif.: Stanford University Press, 1994.
―――. "The Written Word and the Bound Foot: A History of the Courtesan's Aura." In *Writing Women in Late Imperial China*, edited by Ellen Widmer and Kang-I Sun Chang. Stanford, Calif.: Stanford University Press, 1997.
Kristeva, Julia. *About Chinese Women*. Translated by Anita Barrows. New York: Urizen Books, 1977.
―――. *Desire in Language: A Semiotic Approach to Literature and Art*. New York: Columbia University Press, 1980.
―――. *Powers of Horror: An Essay in Abjection*. Translated by Leon Roudiez. New York: Columbia University Press, 1982.
―――. *Revolution in Poetic Language*. Translated by Margaret Waller. New York: Columbia University Press, 1984.
Kuriyama, Shigehisa. "The Imagination of Winds and the Development of the Chinese Conception of the Body." In *Body, Subject, and Power in China*, edited by Angela Zito and Tani E. Barlow. Chicago: University of Chicago Press.
Lee, Thomas H. C. "Books and Bookworms in Song China: Book Collection and the Appreciation of Books." *Journal of Sung-Yuan Studies* 25 (1995): 193–218.
Legge, James, trans. *Confucius, Confucian Analects, The Great Learning and The Doctrine of the Mean*. New York: Dover, 1971.
Lepenies, Wolf. *Between Literature and Science: The Rise of Sociology*. Translated by R. J. Hollingdale. Cambridge, U.K.: Cambridge University Press, 1988.
Leung, Angela Ki Che. "To Chasten Society: The Development of Widow Homes in the Qing (1773–1795)." *Late Imperial China* 14, no. 2 (December 1993): 1–32.
Lévy, André. *Etude sur le Conte et le Roman Chinois*. Paris: Ecole Francaise d'Extreme-Orient, 1971.
―――. "Perspectives on the Jin Ping Mei: Comments and Reminiscences of a Participant in the Jin Ping Mei Conference." *Chinese Literature: Essays, Articles, Reviews* 8 (1986): 1–6.
―――, trans. *Fleur en Fiole d'Or (Jin Ping Mei cihua)*. Introduction by André Lévy. 2 vols. Paris: Gallimard, 1985.
Levy, Dore. *Chinese Narrative Poetry: The Late Han through T'ang Dynasties*. Durham, N.C.: Duke University Press, 1988.

Li, Wai-yee. *Enchantment and Disenchantment: Love and Illusion in Chinese Literature.* Princeton, N.J.: Princeton University Press, 1993.

———. "The Idea of Authority in the *Shi chi* (Records of the Historian)." *Harvard Journal of Asiatic Studies* 54, no. 2 (1994): 345–403.

———. "The Rhetoric of Spontaneity in Late-Ming Literature." *Ming Studies*, no. 35 (August 1995): 32–52.

Liao, Chaoyang. "Three Readings in the *Jinpingmei cihua*." *Chinese Literature: Essays, Articles, Reviews* 6 (1984): 77–99.

Lin Yutang. *The Importance of Living.* New York: John Day, 1937.

Liu, Jen-Peng, and Naifei Ding. "Reticent Poetics, Queer Politics." *Working Papers in Gender/Sexuality Studies*, nos. 3 and 4 (September 1998): 109–55.

Liu, Ts'un-Yan. "Taoist Self-Cultivation in Ming Thought." In *Self and Society in Ming Thought*, edited by W. T. de Bary. New York: Columbia University Press, 1970.

Long, Elizabeth. "Textual Interpretation as Collective Action." In *The Ethnography of Reading*, edited by Jonathan Boyarin. Berkeley: University of California Press, 1993.

Lu, Sheldon Hsiao-Peng. *From Historicity to Fictionality: The Chinese Poetics of Narrative.* Stanford, Calif.: Stanford University Press, 1994.

Lu, Tonglin. *Rose and Lotus: Narrative of Desire in France and China.* Albany: State University of New York Press, 1991.

Lu, Xun. *A Brief History of Chinese Fiction.* Peking: Foreign Language Press, 1976. Trans. Yang, Hsien-yi and Gladys Yang.

Mann, Susan. "Learned Women in the Eighteenth Century." In *Engendering China: Women, Culture, and the State*, edited by Christina Gilmartin et al. Cambridge, Mass.: Harvard University Press, 1994.

———. *Precious Records: Women in China's Long Eighteenth Century.* Stanford, Calif.: Stanford University Press, 1997.

Martin, Henri-Jean. *The History and Power of Writing.* Translated by Lydia G. Cochrane. Chicago: University of Chicago Press, 1994.

Martinson, Paul. "Pao, Order, and Redemption: Perspectives on Chinese Religion and Society Based on a Study of the *Chin P'ing Mei*." Ph.D. diss., University of Chicago, 1973.

———. "*Chin P'ing Mei* as Wisdom Literature: A Methodological Essay." *Ming Studies* 5 (fall 1977): 44–56.

Maspero, Henri. *Taoism and Chinese Religion.* Translated by Frank A. Kierman Jr. Amherst: University of Massachusetts Press, 1981.

McLaren, Anne E. "Chantefables and the Textual Evolution of the *San-kuo-chih-yen-i*." *T'oung Pao* 71 (1985): 217–21.

———. *The Chinese Femme Fatale: Stories from the Ming Period.* Honolulu, Hawaii: University of Hawaii Press, 1994.

McMahon, R. Keith. "The Gap in the Wall: Containment and Abandon in Seventeenth-Century Chinese Fiction." Ph.D. diss., Princeton University, 1984.

———. "A Case for Confucian Sexuality: The Eighteenth-Century Novel *Yesou Puyan*." *Late Imperial China* 9, no. 2 (December 1988): 32–55.

---. "Shrews and Jealousy in Seventeenth- and Eighteenth-Century Vernacular Fiction." Manuscript.

Meskill, John. "Academies and Politics in the Ming Dynasty." In *Chinese Government in Ming Times*, edited by Charles Hucker. New York: Columbia University Press, 1968.

---. *Gentlemanly Interest and Wealth on the Yangtze Delta*. Ann Arbor, Mich.: Association for Asian Studies, 1994.

Mote, Frederick W., and Denis Twitchett, eds. *The Ming Dynasty, 1368–1644 (Part I)*. In *The Cambridge History of China*. Taipei, Taiwan: Cave Books, 1988.

Mulvey, Laura. *Visual and Other Pleasures*. Bloomington: Indiana University Press, 1989.

Naquin, Susan, and Evelyn S. Rawski. *Chinese Society in the Eighteenth Century*. Taipei, Taiwan: Southern Materials Center, 1988.

Needham, Joseph. *History of Scientific Thought*. In vol. 2 of *Science and Civilization in China*. Cambridge, Mass.: Cambridge University Press, 1956.

---. *Spagyrical Discovery and Invention: Magisteries of Gold and Immortality*. In vol. 5, part 2 of *Science and Civilization in China*. Cambridge, U.K.: Cambridge University Press, 1974.

---. *Chemistry and Chemical Technology, Part V: Physiological Alchemy*. In vol. 5, part 5 of *Science and Civilization in China*. Cambridge, U.K.: Cambridge University Press, 1983.

---. *Spagyrical Discovery and Invention: Physiological Alchemy*. In vol. 5, part 5 of *Science and Civilization in China*. Cambridge, U.K.: Cambridge University Press, 1983.

Ning, Zongyi. "Entering Uncertainty." In *Jin Ping Mei and I (Wo yu Jin Ping Mei)*. Chengdu: Chubanshe, 1991.

Nivison, David, and Arthur F. Wright, eds. *Confucianism in Action*. Stanford, Calif.: Stanford University Press, 1959.

---. "Protest against Convention and Conventions of Protest." In *The Confucian Persuasion*, edited by Arthur F. Wright. Stanford, Calif.: Stanford University Press, 1960.

Okada, Takehiko. "Wang Chi and the Rise of Existentialism." In *Self and Society in Ming Thought*, edited by W. T. de Bary. New York: Columbia University Press, 1970.

Oyama, Masaaki. "Large Landownership in the Jiangnan Delta Region During the Late Ming-Early Qing Period," in *State and Society in China: Japanese Perspectives on Ming-Qing Social and Economic History*, Linda Grove and Christian Daniels, eds., Tokyo: Univ. of Tokyo Press, 1984. 101–164.

Parsons, James Bunyon. *Peasant Rebellions in the Late Ming Dynasty*. Ann Arbor, Mich.: Association for Asian Studies, 1970.

Paul, Diana Y. *Women in Buddhism*. Berkeley: University of California Press, 1979.

Pearl S. Buck, trans. *All Men are Brothers [Shui Hu Chuan]*. Introduction by Lin Yutang. New York: Heritage Press, 1933.

Petersen, Jens Ostergard. "Which Books Did the First Emperor of Ch'in Burn? On the Meaning of *Pai Chia* in Early Chinese Sources." *Monumenta Serica: Journal of Oriental Studies* 43 (1995): 1–52.

Plaks, Andrew H. "After the Fall: *Hsing-shih yin-yuan chuan* and the Seventeenth-Century Chinese Novel." *Harvard Journal of Asiatic Studies* 45, no. 2 (December 1985): 543–80.

———. "The Chongzhen Commentary on the *Jin Ping Mei*: Gems amidst the Dross." *Chinese Literature* 8 (1986): 19–30.

———. *The Four Masterworks of the Ming Novel*. Princeton, N.J.: Princeton University Press, 1987.

———. "Where the Lines Meet: Parallelism in Chinese and Western Literatures." *Chinese Literature: Essays, Articles, Reviews* 10 (1988): 43–60.

———, ed. *Chinese Narrative: Critical and Theoretical Essays*. Princeton, N.J.: Princeton University Press, 1977.

Porkert, Manfred. *The Theoretical Foundations of Chinese Medicine: Systems of Correspondence*. Cambridge, Mass.: MIT Press, 1985.

Porter, Deborah. "Toward an Aesthetic of Chinese Vernacular Fiction: Style and the Colloquial Medium of Shui-hu Chuan." *T'oung Pao* 79 (1993): 113–53.

Rickett, Adele Austin, ed. *Chinese Approaches to Literature from Confucius to Liang Ch'i-ch'ao*. Princeton, N.J.: Princeton University Press, 1978.

Robinson, David. "Notes on Eunuchs in Hebei during the Mid-Ming Period." *Ming Studies*, no. 34 (July 1995): 1–10.

Rolston, David. *Traditional Chinese Fiction and Fiction Commentary*. Stanford, Calif.: Stanford University Press, 1997.

———, ed. *How to Read the Chinese Novel*. Princeton, N.J.: Princeton University Press, 1990.

Ropp, Paul S. "Ambiguous Images of Courtesan Culture in Late Imperial China." In *Writing Women in Late Imperial China*, edited by Ellen Widmer and Kang-I Sun Chang. Stanford, Calif.: Stanford University Press, 1997.

Roy, David T. "Chang Chu-po's Commentary on the *Chin P'ing Mei*." In *Chinese Narrative: Critical and Theoretical Essays*, edited by Andrew H. Plaks. Princeton, N.J.: Princeton University Press, 1977.

———. "A Confucian Interpretation of the *Chin P'ing Mei*." In *Proceedings of the International Conference on Sinology, Section on Literature*, August, 1980.

———. "The Case for T'ang Hsien-tsu's Authorship of the *Jin Ping Mei*." *Chinese Literature: Essays, Articles, Reviews* 8, nos. 1–2 (1986): 31–62.

———. "How to Read the *Chin P'ing Mei*." In *How to Read the Chinese Novel*, ed. David Rolston. Princeton, N.J.: Princeton University Press, 1990.

———, trans. *The Plum in the Golden Vase or Chin P'ing Mei*. Princeton, N.J.: Princeton University Press, 1993.

Rushton, Peter. "The Daoist's Mirror: Reflections on the Neo-Confucian Reader and the Rhetoric of *Jin Ping Mei*." *Chinese Literature: Essays, Articles, Reviews* 8, nos. 1–2 (July 1986): 63–82.

Sakai, Tado. "Confucianism and Popular Educational Works." In *Self and Society in Ming Thought*, edited by W. T. de Bary. New York: Columbia University Press, 1970.

Saso, Michael. *The Teachings of Taoist Master Chuang*. New Haven, Conn.: Yale University Press, 1978.

Satyendra, Indira Suh. "Toward a Poetics of the Chinese Novel: A Study of the Prefatory Poems in the *Chin P'ing Mei tz'u-hua*." Ph.D. diss., University of Chicago, 1989.

Saussy, Haun. *The Problem of a Chinese Aesthetic*. Stanford, Calif.: Stanford University Press, 1993.

Schipper, Kristofer. *The Taoist Body*. Berkeley: University of California Press, 1993.
Scott, Mary. "The Image of the Garden in Jin Ping Mei and Hongloumeng." *Chinese Literature: Essays, Articles, Reviews* 8, nos. 1–2 (1986): 83–94.
Sedgwick, Eve Kosofsky. *Between Men: English Literature and Homosocial Desire*. New York: Columbia University Press, 1985.
———. "Privilege of Unknowing: Diderot's The Nun." In *Tendencies*. Durham, N.C.: Duke University Press, 1993.
Serres, Michel. *The Parasite*. Translated by Lawrence R. Schehr. Baltimore, Md.: Johns Hopkins University Press, 1982.
Shigeta, Atsushi. "The Origins and Structure of Gentry Rule." In *State and Society in China: Japanese Perspectives on Ming-Qing Social and Economic History*, edited by Linda Grove and Christian Daniels. Tokyo: University of Tokyo Press, 1984.
Shih, Vincent Yu-chung, trans. *The Literary Mind and the Carving of Dragons*. Hong Kong: Chinese University of Hong Kong, 1983.
Sieber, Patricia. "Corporeality and Canonicity: A Study of Technologies of Reading in Early Modern Zaju Drama." *Graven Images* 2 (1995): 171–82.
———. "Rhetoric, Romance, and Intertextuality: The Making and Remaking of Guan Hanqing in Yuan and Ming China." Ph.D. diss., University of California at Berkeley, 1994.
Snitow, Ann, Christine Stansell, and Sharon Thompson, eds. *Powers of Desire: The Politics of Sexuality*. New York: Monthly Review Press, 1983.
Sommer, Mathew. *Law, Society, and Culture in China*. Stanford, Calif.: Stanford University Press, 2000.
Spivak, Gayatri Chakravorty. "Three Woman's Texts and a Critique of Imperialism." In *"Race," Writing, and Difference*, edited by Henry Louis Gates. Chicago: University of Chicago Press, 1985.
———. *In Other Worlds: Essays in Cultural Politics*. London: Methuen, 1987.
———. "Literature." In *Critique of Postcolonial Reason*. Cambridge, Mass.: Harvard University Press, 1999.
Spyer, Patricia, ed. *Border Fetishisms: Material Objects in Unstable Spaces*. London: Routledge, 1998.
Sugarman, Richard. *Rancor against Time: The Phenomenology of "Ressentiment."* Hamburg: Meiner, 1980.
Suleiman, Susan Rubin. "(Re)writing the Body: The Politics and Poetics of Female Eroticism." In *The Female Body in Western Culture: Contemporary Perspectives*, edited by Susan R. Suleiman. Cambridge, Mass.: Harvard University Press, 1985.
Tanaka Masatoshi. "Popular Uprisings, Rent Resistance, and Bondservant Rebellions in the Late Ming." In *State and Society in China: Japanese Perspectives on Ming-Qing Social and Economic History*, edited by Linda Grove and Christian Daniels. Tokyo: University of Tokyo Press, 1984.
Tang Chun-i. "The Development of the Concept of Moral Mind from Wang Yang-ming to Wang Chi." In *Self and Society in Ming Thought*, edited by W. T. de Bary. New York: Columbia University Press, 1970.
T'ien Ju-K'ang. "Traditional Chinese Beliefs and Attitudes toward Mental Illness." In

*Chinese Culture and Mental Health*, edited by Wen-Shing Tseng and David Y. H. Wu. London: Academic Press, 1985.

———. *Male Anxiety and Female Chastity: A Comparative Study of Chinese Ethical Values in Ming-Ch'ing Times*. Leiden, Netherlands: E. J. Brill, 1988.

Tillman, Hoyt Cleveland. "Ho Ch'u-fei and Chu Hsi on Chu-ko Liang as a 'Scholar-General.'" *Journal of Sung-Yuan Studies* 25 (1995): 77–94.

Tomasko, Nancy Norton. "Chung Hsing (1574–1625): A Literary Name in the Wan-Li Era (1573–1620) of Ming China." Ph.D. diss., Princeton University, 1995.

Tsai, Shih-shan Henry. *The Eunuchs in the Ming Dynasty*. Albany: State University of New York Press, 1996.

Tsai, Ying-chun. "Text, Meaning, and Interpretation: A Comparative Study of Western and Chinese Literary Theories." Ph.D. diss., University of Warwick, 1997.

T'sao Jr-lien. "Remembering Suzhou: Urbanism in Late Imperial China." Ph.D. diss., University of California at Berkeley, 1992.

Tu Wei-Ming. *Humanity and Self-Cultivation: Essays in Confucian Thought*. Berkeley: Asian Humanities Press, 1979.

Unschuld, Paul U. *Medicine in China: A History of Ideas*. Berkeley: University of California Press, 1985.

Waltner, Ann. *Getting An Heir: Adoption and the Construction of Kinship in Late Imperial China*. Honolulu: University of Hawaii Press, 1990.

Wang, John C. Y. *Chin Sheng-t'an*. New York: Twayne, 1972.

Wang, Richard. "The Cult of Qing: Romanticism in the Late Ming Period and in the novel *Jiao Hong Ji*." *Ming Studies*, no. 33 (August 1994): 12–43.

Ware, James R., ed. and trans. *Alchemy, Medicine, and Religion in the China of A.D. 320: The Nei P'ien of Ko Hung*. Cambridge, Mass.: MIT Press, 1966.

Welch, Holmes, and Anna Seidel, eds. *Facets of Taoism: Essays in Chinese Religion*. New Haven, Conn.: Yale University Press, 1979.

Widmer, Ellen. "The Huanduzhai of Hangzhou and Suzhou: A Study in Seventeenth-Century Publishing." *Harvard Journal of Asiatic Studies* 56, no. 1 (June 1996): 77–122.

Widmer, Ellen, and Kang-I Sun Chang, eds. *Writing Women in Late Imperial China*. Stanford, Calif.: Stanford University Press, 1997.

Wiens, Mi Chu. "Socioeconomic Change during the Ming Dynasty in the Kiangnan Area." Ph.D. diss., Harvard University, 1973.

Wilbur, C. Martin. *Slavery in China during the Former Han Dynasty, 206 B.C.–A.D. 25*. New York: Russell and Russell, 1967.

Wilhelm, Helmut. "The Scholar's Frustration: Notes on a Type of 'Fu.'" In *Chinese Thought and Institutions*, edited by John K. Fairbank. Chicago: University of Chicago Press, 1957.

Williams, Raymond. *Marxism and Literature*. Oxford: Oxford University Press, 1977.

———. *Problems in Materialism and Culture*. London: Verso, 1980.

Wright, Arthur F., ed. *Confucian Personalities*. Stanford, Calif.: Stanford University Press, 1962.

———. *Confucianism and Chinese Civilization*. Stanford, Calif.: Stanford University Press, 1975.

Wu Pei-yi. *The Confucian's Progress: Autobiographical Writings in Traditional China*. Princeton, N.J.: Princeton University Press, 1990.

Wu, Hua Laura. "From Xiaoshuo to Fiction: Hu Yinglin's Genre Study of Xiaoshuo." *Harvard Journal of Asiatic Studies* 55, no. 2 (1995): 339–71.

Wu, Laura Hua. "Jin Shengtan (1608–1661): Founder of a Chinese Theory of the Novel." Ph.D. diss., University of Toronto, 1993.

Wu, Nelson. "Tung Ch'i-ch'ang: Apathy in Government and Fervor in Art." In *Confucian Personalities*, edited by Arthur F. Wright. Stanford, Calif.: Stanford University Press, 1962.

Wu, Yenna. "The Inversion of Marital Hierarchy: Shrewish Wives and Henpecked Husbands in Seventeenth-Century Chinese Literature." In Harvard Journal of Asiatic Studies 48.2 (1988): 363–82.

Xiao Jie-fu. "The Enlightenment of Anti-Neo-Confucian Thought during the Ming-Qing Dynasties." *Journal of Chinese Philosophy* 16, no. 2 (June 1989): 209–35.

Yang, Hsien-yi, and Gladys Yang. *A Brief History of Chinese Fiction*. Peking: Foreign Language Press, 1976.

Yu, Anthony. "History, Fiction, and the Reading of Chinese Narrative." *Chinese Literature: Essays, Articles, Reviews* 10 (1988): 1–19.

Zeitlin, Judith. *Historian of the Strange: Pu Songling and the Chinese Classical Tale*. Stanford, Calif.: Stanford University Press, 1993.

INDEX

Abjection, 218–19; and fear, 99
Aphrodisiac pills, 202–3, 213
Armstrong, Nancy, 249 n.30

Bad/unchaste women (bu liang fu), xv, 273 n.51. See also Woman/women and womanhood
Barthes, Roland, 189, 247 n.3, 263 n.37
Bataille, George, 276 nn.19, 20, 22, 280 n.12, 283 nn.62, 64
Baudrillard, Jean, 145, 280 n.14, 281 n.46
Benjamin, Walter, 259 n.72
Besio, Kimberly, 17, 294 n.14
Bestial desires (shouxing de rouyu), 3, 18
Big Sister Ximen (Ximen Qing's daughter), 205
Blood: of a cat (Snow Thief), 211; of Guange, 211; of Li Ping'er, 213–15; of Qiuju, 210; on Ximen's penis, 214, 216
Bondmaid-concubine(s) (biqie): allotted space-time, 170–71; bondmaid becomes concubine (in JPM), 196; and bondmaid-prostitute, 196–97; as cat-like base persons, 222–23; in colonial Hong Kong, 197–98; court case descriptions of, 290 n.44; deaths of (in JPM), 212; disciplinary bondage of, 165, 190–93; domestic and sexual appendages, 196; epitome of "obscene things," 195; and famous prostitutes, 284 n.1; femininity of, 206; as human part-objects (half-human half-object), 189, 196, 219; Jinlian as, 206–7; as life trajectory, 199; Li Yu on, 284 n.2; Maria Jaschok on, xxii; modern polarized memories of, 287 n.14; obsession with sex, 282 n.57; representation and historical transformation of, xx, xxi–xxii; sexual opportunism of, xiii, xv, xx, xxviii; termination of bondmaid status, 287 n.11; uses of, 194; Xue'e's demotion

Bondmaid-concubine(s) (*continued*)
to kitchenmaid, 182; as yinfu, 212. *See also* Bond servant(s); Yinfu (licentious woman/women)
Bond servant(s): xxiv, 145, 152, 163–64, 171, 180, 183, 189; in colonial Hong Kong, 196–97; court cases of, 290 n.44; jiaren as, 279 n.10; and kinship terms, 197–98; in late Ming, 284 n.1; lines of flight from, 278 n.40; Maria Jaschok on, 197–98; in Ming-Qing, 196; as soccer players, 177; termination of bond servant status in Hong Kong, 287 n.11; in twentieth century, 198
Book(s): as aesthetical/ethical object, 111; bookmaking, 54; book market, 51, 54, 76–78; economic and symbolic profit of, 51; late Ming minke or Fujian print shops, 52–53; medicinal qualities of, 112–14; Qin Emperor's book burning, 53–54, 70–73
Bound feet: 167, 173–75, 192–93; feet wraps (foot bindings), 185–86, 192–93
Bourdieu, Pierre, 47, 253, 269 n.8, 293 n.1
Brokaw, Cynthia, 52, 256 n.20, 285 n.6, 286 n.9
Brook, Timothy, 17, 254 n.18
Bu Jian, 44

Cai Yong, 267 n.68
Campbell, Harry, 237
Carlitz, Katherine, 17, 28, 41, 272 n.34, 294 n.14
Cass, Victoria, 41
Cats and dogs, xxiii; akin to concubines and bond servants, 200, 222; cats, 288 nn.20, 21; dog pee, 209–10, 291 n.50; Snow Thief (Snow Lion), 200–2, 207–8, 211
Chang Chun-shu and Shelley Hsueh-lun Chang, 254 n.8

Chao Yen-ning, 296 n.29
Chastity discourse, xx
Ch'en, Kenneth, 295, n.16
Chen Duxiu, 18
Cheng Dongyou, 27–30
Chen Jingji, 213
Chen Jiru, 50, 55, 87
Chen Longzheng, 68
Chen Wanyi, 254 nn.9, 16
Chen Xue, xxxi, 225, 228–29, 234–43, 294 n.7, 295 n.22, 296 nn.29, 31
Cherniack, Susan, 50, 254 n.16
Chinese soccer, 176
Chou Chih-p'ing, 56, 82, 88, 93, 248 n.25, 259 n.1, 260 n.15, 263 n.36
Chow Kai-wing, 245 n.7, 254 n.18, 269 n.12, 274 n.60
Chunmei, 164, 177, 178, 185, 189, 190, 200
Cinnabar pills: 291 n.49; and mercuric sulfide poisoning, 212
Clastres, Pierre, 144, 275 n.6
Clunas, Craig, 17, 256 n.26, 258 n.48
Consumption: conspicuous consumption, 189; cultured or refined consumption, xiii, xvi; greedy or gluttonous consumption, xvi; new subjects of, xxx; sensual/sexual, xxx; visual devouring, 176; wine drinking, 277 n.30
Counting (numbers): 251 n.53; of Jinlian's shushu's, 158; of shoes, 193; of Ximen's tears, 215. *See also* Jin Ping Mei (JPM); Zhang Zhupo

Dane, Joseph A., 251 nn.63, 64
Death: Li Ping'er's, 212–17; Huilian's suicide, 185–86; orgiastic implosion, 176, 222; sacrificial, 147, 150, 152, 193, 215, 216; and sex, 188; Snow Thief's, 211; Ximen's, 184, 219
Dijkastra, Bram, 237
Djebar, Assia, 296 nn.36, 37
Dong Qichang, 55, 82, 93, 108, 111–12

Douglas, Mary, 199, 283 n.60, 288 n.17, 289 n.33
Dumont, Louis, xxi, 196–97, 285 n.5

Egerton, Clement, 189, 282 n.55
Eisenstein, Elizabeth, 254 n.16, 258 n.47
Ellis, Havelock, 29
Ěnu (bad/evil/queer women), xxix, 243; correct representation of, 239; embodiments of, 239–40; guilt and, 234, 240; as late Ming feinu, 241
Ěnu Shu, 225, 234–43; false consciousness in, 236; as inauthentic, 238–39; lesbian sentiment in, 235; as obscene book, 242; queer uses of, 240–41; shamelessness in, 241; Yang Zhao's relation of desire to, 228
Epstein, Maram, 17, 253 n.93

Fan Lien, 278 n.40
Fascination, 177, 193
Faure, Bernard, 274 n.61
Female sexuality, 237; narratives of, 242
Feminism: and bondmaid-concubine, 287 n.14; feminist debates on prostitution, xxviii; and feminist reading, xvi, xx–xxi, xxvii–xxix; feminist woman-intellectual reader, xxix; institutional discourses and practicing prostitutes, 198
Feng Menglong, 50, 55, 87, 91
Filiality, 215; perversion of, 219;
Flaubert, Gustave, 294 n.6
Fu (prose-poem) narrative, xxvi; as cure, 90, 95–99, 102–4; early fu, 95; "exorcising fu," 99
Furth, Charlotte, 265 n.43, 296 n.32

Games: aiming at the gourd, 283 n.63; soccer, 177
Genette, Gérard, 293 n.1
Gongan School, 82, 83
Grand Canal economy and culture, 27–28

Grape Arbor, 188–93, 222
Guange, 201–2, 208–12; death of, 292 n.60; fragile as (all) firstborn son(s), 208, 290 n.47; infantile convulsions, 211; Li Ping'er's son, xii; as reincarnation of Hua Zixu, 213, 216
Guattari, Felix, 294 n.6, 295 n.17
Gu Yenwu, 270 n.20

Half-human half-object, xxiv, 196, 219, 243; bondmaid-concubine as, 189, 196, 219. *See also* Personhood
Hanan, Patrick, 284 n.2, 288 n.21
Hegel, Robert, 14, 253 n.5
He Liangjun, 279 n.10
Heroes (haohan): 144; as base heterogeneous elements, 151; counterpart to yinfu, 152; as sovereign element, 152
Hierarchy, xxiv, 196–97, 223, 289 n.33; and Confucian ritualist ethics, 44; and familial-social power negotiations, xv; Louis Dumont on, xxi; and self-discipline, 45
Ho, Josephine, 247 n.22
Homology, 226
Hong Lou Meng (*Dream of the Red Chamber*), 281 n.46
Hsia, C. T., xvi, 5, 12–14, 17, 33–36, 274 n.2
Huang, Martin, 17
Huang Lin, 5, 25–27, 32, 252 n.65
Hua Zixu, 171
Huilian (Song), 170–75, 177–88
Human(e)ness (ren): civility and, xxiii
Hung Ming-Shui, 247 nn.21, 7, 259 n.1, 263 n.35
Hu Shi, 6, 12–13, 18–20, 28, 249 n.32

Imperialism, xx
Imperial service: alienation from, xiv; shift to market management, xxix
Incest: 213; mother-daughter, 235
Intimacy, 197
Intimate politics, xiv, xvi

Jaschok, Maria, xxii–xxiii, 197–98, 280 n.22, 282 n.57, 285 n.8, 287 nn.11, 14, 290 nn.39, 44, 47, 291 n.53
Jian: as contaminating, xxiii; as innate moral depravity, xv, xx; as social baseness, xv, xx
Jiang Dongwei, 273 n.51
*Jiangsu Keshu*, 257 nn.35, 36
Jiao Hong, 55
Jia Sanjin, xviii
Ji Dawei, 293 n.3
*Jin Ping Mei* (JPM): xxvi, 153, 225; abjection in, 218–19; aesthetic-ethical reading of, xviii, xxvii; "ancient filth," 21–25; authorial and textual control, 36–37; authorship, xviii; bad sex in, 38–39; borderline work, xiv, xix; in China, 18–30, 43–45; *Chongzhen ben Jin Ping Mei* (XXPJPM), xxiv; circulation and cultural myths of, xi–xvi, xxvi; contemporary revisions, xv; earliest readers and editors, xii, xvii, xxx; enthralled readers, 281 n.27; as exorcistic rite for voyeurs, 39–43; feminist reading of, xvi, xx; free indirect style in, 291 n.51; for literati readers, xiv; gender taboo of, xv; half-human half-object in, 108, 196, 219; heterosexual male subject in, 227–28; interventionist readings of, xxx–xxxi; intimate politics in, xiv; irony in, 15–16, 31–32; *Jin Ping Mei Cihua* (JPMC), xxiii–xxiv, 145, 158; Jin-ology (jin xue), 3–45 passim, 247 n.1; and *Lady Chatterley's Lover*, 251 n.57; legacy of readings, xxvii; low culture/common mind of author, 35, 39; manuscript copy of, 82; misogyny in, xiv, 4–5; moral obscenity in, 186, 188, 212; as "negative" representation of bondmaid-concubines, 196, 198, 212; and New Criticism, 16, 30–33; Pearl-Juggler of Eastern Wu on JPMC, 109–10; and the Peony Pavilion (*Mudan Ting*), 44; percentage of or quantifying "sex" in, 24, 28, 33; pornography and censorship (*yinshu* issue), xvi, xvii–xviii, xxvii, 6, 18–19, 24; "pounding hearts and sweaty palms" while reading, 20–21; prostitution in, 280 n.15; reality effect in, 189, 290 n.44; as record of enchantment with things, 163–64; representation of women and sex (female sexuality), xiv, 4, 7, 24, 29, 32, 33–39, 44–45; retributive logic of, xix; seduction and fascination in, xxxi; sexual services and sexual opportunism in, xi, xxvi; and SHZ, 145, 268 n.6; in Taiwan and Hong Kong, 30–33; three main recensions, xxv, 268 n.1, 275 n.7; three Wanli prefaces, 266 n.62; in the twentieth-century, xiii, xxix, 4–7, 18–45; twentieth-century Chinese critics on, 237; unethical aesthetics of, 23; urban mercantilism in, 144–45, 152; in the United States, 33–43; woman-sex-phobic narrative logic in, 156; "worldly sensibility," 20; writer's pseudonym, 276 n.20; younger generation Chinese scholars on, 43–45; young Jinlian in, 272 n.49; *Xinke Xiouxiang Piping Jin Ping Mei* (XXJPM), xxiv, 145, 202, 204, 206, 214, 218, 221; *Zhang Zhupo ben Jin Ping Mei* (ZZPJPM), xxvi, 158; Zhang Zhupo's relations of desire to, 228. See also *Xinke Xiouxiang Piping Jin Ping Mei* (XXJPM)
Jin Shengtan, xxix, 47–49, 51, 58, 63–75, 78, 92, 93, 146, 148, 241, 274 n.1, 275 n.10, 276 nn.13, 19; aesthetic consumption of fiction, 57; and authority in writing, 49, 66; counting Jinlian's shushu's, 158; first preface to SHZ, 68–76; as gatekeeper of textual empire, 75; "megalomania," 49, 78, 253 n.5; on Qin Emperor's book burning as bookmaking, 71–73; SHZ as prohibitive text, 63–68, 78–79; on

SHZ as youth primer, 74; on transmission of texts, 67–68; on writing as embodied disposition, 69

Ko, Dorothy, 51, 52, 254 n.16, 287 n.15
Kristeva, Julia, 283 n.60
Kuriyama Shigehisa, 271 n.29

Lady Lin, 278 n.39
Laiwang, 179, 180–83, 187
Laixing, 180, 182
Lang Ying, 52–54
Late Ming: authenticity of emotions, 89; bond servitude in, 196; economic and social historians of, 196; enchanted objects, 163–64; erotic writings, 193; parvenu subjects, 107; print culture, 9–10; pursuit of fame, 88; space/time of leisure, 89; urban material culture, 8; urban mercantilism, 28; valuing of trivial/everyday, 86; wealth and consumption, 87, 107
Late Ming Jiangnan literati (wenren): creative genius of, 16; imperial examination and bureaucratic service, 49; involvement in book market and print culture, 48–52; Lin Yutang on, 7–11; and modern "Chinese" sensibility, 4, 6; as prefiguring modern "Chinese" literatus (fantasmatic recognitions), 6, 7–18
Laughter: the author's (of JPM), 178, 187; George Bataille on eroticism, death, and, 150; Jinlian's, 177–78; Jin Shengtan's, 150
Lawrence, D. H., 28–30; *Lady Chatterley's Lover*, 251 n.57
Lesbian: erotic short stories, 225; existence and sentiment in Taiwan, 239; "lesbianism per se," 235–36, 238, 243; representation, 239; and queer fiction, xxxi; stories (gossip) of, 240; "women discovering women," 238
Levy, Dore, 96
Li Ang, 275 n.12

Li Jianzhong, 251 n.57
Li Jiao'er, 203
Li Kaixian, xviii
Ling Mengchu, 50, 91
Lin Yutang, 7–11, 17, 248 n.8, 260 n.15, 277 n.30
Li Ping'er, xii, 171, 176, 178, 188, 190, 200–201, 203, 205–16, 282 n.51, 288 n.26, 290 n.42
Li Rihua, 91, 111
Liu Hui, 246 n.20, 268 n.3
Liu Jen-peng, 245 n.5, 246 n.9, 287 n.13
Liu Liangya, 293 n.4
Liu Xie, 104–5, 268 n.1, 270 n.16
Li Wai-yee, 270, n.22
Li Xifan, 23–24, 25
Li Yu, xii, 87, 88, 112–14, 196, 262 n.28, 284 n.2, 288 n.21, 293 n.79; on grooming of bondmaid-concubines, xiii, xxiii
Li Zhi, xxix, 82, 92, 48–51, 55–63, 65–67, 76–77; and authenticity in writing, 49; ethical affect of reading, 58; and political alienation, 61; preface to *Shuihu Zhuan* (SHZ), 56–63, 65–66
Long, Elizabeth, xxv
Lung Zunxu, 272 n.42
Lu Tonglin, 3
Lu Xun, 5–6, 18–20

Ma Sen, 293 n.3
McLaren, Anne E., 254 n.16
McMahon, Keith, 17
Mei Sheng (Ch'eng), 90, 94, 105, 113
Melancholy: everyman's, 107–11, 115; and illness, 83–86, 88–90, 104, 106–7, 108; and poetry, 84–86; princely melancholy, 106–7, 114
Meng Yulou, 180, 183, 190, 217
Meskill, John, 87, 161 n.17, 254 n.10, 261 n.21, 278 n.40, 282 n.47
Mimicry, xxiv; Jinlian's *xueshe*, 291 n.51; women who read JPM, xiv

Ming-Qing fiction, 13–14, 18–20; fictional aesthetics, 49; fiction commentaries, xxiv; market in fiction, 49; and modern love, 19; New Critical reading of, 16, 30–33; prefacing and reading tactics, 49; rhetorical uses of irony in, 15–16
Mirror: and the market, 259 n.67
Misogyny, 4–5, 43; class-status based, xiv-xv
Modern Chinese (masculine) subject, 6, 8–9; formation of, 10–11, 17; in Taiwan and Hong Kong, 12
Modern/premodern: 9–12; modernity as biological maturity, 13; myth of radical rupture, 11–12; other (alternative) modernities, 10–11
Moral sadism: 186

Nationalist sentiment, xxviii
Needham, Joseph, 292 n.72
Ning Zongyi, 24, 249 n.33, 250 n.43
Nun Wang, 203, 289 n.34
Nüse (woman-sex), 221; dangers of, xv
Numbers (counting): of Jinlian's shushu's, 158; quantifying "sex" in JPM, 24, 28, 33; of shoes, 193; of Ximen's tears, 215

Obscene (yin): 5, 33; instruments (toys), 203, 278 n.40; matters, xvi-xix; mother, 212–17; objects, xvii; voiding of, 186–87
Obsession (pi), 88–89; as embodiments of one's qi, 89
Old Woman Liu (Liu Po), 208, 212
Oyama Masaaki, 284 n.1, 286 n.10

Pan Jinlian, 146, 152–64, 166–68, 171–94, 200–22, 282 n.54, 285 n.4, 287 n.12, 288 nn.26, 27, 290 n.43; archyinfu, xxviii, xxx; "art of maneuvering power," 175, 184; "art of playing up to others" (techniques of servitude), 156; barren because lascivious, 215; bondmaid-concubine, xi; covert operations of, 187; cruelty of, 291 n.53; and death of Guange, 208–12; decapitation of, 276 n.21; as fox spirit, 291 n.54; inappropriate sentiments, 205; most licentious woman in history of Chinese fiction, 45; and mother, 210; piss-swallowing, 218–19; "riding" her partners to death, 37–38; and shushu (Wu Song), 278 n.34; and Snow Thief, 200–208; and Ximen's death, 220–23; Ximen's fifth concubine (sixth wife), xi; xueshe, 291 n.51
Parasite (interceptor): 162–63, 219
Parry, Amie, 296 n.31
Parsons, James Bunyon, 52, 256 n.20
Paul, Diana, 295 n.16
Peony Pavilion, xxii, 44
Personhood: half-human half-object, xxiv, 196, 219, 243; hierarchical, xxi. See also Half-human half-object
Plaks, Andrew H., 4, 14–17, 28, 36–39, 246 n.20, 251 n.53, 252 n.80, 268 n.1, 274 n.1
Polygamy: good behavior in, 204; household spatial arrangements, 170–71
Preface(s), 48, 229, 241–43; and literary field, 226, 237; politics and erotics of, 225
Print culture, xvi, xviii, xxix, 9–11, 33; authorial control of texts, 51; author's name as commercial tactic, 55–56; consumption of erotic textual objects, 93; and literati subjectivity, 50; in late twentieth-century Taiwan, 225; market in fiction (commodification/aestheticization of fiction), xvii, 49, 92; in Ming China, 12, 225; new vernacular forms, 92; printing innovations in late Ming, 54–55; private, commercial, and official printing, 52, 55; and textual empire, 51–52, 75; and textual repu-

tation, 53; vicarious sex of, 42; "way of the market" in, 56, 75–78
Prostitutes and prostitution, 171; prostitution in JPM, 280 n.15; Taipei-licensed prostitutes, xxviii, 243

Qian Xuantong, 18–19, 249 n.27
Qifa (Seven stimuli), xxix, 90–107, 108; abjection, 102–3; bore (wave), 99–103; consumption of pleasures, 102; "essential words and marvelous doctrines" in, 97–98; fantasies/sensualities, 98–99; illness of prince in, 96; language, 105; metastases of desires, 104, 108; poet-shaman in, 99, 104; representation of sensualities in, 114–15; teachings of sages in, 97; transformational affective powers, xxvi; "word magic" in, 96
Qiuju, 210
Qiu Miaojin, 238

Read/write. See Readers and reading; Writing
Readers and reading: aestheticization as reading strategy, xxx; counter-ethical feminist reading, xvi, xx, xxvii–xxix; dominant institutions of, 225; embodied process of, 93; heterogeneous reading, xxvi; histories of readings, xvii; interventionist readings, xxx–xxxi; literacy and ethical acculturation, xxiii; masculine/male literati readers, xiv, xx; medicinal qualities of, 112–14; new cultural object (manuscript), 91; of JPM, xviii; parvenu (improperly literate) readers, xvii, 273 n.55; pity and horror, 214–15; politics of reading, 6; positionalities of reading, xxv; production and consumption of, 10; professional readers, 5, 32; queer modalities of reading, 240; reading as social practice, xxv; in solitude, 27

Red shoe: 192, 209–10, 282 n.59. See also Shoes
Representation: of objects, 189–90; of women, 161–62; of women and sex (female sexuality), xiv, 4, 7, 24, 29, 32, 33–39, 44–45
Ricci, Mathew, 275 n.8, 286 n.9
Rolston, David, 48, 252 n.5, 253 n.2, 256 n.22, 257 n.42, 271 n.27, 276 n.18
Ropp, Paul S., 284 n.1
Roy, David T., 5, 39–41, 259 n.55, 266 n.63, 268 n.1, 275 n.7, 278 n.39, 294 n.6
Rui'er (the wetnurse), 201–2, 217–19
Rushton, Peter, 268 n.1, 295 n.15

Saleswoman Wu, 278 n.40
Schipper, Kristofer, 265 n.54
Sedgwick, Eve Kosofsky, 296 n.30
Seduction: 149–63, 170; the eye and the gaze in, 161–63; and fascination, 96, 98, 99; hero's refusal of, 157; orchestration of shushu's in, 158; as pas de deux, 160; reciprocal seduction, 149; reversible power of, 145; and sa jiao, 278 n.33; and violence, 144–46; and wine drinking, 155
Sensualism and curiosity, 92–93
Sex and sexuality: 4, 26; as bad objects, 232; and death, xii; erotic/hygienic self-care, xiii; excesses, xix; and gender, 7; percentage of sex in JPM, 24, 28; politics of sexuality, xxviii; sexuality and affect, 21; sexual desire as narcissistic and autoerotic, 236; sexual ideology, xxix; sexual/sensual contact, xiii; as transhistorical realm of representation, 29–30. See also counting (numbers)
Shamanism: in fiction, xxx
Sha Wenhan, 276 n.21, 286 n.9
Shen Defu, 273 n.55, 288 n.20
Shigeta Atsushi, 262 n.21, 279 n.10
Shoes: red, 192, 282 n.59; soiled red,

Index 331

Shoes (continued)
    209–10; Zhang Zhupo's counting of,
    193
Shui Hu Zhuan (SHZ): xi, xxix, xxx, 143–
    52; base heterogeneous elements in,
    277 n.25; 278 n.32; infamous women
    in, 275 n.11; and JPM, 145; political
    uses of, 274 n.4; progressiveness of,
    276 n.23; San Guo Yanyi (Romance of
    the three kingdoms) and, 143–44;
    textual history of, 274 n.1; warrior
    ethos in, 143–44
Sieber, Patricia, 17, 259 n.58, 269 n.7,
    270 n.23, 272 n.34, 294 n.14
Sima Qian, 270 n.24
Sinology: in the United States, 9, 11
Slavery, 286 n.9
Sommer, Mathew, 245 n.1, 246 nn.10,
    11, 16
Song Mouyang, 250 n.42
Spivak, Gayatri, xx, xxv, 296 n.36
Structure of feeling, 5–6, 8–9
Sugarman, Richard, 270 n.17
Sun Chengen, 282 n.47
Sun Shuyu, 30–33, 252 n.65
Swing, 176–79

Taiwan, xvi, 225; Chang De Road incident, 243; emergence of lesbian and gay groups in universities, 229; JPM in, 30–33; lesbian, 296 n.28; lesbian erotic stories, xxxi; literary field of the 1990s, 238, 241–43; penumbra queers in, 287 n.13; residual master-bondservant affect in, 285 n.7; reticent homophobia in, 246 n.9; state feminist reforms in, 245 n.5; Taipei-licensed prostitutes, xxviii, 243; The Wedding Banquet in, 229
Tanaka Masatoshi, 262 n.21, 284 n.1
Tang Xianzu, xviii
Tao Muning, 280 n.15, 284 n.2
Tao Xiaoruo, 83–84
Tomasko, Nancy Norton, 257 n.34, 263 n.34

Trajectory, 287 n.16
Transmission: of culture, 10; of literary traditions and authority, 17; of orthodoxy 50
Tsai Shih-shan, Henry, 261 n.16, 285 n.4, 6, 286 n.9
Tsao Jr-lien, 17, 260 n.3, 261 n.17, 266 n.61, 273 n.55
Tu, Joy, 293 n.3
Tu Long, xviii, xix, 87

Unschuld, Paul, 289 n.28, 35
Urine, 196, 218. See also Cats and dogs

Van Gulik, Robert H., 283 n.62

Wang, John C. Y., 253 n.5
Wang Liu'er, 203, 213, 219, 280 n.16, 23
Wang Po (Dame Wang), 153, 162–63
Wang Rumei, 293 n.2
Wang Shizhen, xviii, xix
Wang Yijia, xv
Wang Zhideng, 87
Wanli (Ming): connoisseurs, xvii; mental world of literati of, xxix
Wei Ziyun, 264 n.40
Wen Long, 195
Wiens, Mi Chu, 256 n.24
Wilbur, C. Martin, 286 n.9
Williams, Raymond, 5, 10, 294 n.11
Wine drinking, 277 n.30; and seduction, 155
Woman/women and womanhood: bad/unchaste (bu liang fu), xv, 273 n.51; base, xii, xiv, xx; general category of, xx, xxii; good/chaste (liang fu), xx; half-object half-human, 163; mimetic model of reading, xiv; as pastiche or collage, 161–62; as reproductive bodies, xiii; women and sexuality, xiii; woman-sex (nüse), xv; women scholars and female intellectuals, xiv, xxiii; and young boys, 176. See also Nüse; Yinfu
Writing: authority and authenticity, 49;

332   Index

commentaries, 48; dominant institutions of, 225; everyday trivialities as figure and value of, 86; good writing and ethical speech, 105–6; and literary field, 226; "miscellaneous writings" (*zawen*), 105; pictorial effect of, 192; produced in leisure, 105
Wu, Laura Hua, 254 n.7, 258 n.8
Wu Da, 151, 221–22
Wu Gan, 270 n.15, 293 n.2
Wu Han, 21–22
Wu Hu Laoren (Old Man of the Five Lakes), 62
Wu Song, 145–59, 159–63, 216; and Oedipus, 147; as object of desire, 150; in SHZ and JPM, 277 n.27; and Wu Da, 151

Xiao Tong, 105
Xie Zhaozhe, 91, 111, 112, 267 n.68
Ximen Qing, 145, 146, 148, 159, 166–77, 179–85, 187–89, 190–92, 194, 202–5, 207–9, 211, 213–23, 280 n.23, 282 n.51, 287 n.12, 289 n.36, 292 n.63; death of, 217–22; object of the gaze, 161; parvenu merchant-militaryman, xi; and Ping'er's death, 213–17; tears of, 215
*Xinke Xiouxiang Piping Jin Ping Mei* (XXJPM), 145; fascination with Jinlian's language, 292 n.66; unknown commentator of, 202, 204, 206, 214, 218, 221, 282 n.56; 289 n.36. See also *Jin Ping Mei* (JPM)
Xue'e, 179, 181–82, 186, 209
Xue Gang, 87, 111
Xunzi, 39

Yang Zhao, xxviii, 225–27, 234–41, 242
Ye Lang, 294 n.11
Ye Sheng, 273 n.55
Yinfu (licentious woman/women): 185, 196, 216, 243; becoming, 229–34; debasing strategy toward, 276 n.12; and ěnu, 225; fear and hatred of, xiii; historical yinfu and contemporary ěnu, xxix, xxxi; Pan Jinlian as, xxviii, xxx; symbolic effects of, xiv; xxi; and tiger, 143–50, 152; "verisimilar," 242
Ying Bojue, 282 n.54
Yingchun, 201–2
Yuan Hongdao, xii, xvi, xix, xxvi–xxvii, xxix, xxx, 50, 55, 56, 81–94, 107–8, 111–2, 115; on drinking, 277 n.30
Yuan Zhongdao, 82, 111–12
Yueniang, 176, 201–3, 205, 215, 216, 217, 281 n.28, 289 n.34, 291 n.54

Zeitlin, Judith, 262 n.23
Zhang Guofu, 44–45
Zhang Yuanfen, 3
Zhang Zhenjun, 280 n.21, 284 n.2
Zhang Zhupo, xii, xvi, xix, xxvi–xxvii, 5, 27, 48, 78, 93, 179, 184, 185, 186, 202, 204, 214, 215, 221, 225–34, 242, 251 n.53, 266 n.62, 269 n.15, 270 n.21, 271 nn.27, 31, 32, 273 n.55, 280 nn.16, 20, 289 n.36; aesthetics of ressentiment, xviii, xxx; on becoming yinfu, 231–34, 295 n.17; and Bhuddist misogyny, 274 n.61; counting (number of) shoes, 283 n.61; counting Jinlian's shushu's, 158; on nuns, 289 n.34; quasi-queer reading of Buddhist rhetoric, 231–34; shades of, 252 nn.65, 80, 272 n.49; sobbing laughter, 292 n.62; on "truth effect" of representation of yinfu, 229–31; use of Buddhist rhetoric, 226, 229–34; on women readers of JPM, xiv; and Yang Zhao's preface to Chen Xue, xxxi; on Yueniang, 281 n.28; *Zhang Zhupo ben Jin Ping Mei* (ZZPJPM), xxvi, 158
Zheng Zhenduo, 22–23, 250 n.36
Zhong Xing, 87, 263 n.34
Zhu Guozhen, 257 n.40
Zhu Hanmin, 277 n.26
Zhu Tianwen, 238
Zhu Xi, 51

Naifei Ding is Professor of English at the National Central
University in Taiwan.

Library of Congress Cataloging-in-Publication Data
Ding, Naifei.
Obscene things : sexual politics in Jin Ping Mei / Naifei Ding.
p. cm.
Includes bibliographical references and index.
ISBN 0-8223-2901-8 (alk. paper)
ISBN 0-8223-2916-6 (pbk. : alk. paper)
1. Xiaoxiaosheng. Jin Ping Mei ci hua.  2. Sex in literature.
3. Women in literature.  I. Title: Sexual politics in Jin ping mei.
II. Title.
PL2698.H73 C5337   2002
895.1'346—dc21   2001008589

www.ingramcontent.com/pod-product-compliance
Lightning Source LLC
Chambersburg PA
CBHW061343300426
44116CB00011B/1971